'Alive in Time':

The Enduring Drama of Tom Murphy

New Essays

Edited by **Christopher Murray**

With a Preface by Fintan O'Toole

Carysfort Press

A Carysfort Press Book
'Alive in Time': The Enduring Drama of Tom Murphy,
New Essays
ed. Christopher Murray
With a Preface by Fintan O'Toole

First published as a paperback in Ireland in 2010 by
Carysfort Press Ltd
58 Woodfield
Scholarstown Road
Dublin 16
Ireland

ISBN 978-1-904505-45-7

© Tom Murphy
All play extracts by Tom Murphy
All performance rights reserved

Typeset by Carysfort Press Ltd

Printed and bound by eprint limited
Unit 35
Coolmine Industrial Estate
Dublin 15
Ireland

Cover design by eprint

This book is published with the financial assistance of
The Arts Council (An Chomhairle Ealaíon) Dublin, Ireland

Table of Contents

History, Politics, Society

Comparative Essays

Performance and Text

Identity, Family, Religion

Acknowledgements

Thanks are due to Tom Murphy for supplying an extract from his typescript of *The Last Days of a Reluctant Tyrant* six months before the play went into rehearsal at the Abbey Theatre, Dublin. He points out that the text underwent many changes in rehearsal, but the editor feels that the extract here published gives a very good sense of the sharp dialogue and disturbing subtext characterized by the play on stage.

The nature of this book of essays demands much quotation from Tom Murphy's work, and due acknowledgment is here made to Methuen Drama for permission to quote from the five volumes (to date) of his *Plays* comprising the revised editions. Thanks are also offered to Gallery Press, Mercier Press and Poolbeg Press for permission to quote from other editions of the plays. The late Robert Hogan is remembered as the first to publish *The Orphans* and *The Fooleen*, precursor of *A Crucial Week in the Life of a Grocer's Assistant*, for Proscenium Press.

Acknowledgement is made also to the Board of Trinity College Dublin, for permission to quote from unpublished drafts of Tom Murphy's plays contained in the Tom Murphy Collection, Manuscript Department.

The cover photograph of Marie Mullen as Arina in *The Last Days of a Reluctant Tyrant* (2009) is reproduced by permission of Ros Kavanagh. Thanks are due to Jane Brennan for the pictures of Tom Murphy which form the frontispiece, its counterpart in verso (photographer Johnny Hippisley), and the picture on the back cover (photographer Anthony Woods).

Finally to Lilian Chambers of Carysfort Press, whose idea this book was in the first place, my sincere thanks for inviting me to undertake the commission, to Dan Farrelly for his meticulous work on the text and for the index, to Eamonn Jordan for his expert advice, to Fintan O'Toole for taking the time to write the preface, and to the contributors who have been wonderfully supportive from start to finish.

Christopher Murray

Preface: Tom Murphy's Times

If, in recent years, you have gone to see plays by some of the best writers of the new generation of Irish playwrights, you may have found it hard not to think of Tom Murphy. *Bailegangaire*, for example, hovers around both Martin McDonagh's *The Beauty Queen of Leenane* and Conor McPherson's *The Weir* and *The Gigli Concert* haunts the latter writer's *Shining City*. Owen McCafferty's *Scenes From the Big Picture* owes much to *Conversations on a Homecoming* and *A Whistle in the Dark* is a kind of springboard for Enda Walsh's *The Walworth Farce*. None of this has anything to do with mere imitation. It draws attention, rather, to the ways in which Murphy has never become a figure of Irish theatre's past. Just as *The Gigli Concert* seemed utterly immediate and of-the-moment when it toured Ireland in Druid's revival in 2008, the reworking of Murphy's theatrical tropes by younger writers draws attention to the ways in which they slip free from their moorings in a specific decade.

When we celebrate a writer's seventy-fifth birthday – and incidentally mark just over fifty years of professional playwriting – the temptation is to place him in the context of his times. This is especially so with Murphy who has written, in effect, a secret psychic history of the Ireland he has lived through, responding in turn to the despair of the 1950s, the modernizing fantasies of the 1960s, the disillusionment of the 1970s and 1980s, and the return and collapse of illusions in the Celtic Tiger years. Yet, as the continuing dialogue of younger Irish playwrights with his works suggests, any kind of linear or mechanical notion of the relationship of those plays to Ireland and the world is rather inadequate. His great dramas may encapsulate the successive eras in which they were created but they also elude them. If we ask what are Tom Murphy's times, the only convincing answer is that which we must give for all the great playwrights – *now*. What makes him so thoroughly a dramatist is that the tense of all his works is the continuous present.

In contemporary theatre, there has been so much concern with space that it is easy to forget the other essential medium of the form – time. For just as the co-presence in space of the actor and the audience is at the core of theatre, so too is their co-presence in time. One of the distinctive features of Tom Murphy's work is its especially vivid awareness of this reality. His work, however dark and pained, is marked always by the celebration of what JPW King says to Mona in *The Gigli Concert*: "[you are] alive in Time at the same time as I... You and I are alive in Time at the same time". One of the things that makes him a major playwright is the subtlety and complexity of the ways in which he both acknowledges and complicates that basic fact of theatre.

Because, no matter what physicists or philosophers may tell us, our experience of time is always sequential, theatre is always one damn thing after another. However fractured or convoluted a theatrical narrative may be, however many flashbacks or flash-forwards it may use, it will always have to reveal itself in a linear way. Much dramatic ingenuity goes into making us forget this linearity, into creating for the audience the illusion that we are somehow out of time, even while we are in fact experiencing time in a heightened and self-conscious way. Murphy's work is not greatly concerned with these illusions. It is, indeed, sharply focused on the basic dramaturgical question: why is this happening *now?* The sense of urgency that gives his plays their dynamism seldom allows for narrative tricks or shifts.

What Murphy tends to do, rather, is something more profound. Appropriately for a dramatist whose work is so saturated in music, he often complicates time by using two different measures of time at once. Put simply, *now* in Murphy is plural. The point is not that, in his plays, two different things can be happening at the same time – this is pretty much the definition of all good theatre. Rather, those things happen simultaneously but in different time frames.

This is true, of course, of much great theatre. A play by Euripides unfolds both in mythic time and in human time. *King Lear* is set both in the far distant past and in the urgent, politically-charged present. Chekhov's people exist both in their own present tense and in a future that is fast arriving to obliterate them. Brecht's *Life of Galileo* happens both in the seventeenth century and in the nuclear age. All theatre that successfully moves from simile (this is like that) to metaphor (this *is* that), shares this quality of narrative doubleness.

The easiest way to get a sense of this dimension of time in Murphy's work is to consider briefly the history of *The White House/Conversations on a Homecoming*. The original play, *The White House*, is highly unusual in Murphy's work in having two halves set in different periods. One (*Conversations on a Homecoming*) is set in 1972, when the play was first staged at the Abbey. The other (*Speeches of Farewell*) happens in the same space in 1963, at the time of the death of John F. Kennedy on whom the central character JJ Kilkelly models himself. In itself, this structure works very well but Murphy was deeply unhappy with it. He could not settle on a sequential structure of two separate time periods. During the course of the Abbey run, he actually changed the running order of the halves, moving from a reverse order to a more straightforward timeline.

This tinkering did not satisfy him, and the play clearly nagged at Murphy. In 1985, he entirely re-wrote it as *Conversations on a Homecoming*, staged by Garry Hynes for Druid in Galway. The nature of that re-write is illuminating. At one – deceptive – level, it seems to simplify the time frame: the play returns to the classical unities of *A Whistle in the Dark*, and the action happens on one night in the pub. In fact, however, the 1963 part of *The White House* is subsumed into the 1972 part. The past that is played out is barely visible. There is a faded picture of JFK on the wall. JJ, his imitator, exists now as a potent absence, off on a binge in another pub, referred to as a touchstone for the ironies and bitterness of the present, but never seen. What we get is a single, apparently robust time frame, around which another shadow time flits and hovers. As each hour passes in the pub, the passage of time is marked, almost subliminally, by two clocks. First the town clock sounds the hour, then, a few minutes later, we hear the church clock. The divergence is noted at the beginning of the play – 'Another discrepancy', Tom notes, 'between church and state' – but its function is not naturalistic or political. It is a deceptively simple way of making us both conscious of time itself and aware that it is out of kilter.

This double time frame exists internally within *Conversations* and it is also, of course, stitched into the very structure of *Bailegangaire*, in which the contemporary action and Mommo's strange story of the past hold the stage alternately until they gradually begin to cohere as the two times become one. To some extent the same, less explicitly, is true of many Murphy plays. The arrival of Dada into Michael's world in *A Whistle in the Dark* brings the past into his present. The Irishman's appropriation of Beniamino Gigli's 'memories' in *The Gigli Concert* makes him exist simultaneously in his own time and in a borrowed past. The clash of the demotic and the archaic in the language of *The Morning After Optimism* is also a clash of a time-bound reality with an apparently timeless archetype.

Yet, as well as this internal disjunction of time, there is also, more rarely, an external one. By external I mean that the slippage between time frames happens, not within the play itself, but between the play and its audience. There is, on the one hand, a specific historical setting. And on the other hand there is the time of the production, the audience's present tense. Between them, there is a shadowy zone of uncertainty. We begin with the relatively comfortable sense that we are watching an aspect of our history and gradually enter into the notion that, as Mary Tyrone puts it in Eugene O'Neill's *Long Day's Journey Into Night*, 'the past is the present, isn't it? It's the future, too.'

This sensation is not that of the Brechtian audience, which observes, for example, the seventeenth-century action of *The Life of Galileo* and is continually invited to retain the critical distance necessary to see it, not as lived history, but as political metaphor. On the contrary, when it occurs in Murphy, it is a much more uncertain feeling. It is our very sense of the sequence of historical time that is at stake. The past is presented vividly, in realistic detail. This compelling historical evocation should give us a sense of distance and difference. Instead it gives us the deeply unsettling sense of a past that is not over, and of a historical 'them' that is also 'us'.

This happens, I would suggest, just three times in Murphy's extensive canon. The first time is with *Famine*. At one level, *Famine* is a play of precise historical specificity. It is set in an exact time: 'Autumn 1846 to Spring 1847'. It delineates in accurate, thoroughly researched, historical detail the course of well-known events. Its private drama is bolstered and lent authority by an extensive public apparatus of policy and administrative realities. It can be seen as a straightforward historical tragedy, a re-enactment of a crucial episode in Irish history. At one level, that is precisely what it is.

There is, however, another, more insidious level at which the play operates for its audience. For as well as being a play about the Irish nineteenth century, it is also a play about the Irish twentieth century. There is not a single explicit moment in *Famine* at which this is stated. Although the play uses Brechtian techniques, it does not break the frame to include its audience and demand that it think about what it is seeing. Yet it exerts a fierce pressure on the present. At this other level, it is a play, not about literal hunger but about emotional hunger. It enacts for the Irish audience the process by which they came to have certain kinds of openness and generosity squeezed out of them. It shows the cause of which the audience itself is the consequence. This happens slowly and subtly and it builds up to a closing line whose mordant intensity is matched by its simplicity. The two youngsters Maeve and Liam are left on stage. Liam offers Maeve bread. She refuses, saying 'No! There's nothing of goodness or kindness in this world for anyone. But we'll be equal to it yet.' Liam wonders 'Well maybe it will get better.' Maeve again says 'No.' Liam says 'And when it does we'll be equal to that too.' The lines project into the future that the audience inhabits. It leaves us to wonder what exactly these awful figments are equal to.

The second play in which this effect is found is *The House*. Its basic texture is not unlike that of *Conversations on a Homecoming*: it is set in a version of Tuam, with much of the action unfolding in a pub; its central character is a temporarily returned emigrant; it uses songs for dramatic effect. And, like *Conversations*, it has a dual time frame of past and present. Unlike *Conversations*, that duality is expressed in geographical terms – there are two speeds of life. Early on, Christy, the emigrant to England home on his holidays, marks for the audience 'the changes that's happening over there'. A few moments later, he celebrates, by contrast, the fact that 'this place will never change. Absolutely!' The paradigm is in part an ironic twist on Goldsmith's *The Deserted Village* – quoted at some length in scene 7 – with its Irish exile's nostalgia for a rustic idyll back home. But it also opens up the gap in which a tragedy will unfold. Christy's belief that there is one world (England) in which time operates and one (Ireland) in which it does not, will ultimately trap him into self-destruction. His statement that 'this place will never change' is immediately followed by Mother's announcement that 'We're selling ... We're on the move too.' His inability to accept this evidence that time and change will also unfold at home drives his relentless obsession. In order to live with change and disruption he needs a fixed, unchanging point of reference – a need that can never be fulfilled in a time-driven world.

This internal slippage between two time frames is matched, however, by a disjunction between its apparent setting and its resonance for a contemporary audience. Just as *Famine* is 'about' the 1840s but also the 1950s, so *The House* is 'about' the 1950s but also the early twenty-first century. At its heart is the notion of a circular time, of things passing and recurring, disappearing and reappearing. What Louise calls 'the returning – exodus', of which Christy is part, is a human cycle of homecoming and departure. Kerrigan likens Christy to 'the swallow, golondrina', evoking a natural image of seasonal cycles. But the implied romanticism is again ironic. A 'returning exodus' is a contradiction in terms, containing a profound instability. It has an inevitably tragic tinge.

Premiered as it was in Dublin in 2000, when the Celtic Tiger was at its height, this notion of an unstable, cyclical time was profoundly unsettling. The audience was living with a powerfully linear national narrative. Ireland was poor, benighted and unstable. It had become rich, fortunate, and fixed. Emigration had been replaced by immigration. History was over. We had, in the fatuous phrase much favoured by politicians, 'put the past behind us'. Against this comforting linear narrative, the cyclical time of *The House* presented an uneasy set of alternative possibilities. What if, contrary to Mother's warning to Christy that 'the past is the past', the past is also the future? What if this 1950s Ireland is also, psychically, now? What if, like the returning exodus, Ireland was still geographically and psychologically unsettled, not at a fixed point of long-awaited consummation but merely in another phase of flux? What if the idea of home that so haunts Christy was still elusive and tantalizing rather than comforting and reassuring? What if, like the swallows and the exiles, everything that had gone could come back again?

In *The Last Days of a Reluctant Tyrant*, the third of the plays that have this quality of deliberately creating a zone of temporal uncertainty, somewhere between the world of the stage and that of the audience, Paul suggests that 'whether going up a ladder or down, your position is shaky.' If *The House* captured the shakiness of a society ascending the ladder of prosperity, *The Last Days* enacted the unsteady descent from the top. It is, in many ways, among the most timely of Murphy's plays, enacting as it does the rise and fall of a driven, acquisitive self-made matriarch whose story parallels that of the Irish economic boom and its collapse into crisis. Yet, perhaps because the parallels are so obvious, the play is also the most distanced in the Murphy canon. It is refracted through a whole set of literary prisms – Mikhail Saltykov's *The Golovlyov Family*, Brecht's *Mother Courage and Her Children*, *King Lear*, the songs and poems of, amongst others, John Wilmot and Heinrich Heine.

The place of the play is thus neither Russia nor Ireland, but some fictional space contiguous to both. More importantly – and more disturbingly – the time of the play is no time at all. The setting is 'once upon a time in a provincial rural area'. We are in the territory of folk tales, where narratives unfold according to their own internal chronologies. The suggestions of time are deliberately ambiguous. Arina wants a motor car but still uses a horse-drawn carriage. And time itself in the play is extensive rather than intensive – the action seems to unfold over a period of about a decade. It is episodic – the play is in twenty scenes, and the fact that some changes of order from the published text made relatively little difference to the workings of the Abbey production says much for the elasticity of the structure.

Most importantly, there is Arina herself. In a playing with time that was superbly articulated in Marie Mullen's performance, her age seems to bear no strict relationship to the sequence of the action. It is a function of psychology rather than of chronology – she is very old when she is beaten down by events and much younger when she asserts herself against them. This elasticity of time meant that the play both was and was not a metaphor for the contemporary situation, both invited and resisted an identification with Arina's story.

The paradox is that all of Murphy's ways of playing with time are themselves responses to his deep engagement with his own times. He is, at one level, a figure of the 1950s, the 1960s, and every decade since. But he is above all a figure of the theatre, a world in which the only time that really matters is the enriched present that is shared by the actors and the audience. It is his refusal to believe that time moves in a straight line that has allowed him to transcend its implacable logic. Even as we celebrate the chronology that has brought him to his seventy-fifth birthday, we rejoice even more in his great gift of eluding it.

Fintan O'Toole
Dublin
15 January 2010

1 | Introduction: Reading Murphy Reading Ireland

Christopher Murray

Situating Tom Murphy today involves seeing him within two contexts: Ireland and the world at large. This is the focus here. There are other ways, other parameters. There is, for example, the British theatre: after all, Murphy's first major play, *A Whistle in the Dark* (1961), was first staged in London and not in Dublin, and at the Theatre Royal, Stratford East and not where one might expect, at the Royal Court, where John Osborne had with *Look Back in Anger* (1956) revolutionized drama in ways a lot closer to Murphy's style. We tend to associate Littlewood's former theatre with Brendan Behan, since it was there that *The Quare Fellow* and *The Hostage* were acclaimed and transformed. History plays strange tricks, in theatre as on the world stage, and although it turned out that Murphy's critique of modern Ireland in the considerable body of drama he has created contains sharpness, humour and satire to equal Behan's – as Alexandra Poulain shows in her essay in this volume – it is less of Behan we usually think when listening to Murphy's powerful language than of Osborne and the diatribes of Jimmy Porter and Bill Maitland.

But the main lines of definition for any comprehensive assessment of Murphy's plays must be drawn from the Irish dramatic tradition and the American drama. In that regard, as will be seen later on, it is noteworthy that the European stage, the French or the German twentieth-century theatre, has had surprisingly little to do with Murphy's work: Boston rather than Berlin, to use the polarity famously invoked by a noted politician in recent times, has proved the major axis after the matrix provided by the

Abbey tradition. Mary Harney, Ireland's Minister for Health, put the broad point thus: 'As Irish people our relationships with the United States and the European Union are complex. Geographically we are closer to Berlin than Boston. Spiritually we are probably a lot closer to Boston than Berlin.'[1] There is more of Tennessee Williams than of Bertolt Brecht in the plays of Tom Murphy.

Almost fifty years after *A Whistle in the Dark*, having been rejected by the Abbey Theatre, exploded onto the London stage Murphy stands out as one of the two major and enduring (major because enduring) Irish playwrights since 1960. Wesker with an Irish accent, he was the first to show the new realism in Irish guise, early on providing kitchen-sink drama which exposed the moral squalor behind the hypocrisy of small-town Irish life. Above all, Murphy has managed to turn the fabled Syngean and post-Syngean 'poetry talk' established as the classic discourse of the Abbey stage into a new direction: into the eloquence of the powerless, the confused and the bitterly angry and disappointed children of de Valera's pastoral fantasy of an Ireland that would be 'the home of a people who valued material wealth only as the basis of right living, [and] of a people who were satisfied with frugal comfort and devoted their leisure to the things of the spirit'.[2] While Hugh Leonard was writing about the Dublin middle class and hilariously satirizing their pretensions and their aspirations, masking their roots in poverty and ignorance, and while Brian Friel was delicately selecting the themes which went to the heart of Irish loneliness and historical displacement, Murphy was finding metaphors in rural Irish life for the urban alienation and sexual desire of Ireland's new class, the young disaffected generation demanding a place in the world. Looking backwards, one can perhaps see that Murphy's real counterpart in the 1960s and 1970s Irish theatre was John B. Keane, a lesser artist and yet one whose anger was also directed with superb purity against the restrictions of church and state denying the fulfilment of natural appetites and freedoms, towards a utopian space where community values and traditional allegiances might find renewal and harmony. Simple though they were in some respects, such plays by Keane as *Many Young Men of Twenty* (1961), *Hut 42* (1962), and even the sub-standard *Chastitute* (1981), raised a strong voice of protest, though not as dramatically embodied as in Keane's better-known plays *Sive* (1959), *The Field* (1965) and *Big Maggie* (1969). In contrast, Murphy's focus is more urban, his voice more urbane; yet the comparison will stand, for both playwrights had the courage of their convictions at a time when to speak out against established values was to court rebuke. In general more embittered and more disillusioned with Irish traditionalism than Keane, Murphy never imagined its transformation as Keane did: for Murphy nostalgia was always suspect, despised as the great Irish temptation, and dystopia the condition to be frankly exposed and acknowledged in play after play, with blistering humour and terrible, sometimes heart-stopping, force. Indeed, Murphy's work, such as *The Morning after Optimism* (1971), *The Sanctuary Lamp* (1975) and *The Gigli Concert* (1983), was to range irreverently into metaphysical and even theological territory in ways that prophesied, it can now be seen, the faltering hold of the Catholic church on Irish society and the necessity of some kind of revolution. (It needed the then president of Ireland, the cultivated Cearbhall Ó Dálaigh, to defend *The Sanctuary Lamp* in its Abbey premiere against the charge of blasphemy.) If a culture is built on the words, images and narratives of its angry prophets as well as on the coded rhetoric of its politicians then Murphy is one of those who, like Joyce, O'Casey and Beckett before him, through art brought the Irish people to a new plane of self-understanding.

Yet the invoking of Joyce, O'Casey, and Beckett in this context should remind us of one major difference. Murphy exiled himself and then returned to Ireland. The move back from London (in 1970) was deliberate: 'I believe there is a make-up in the body which comes out of the particular earth of the place in which a man is born.'[3] Dislocation and emigration were major and inter-connected themes in Murphy's early work. The refrain from the popular Mayo ballad, 'So boys stand together in all kinds of weather, / Don't show the white feather wherever you roam', became a threatening declaration of a new community based on violence when rendered in chorus by the Carney brothers in Coventry in *A Whistle in the Dark*. Everything in Murphy starts from here. The achievement lies in the resistance, the radical opposition to the way 'things' (Iggy's word) seemed destined by immutable history to remain, firmly and boldly offered through Murphy's semi-articulate but street-wise characters. The response to hegemony was to recommend in ironic terms a fresh 'band of brothers' with nary an Agincourt in sight but badly lost in a tangle of Irish-English relations. Smouldering beneath that response was a fierce violence, a rage bound up in a confused sense of history felt as injury and grudge, pent up, on a hair-trigger certain to let loose within the family as well as without as *A Whistle* reached its overwhelming climax. Nicholas Grene and Aidan Arrowsmith explore the nature of this violence in some detail in two essays coming from different perspectives in this book. Other contributors inevitably touch on it also, for it is the bedrock of Murphy's savage indignation, ever likely to cast up its volcanic lava through play after play in Swiftian witness to the horror behind the desperation and folly on which modern Irish culture is built. This violence is to be felt all the way to *The House* (2000) and *Alice Trilogy* (2005), and the ominous characterizations respectively of Christy and Jimmy. There is a book in this theme alone. It might, with nods in sequence to Orwell and Osborne, ironically be entitled *Damn You, Ireland!*

As an exile in London, Murphy was acutely aware of what he called, citing Goldsmith's poem *The Traveller*, 'the lengthening chain' binding the Irish person to home.[4] Murphy's gloss reveals the violence released through the recognition of resentment attending experience of exile: 'The man who goes to England and belongs neither to England nor Ireland lives in a vacuum', and in drink 'he will say that his ambition is to go back to Ireland to buy up his home town and burn it to the ground.'[5] In *A Crucial Week in the Life of a Grocer's Assistant* (1969) the emigrant Pakey gives voice to just this ambition as, home for his father's funeral, he engages in conversation with his former employer:

> **MR BROWN**. Ah – well – yes. But you're doing well?
> **PAKEY**. Oh, yes, Mr Brown.
> **MR BROWN**. Saving your money, Patrick?
> **PAKEY.** Oh yes. And when I have enough saved –
> **MR BROWN**. You'll come home.
> **PAKEY.** I will.
> **MR BROWN**. And you'll be welcome.
> **PAKEY.** And I'll buy out this town, Mr Brown.
> **MR BROWN**. You will, sir.
> **PAKEY:** And then I'll burn it to the ground.
> **MR BROWN**. Hah-haa, hah-haa, joker, joker! [...][6]

But Pakey was not joking. His anger has no clear political focus, and yet its cultural origins have very much to do with what Paul Murphy refers to in his essay as 'the syntax of Irish history'. It has to do also with what Seamus Deane calls the distinction between 'strange' and 'normal' as applicable to Ireland in a series of sliding prevarications defining nationalism since the age of Edmund Burke (and Goldsmith):

> The paradigm prevails; in order to be understood, Ireland must
> be split between the rational and the national. It is a strange

country, resistant to the normalization that is offered to it by the historian [F.S.L. Lyons] who has been emancipated from the strangeness that his version of normality constitutes. [...] The country remains strange in its failure to be normal; the normal remains strange in its failure to be defined as anything other than the negative of strange. Normality is an economic condition; strangeness a cultural one. Since Burke, there has been a series of strenuous efforts to effect the convergence of the twain, even though the very premises of their separation has been powerful in assuring that the twain will never meet.[7]

For his part, Goldsmith had an idea, perhaps even an ideal, of his native, rural Ireland in the eighteenth century as 'normal', as antidote to the 'strange' London life where he had to wear a mask and even to adopt the persona of a Chinese traveller in order to make sense of English manners and values. As ever, it depends which end of the telescope the traveller is looking through. Yet Deane is obviously right: Irish identity is polarized, definable only in its indissoluble relationship to England. For the Irish writer this relationship is at once energizing and damaging. In his better-known long poem, *The Deserted Village* (1770), Goldsmith avowed that he still had hopes, his 'long vexations passed', to leave London, return to Ireland, and 'die at home at last'. The 'long *vexations*' (line 95, my emphasis) refer to Goldsmith's chronic Irish unease in London. He died there nevertheless, in his misery. Murphy got out at age thirty-five, to carve out a successful career at home as postcolonial prophet in his own country. Goldsmith was to remain a tutelary presence in his working life: for the Abbey he adapted *She Stoops to Conquer* and *The Vicar of Wakefield* to an Irish setting, and as always with this artist the few writers he adapted literally speak volumes about his own deepest thoughts and emotions. (So, his adaptations of Liam O'Flaherty's *The Informer*, of Synge's essay 'Under Ether', of Chekhov's *The Cherry Orchard*, of Shchedrin's *The Golovlyov Family,* and even of the nineteenth-century English melodrama *The Drunkard*, in various ways help to define Murphy's own artistic ideals.) The kindly Goldsmith offered Murphy another possibility of representing the Irish experience: the pastoral world rid of any de Valerian nostalgia or of any post-civil-war legacy of violence from this 'strange country'. Such representations, however, could ever only be interludes, vacations from Murphy's darker purpose.

In the early and neglected play in Chekhov's vein and set in England, *The Orphans* (1968), about which Bernard McKenna writes in this book, a young Englishman upbraids the ex-priest Dan,

who is Irish: 'Cromwell is dead a long time. The bogmen should get
with [i.e. over] it.'[8] But the bogmen know the bogs, if nothing else,
and know them, as Seamus Heaney has shown in masterly fashion
in *North* (1975) and elsewhere, as repositories of history and
memory. In his book on Synge, however, Daniel Corkery argues that
'everywhere in the mentality of the Irish people are flux and
uncertainty. Our national consciousness may be described, in a
native phrase, as a quaking sod. It gives no footing.'[9] One false step
and you're into the bog yourself. *The Orphans* is all bog, but
interesting on that account. It is about the moral 'flux and
uncertainty' of the later 1960s as Murphy saw them.

If the Troubles were just around the corner in the North they
could stay there while the national epic *Famine* was being written,
for *Famine* is no less than a masterpiece. In her essay, Hiroko
Mikami links it back to the folklore deriving from memories of the
Great Famine and, citing Murphy himself, forward to the 1940s and
after, when the psychological legacy of the famine was felt by every
bogman in the impoverished country. What price culture versus
anarchy here? To his credit, F.S.L. Lyons keenly appreciated the
famine's long-lasting political effects, traceable from the rise of
violent Fenianism:

> Although as an attempt at insurrection Fenianism was totally
> inadequate, as a phase in the evolution of Irish nationalism it
> was of central importance. Not merely was it a vital link in the
> chain connecting the men of 1848 with the men of 1916, but in
> its brief high noon it established, or restated, certain
> fundamentals of the separatist ideal. By its resistance to ecclesi-
> astical censure and its rigorous attempt to separate Church and
> State it proclaimed that the independence for which it fought
> was intellectual, even spiritual, as much as political. By its
> appeal to the lower classes it indicated that, however innocent
> of Marxist theories of society it might be, it had grasped where
> the real base for a genuinely radical movement might lie in the
> future.[10]

A propos, Murphy wrote only one directly political play, perhaps
written in the communal heat of the 1966 moment when ill-
considered commemorations of 1916 were seemingly everywhere
encouraged, but not actually staged until the 75th anniversary of the
Rising in 1991. This was *Patriots*, a documentary play. 'Its theme is
nationalism', Murphy frankly conceded, annoyed by the official
decision to ignore the anniversary and arguing that 1916 'was the
birth of the Irish nation. I believe in the individuality of races and
cultures *and* I believe in internationalism; they are not contra-

dictory.' He went on to defend this position: 'I believe that nationalism is an elemental and dangerous emotion, intrinsic to us all: but I believe that it is more dangerous not to acknowledge it or to pretend otherwise.'[11] *Patriots* was not welcomed in Dublin in 1991, but voicing the consciousness of a necessary violence it may now be considered as the flip side of *Famine*.

In theme Murphy is not confined to the 'state of the nation' play. To be sure, his plays often focus on the neuroses and malaise afflicting the body politic, but as often as not the real interest of a Murphy play lies in its spiritual or religious embattlement – as Csilla Bertha brilliantly demonstrates in her contribution to this book – or in investigating the individual's relation to family and place – as Shaun Richards demonstrates with characteristic thoroughness. Incidentally, in relation to the religious theme Murphy is entirely original. No other Irish playwright grapples so intensely as he with matters of guilt, sin and redemption; none has the power or the conviction. Strangely, because Yeats's drama is in many ways esoteric, Yeats is the only significant predecessor Murphy has as dramatizer of the 'war of the spiritual with the natural order'.[12] Yeats defined his plays as 'rituals of a lost faith'[13], and arguably this phrase sums up much of Murphy's oeuvre also. Leaving Yeats to one side, however, there are few other such counterparts (Paul Vincent Carroll, of course, Seamus Byrne[14], maybe, Brian Friel's work intermittently). Thus, in situating Murphy within the contexts of modern drama one must not assume either that he is a slice-of-life playwright or that he is limited to one tune.

The point is worth emphasizing since sometimes critics are blind to it and measure Murphy by a one-size-fits-all aesthetic. For example, Joe Cleary insists on seeing Murphy alongside the fiction writer John McGahern as at once the proponent and prisoner of nineteenth-century naturalism. A Murphy play 'struggles more than other texts of the period to think its way through the assumptions that define Irish naturalism' yet 'remains nevertheless completely trapped within the logical binds it strives to overcome.'[15] Is it necessary to advance a list of Murphy's non-naturalistic plays in refutation? Happily, several essays in the present collection do this far better than I could attempt. I mention here Helen Lojek on *A Crucial Week*, Alexandra Poulain on *The Blue Macushla*, José

Lanters on *Too Late for Logic*, Harry White on Murphy and music, and Ben Barnes on *The Gigli Concert* and feel confident that Joe Cleary is answered. I take the point that naturalism is not enough, that in its very form it fails to take the argument to the audience for radical adoption. But I would hold that Murphy's dramaturgy is not so naïve or so ill-informed as to leave his audience, as Zola left his, without a sense of what the problem to be taken up is. In addition, I would go along with Bert O. States when he reminds us of 'the falsity of the idea, still assumed by some postmodern critics, that mimetic theorists have always been deluded into thinking art is imitating reality in the sense of copying something one can find in the empirical world. The truth is, mimesis has never had much to do with reality, except – in the trivial sense' but as with art in general 'has an infinite capacity to enlarge its confine, even to include itself in its subject matter, one of drama's favorite indulgences at least since Shakespeare, if not since Aristophanes.'[16] In other words, drama in whatever form is revelation, and that revelation is pleasurable for an audience even if it be painful. The ending of a Murphy play – and one may freely generalize here because he is consistent in the matter – involves transformation. The lights do not go down on stasis but on a new dynamic. Liberation is usually incorporated, if not always hope or transcendence (though these are certainly emphasized more in the later work). Ergo, Murphy's drama is radical.

Finally, to address the question of Murphy in an international context. Because Murphy's dramatic language is invariably polished idiom, his style is poetic in the sense that Pinter's style or Mamet's style is poetic: demotic speech, urban dialogue, is raised to new heights in the work. In his early days as writer he admired the plays of Lorca and of Tennessee Williams – and what modern dramatist of the 1950s did not? – but the plays of Arthur Miller tended to leave him cold. Because Williams self-consciously emphasized 'a new, plastic theatre which must take the place of the exhausted theatre of realistic conventions' he got Murphy's vote.[17] Williams's colourful romanticism with characters cornered by life and with big, bravura speeches steeped in anguish and a sense of doom answered better to Murphy's own exploitation of mood in drama than did American social drama and its preoccupation with the American dream. 'We have in our conscious and unconscious minds', wrote Williams, 'a great vocabulary of images, and I think all human communication is based on these images as are our dreams; and a symbol in a play has

only one legitimate purpose which is to say a thing more directly
and simply and beautifully than it could be said in words.'[18]
Murphy's plays, likewise, are full of powerful images, stage metaphors and symbols representing human aspiration, longing,
loneliness, guilt and failure in the struggle to survive and hopefully
transcend potentially tragic circumstances. To him, Williams was 'a
great punctuation mark in my life'.[19] Helen Lojek's essay points to
the fertile common ground between Murphy and Williams, and
opens up the topic inspiringly.

Patrick Burke draws together for comparison Murphy's *The
White House* (1972) and Robert Patrick's *Kennedy's Children*
(1973). Here is a clear example of the range and scope of Murphy's
imagination. He seized independently on the assassination of JFK as
a symbol of hope destroyed for a community and by extension of a
culture and a nation. Set in a small western town, Tuam in disguise,
in 1963, the second act of Murphy's original script celebrated the
Irish need for and response to the hero, with J.J. Kilkelly as, on the
one hand, a version of Synge's enabling Playboy and the mes-
merizing power of his rhetoric and, on the other, the vulnerability of
this figure when his identity is too bound up in the appearance,
language and example of an ideal. The death of Kennedy explodes
the attendant dream of an Irish community. All that is left is
disillusion, which the first act of *The White House*, set in 1972, so
powerfully expressed that it salvaged the play in its rewritten form
as *Conversations on a Homecoming* (1985). Murphy's original idea,
it seems to me, was far stronger than Patrick's. *Kennedy's Children,*
while a monologue play, has a broader writ, including the Vietnam
war in its registering and evaluation of the fallout from JFK's
sudden loss to the American nation but formally, dramatically,
Murphy's play holds the advantage.

Not only that, but by making the JFK look-alike committed to art
and its social purposes Murphy laid down his own creed. The
Bostonian Kennedy is quoted in *The White House*: 'Art and the
encouragement of art is political in the most profound sense – not
as a weapon in the struggle, but as an instrument of understanding
the futility of   struggle between those who share man's faith. [...]
After the dust of centuries has passed over our cities, we, too, will be
remembered not for our victories or defeats in battle or politics but
for our contribution to the human spirit.'[20] The nobility of the
speech survives the irony of the quoter's collapse in Murphy's play.

Another American writer Murphy has admired is David Rabe, whose *Streamers* (1976) had a brief run in Dublin. Something of Rabe's roughness and toughness finds a correspondence in Murphy's work, but to my mind the Vietnam experience makes Rabe's peculiarly American and time-specific. I believe influence is not a factor here. Likewise, Sam Shepard's work sometimes awakens echoes in an Irish ear, and *True West* (1980) seems to retrace Murphy's interest in brothers, doppelgangers and violent rivalry pushed to extremes. Behind Shepard lies Eugene O'Neill, who has his own dramatic conversations on a homecoming or two, as in *Mourning Becomes Electra* and elsewhere. At times, indeed, *The Iceman Cometh* seems like a typical Murphy play. But then we remind ourselves that behind O'Neill in turn lay Synge, Lady Gregory and T.C. Murray, whose plays – especially Murray's *Birthright* (1910), another tale of two warring brothers – came to him as a revelation when the Abbey Players toured to Boston and New York in 1911.[21] Therefore, the initial influence came from the Irish side, and in the course of time kinship was established and endures, although Boston is not perhaps historically the greatest supporter of off-beat Irish drama. The Irish-American diaspora gave short shrift alike to Synge's *Playboy* and O'Casey's *Within the Gates* in their time. The American diaspora seems to care little for Murphy's disturbing plays today, although one cannot afford to be glib about this. The topic is a complex one, recently given attention in John Harrington's *Irish Theater in America* (2009). There we read that Irish plays which challenge old stereotypical views of Ireland 'fight a predominantly uphill battle' in the United States as at home.[22] It is clear there are diverse strands among Irish-American audiences, with room, though not much, for Murphy somewhere on the theatrical fringe.[23]

Likewise Murphy's plays are seldom performed in Germany (or in continental Europe in general). One is told they are too 'difficult' for non-Irish audiences. The problem may partly be more that of Murphy's uncompromising fidelity to the local as a priority, less to the state of a nation than to the state of a specific nation's soul. It is also true that Murphy's work is basically expiatory: the fables offered often deal with guilt and redemption, not exactly the material to attract your average punter in search of a John-McGrath-style 'good night out'; and yet Murphy is at least as funny and as entertaining as Beckett (though his plays are considerably longer). The fact is, audiences whether located in Boston or Berlin cannot expect to approach Murphy's plays cold: they need to know what to expect, and they need to welcome a tough-minded drama. Perhaps the problem lies squarely there, with foreign audiences confronted with what they fear as a foreign play. Undoubtedly, there remains also the problem of translation. To date the situation is not encouraging – even in Berlin – and productions of Anglophone drama in Europe depend on translation. Outside Europe, in Australia and New Zealand, for instance, the problem seems much the same. Time must resolve this question of reception abroad.

Even in England, so close in many ways and yet sometimes so far off the mark, critics of Irish drama can seem obtuse, as Peter Harris's report on the London premiere of *Alice Trilogy* frankly demonstrates. Ever since Kenneth Tynan recoiled from *A Whistle in the Dark* the English critics have been unable to tame Murphy and make the work biddable. Is it merely a postcolonial thing or something more complex? Yeats once commented:

> The critical mind of Ireland is far more subjugated than the critical mind of England by the phantoms and mis-apprehensions of politics and social necessity, but the life of Ireland has rejected the dominion of what is *not* human life.[24]

In the Irish theatre, meantime, Murphy maintains a pre-eminent place. He is still writing. In 2009 his dramatization of a Russian novel (Shchedrin's *The Golovlyov Family*) commanded the Abbey stage under the title *The Last Days of a Reluctant Tyrant*, a parable for our time. He has become that strange hybrid: an Abbey playwright who is primarily experimental and radical. In 2001 the Abbey accorded him the honour of a season of five of his plays, an open recognition of his status as national playwright. More recently, new companies such as Livin' Dred (*Conversations on a Homecoming*) and B*spoke Theatre (*The Sanctuary Lamp*) have proven that the work is still powerfully attractive.[25] Productions continue to be a sell-out, for example when the Druid Theatre marked its renovation with *The Gigli Concert* in July 2009 it sold out on-line before the box-office even opened. A new generation of playgoers is discovering the work with wonder at its freshness, energy and relevance. Young playwrights, too, such as Conor McPherson (*The Weir* and *Shining City*), Eugene O'Brien (*Eden*) and Mark O'Rowe (*Crestfall* and *Terminus*), are obviously marked by Murphy's influence. He has become a shamanic figure; he reads Ireland better than anyone else alive in his time and ours. Such is the conviction behind this book.

1 See Richard Aldous, ed., *Great Irish Speeches* (London?: Quercus, 2007): 185. The speech was delivered on 21 July 2001.

2 Ibid : 93. De Valera's speech was delivered on St Patrick's Day 1943.

3 Interview, 'Two Playwrights with a Single Theme', in *A Paler Shade of Green*, ed. Des Hickey and Gus Smith (London: Leslie Frewin, 1972): 227.

4 Oliver Goldsmith, *The Traveller, Or, A Prospect of Society* (1764): 'Where'er I roam, whatever realms to see, / My heart untravelled fondly turns to thee; / Still to my brother turns with ceaseless pain, / And drags at each remove a lengthening chain' (lines 7-10).

5 In *A Paler Shade of Green*: 227. The reference to 'a lengthening chain' is on the same page.

6 Tom Murphy, *Plays: 4* (London: Methuen, 1997): 103.

7 Seamus Deane, *Strange Country: Modernity and Nationhood in Irish Writing since 1790* (Oxford: Clarendon, 1997): 196-97.

8 Thomas Murphy, *The Orphans: A Play in Three Acts*. The Contemporary Drama: 2 (Newark, DE: Proscenium Press, 1974): 32.

9 Daniel Corkery, *Synge and Anglo-Irish Literature* [1931] (Cork: Mercier Press, 1966): 14.

10 F.S.L. Lyons, *Ireland since the Famine* [1971], revised edition (London: Collins/Fontana, 1973): 137-38.

11 Tom Murphy, Introduction, *Plays: One* (London: Methuen, 1992): xvii-xviii.

12 Cited by James W. Flannery, *W.B. Yeats and the Idea of a Theatre: The Early Abbey Theatre in Theory and Practice* (New Haven: Yale UP, 1976): 37.

13 *W.B. Yeats and T. Sturge Moore: Their Correspondence 1901-1937*, ed. Ursula Bridge (London: Routledge, 1953): 156.

14 Seamus Byrne (1904-68) caused controversy at the Abbey with his *Design for a Headstone* (1950), a political play in which a radical IRA man denounces the clergy in uncompromising terms anticipating Murphy's *The Sanctuary Lamp*.

15 Joe Cleary, *Outrageous Fortune: Capital and Culture in Modern Ireland* (Dublin: Field Day Publications, 2006): 129.

16 Bert O. States, *The Pleasure of the Play* (Ithaca and London: Cornell UP, 1994): 102.

17 Tennessee Williams, 'Production Notes', *The Glass Menagerie*, in *Sweet Bird of Youth, A Streetcar Named Desire [and] The Glass Menagerie*, ed. E. Martin Browne (Harmondsworth: Penguin, 1962): 229.

18 Tennessee Williams, 'Author's Foreword' to *Camino Real*, in *The Rose Tattoo and Camino Real*, ed. E. Martin Browne

(Harmondsworth: Penguin, in association with Secker and Warburg, 1958): 121.

19 In conversation with Michael Billington, *Talking about Tom Murphy*, ed. Nicholas Grene (Dublin: Carysfort Press, 2002): 95.

20 Tom Murphy, 'The White House', MS 11115/2/7a: 22, Trinity College Dublin. Kennedy's speech was given on behalf of the National Cultural Center, National Guard Armory, 29 November 1962.

21 Arthur and Barbara Gelb, *O'Neill* (London: Jonathan Cape, 1962): 172. Travis Bogard points out that O'Neill's 'more particular debt' was to Murray's *Birthright*, a play in which two brothers fight to the death. 'His borrowing from it was extensive and continuous throughout his life.' *Contour in Time: The Plays of Eugene O'Neill* (Oxford: OUP, 1972): 120.

22 Christopher L. Berchild, 'Ireland Re-Arranged: Contemporary Irish Drama and the Irish American Stage', in John P. Harrington, ed., *Irish Theater in America: Essays on Irish Theatrical Diaspora* (Syracuse: Syracuse UP, 2009): 39.

23 See Christina Hunt Mahony, '"The Irish Play": Beyond the Generic?' for a thorough examination of the diverse contemporary Irish-American audiences and the difficulties involved in weaning audiences away from nostalgia and conservatism, in *Irish Theater in America*, ed. Harrington: 163-76.

24 *Explorations*: 148, emphasis added.

25 The Livin' Dred's production of *Conversations*, directed by Padraic McIntyre, took place within the NOMAD Network (touring circuit) of the Irish northern midlands in October-November 2007. See Phelim Donlon, 'Theatre Tour Case Study', *A Future for Arts Touring in Ireland* (Dublin: Arts Council, 2009), Appendix 4. B*spoke Theatre Company, founded in 2002 by Jane Brennan and Alison McKenna, scored a major success with *The Sanctuary Lamp*, directed by Murphy himself, at the Beckett Theatre, Dublin, in July-August 2008.

2 | From *The Last Days of a Reluctant Tyrant* (2009)[1]

Tom Murphy

[inspired by *The Golovlyov Family* (1876), by Mikhail Saltykov-Shchedrin]

SCENE FOUR

PETER *and* PAUL *have arrived* (*summoned by* ARINA). ULITA *and* VERA *take their coats.* ULITA *always tends to* PETER. *Manservant* (KIRY) *is present or walks through.* (PETER, *ex-seminarian, now a civil servant, believes everything he himself says; he's your average man.*)

ARINA. He's been here for two weeks. He arrived quite pleased with himself, as though he'd just done a good thing. (*Makes a soldier's salute:*) 'Reporting for duty, Field Marshall' (*he said to her*). The dead of night, the dog barking, the watchman sounding the clapper, the whole house woken up. I can play the goat for as much and for as long as I like, my old fool of a mother will always be here for me. I don't understand it. I had him educated, tried to make an accountant of him, I got him a position, when he lost that I got him another, and another, until: 'What can I do with him?' Maybe if he has a house, some money, he'll sober down. He runs up debts – drink! – the bank possesses the house I

bought him and sells it for 22,000. That was a nice
thing to happen? I paid twenty-nine for it. That house,
managed, could have brought in 15% a year and
appreciated.

PETER. Tssssss!

ARINA. (*testily to* PETER) What does that mean?

PETER. That is no way to deal with a mother's blessing.

ARINA. He runs off and joins the army, a private soldier. Well,
thank Christ, maybe that's the last we'll see of him. (*To*
PAUL) Are you interested at all in any of this?

PAUL *gestures, shrugs, that he doesn't see that the matter has
anything whatsoever to do with him.*

PETER. You did everything for him, mamma.

ARINA. How much longer can I stand it? Now he's back to
sponge on me again.

PETER. If an undeserving child cannot appreciate a mother's
love, then look to the one who can.

ARINA. It wasn't by going 'on the razzle' that I made out. Where
was I born? Nearly on the top of the mountain! What
was there when I married that windmill upstairs? –
And *he* won't even get out of bed anymore! – What was
there when I married him? Now everyone refers to the
whole district as 'Arina'! My name. Is that – failure?

PETER. (*cueing her*) The first big purchase of land. (*And he
claps his hands silently as in anticipation.*)

ARINA. Yes. ('*We were*') Living on the farm, the slopes of the
mountain, rocks, an inhospitable place. Then Rill's
came on the market, good fertile land, mostly a plain,
nearly all of it adjoining what we had, only Townsend's
in between – *still* in between. What age was I, how

much money had I? With what I had put by, I got rid of
the land on the far side of the mountain, fast, to the
sheepman for 11,000. I had 30,000. No joke this!
(*Though she is growing in inner excitement.*) I had a
mass said. When the priest asked 'What for?', 'For a
purpose' I said: I wouldn't even publish my business
with God! Sleepless nights: the waiting! I visited Our
Lady's shrine. I wept there. And I went to town to try
my hand at the auction. The men there were shouting
this sum and that, wrangling like children playing a
game, until the auctioneer said, 'Let us be serious,
gentlemen'. 30,000, I said. It was marvellous. You
could hear a pin drop. It was as if Our Lady had seen
my tears. The auction was over. Then the auctioneer
came down and shook my hand and I didn't
understand a word he was saying. I stood there like a
post.

PETER. (*claps his hands, silently*) Mamma!

ARINA. And I still think of the Lord's mercy – sleepless nights
still: what if someone had sensed out my distracted
state and shouted – out of trickery, mischief? –
'35,000!' What would I have done? Lost the place
which was the beginning of all this? Or would I have
called '40!', '50!' and where would I have come by it?
What would have happened?

PETER. Sleepless nights.

ARINA. And that dolt thinks – and you think, maybe – that
what I have done cost me nothing, *means* nothing?

PETER. 'You can't have a pimple on your nose for nothing'.

ARINA. (*To* PAUL) Mind you don't bite me with that face.

PAUL.   I heard it all before!

PETER. Tsssss!

ARINA. Well here's something you haven't heard before: I want you now to judge between your brother Steven and me, your mother.

This is, indeed, something they haven't heard before. And it's most strange.

PETER. Judge, mamma?

ARINA. Judge, rule, decide between us – That's why I called you here. And whatever you decide will be right. Find me guilty, say that everything I did in my life was wrong, a mistake, say that property doesn't matter, say that I shouldn't complain ever again about anything, let alone about money being flung on a dung heap. Find against him, then his way of life is wrong, and you'll tell me what to do with him.

PETER. If you'll allow me, mamma, to express an opinion.

ARINA. I just asked for it.

PETER. Then, in two words: Children belong entirely to their parents, parents may therefore judge their children, but children their parents? Never. That's all.

ARINA. That's all?

PETER. Even if it were true that parents wronged their children, it would never be lawful for children to meet parents with the like.

ARINA. What're you saying behind what you're saying?

PETER. Mamma! Children must obey their parents, must follow their guidance without question and take care of them in their old age.

ARINA. All right, you won't judge me, judge him then and rule in my favour.

PETER. We can't do that either, we daren't: You are our mother.

ARINA. (*grimly*) Settle your troubles for yourself, mamma, as always.

PETER. But –

ARINA. (*flips*) I'm tired! What is it all about? I don't know why or what or who I've been doing it all for!

PETER. ... To make decisions, mamma, a person would first have to be in a position of authority.

ARINA. (*To* PAUL) You! What do you say?

PAUL. Nothing.

ARINA. Stupid!

PAUL. (*Yes!*) So should it matter what I say?

PETER. Without first being in a position of authority, a –

ARINA. I heard you the first time. It's a bit too soon to bury me.

PAUL. Shoot him – He's guilty – and it's all settled!

ARINA. That's disrespectful.

PAUL. What is disrespectful in saying nothing?!

PETER. Tssssss!

ARINA. Mind, be careful – both of you – I have grandchildren!... (*Under her breath, 'For'*) Christ's sake! ... All right: I'll try kindness again. The Valley, that parcel of land that came from your father's sister: I'll give him that. If he applies himself, he'll get some kind of keep from it, and he's out of my sight. So there we are, the matter's settled. (*And she waits.*)

PETER. ...That is more than kind.

She nods; waits.

    It's generous.

She nods; waits.

    It's very generous ... When one thinks of the shameful way he's treated you. Nice valley. And you forgive and forget.

She nods.

(PETER *appeals to* PAUL) Paul?

PAUL *is helping no one.*

    But dear friend, mamma, excuse me.

ARINA. Yes?

PETER. I wouldn't do it.

ARINA. You wouldn't do it.

PETER. I wouldn't.

ARINA. Why not?

PETER. I don't know.

ARINA. You don't know.

PETER. I don't. Paul? I just keep thinking, my brother Steven appears to be naturally depraved – I didn't like saying that – and what if he treats this gift the same as everything else you've done for him?

ARINA. The Valley has remained solely in your father's name: Sooner or later your brother would have to come into his share of it.

PETER. I understand that, but –

ARINA. Understand then, too, he will have a legal claim to a share of all the *rest* (*of her 'empire'*). Before settling the Valley on him, he can be made to sign a declaration that he has a claim on nothing whatsoever else – patrimony, matrimony – that he is content with the Valley and that that's that, forever.

PETER. But shouldn't you have done that when you bought the house for him?

ARINA. Did you say that to me at the time?

PETER. He'll squander it and he'll be back to you again.

ARINA. He won't be back to me again, not for a crust of bread, a drop of water! He's been nothing but a disgrace and an embarrassment. His life mocks me!

PETER. Mamma, mamma –

ARINA. *Your* lives mock me!

PETER. You are so angry!

ARINA. I should dance a jig?

PETER. So angry, beautiful mamma, and I thought you were a good girl. And what does the gospel counsel? Possess your soul in patience. Do you suppose God doesn't see us here now, planning this, planning that, while up there he's made up his mind already? Up there, he's said 'I think I'll send Arina a little trial'.

ARINA. How d'you know that? Tell me, straight out, what you're thinking! Don't keep throwing dust in my eyes. Do you want me to keep him here, saddle me with him forever?

PETER. If that's what you've decided on! And make him sign away his claim to everything else for keeping him here.

ARINA. ... All right. He'll stay here. But-not-in-this-house. We'll find a place for him in the yard. He won't starve, he won't get fat either.

PETER. The return home of our poor prodigal Steven: thanks be to God! Allow me, mamma, to have a word with him and give him some advice. I'm happiest serving a poor person, the rich don't need it, bless them. Do you recall what Our Saviour said about the poor?

ARINA. At the moment, no. (*As she walks out*)

---

[1] *The Last Days of a Reluctant Tyrant* copyright Tom Murphy. Reproduced with the permission of Methuen Drama.

History, Politics, Society

3 | Voice and Violence in Murphy

Nicholas Grene

'I was born with a voice and little else' (*Plays 3*: 176) says Irish Man in *The Gigli Concert*, when JPW King asks for his life story.[1] Of course it is not true: he is here mouthing the autobiography of his idol Benamino Gigli. Irish Man is not much of a talker, much less a singer. One of the symptoms of the crisis that drives him to seek the help of the 'dynamatologist' is the inability to say what he wants to say. When he tries to speak words of love to his wife, all that comes out is 'Fuck you, fuck you ... fuck you' (*Plays 3*:185). One climax of the play comes in Scene Five, with the terrifying aria of weeping anger initiated by the words 'I hate! I f-f-f-f-h-h-h-ate ...' The stage direction says:

> A few whimpers escape ... fixed, rooted in his position, he starts to shout, savage, inarticulate roars of impotent hatred at the doorway ... developing into sobs which he cannot stop ... He is on his hands and knees. Terrible dry sobbing, and rhythmic, as if from the bowels of the earth. (218)

(No-one who saw Godfrey Quigley perform this scene in the play's first production at the Abbey in 1983 will ever forget it.) The mad, impossible desire to sing with the tender expressiveness of Gigli stands as antithesis to all this blocked and frustrated inarticulacy.

In *The Gigli Concert* Murphy reverses the standard national stereotypes. It is the Englishman King who is the fluent fantasist with the gift of the gab; Irish Man, who has no other name, is solid, practical, laconic. From his earliest plays, Murphy appears to be in reaction against the tradition of attributing to the Irish a native speech of flowing high colour. His people of Galway and Mayo are not gifted with Synge's 'popular imagination that is fiery and magnificent, and tender'. On the contrary, they speak a brutish and broken language, a halting dialect of stops and starts, rags and patches. It must have been this, among many other objectionable features, which led Ernest Blythe, custodian of conservative Abbey orthodoxy, to reject *A Whistle in the Dark* so emphatically.[2]

From his earliest plays Murphy seeks to give voice to the voiceless, to find a theatrical speech for people who mumble and mutter, stammer and shout. He contrives, somehow, to give an expressiveness of force and feeling to a whole variety of characters who are without fluency or conventional eloquence. For many of them, like the Irish Man in *The Gigli Concert*, the obstructed need for speech issues in violence. But that violence is more than merely the symptom of the blocked energies that cannot find expression in language. It becomes itself a language of the theatre. It is a language that persists through many of Murphy's plays from *A Whistle in the Dark* (1961) right through to *The House* in 2000. In this essay, however, I want to concentrate on three early plays, *A Whistle*, *Famine* (1968) and *The Sanctuary Lamp* (1975) and to explore in them the range of different forms of speech and the interplay of voice and violence because I see in them developments that were to take Murphy on to the great achievements of the 1980s, including *The Gigli Concert*.

Originally it seems Murphy had *A Whistle* (*The Iron Men* in its first incarnation) beginning with a standard expository scene between Michael and Betty; in production it was decided that it would be more 'arresting' to begin with the sight and sounds of Michael's brothers overrunning the couple's house.[3] Harry searches for a lost sock, Hugo sings as he hair-oils himself before a mirror, Iggy sits impatiently fully dressed waiting for the others, while Betty runs around trying to prepare the house for the arrival from Ireland of the father Dada and the remaining brother Des:

> **HARRY**. (*looking for sock*). Sock-sock-sock-sock-sock? Hah? Where is it? Sockeen-sockeen-sockeen?
> **HUGO** (*singing*). 'Here we go loopey loop, here we go loopey laa'
> **HARRY**. Now-now-now, sock-sock!
> **BETTY.** Do you want to see if that camp-bed is going to be too short for you, Iggy?
> **HARRY**. (without looking at her, pokes a finger in her ribs as she passes by). Geeks! (Continues search for sock.). Hah? Sockeen.
> **BETTY.** Iggy?
> **IGGY.** Are we r-r-ready? (*Plays 4*: 3)

In this burst of disconnected language, only Betty even attempts communication, and she is ignored by Iggy, insulted by Harry. As Murphy's introductory stage direction has it, 'all of them are preoccupied with themselves'. The inadequacies of language and communication are matched by their physicality. Iggy, the biggest and toughest of the lot, the 'iron man' of the play's original title, suffers from a speech hesitation 'in moments of tension'. His language is the most erratic, even down to the confusion of the gender of pronouns. Against Michael's attempt to keep the young Des out of the fight with the Mulryans, he counters, 'Let her (*Des*) do the choosing. Like Dada said, she's no baby.' (*Plays 4*: 28)

Des's youth and shyness make him all but completely inarticulate, with a particular Irish squeamishness, when he tries to tell how he got into a row with two men in the lavatory of his first English pub: 'Two fellas in the – yeh know, of the pub. And they were laughing, yeh know, and talking about – well, Paddies.' (*Plays 4*: 22) Michael wants to shield his youngest brother from the life of the other siblings, to find a way upwards for him through education and a better class of job. But education for the likes of Harry, with bitter memories of humiliation at school, is the enemy. He recalls how the schoolteacher McQuaide asked round the class what the boys wanted to be when they grew up:

> Some said engine drivers, and things. And Dada was then sort of selling things round the countryside. Suits and coats and ties and things. Well, just when he came to my turn, and I was ready to say what I was going to be, he said first, "I suppose, Carney, you'll be a Jewman (*pedlar*). " (*Plays 4*: 43)

It is with this exposure still rankling in his mind that Harry is driven to his most incoherent burst of rage when asked by Michael for his reasons for fighting:

> **MICHAEL.** [...] you've no reason, see.
> **HARRY.** But, see, I have! I have reasons, see, all right! I'll fight anyone that wants to, that don't want to! I'm not afraid of nobody! They don't just ignore me! (*Plays 4*: 44)

The self-contradictions, the significant double negative, 'I'm not afraid of nobody', suggest how pathologically inturned the anger is here. And Michael, for all his belief in education and social mobility, is just as much a prisoner of the self. His very attempt to express his aspirations to Betty breaks down into a sense of its impossibility. 'I want to get out of this kind of life. I want Des – I want us all to be – I don't want to be what I am.' (*Plays 4*: 57) The sentence cannot find a predicate, so ends up banging its head against the wall of the subject.

When he first appears, the patriarch Dada appears to speak with a different order of formality. One notices that he addresses each of his sons by their full names, Henry, Hubert, Ignatius, Desmond as though lifting them out of their casual selves as Harry, Hugo, Iggy and Des. Unlike his sons, he is at least initially polite to Betty: 'How do you do, ma'am! [...] I hope we aren't too much trouble, inconvenience.' (*Plays 4*: 20) (There is unintended irony here, given the 'inconvenience' caused by the family to Betty in the opening scene.) Dada has at least a notion of the grammatical distinction between an adjective and an adverb, even if his self-correction sounds funny coming at the end of a sentence so full of other mistakes: 'If the Mulryans is bragging about what they'd do to sons of mine, then they have to be learned different. Differently.' (*Plays 4*: 29). But his attempts to convince Betty of his high level of literacy in a drunken tête-à-tête at the start of Act III are hardly very convincing: 'I bet you never read *Ulysses*? Hah? – Wha? – Did you? No. A Dublin lad and all wrote *Ulysses*. Great book. Famous book.' (*Plays 4*: 60) And it is in this scene as he sinks to brooding on his own loss of status as a former Garda, that he produces the sudden unexpected outburst: 'I hate! I hate the world! It all! ... But I'll get them! I'll get them! By the sweet, living, and holy Virgin Mary, I'll shatter them!' (*Plays 4*: 60) As with the later Irish Man, the emotion of hatred is anterior to any object, any 'them' to be destroyed in revenge.

Violence is endemic in *A Whistle*, from the roughhouse of the very first scene. The effort of the sons, inspired by Dada himself, is to turn violence into heroics. The coming confrontation with the rival Irish gang, the Mulryans, is treated as an epic conflict, and when they return from the fight victorious, Dada is there to award them their prize: 'I present ye, Carneys, with this cup – trophy – magnificent trophy – for your courage and bravery in the face of the enemy.' (*Plays 4*: 67) They even have the parasitic hanger-on Mush to give a parodic version of a victory ode with his doggerel celebration of the achievements of 'Iggy the Iron Man'. For much of the action, however, the violence remains offstage, narrated rather than acted out. Dada's account of his battle with three unknown strangers, which prevented him from joining his sons for their fight against the Mulryans, is fairly evidently fictitious. His assailants in the backstreets of Coventry are own cousins to the imaginary men in buckram green with whom Falstaff combats in *1 Henry IV*. Dada, indeed, is a tragic variant of the Falstaffian *miles gloriosus*, the boastful soldier.

The first actual assault we see in the play is when Michael is goaded by his brothers into hitting Betty, driving her eventually to leave their home. The triumphantly related battle with the Mulryans, itself a sort of civil war among the Irish immigrants for turf supremacy, is only the prelude to the vicious internal conflicts within the family itself. Harry punches Michael in revenge for his would-be superiority, his failure to recognize and support his brothers. A fight is engineered finally between Michael and Des, the other brothers egged on by Dada who needs to deflect a challenge to himself, needs to see his rebellious oldest son humiliated. Even though it has been prepared for theatrically, with Michael gesturing towards the use of a bottle as weapon at the end of Act Two, in performance the catastrophe always comes as a shock in its suddenness. As Des comes at Michael, he '*hits* DES *on the head with the bottle.* DES *falls and lies still. Silence.*' (*Plays 4*: 86) The tragedy produces a realignment of the family, all the brothers one by one going over to join Michael by Des's dead body, leaving the promoter of the fight Dada, standing on his chair, '*isolated in a corner of the stage*'. In the face of this silent and formalized tableau of mourning, the language of his self-justifying speech unravels:

> Wha'? ... Boys ... Ye're not blaming me. ... No control over it. No one has anymore. ... Did my best. Ye don't know how hard it is. Life. Made men of ye. What else could I have done? Tell me. Proud. Wha'? A man must have – And times were hard. Never got the chances. Not there for us. Had the ability. Yas. And lost the job in the guards, police. Brought up family, proper. Properly. No man can do more than best. I tried. Must have some sort of pride. Wha'? I tried, I did my best ... I tried, I did my best ... Tried ... Did my best ... I tried ... (*Plays 4*: 87)

The very failure to sustain any of these lying and clichéd evasions represents a sort of tragic pathos in itself.

The condition of people like the Carneys, Murphy believed, was not just a result of their own personal situation but of the history of Ireland stretching back into the nineteenth century. Inspired by Cecil Woodham-Smith's popular history, *The Great Hunger*, he created his play *Famine*, and in a much quoted passage from the Introduction to the published collection in which the play appeared, he reflected on the long-term consequences of that terrible event:

> the absence of food, the cause of famine, is only one aspect of famine. What about the other "poverties" that attend famine? [...] The dream of food can become a reality – as it did in the

Irish experience – and people's bodies are nourished back to health. What can similarly restore mentalities that have become distorted, spirits that have become mean and broken? (*Plays 1*: xi)

Among the deprivations dramatized in *Famine* is a breakdown of language.

As the play opens, we hear the keening at the wake of the daughter of John Connor:

DAN'S WIFE. Cold and silent is now her bed.
OTHERS. Yes.
DAN'S WIFE. Damp is the blessed dew of night,
But the sun will bring warmth and heat in the
morning and dry up the dew.
OTHERS. Yes.
MOTHER. But her heart will feel no heat from the sun.
OTHERS. No! (*Plays 1*: 5-6)

These are ritual forms for the collective expression of grief, the traditional verse forms and the antiphonal responses making it clear that this is not merely an individual personal lament.[4] In the foreground we see the men gather and talk compulsively about the prospects of the potato crop – it is 1846, the second year of the Famine:

MARK. [...] And – and – and I seen my own crop last year, and the stalks as black as – as – as – as ...
DAN. And 'twas the fog caused that.
BRIAN. Oh, yis.
LIAM. Ach!
MARK. Yis! And what's on them in there now today but a few speckeleens the flies'd cause?
BRIAN. Oh, you could be right. (*Plays 1*: 8-9)

The interchanges here represent an attempt to allay anxiety, with Brian's perfunctory assents the equivalent of the women's responses in the keen. There is even a suggestion of verse rhythm in Mark's line 'And what's on them in there now today but a few speckeleens the flies'd cause?' that echoes the metrics of the mourning stanzas. But Mark's language keeps juddering to a halt, and Liam (who will take a job as overseer for the villainous Agent) is already in dissent with his cynical 'Ach!' Under the fearful pressure of starvation the solidarity of the community will be broken and the attempt to sustain it with shards of shared language is evidently doomed to failure. One of Murphy's great skills as a dramatist is to orchestrate into theatrical harmony a diversity of voices that, on the page, look like a cacophany of mere discordant sounds and linguistic gestures. The opening sequence of *A Whistle*, quoted above, is one example; the group conversations in *Famine* are another.

The village of Glanconor looks for leadership to John Connor, alleged descendant of high kings. When he is asked by Liam what the people are to do in the face of starvation, he replies:

> What's right!
> *The statement seems to surprise himself as much as it does the others.*
> ... What's right. And maybe, that way, we'll make no mistakes. (*Plays 1*: 22)

It is to this one ethical imperative that John clings stubbornly throughout for all his baffled suffering. He is the very antitype of Dada in *A Whistle*; where Dada blusters, boasts and speechifies, John can only stand upright and silent. Dada foments violence to bolster his spurious cult of masculinity; John restrains the villagers who threaten to mount an attack on the corn-carts leaving the village and the policemen who guard them. This is in Scene Two, ironically entitled 'The Moral Force', for no sooner has John, by a mixture of authority and pragmatics, succeeded in quelling the potential riot than the zealous curate Fr Horan enters and, by his too vehement denunciation of the people's mutinous anger, stirs it up again though in a different direction. Mickeleen, the Thersites-like hunchback fool figure who dares to question the priest's assertion of 'moral force', is turned into a scapegoat and nearly lynched. Again it is only Connor, swinging a protective stick around him, who restores order.

Though it is just averted here, violence mounts through the play as it is bound to do. The O'Learys, Mickeleen and his giant brother Malachy, isolated and estranged from the community, are shown in Scene Six, 'The Quarry', ambushing two policemen to take their weapons, killing one of them in the process. Inevitably, it is the relatively well-intentioned magistrate, identified only as JP, whom Malachy murders with the stolen gun. By the end of the play he has disappeared, rumoured ominously to be 'in America, a gang to him.' (*Plays 1*: 89) If not a mere gangster, Malachy will become the sort of embittered Irish emigrant to spearhead the violent revolutionary movement of coming times. There is nothing John, by his dogged moral exemplum, can do to withstand this dynamic. Instead, he himself is rendered ever more desperate and beleaguered, evicted with his family when he refuses to accept the fraudulent assisted emigration scheme offered him by the Agent. His attempts to keep up hope in 'the Policy', or a change of heart on the part of the government, are increasingly unconvincing, and all he has left is something he refers to mysteriously as his 'sacred strength' kept in reserve.

By the climactic Scene Eleven, 'The Queen Dies', we are back where we started, but it is now Dan's wife, who led the keen in the opening scene, who lies dead. And there is no chorus of voices to wake her, just the aged Dan himself, who rambles through a life-history: 'What year was I born in? 1782 they tell me, boys.' (*Plays 1*: 84) The cottage of the Connors has been levelled and what is left of the family is housed in a make-shift shelter. We hear Dan reprising the keen of the beginning, 'Cold and silent is now your bed ...', filling in the responses as well as the lead verses. Simultaneously, in 'a kind of trio' of voices, there is an altercation between Connor and his wife Mother, who despairingly urges him to the action that he continues to resist: 'Connor, will you move now, or are you still engaged, defying all, standing in the rubble of what you lost?' [...] 'Don't keep on.' (*Plays 1*: 86-87) As the scene moves to its tragic end, theatrical attention remains divided between voice and action. On one side of the stage, lit by a fire, Dan can just be seen meandering away over the historical landmarks of his lifetime to imaginary hearers:

> Aaaa, but the day we got our freedom! Emancy-mancy – what's that, Nancy? Freedom, boys! Twenty-nine was the year and it didn't take us long putting up the new church. The bonfires lit, and cheering with his reverence. Father Daly, yis. And I gave Delia Hogan the beck behind his back. I had the drop in and the urge on me. (*Plays 1*: 88)

In darkness at the other side of the stage, the secret of Connor's 'sacred strength' is revealed, as he takes the action Mother has urged on him:

> JOHN *moves to the shelter. We hear the stick rising and falling. After a moment* MAEVE *rushes out of the shelter and off. The sound of the stick, rising and falling, continues for a few minutes.*
> [...]
> JOHN *comes out of darkness and walks off. He has killed his wife and son.* (*Plays 1*: 88)

In the final scene, John has gone mad and it is left to Maeve, the survivor, to speak the epitaph: 'There's nothing of goodness or kindness in this world for anyone, but we'll be equal to it yet.' (*Plays 1*, 89) The world of the future which Maeve here faces is Murphy's blighted post-Famine Ireland in which the drive for mere subsistence empties language and action alike of full meaning.

Murphy began writing out of his own situation, growing up in a large family in Tuam, with a father and brothers forced to work in England to make a living. In *Famine* he went back to explore imaginatively the nation-wide tragedy that had shaped Ireland as he knew it. But from early in his career, he reached towards a theatre that was not localized or representatively Irish. Already in *The Morning after Optimism*, written shortly after his arrival in England in 1962 following on the great London success of *A Whistle*, he used a non-Irish form of English. And in *The Sanctuary Lamp*, set in a 'church' with no country specified, the Monsignor appears to be English and two of the other three characters also have English voices. This is the more striking in the case of the strong man Harry because his real-life model, the boxer Jack Doyle was actually Irish.[5] In the stage direction describing Harry's speech – '*an affectation in his sound* ('*y'know?*' '*old boy*' *etc.* – *British officer type*)' (*Plays 3*: 101) – there is no indication that this overlays an originally Irish voice. The Jewish Harry is a total stranger to the traditions and rituals of the Catholic church into which he strays, and needs to be instructed by the Monsignor on the significance of the constantly lit sanctuary lamp. Maudie, the adolescent waif who also takes refuge in the church, appears to come from Northern England. At least one of her typical speech forms, 'were' for 'was' – 'I think it were a few years ago' (*Plays 3*: 117) – is characteristic of Northern dialects. Only Francisco, the venomously anti-clerical juggler, is unquestionably Irish.

If Murphy's earlier Irish plays can be seen as post-Famine, *The Sanctuary Lamp* may be taken as post-Catholic, post-Christian. In the first version of the play, which caused so much controversy when produced at the Abbey in 1975, there was a Mass with a heavily satirized sermon by a modish guitar-swinging young priest making facetious jokes about the Holy Spirit.[6] In the revised text, this mockery of the spirit of Vatican II populism is removed, and the church becomes an all but abandoned space. Even the Monsignor uses the confessional as a place to keep cleaning things, and Harry upends it to provide a bed for Maudie and himself with church cushions and vestments as bedding. They both need to confess; Maudie in particular hopes for the absolution of 'forgiveness'. Both of them, however, are completely ignorant of the rituals of Catholicism. It is as though Christian belief and doctrine has to be re-imagined from basics; the 'sanctuary' of the church becoming literally a place for homeless people, Jesus, embodied in the lamp, a puzzling presence to be interrogated about the meaning of the world.

Each of the three major characters speaks a distinctive language, an ideolect of their own. They reach out through speech across a divide of mutual incomprehension. Maudie tells of a night when her grandparents returned from an unsatisfactory film in the cinema:

> **MAUDIE.** [...] grandad come home, sad, with gran, from the ABC.
> **HARRY.** They were unfulfilled.
> **MAUDIE.** Sad. (*Plays 3*: 117)

Harry's inflated synonym, incomprehensible to Maudie, hangs in the air with a significance beyond its context. Variants on a single meaningless speech tag are markers for the characters' gestural efforts at communication. Harry's hallmark 'Y'know?' is an interrogative sentence-ending, indicating a shortfall in articulation. So, for instance, he talks to the Monsignor of 'This compulsion to do this – terrible thing. Y'know?' (*Plays 3*: 102) With Maudie, the question comes at the beginning of the sentence as an invitation into a private world of her own: 'do you know "dreaming"?', 'Do you know "lamp-posts"?' (*Plays 3*: 117, 119) The quotation marks indicate the special meaning these words have for her that Harry cannot be expected automatically to share. When at the start of Act Two we finally meet Francisco, who has lurked around the edge of the action in Act One, he is in mid conversation with Maudie:

> **FRANCISCO.** ... Know what I mean? (MAUDIE's *face is blank*.) (*Plays 3*: 128)

He also uses a post-sentence interrogative, 'What?' (*Plays 3*: 129) to encourage the understanding he has failed to achieve. For these lost people who know nothing securely, 'Y'know?', 'Do you know...', 'Know what I mean?' all represent an aspiration to the communion of shared knowledge.

Harry, Maudie and Francisco each speak a more or less private language of their own, with idiosyncratic scraps of speech and song. Harry tries to cheer up Maudie with the old Al Jolson number 'When the red, red robin goes bob-bob-bobbin' along.' (*Plays 3*: 121) The much younger Maudie responds with the 1970s Kris Kristofferson song, 'Put your head upon my pillow.' Somewhere or other Francisco has picked up a knowledge of Shakespeare's *1 Henry IV*,

which he echoes in his greeting to his former circus partner: 'For
what reason have I this fortnight been a banished pal from my
friend Harry?'[7] In typical Murphy fashion, the characters manifest
their inner feelings in a cryptic code difficult of access for one
another, or indeed at times for the audience. But in both acts, Harry
and Francisco are given at least one opportunity to speak with the
force of eloquence. Harry's expository address alone to the sanctuary lamp, hesitant and fragmented as it it is for most of its length,
culminates in a prayer for vengeance:

> Oh, Lord of Death, I cannot forget! Oh Lord of Death, don't let
> me forget! Oh Lord of death, stretch forth your mighty arms,
> therefore! Stir, move, rouse yourself to strengthen me and I'll
> punish them properly this time! (*Plays* 3:112)

The invocation of Jesus, the life-giving Redeemer, as his opposite
the Lord of Death, is matched by Francisco's great anti-sermon from
the pulpit, with its virulent denunciation of the priests, the 'coonics':

> Those coonics! They're like black candles, not giving, but each
> one drawing a little more light of the world. [...] Hopping on
> their rubber-soled formulas and equations! Selling their
> product: Jesus. Weaving their theological cobwebs, doing their
> theological sums! Black on the outside but, underneath, their
> bodies swathed in bandages – bandages steeped in ointments,
> preservatives and holy oils! – Half mummified torsos like great
> bandaged pricks! Founded in blood, continued in blood,
> crusaded in blood, inquisitioned in blood, divided in blood –
> And *they* tell *us* that Christ lives! (*Plays* 3: 154)

The verbal violence of this fierce invective against a church that
has turned the principles of its founder into its very opposite, with
its echoes of Christ's own denunciation of the Pharisees as 'whited
sepulchres', is matched by the actual violence which threatens from
the beginning of the play, the 'terrible thing' that Harry has
contemplated, and which he prays to the Lord of Death to give him
strength to accomplish. In grief for the death of his young daughter
Teresa, Harry imagines killing his promiscuous wife Olga and
Francisco, his cuckolding friend. His knife is out when he first hears
footsteps in the church in anticipation of the appearance of
Francisco in Act One, and he is goaded into hitting Francisco
repeatedly in Act Two, when the juggler looks as though he is
seducing Maudie away from the protective friendship she has struck
up with Harry. Francisco defends himself against Harry's knife with
an empty altar-wine bottle.

In the event, however, Harry's physical force is diverted into
lifting the pulpit, the task he has repeatedly set himself and failed to

achieve earlier, lifting it indeed with Francisco in it. The image of
the strong man shaking the church pulpit has resonances of Samson
pulling down the pillars of the temple on the Philistines. As such it is
related to the anti-clerical iconoclasm that is one of the driving-
forces of the play as a whole. But Harry's recovery of his strength
here, together with Francisco's outburst of anger against the corrupt
priesthood, represents an exorcism allowing them to move towards
reconciliation, something like the 'forgiveness' all three characters
need. In the last scene, Maudie falls peacefully asleep and the two
men '*have talked themselves sober.*' (*Plays 3*: 158) The ritual of replacing the candle in the sanctuary lamp suggests a re-conception of
the Christian religion of love, freed of its church institutiona-
lization. In Harry's case it is an imagination of heaven as the reunion
of soul-silhouettes, perfected together: 'And the merging – y'know?
Merging? – merging of the silhouettes is true union. Union forever
of loved ones, actually.' (*Plays 3*: 159) Francisco has an equally be-
atific vision of the Limbo where unbaptized infants go: 'With just
enough light rain to keep the place lush green, the sunshine and red
flowers, and the thousands and thousands of other fat babies sitting
under the trees, gurgling and laughing and eating bananas.' (*Plays
3*: 160) Their characteristically different voices express a shared
Utopian metaphysic transcending the violent suffering that has
tormented them throughout.

෨   ෨

The first collection of Murphy's three great plays of the 1980s, *The
Gigli Concert*, *Bailegangaire*, and *Conversations on a Homecoming*, was given the collective title *After Tragedy*.[8] It was an apt
name for the new dimension to his work at that time. But in *The
Sanctuary Lamp* we can see in retrospect that this was where his
theatre was headed. *A Whistle* and *Famine* certainly are tragedies,
tragedies all the more powerful because they show the impossibility
of certain traditional features of tragic form. The tragic heroes of
Greek and Shakespearean theatre articulate eloquently the significance of the suffering they undergo: that is what constitutes their
heroism. Dada and the Carney sons in *A Whistle* are antiheroes in
their inability to speak themselves, to resist the violence that grips
them in default of speech, and which brings them inevitably to their
tragic ending. John Connor is the stuff of which traditional heroes
are made, but in a situation where his heroic qualities of leadership
and resolution can be of no avail. His tongue-tied affirmation of the

rule of right only ends in the horrible mercy-killing of his starving wife and son and his own madness. The situation in *The Sanctuary Lamp* gives us characters in comparable emotional extremities and, initially, as little able to communicate with one another. Yet they find through the play a self-expressiveness that releases them from the torments of their anguish and anger. In this it anticipates the movement of those later dramas that work through violence and tragedy towards some sort of healing through talking, singing or laughing.

---

[1] Except where specified, all the quotations from Tom Murphy's plays are taken from the five volumes published by Methuen from 1992 to 2006 with abbreviated references in the text.

[2] See Fintan O'Toole, *The Politics of Magic* (Dublin: Raven Arts, 1987): 42 for the terms of this rejection.

[3] O'Toole: 43.

[4] For the original keen which Murphy appears to have used as source here, see my 'Tom Murphy: Famine and Dearth' in George Cusack and Sarah Goss (eds.) , *Hungry Words: Images of Famine in the Irish Canon* (Dublin and Portland, OR: Irish Academic Press, 2006): 245–62.

[5] See O'Toole, *The Politics of Magic*: 144.

[6] Thomas Murphy, *The Sanctuary Lamp* (Dublin: Poolbeg, 1976): 12-15.

[7] *Plays 3*: 134. The lines Francisco recalls are Lady Percy's appeal to Hotspur: 'For what offence have I this fortnight been / A banished woman from my Harry's bed?' (*1 Henry IV*, 2.4.38-9)

[8] Tom Murphy, *After Tragedy* (London: Methuen, 1988).

4 | *Famine* in Context[1]

Hiroko Mikami

Murphy and 'the Feeling of Life'

Tom Murphy states in his introduction to a 1992 collection of his plays: 'In writing a play I attempt to create or recreate the *feeling* [original emphasis] of life' (*Plays 1*: ix). In an interview held in 2004 he again comments on this issue: 'I feel that the stage is a place [...] to achieve some sort of pure form of emotion. [...] On stage you get closer to the human condition in terms of what the human feels and what he or she is longing for, without even being able to intellectualize it.'[2]

Murphy's emphasis on 'feeling' or 'emotion' evokes the Annales School's approach to history that focuses on the lives of ordinary people and their mentalities while aiming at achieving a 'total history'. Robert Darnton, an Annales School scholar, in his discussion of the French Revolution, defines 'the history of mentalities' as 'the examination of the common man's outlook and perception of events rather than the analysis of the events themselves'. He continues: 'It is a sort of intellectual history of non-intellectuals, an attempt to reconstruct the cosmology of the common man or, more modestly, to understand the attitudes, assumptions, and implicit ideologies of specific social groups.'[3]

Murphy undertakes to create the cosmology of the common people who suffered during the time of the Great Famine in the mid-nineteenth century. Instead of analyzing the phenomenon, Murphy, like an Annales scholar, deals with, what he describes as, 'the contradictions and the complexities – the extremes – in people who are ordinary and who are abject.' (*Plays 1*: xvi) *Famine* is unmistakably a history play, in a sense that it deals with a traumatic event in Irish history, but at the same time, as Murphy told an interviewer, the play was written as a response to the Irish society of the 1950s. After conducting intensive research on the subject, he reaches the conclusion that he is a victim of the famine: 'Was I, in what I shall call my times, the mid-twentieth century, a student or a victim of the Famine? It was that thought/feeling, I believe, that made me want to write the play, the need to write about the moody self and my times.' (*Plays 1*: xi) In order to convey this realization of the playwright, the play evolves to show how a racial memory and the nation's memories and cultural patterns were carried over to modern Ireland, or to be precise, to post-Emergency Ireland.

The Cosmology of Glanconor

Famine is set in the fictional village of Glanconor in the early years of the Great Famine, from the autumn of 1846 to the spring of the following year. The village is called after the Connors, who used to be 'kings and chieftains [there] in days of yore.'[4] John Connor, their descendent, is 'the village leader' and the central character of the play. Murphy describes John and his wife, Sinéad,[5] a starving couple in tattered clothes, as 'the King and the Queen' (*Plays 1*:80) in the caption of Scene Ten.[6] This might be taken as a metaphor according to poetic licence, but it has a certain historical relevancy. Cecil Woodham-Smith writes in *The Great Hunger* that their type was actually observed in the Victorian period:

> Until the famine, it was by no means uncommon for poor peasants in mud cabins to make wills bequeathing estates which had long ago been confiscated from their forefathers, and that figure of fun in Victorian days, the Irish beggar who claimed to be descended from kings, was very often speaking the truth. [7]

This is just one example of something which appears to be a product of the playwright's sheer imagination, but which, in fact, has its roots in reality. In constructing the play, it seems that the author sought after historical details to support the cosmology of Glanconor. The play is, of course, a piece of fiction, and as its creator, Murphy certainly makes use of his writer's licence. Everything, the fictional setting, the characters, and their relations, are under control. However, Murphy's preoccupation with historical details and relevancy is obvious. One of the reasons for this, perhaps, is that truth is more poignant than fiction in the case of such a catastrophe as the Great Famine in Ireland. And a formidable question always lingers, as the narrator of Carleton's *The Black Prophet* asks himself: 'But how shall we describe it?'[8] After quoting from George Steiner on the Holocaust, 'to speak of the *unspeakable* [original emphasis] is to risk the survivance [*sic*] of language as creator and bearer of humane, rational truth', in her argument for the famine-themed Irish prose fiction, Margaret Kelleher concludes: 'In Irish famine literature, questions about language's competence give way to a detailed attempt at representation.'[9]

This is also true of *Famine* and Murphy drew heavily on folk memories in his 'detailed' attempt at representing the famine on stage. The collection of the Irish Folklore Commission[10] was, according to Nicholas Grene[11], a vital source for the playwright. Cathal Póirtéir explains the characteristics of this collection:

> This oral history gives us a rare opportunity to hear about the Great Famine from the perspective of the people whose voice is usually lost or silenced by the passage of time. It comes to us in their words, with memories and images strongly linked to local places, individuals and events. These are the words of men and women who grew up surrounded by the physical and psychological legacy of the Famine. They echo what they heard from their parents and neighbours who experienced the reality of the Famine.
>
> These testimonies have *a simple emotional power* that has carried them forward from one generation to the next. Here they have etched the intricate details of vivid human tragedy. It's not the type of statistical material you'll find in official documents. It's not an overview or analysis of the catastrophe in context, but a series of memories and interpretations from below.[12]

The nature of the collection of the Irish Folklore Commission is again very similar to the Annales School's approach to history. It certainly attracted the playwright as a source. Murphy took, according to Grene, the words and phrases of two key moments in the play, a traditional keen at the opening and the ballad of Colleen Rua sung in Scene Four, from this archive.[13] Many other haunting anecdotes or everyday details in the play seem to have been taken from the same source and we can read part of this huge archive in Mc Hugh's 'The Famine in Irish Oral Tradition' in *The Great Famine* (1956), a book which Murphy had in his possession.[14] In its attempt to present a picture of the famine McHugh's chapter is 'highly original in the methodological sense'.[15] It is based on folk memories 'of the men and women who were caught up, un-comprehending and frantic, in that disaster'[16]. Its six sections, 'the blight', 'food during the famine', 'relief: food and work', 'disease', 'death and burial', and 'changes in the Irish countryside', certainly provide the framework of the common people's cosmology and vivid insights into their 'feeling of life'.

McHugh relates an account about a baby at its dead mother's breast:

> I heard my grandmother saying – she was from the Kenmare side – that the worst sight she ever saw was a woman laid out on the street [in Kenmare] and the baby at her breast. She died of famine fever – nobody would take the child, and in the evening the child was eating the Mother's breast.[17]

In Scene One of *Famine*, this anecdote is introduced as the worst sight witnessed by Brian, a sixty-year-old villager, during the famine back in 1836. Stumbling over his words, Brian starts telling the story: 'And in '36 [...] The worst I seen ... The worse I seen was a child [...] A child, an infant – [...] A child under a bush, eating its mother's breast. And she dead and near naked' (*Plays 1*: 13). Being told as a story of the past famine in the very first stage of the play, this horrifying episode, which actually happened during the historical Great Famine, foreshadows and intensifies the catastrophe to come, which is even worse than the worst. Dan, another villager who is sixty-five years of age, responds to Brian, like an antiphon, with yet another haunting memory of the past. Dan recalls the famine in 1822 with his fear of the rats in 1822: 'I counted eleven dead by the roadside and my own father one of them. Near the water, Clogher bridge, and the rats. I'm afeared of them since.' (13)

This is the process whereby personal recollections accumulate to become collective memories after being shared among a community. Young people who were not born in 1822 live through the horror and distress by listening to the senior members of society. As the play progresses, this process also has an effect on the audience, who are sitting in a quasi-community called the theatre. Stories told there become part of the audience's own memories and this is often reinforced by repetition. Dan repeats his fear of the rats throughout the play and almost at the end of the play, he articulates the precise reason behind his terror: he saw the body of his own father, almost completely devoured by them, 'near the water, 1822, and little on him for the maggot after the rat had pleased himself.' (85) In 'The Famine in Irish Oral Tradition' McHugh records a similar story:

> The hunger brought on the sickness – the fever – God bless us – and the two sons were buried [...] the poor mother was not able to go to the graveyard with them. Some time after [...]

when some neighbour went to see the old woman, she was found dead and her body almost eaten away with the rats.[18]

Memories, or feelings of horror, of this kind are rarely dealt with in the writings of mainstream professional historians, who provide context and analysis where facts and figures are vital and indispensable. Murphy regenerates such folk memories, which have been passed down by the oral traditions, by having them retold and enacted on stage for a modern audience.

McHugh also describes the communal life characteristic of rural Ireland in pre-famine days: 'There was much sharing of food; if a farmer slaughtered a beast his family would share the meat with others, [and] they did not eat it aright without the neighbours being thankful.'[19] This spirit is seen in John Connor, who insists that others share whatever his family has. At the time when anything edible, such as roots, weeds, nettles, cabbage and turnips (*Plays 1*: 22), is desperately sought after,[20] he says: 'We'll all have a share. No one ever went hungry from the house of a Connor.'(41) Sinéad, as the mother of two starving children, is unwilling to follow the custom of the good old days, and in a roundabout way suggests the visitors leave. John, however, insists that she give the neighbours whatever they have at home.[21]

This is a transitional moment when such dysfunction of a traditional custom in the community is seen and captured. Here Murphy does not just lament the loss of such culture, but shows the deep gap between the old culture and the plight people were confronted with during the famine, by contrasting John and Sinéad, the King and the Queen. For Sinéad, to follow her husband's wish means letting her children starve. It is reported that two of their children already died of hunger before the play starts. If they share the soup, no portion will be left for the children. McHugh explains: '[H]ardship and hunger broke the communal spirit of the people, who became preoccupied with the struggle to survive and lost their sympathy for each other.'[22] Sinéad is trapped in this very situation. For sheer survival, she steals the turf from Brian, her neighbour, who later dies as a result of her theft. As Murphy says, 'the mother figure has to face reality ... A man can get lost in abstracts.'[23] John, the righteous husband, who gets lost in abstractions, cannot accept her act of disgrace. But it is true that John's insistence on generous hospitality at the cost of the well-being of his own family members, drives her to steal. Here Murphy displays sympathy and understanding for Sinéad, instead of passing judgment and allows her to die as the Queen. In Scene Eleven, captioned 'The Queen Dies', Sinéad's bitterness is turned into the noble defiance of a tragic heroine:

> – but how, Lord, did he think us to live here? No rights or wrongs or ráiméis talks, but bread, bread, bread. From where, but myself – Not him, not You – but always the slave, the slave of the slave, day after day, to keep us alive for another famine. (*Plays 1*: 87)

Sinéad is proud of the fact that she is the supplier of the food to her family, even though she knows that hers is a slave's pride. Not her husband or God, but herself supports them. She then goes into the shelter and lies down to be killed by her husband John, for whom Murphy also shows sympathy and understanding. After the killing of his wife and son John wanders about the village as if he has lost his senses. His frenzy like that of King Lear[24] in the final scene aptly symbolizes the breakdown of Glanconor as a community.

Murphy also shows the process of the disintegration of a community by the change in the ways in which people were buried. In Scene One, John Connor's daughter, who died of starvation, can still receive a decent burial in a coffin as well as a decent wake. Some months later (Scene 8), villagers are making coffins at Sinéad's suggestion in order 'to sell to the countryside' (*Plays 1*: 42). These coffins 'with trap-bottom' (70) are meant for repeated use, somewhat unusual considering the nature of a coffin. McHugh gives a full account of 'communal coffins' made and used during the famine period:

> Sometimes these were ordinary coffins which were carried to the graveyard and when the corpses were emptied out of them were left by the graveside for the next people who needed them. Coffins with hinged or detachable bottoms were also used: 'they opened it the same way as you'd open the bottom of "bawrthogs" when putting out dung'; 'they were on sort of hinges or something and when you'd take a corpse to Creggan burying-ground, you'd let the corpse out of the coffin and use it again.'[25]

It is ironical that people had to share coffins when it became difficult to share food. Here, the corpses are regarded as something like loads, even likened to dung, to be carried away to be dumped. As if reflecting this disrespect towards the dead bodies, people become uncaring to the living. John puts Donaill, his ten-year-old son, into the coffin in the making to see if the trap-bottom works properly. When the catch is loosened, the boy tumbles out on the floor and the people laugh at the boy's dismay. John's comment follows: 'it's only a bit of sport we're having.' (*Plays 1*: 77) This is a remarkable and also ironical device to present both the callousness of the father, who always insists on 'doing the right', through the way he treats his son, and the function of the coffin – which is totally unfamiliar to the modern audience – on stage at the same time.

While working at the coffin Dan tells how his neighbour had to bury his wife without a coffin:

> Carney buried the wife in a bag last night.[...] A person'd soon go rottening through a bag. The maggots is the boyos to the dead. But isn't the rat worse to living dead? Hah? A strange little animal. Buried Nell Carney in a bag. But, isn't it the same with this style – Lord, a chuid, style: trapdoors in coffins, a Thighearna! (*Lord!*) (71)

Dan does not see much difference between a burial in a coffin with a trap-bottom and a burial in a bag, if the dead bodies are to be thrown into the grave from such coffin. Again, McHugh explains the variations of a burial without a coffin: 'People buried their relatives in sheets when they could obtain them; others wrapped corpses in sacking, in straw mats, in barrel-staves wrapped about with *súgán ropes* (straw ropes) and in places where the art of basket-making was practised, in basket-coffins.'[26]

In Scene Four, the corpses of a family are lit by the moonlight and contrasted with 'the Love Scene' between the young villagers, Maeve and Liam, the caption ironically given to the scene. In the final scene (Scene 12) the corpse of Mickeleen, one of the villagers, lies and is watched by Maeve. All the corpses in both scenes are exposed to the air without any kind of burial: however, the effects are different. While Maeve is frightened by the sight of the anonymous corpses in the earlier scene and runs off, some months later she looks indifferently at the dead body of Mickeleen, whom she knew very well. The audience's reaction is probably quite the opposite: while the corpses of a family (Scene 4) intensify the horror but arouse little sympathy, as if they are simply part of the stage props, Mickeleen's corpse, in contrast, has an emotional impact on the audience. Mickeleen is remembered as an individual who had his own life but nobody mourns and buries him on stage. This harrowing tableau suggests the devastation of the whole village.

Famine and the History of Irish Theatre

In *Famine*, Murphy deals with a time-span of 120 years between the historical famine of the late 1840s and the time when the play was written in 1968.[27] In order to make the audience/readers aware of the span of Irish history covered, the text subtly alludes to several plays of the Irish dramatic canon. One of the villagers says that 'some people like the dirty word. And the dirty deed' (*Plays 1*: 17). In the scene that follows, an example of such a deed is enacted by the villagers. They hysterically kick a man unconscious, because he received some food from a Protestant soup-kitchen. Being a 'souper' meant a terrible betrayal for Catholics. This phrase, 'the dirty deed', immediately evokes, in the context of Irish theatre, the famous speech of Pegeen Mike in *The Playboy of the Western World*. She derides 'a dirty deed' of Christy's, saying that 'there's a great gap between a gallous story and a dirty deed.'[28] But it will be remembered that Pegeen, contradicting her own words, burns Christy's leg at the very end of the play and that the villagers encourage her to do so. Initially, we see Murphy's peasants, with their violence and harshness, as the direct descendants of those of Synge. Then, we realize that Synge's peasants are in fact the imaginative offspring of those who suffered the Famine: in other words, the Irish peasants of the mid-nineteenth century prefigure those in Synge's play written in 1907. In a fictional way, Murphy's villagers could be perceived as the ancestors of Synge's peasants. The reference to *The Playboy*, which is set in the very middle of the time-span of 120 years, objectifies and makes visible the historical sense of continuation: such mentalities of violence had been passed on to the modern Ireland, through the 1950s to the 1960s.

Murphy uses another canonical play, *Juno and the Paycock*, in the same manner. This reference serves to underline the continuation of the nation's poverty and chaos following the Great Famine. One villager, who refused the emigration scheme, an official form of eviction, makes an insinuating remark about his neighbour who accepted it: 'The peacock! Look at the strut of him!' (*Plays 1*: 72) The way he walks, however, is far from the peacock's way as the stage direction here tells: '*He enters timidly, slowly, his eyes on the road all the while.*' The discrepancy between 'what is told' and 'what is seen' on stage brings the audience's attention to the very word 'peacock' and its variant 'paycock': the mention of the word suggests that the 'terrible state of chassis' in the early 1920s, the time of Captain Boyle and also of O'Casey, was foreshadowed in the Famine time. But of course, as with the case of *The Playboy*, the fictional effect is the other way round.

Another example which alludes to the tradition of Irish theatre is the transformation of an old hag into a young girl. When Maeve,[29] a sixteen-year-old girl, appears in Scene Four, titled 'Love Scene', her harshness is depicted as *'more suited to a bitter old hag'*. (43) When given a sour apple, Maeve or Murphy's hag progressively *'becomes a sixteen-year-old girl again'* (45) by simply devouring the apple. The sense of *déjà entendu* about this transformation on the Irish stage is overwhelming. In the final scene of Yeats and Gregory's *Cathleen ní Houlihan*, Cathleen's off-stage transformation is reported: 'I did not [see an old woman] but I saw a young girl, and she had the walk of a queen.'[30] Cathleen was reborn as a young girl by devouring the blood of young patriots. In spite of the difference in appearance, these two hags, Maeve and Cathleen, still have something in common: they symbolize the starving Ireland – Maeve starving for food, and Cathleen starving for blood.

Here, another sense of expansion in the time spectrum is at work. Yeats and Gregory's *Cathleen ní Houlihan* is set at the time of Wolfe Tone's rising in 1798, the failure of which eventually led to the Act of Union in 1800. This political framework, or euphemism for British colonial rule over Ireland, was, of course, the background of the historical Famine. The recognition of the year of 1798 adds another fifty years to the whole notion of history in Murphy's *Famine*. A villager makes a comment on the Rising in the play: 'the men of '98 shed their blood!' This commentary on the blood sacrifice draws an angry response from a priest, who thinks of the rebellion as 'butchery': 'What advantage is worth a single drop of blood?' (*Plays 1*: 27) This short exchange aptly summarizes the argument concerning the other Rising of 1916, the 50th anniversary of which took place in 1966 while Murphy was researching the Famine for his play.

Certainly, *Cathleen ní Houlihan* is a play which is remembered with its strong connection to the Easter Rising. Its first production in 1902 marked a watershed in the development of the modern Irish theatre, and also had an enormous impact on Irish society. The play was at the very least indirectly responsible for encouraging men to take part in the Easter Rising, as Yeats, near the end of his life, posed himself the question in 'The Man and the Echo': 'Did that play of mine send out/Certain men the English shot?' At the time of the first production of *Famine* in 1968, the Easter Rising was fresh in people's minds, its recent anniversary having taken place only two years before. *Cathleen ní Houlihan*, alluded to in Murphy's play, objectifies the span of time following the Wolfe Tone rising through the Easter Rising to Ireland of the 1960s. With the revived memory of the fiftieth anniversary of 1916, it also foreshadows the uneasiness of the Troubles that were to come in Northern Ireland. The haunting shadow of Cathleen connects the past through the present to the future.

The most contemporary playwright we see in Murphy's *Famine* is Samuel Beckett.[31] At the opening of the play Brian, one of the villagers, is '*sitting on a ditch by the roadside*' (*Plays 1*: 5), and is soon joined by Mark, another villager. This opening tableau, in which a man sitting on the roadside is met by another, shows a striking resemblance to that of *Waiting for Godot*. John Connor, the leader of the village, after '*staring vacantly at the crop of potatoes*', says to himself: 'How am I to overcome it?' (7) This is John's first utterance on stage and could be read as a question which is to be answered in the first speech of *Waiting for Godot*, 'Nothing to be done.'[32]

'The Famine and Young Ireland', a section in *The Field Day Anthology of Irish Writing*, introduces an extract from a recorded narrative of 1846 by a woman from Co. Donegal. Its English translation reads: 'when the blight came [the potatoes] developed no further. Nothing could be done with the potatoes.'[33] In 1877, a generation after the famine, A. M. Sullivan also recorded the similar memory of state of inertia: 'Blank solid dismay, a sort of stupor, fell upon the people. [...] It was no uncommon sight to see the cottier and his little family seated on the garden-fence gazing all day long in moody silence at the blighted plot that had been their last hope. Nothing could arouse them.'[34]

Phrases, such as 'nothing could be done' and 'nothing could arouse them', are reflections of the feeling of inertia in the specific context of Irish history and of Murphy's characters. But they also echo throughout Beckett's *Godot*. Indeed, the phrase, 'nothing to be done' is repeated over and over again like a *basso continuo* and determines the mood of the play. The two tramps in *Godot* are 'gazing into distance off', as the farmers of the Famine period were gazing all day long in moody silence, facing the loss of their last hope, as Sullivan noted. Seeing elements of the Irish Famine in this postmodern, cosmopolitan play, is not as far-fetched as it first looks, and it could be argued that the prevailing apathy of *Godot* is a memory that has been passed down from the famine time as a national trauma.[35]

Murphy's *Famine* is also a play about waiting: John starts his speech by saying that 'everyone to be doing something more than waiting until ... until ...' (*Plays 1*: 34), but he is unable to finish it. Soon after when he is expected to give some guidance as a leader, this time he insists on waiting, in spite of the impatience of the villagers: '(*angrily*). Well, we'll withstand it!' (36-37) One of the villagers (Mickeleen) asks John later: 'But what thing is it ye're waiting for? John?' His reply is 'Not for you.' (77) A recurrent theme in modern theatre since Beckett, that of waiting for something uncertain, is carried throughout the play.

We have seen several allusions to plays of the Irish canon, such as *Cathleen ní Houlihan* (1902), *The Playboy of the Western World* (1907), *Juno and the Paycock* (1924), and *Waiting for Godot* (in French, 1953), in Murphy's *Famine*. It seems that even a short history of Irish theatre in the first half of the twentieth century could be written using these four plays: certainly the authors of these plays, Yeats, Gregory, Synge, O'Casey and Beckett, played decisive roles in that context. It seems that Murphy's play is a container for such a literary tradition and that Murphy is positioning himself as a successor of such a tradition.

Seventeen years later in 1985 Murphy wrote two plays about a fictional town called Bochtán, *Bailegangaire* and *A Thief of a Christmas*. It seems that the playwright expanded the time-span covered in *Famine* slightly further to include the 1980s. It has been argued that *Famine* and these two plays about Bochtán are imaginatively connected: 'the miseries of the semi-modernized Ireland of the 1980s [...] have their origins in these antecedents two or more generations back.'[36] Certainly, the following stage direction for the crowd scene in *A Thief of a Christmas* is almost equivalent to the setting of *Famine*:

> Those who have arrived in the last two hours are shaped and formed by poverty and hardship. Rags of clothing, <u>deformities</u>. But they are individual in themselves. If there is a beautiful young woman present she, too, looks freakish because of her very beauty. [37]

In this description of a poverty-stricken Irish village, set sometime in the 1930s (about fifty years before the play's first production in 1985), 'deformity' and 'freakishness' are the keywords, which strongly combine the two worlds of *Famine* and *A Thief of a*

Christmas. Indeed, *Famine* is a play about deformity and Murphy knew how to make the right use of the whole power of deformity and freakishness in his play.

Among the villagers in *Famine*, Mickeleen is an obvious and visible example of deformity, with his '*hunchbacked figure*' (*Plays 1*: 15). He is a pointer to help the audience/readers to look at other villagers' deformities in one way or another. John Connor is possessed by the notion of 'doing the right'. If John had lived in the right place at the right time, his insistence on this commitment would have been regarded as a noble quality of leadership, but in the circumstances in which he is forced to live he is just an obstinate and incapable leader who is unfit for survival. He cannot even protect his own family, let alone the village as a whole. This inflexibility is an example of deformity represented by John Connor.

His wife Sinéad, who, in the list of characters is just called 'Mother', works hard to keep the family together, as O'Casey's Juno does. Her instinct for survival is an innate quality of motherhood. She has wisdom, too. In the meeting in which male villagers are utterly unable to devise any appropriate measures to cope with the situation, it is Sinéad who suggests something practical. She, however, turns out to be too selfish and steals from a neighbour, who dies as a result of her act. This shows that excessive flexibility and an overly strong desire for survival lead to another representation of deformity.

Dan, the village historian and storyteller, is always talking about the past. He is a storehouse of the village memory, but in the course of the play, he becomes too obsessed with talking and cannot tell the present from the past, a condition which is akin to insanity. Malachy represents, according to Murphy, 'a violent part of the future.' He kills a policeman to steal a gun, with which he commits another murder. He kills the Justice of the Peace, the good-willed engineer in charge of the roadworks provided for the villagers. His indiscriminate killing is 'a foretaste of the atrocities that were to follow in the Land Wars' (*Plays 1*: xvii) and, no doubt, also in the Northern Ireland Troubles in the twentieth century. Malachy's inclination to violence is another form of deformity. Liam is a well-balanced young man and the fittest for survival. Just as a young beautiful girl in *A Thief of a Christmas* looks freakish because of her very beauty, Liam looks the same because of his reasonableness in the circumstances.

The effects achieved in Murphy's crowd scenes resemble those of an orchestra which creates harmony without suppressing the dynamism of individual performance. It seems that *Famine* is a play about deformities and every single character serves to orchestrate the harmony of the gigantic deformity in Irish history, the Great Famine.

In this cosmology of deformity, one young couple, Maeve and Liam, remain in the final scene as survivors. Liam twice offers Maeve bread, which she twice refuses, and her rejection contains bitterness and resentment: 'There's nothing of goodness or kindness in this world for anyone, but we'll be equal to it yet.' Liam tries to pacify her, using Maeve's own defiant terms, but in a positive manner: 'Well, maybe it'll get better. [...] And when it does we'll be equal to that too.' (*Plays 1*: 89)[38] This is the final speech of the play and the diversion of the tone here is crucial, because it enables Maeve to cry, as the stage direction tells: '*He puts the bread into her hand. She starts to cry.*' Maeve, who was bitterly accused by her own mother of having 'eyes without notion of a tear' (87), is now crying.

Famine is one of many of Murphy's plays that end with tears shed by the central character(s): for example, *Morning After Optimism* (1971), *Bailegangaire* (1985), *The Wake* (1997), and *The House* (2000). As Mommo in *Bailegangaire* says, 'a tear isn't such a bad thing.' (*Plays 2*: 169) Murphy's characters obtain the power to cleanse themselves 'in this valley of tears' (*Plays 2*: 162), after they pursue their respective journeys. Christopher Murray writes that 'the harrowing peculiarities of *Famine* provide also a sturdy sense of resilience, of man resolutely scrambling for survival.'[39] Indeed, the ending of *Famine* with Maeve's tears creates a strong feeling of empathy in the audience, who along with the playwright know that 'the historical worst [is] yet to come, Black '47' (*Plays 1*: xvii). Here, the play eventually opens into a wider sphere which transcends common experience. The rage and bewilderment, crystallized in Maeve's tears become a sense of purgation, a form of catharsis which is always connected with hope, as Murphy says even more revealingly: 'There is *always* hope at the end of the play. [...] I seem to be looking for hope, always.'[40]

---

[1] The writing of this article was made possible by a grant 20320047, Grant-in-Aid for Scientific Research (B) from the Japan Society for the Promotion of Science. It had its origin in a paper read in a MA seminar on 'Drama in Performance', conducted by Professor Frank McGuinness, on 5 February 2008 at University College Dublin. The

article's latter half was read at the Annual Meeting of the International Association for the Study of Irish Literatures (IASIL) held at University of Porto on 30 July 2008.

2 Interview with Anne Fogarty, in *Theatre Talk: Voices of Irish Theatre Practitioners*, eds Lilian Chambers et al (Dublin: Carysfort Press, 2001): 356. Later in the interview, Murphy emphasized 'creation' rather than 'recreation': 'I used to say "Recreate the feeling of life", now I'm saying: "Create the feeling of life", because the feelings and emotions that we express are quite inhibited in life or at least they are repressed. They don't get out, we suppress them ourselves. I feel that the stage is a place [...] to achieve some sort of pure form of emotion.'

3 Robert Darnton, *The Kiss of Lamourette: Reflections in Cultural History* (New York: Norton, 1990): 257.

4 Tom Murphy, *Famine*, in *Plays: One* (London: Methuen, 1992): 15. Subsequent quotations from *Famine* are from this edition, referred to as *Plays 1* with page numbers in parentheses.

5 Sinéad is just called 'Mother', by which her motherhood is intensified in the list of characters.

6 Christopher Morash writes that this Brechtian title for each scene 'is projected on the back of the stage throughout the scene' for the audience to notice the playwright's intention. See 'Sinking Down into the Dark: The Famine on Stage', *Bullán* 3.1 (1997): 83.

7 Cecil Woodham-Smith, *The Great Hunger* [1962] (repr. Dublin: Lilliput Press, 1994): 26. The encounter with this book was, according to Murphy, the genesis of *Famine* (Murphy, *Plays 1*: x).

8 Cited by Margaret Kelleher, 'Irish Famine in Literature', in Cathal Póirtéir, ed. *The Great Irish Famine* (Dublin: Mercier Press, 1995): 232.

9 Ibid.: 232.

10 Cathal Póirtéir explains the history and nature of the collection. 'It was collected systematically in two ways. About half of it in 1945 as the result of a questionnaire from the Irish Folklore Commission, the other half was collected from 1935 on by the Commission's full-time and part-time collectors who had expert local knowledge and understanding of the people, places and material they were dealing with.' Póirtéir, 'Folk Memory and the Famine' in *The Great Irish Famine*: 219.

11 Nicholas Grene, 'Tom Murphy: Famine and Dearth', in *Hungry Words: Images of Famine in the Irish Canon*, George Cusack and Sarah Goss, eds (Dublin: Irish Academic Press, 2006): 248.

12 Cathal Póirtéir, 'Folk Memory and the Famine': 219-20.

13 Grene introduces Murphy's unpublished papers, now in MS library of Trinity College Dublin, in which the words of a traditional keen are

transcribed. They are taken from the collection and used in the opening wake scene. Also, the ballad of Colleen Rua, sung in Scene Four, is taken from the same archive (Grene: 248-49). These two materials are not included in Roger McHugh's chapter in *The Great Famine: Studies in Irish History*, R. Dudley Edwards and T. Desmond Williams, eds (1956) (repr. Dublin: Lilliput Press, 1994): 389-436.

14 In addition to *The Great Famine* (1956), cited n. 11, Murphy also read: Cecil Woodham-Smith, *The Great Hunger* (1962), James Connolly, *Labour in Ireland* (1916), John O'Rourke, *The History of the Great Irish Famine of 1847* (1875), Charles Gavan Duffy, *Four Years of Irish History, 1845-1849* (1883), Charles Trevelyan, *The Irish Crisis* (1848), William Carleton, *Valentine McClutchy* (1845), *The Black Prophet* (1847) and *The Emigrants of Ahadarra* (1848). See Grene: 247-48.

15 Cormac Ó Gráda, 'Introduction', *The Great Famine*, R. Dudley Edwards and T. Desmond Williams, eds, 1994 reprint: xxiii. Having read McHugh's chapter, Edwards was prompted to note about John Mitchel (1815-75), a leader of the Young Ireland: 'Mitchel's popularity is explainable [...] because he correctly interpreted "*the feeling of the people*".' Ó Gráda: xxiii, emphasis added.

16 Roger McHugh, 'The Famine in Irish Oral Tradition' in *The Great Famine: Studies in Irish History*: 436.

17 Ibid.: 419.

18 Ibid.: 418.

19 Ibid.: 433.

20 Ibid.: 397-400. All items are mentioned as substitutes for potatoes in the section 'Food During the Famine'.

21 She offers soup made from cow's blood and says: 'there's nourishing in it' (*Plays 1*: 41). McHugh also gives a detailed account about the blood extracted from cows for food. He describes how to extract and how to cook blood, including Sinéad's way of boiling it with herbs, and concludes that 'it was generally estimated to be a good strong nourishing food' (McHugh: 400).

22 McHugh: 434.

23 In interview with Anne Fogarty, *Theatre Talk*: 363.

24 Several critics commented on the King Lear aspect of John Connor, See Fintan O'Toole, *Tom Murphy: The Politics of Magic* (Dublin : New Ireland Books; London: Nick Hern, 1994): 114; and Nicholas Grene, 'Tom Murphy: Famine and Dearth': 251.

25 McHugh, 'The Famine in Irish Oral Tradition': 423.

26 McHugh: 422.

27 The year 1968 was a time of two major worldwide upheavals; firstly, the Civil Rights Movement in the USA, which had spread all over the

world as a students' movement, and secondly the Troubles which broke out in Northern Ireland. This was also the year when a terrible famine broke out in Biafra during the Nigerian civil war.

28 J. M. Synge, *Collected Works IV: Plays Book 2*, ed. Ann Saddlemyer (Oxford: Oxford UP, 1968): 169.

29 Her name, Maeve, is associated with the legendary queen of the same name.

30 W.B. Yeats, *Collected Works*, vol. 2, *The Plays*, R. Clark and Rosalind E. Clark, eds (New York: Palgrave, 2001): 93.

31 In interview with John Waters, Murphy denied Beckett's influence on himself: 'Beckett is my most unfavourite playwright and to the best of my knowledge I'm not influenced by him at all. [...] *I can't stand his plays*'. Later in the interview, however, he explains his writing process by invoking Beckett: 'Sometimes in the middle of the first draft you get into such a state of the crisis of will, of confidence, that there seems no point in getting out of bed at all. Perhaps for two weeks you just grind your teeth at the ceiling and stay there. And then you get up one day and something happens, and you get a bit further. And sometimes you say to yourself – and now I'm into Beckett (*laughs*) – "I can't go on," "What's the point?", "What could this possibly mean to anybody?", "What does this possibly mean to myself?". So you give up and you say "I can't do it," and perhaps because you say that, I wonder sometimes is that an unconscious act of humility? And perhaps a few days or a week later, you're rewarded for your humility, and again perhaps the muse, or whoever, shows you what is the next step.' John Waters, 'The Frontiersman', *In Dublin* 15 May 1986: 28-9 (emphasis added). Despite Murphy's lack of respect for Beckett and denial of any Beckett influence in his writing, it is obvious that he cannot totally ignore this giant of contemporary theatre.

32 In the seminar at UCD (see n.1), Professor McGuinness drew attention to John Connor's first utterance in *Famine* in connection with *Waiting for Godot*.

33 *The Field Day Anthology of Irish Writing*, ed. Seamus Deane et al (3 vols., Derry: Field Day Publications, 1991), 2: 204.

34 Ibid.: 194.

35 As for elements of the famine in Beckett's Endgame, Julieann Ulin brings forward a convincing argument in her article, '"Buried! Who would have buried her?": Famine "ghost graves" in Samuel Beckett's Endgame', in Hungry Words: Images of Famine in the Irish Canon, ed. Cusack and Goss: 197-222.

36 See Nicholas Grene, 'Tom Murphy: Famine and Dearth': 259.

37 Tom Murphy, Plays: Two (London: Methuen, 1993): 215.

38 According to Nicholas Grene, Murphy made a note from Carleton's novel: 'This world has nothing good or kind in it for me – and now I'll be equal to it.' Tom Murphy, unpublished papers, TCD MS 1115 3/1 fol.80r. See Grene: 248.

39 Christopher Murray, 'Introduction: The Rough and Holy Theatre of Thomas Murphy', *Irish University Review*, Special Issue: Thomas Murphy, 17.1 (1987): 10-11.

40 In interview with John Waters, 'The Frontiersman': 28.

5 | Tom Murphy and the Syntax of Irish History[1]

Paul Murphy

If there is a political leitmotiv which threads its way through Tom Murphy's canon it is a concern, whether implicitly or explicitly stated, with social justice; from *On the Outside* and *On the Inside*, to *A Crucial Week in the Life of a Grocer's Assistant* and on to *Bailegangaire* and *A Thief of a Christmas*. In these plays Murphy's focus is not on the great men of Irish history, but on socially subordinate figures who played only minor roles in the national epic. I will argue that Murphy brushes Irish history against the grain by representing those discourses which the nationalist metanarrative has consigned to the margins of history. In parallel with this analysis of Murphy's plays I will engage with the debate on Irish historiography, particularly as it is manifest in the antagonistic relationship between nationalism and revisionism. I will suggest that Murphy synthesizes the dialectic between past and present by representing history as a process of story-telling, where hegemonic Catholic, bourgeois, nationalist history is challenged by countervailing discourses of class and gender. The aim is to move beyond a reading of Irish theatre grounded in identitarian paradigms of nation and nationalism, towards an engagement with ethical issues of class and gender subordination which are as much a part of Irish history as the nation is or ever was. *On the Outside* was written in 1959 during the first year of the First Programme for Economic Expansion under the administration of Taoiseach Sean Lemass and implemented by Minister for Finance T.K. Whitaker. It was produced as a radio play for Radio Eireann in 1962, and had its first stage production in Dublin at Project in 1974. Just as Lemass and Whitaker's Programme aimed to drag Ireland out of the economic morass of protectionism inherent to the post-indepen-dence governments, so *On the Outside* deals with the impact of that period on the inhabitants of small, rural towns. The play works on the dichotomy between those characters whose status keeps them outside of a country dancehall, typfied by the proletarians Joe and Frank, and those predominantly middle-class characters whose status allows them entry to the bourgeois tedium within. The spatial dichotomy enhances the class disparity made clear in the description of Frank as '*aware of the very rigid class distinctions that pervade a small, urban-rural community and resents "them" with the cars and money because he has not got the same.*'[2] Frank and Joe do not have enough money to pay the entry fee to the dancehall and Frank has been pretending to his putative sweetheart Anne that he is a man of means. The relative poverty of the two apprentice tradesmen is juxtaposed with the ostentatious Mickey Ford, whose pretentiousness is enhanced when he '*affects a slight American accent whenever he thinks of it.*' (4:175) In spite of his brazen wealth Ford refuses to lend the two indigents the entry fee and they are reduced to begging the Drunk for his own meagre finances.

Frank's acute class consciousness serves to fuel his frustration at the evident class disparity between himself and the likes of Mickey Ford who have either inherited their money from 'an uncle in America' or are the children of strong farmers and traders who have long since achieved embourgeoisement. In one sardonic observation Frank describes the local class divisions:

> The whole town is like a tank. [...] And we're at the bottom, splashing around all week in their Friday night vomit, clawing at the sides all around. And the bosses – and the big-shots – are up around the top, looking in, looking down. [...] Spitting. On top of us. And for fear we might climb out someway – Do you know what they're doing? – They smear grease around the walls. (4:180)

When Frank and Joe sing nationalistic songs to relieve their boredom, the reference to Patrick Sarsfield and the solidarity inherent in patriotic nationalism rings hollow in independent Ireland where British rule has been replaced by the hegemony of Catholic bourgeois nationalism. Indeed the Ireland which Murphy portrays in *On the Outside* and the later *A Crucial Week in the Life of a Grocer's Assistant* is of a country riven by cronyism, gombeenism and a general sense of Shaft Thy Neighbour. As the play draws to a close Ford leaves the dancehall with Anne on his arm, and it is clear that during his seductions he has revealed Frank's deceptions as Anne exclaims 'You're only a liar. I wouldn't have anything to do with you. (*As she exits.*) Are you coming, Mickey?' When Frank pleads with Anne, Ford dismisses him with the callous indifference of the risen bourgeoisie: 'What about all the lies you told her? Pick on someone your own class now.' (4:191)

The play ends with Frank venting his frustration as he rushes over to the poster advertising the night's entertainment '*and hits it hard with his fist. He kicks it furiously.*' Joe has the final line which crystallizes their exasperation as he invites his comrade to 'Come on out of here to hell'; the final image is of the drunkard Daly mimicking Frank's futile rage in '*giving a few impotent kicks to the poster as the lights fade.*' (4:192) The situation depicted in *On the Outside* is symptomatic of the socio-economic predictament Ireland found itself in during the 1950s. As Tom Garvin argues, 'it took what was seen as the economic disaster of the mid-1950s and the ageing of the Boys of the Old Brigade to force real change; there was a genuine problem of gerontocracy.' In the 1950s, 'the facts of economic life and electoral pressure began gradually to nullify the special interests of older business, ecclesiastical, cultural and labour elites, the people who had, essentially, carved up the entire country into a set of fiefdoms after 1920 and 1932.'[3] The impact of these special interests on the personal lives of people in small town Ireland are dealt with in *On the Inside*, first produced on the Peacock Stage of the Abbey Theatre, Dublin in 1974, and is deliberately constructed as the companion to *On the Outside*. The characters are predominantly school teachers whose sexual interactions are delimited by the rigours of the highly conservative form of Catholicism pervasive in Irish society since its institution in Taoiseach Eamonn de Valera's 1937 Constitution, and whose taut etiquette is defined by the snobbery inherent to bourgeois pretentiousness.

Where the issue of class politics is foregrounded in *On the Outside*, the issue of sexual politics is highlighted in *On the Inside*. In the opening scene the '*neurotic, staccato-voiced*' teacher Miss D'Arcy says that the men in the dancehall are 'only a bunch of mullackers', and when her younger colleague agrees Miss D'Arcy states that 'they're worse outside', indicating her contempt for her social inferiors typified in Frank and Joe from *On the Outside*.[4] Mr Collins is the staunch Headmaster who personifies the unflinching conservatism of the Catholic bourgeois subject, and frequently displays his naked disapproval of the younger teacher Kieran and his 'layabout' friend Malachy in their haphazard attempts at debauchery. The moral frigidity characteristic of Ireland during the early decades of independence is thrown into relief by the furtive attempts at sexual congress made by Kieran and his generation: 'We're all only disgracing ourselves. [...] This Sunday-night job. (*He demonstrates the close dancing style.*) And if not that, we're lurking somewhere; in doorways, or dirty old sheds, or mucky old laneways.' (4:199) Kieran becomes increasingly frustrated with having to 'welter for years in guilt and indignity' and intends to get 'away from it all' and emigrate until, during a moment of clarity after a drunken outburst, he acknowledges his devotion to his pregnant sweetheart Margaret and determines to stay with her. The profundity of true love prevails over the tedium of their quotidian existence, and is crystalized in the sublime promise of sexual union: 'Will you come somewhere, with me? /*She nods*/ Not the usual places. Malachy has a house all to himself. He might give me the key. (*She nods her agreement.*) We'll do it right this time.' (4:221)

A Crucial Week in the Life of a Grocer's Assistant, written in 1962 and first produced at the Abbey Theatre in 1969, is again set in the 1950s but shifts the focus back to class politics in a more sustained way than the one-act structure of *On the Outside* allowed. John Joe Moran is the titular Grocer's Assistant whose dreary life is illuminated in twelve scenes alternating between dreamy surrealism and stark realism. John Joe too is in his thirties, still confined by financial contingencies to his parents' good graces, who maintain themselves on a barely subsistence level economy. John Joe's mother is worn out through the constant penny-pinching to make ends meet, '*given much to grimacing to emphasize what she says,*' slovenly in appearance, '*harsh in expression and bitter*' and furthermore '*a product of Irish history – poverty and ignorance.*'[5] Mrs. Moran is faced with the impossible yet nonetheless quotidian effort of trying to synthesize desperate economic circumstances with social respectability in the eyes of her neighbours: 'There's Peteen's wife out there and she has a new rig-out on her for every time she wants to be swanking it, and I'm the same old three-and-fourpence Sunday and Monday. He's (*Father*) bringing nothing in here except the few shillings he gets now and again for digging a grave.' (4:108) In spite of her best efforts Mrs. Moran is thwarted at every turn by both her husband's lethargy and the opprobrium consequent on her son's frustration at his diminished prospects of sexual congress and social advancement: 'A bird in the hay is worth two in the dance hall. I wish I was rich.' (4:114)

The opprobrium is amplified when John Joe refuses to continue working for local grocer Mr Brown and in a fit of pique points out the chicanery his employer uses to obtain business in buying out his old employer using money that his 'uncle in America' bequeathed him and leaving the old employer 'broke'. (4:124) The brute mercantilism underpinning the realpolitik of economic advancement is further illustrated when John's uncle Alec assumes he has been informed upon to the Pension Officer and, suspecting the local sycophant Mullins, launches into a vehement indictment of the moral hypocrisy of his neighbour's embourgeoisement: 'All my people, I told him, were decent, respectable people, even if my mother wore a shawl going to mass itself! None of them ever informed to the soldiers one time for twenty-three shillings and got the legs shot off Danny Kelly! [...] And none of them was ever brought up in court for one of them talking about football to the fish man, while the other was stealing the herrings from the back of the van!' (4:139-40) It transpires that Mrs Moran reported uncle Alec to the Pension Officer in a desperate attempt to elevate her son's position, adding poignancy to their circumstances whilst simultaneously eliminating any moral high ground which she may have compared to the hypocrisies of her neighbours.

As with his predecessors in Murphy's earlier plays, John Joe sees emigration as the only solution to his predicament, but as with *On the Inside* the male protagonist is drawn back to the tedium of small town life by the possibility of union with his female counterpart. Where Kieran and Margaret's relationship in *On the Inside* was problematized by the rigidity of Catholic bourgeois mores concerning sexuality, John Joe's penurious circumstances set him a class apart from Mona (Mr Brown's daughter) who, by her own admission, has money. John Joe's indignation at their class disparity boils over into heartless vitriol as he misdirects his anger at her: 'You are a silly, stupid bitch. [...] What means anything to you? Mummy, big farm, daddy; the priest plays golf with daddy; the bishop knows daddy; money in the bank. Where does John-Balls-Joe come in? For favours, pity?' (4:153) John Joe's dismissal of romantic love in the face of brute economic disparity is echoed by his mother's disavowal as she mimics him: 'What's wrong with that word? [love] Wait on, till Fr. Daly sees you.' (4:157) John Joe eventually rejects his mother's dystopian view and confronts her directly: 'The house is filled with your bitterness and venom. [...] Whether it's just badness or whether it came from a hundred years ago, or whether it's your ideas of sex, or whether it's – (MOTHER is *crying*.) No, you'll listen to me –'. (4:159) In the finale John Joe completes his rite of passage to a delayed manhood of individual agency by railing against the hypocrisies of both his own and his neighbours' families as he shouts into the street. The play concludes with John Joe determined to take up the new job which the local priest Fr Daly has secured for him and to consolidate his faltering relationship with Mona.

In *Bailegangaire*, first produced by the Druid Theatre Company, Galway, in 1985, the character Mommo, an elderly grandmother on the verge of senility, recites a prayer of lamentation: 'Hail Holy Queen [...] Mother of Mercy [...] Hail our lives [...] Our sweetness and our hope [...] To thee do we cry [...] Poor banished children of Eve [...] To thee do we send up our sighs [...] Mourning and weeping in this valley of tears.'[6] In dramatic terms Mommo's prayer works on several levels of signification. It is a plea for mercy and forgiveness, but it is also a cry for representation from working-class women in rural communities who were the victims of class and gender hierarchies during the British colonial administration of Ireland, and continue to be repressed in the postcolonial administration of Catholic bourgeois nationalism. The setting for *Bailegangaire* is '1984, the kitchen of a thatched house' (2:90) on the Mayo/Galway border in the west of Ireland. The play centres on Mommo's recollection of traumatic events which occurred some thirty years prior to the temporal setting of *Bailegangaire*: 'An' no one will stop me! Tellin' my nice story ... Yis, how the place called Bochtán – and its *graund* (*grand*) inhabitants – came by its new appellation, Bailegangaire, the place without laughter.' (2:92) Indeed the subtitle to *Bailegangaire* is 'The Story of *Bailegangaire* and how it came by its appellation,' and Mommo's story is a narrative reconstruction of the events that take place in *A Thief of a Christmas*, first produced at the Abbey Theatre in 1985, which Murphy subtitles 'The Actuality of how *Bailegangaire* came by its appellation.' The two plays are intertextually linked through Mommo's discourse which fractures the temporal consciousness of *Bailegangaire* in 1984 with the re-presentation of traumatic events from the temporal unconscious of *A Thief of a Christmas* in the 1950s.

Through this intertextual link between 'actuality' and 'story' Murphy represents the syntax of history which has been fragmented by the traumatic events of *A Thief of a Christmas* leading on to *Bailegangaire* in the troubled relationships between Mommo, Mary and Dolly. In *Bailegangaire* the time is out of joint and by juxtaposing the historical past with the contemporary present,

Murphy opens up a dialogue in broader cultural terms between tradition and modernity. In order to allow this dialogue to emerge and develop, Murphy critiques Eamon de Valera's nostalgically essentialist[7] vision of Ireland in the 1950s through the representation in *A Thief of a Christmas* of the harsh realities of 'peasant' life in the pre-industrial era of the recently established Republic. In *Bailegangaire* Murphy effects a similar critique of the epochalistic, modernizing vision of the Lemass administration which instigated Ireland's economic expansion into the world markets of the 1960s and ended up in the predatory arena of multinational capitalism in the 1980s.

In *A Thief of a Christmas*, however, Murphy not only critiques de Valera's essentialist vision of Ireland as an agrarian idyll, but also demythologizes Synge's representation of the west of Ireland as the last vestige of an essential Gaelic culture, embodied in the life of the peasant still living in unity with nature.[8] As Luke Gibbons suggests 'idealizations of rural existence, the longing for community and primitive simplicity, are the product of an urban sensibility, and are cultural fictions imposed on the lives of those they purport to represent [...] it was urban based writers, intellectuals and political leaders who created romantic Ireland, and perpetrated the myth that the further west you go, the more you come into contact with the real Ireland.'[9] While Murphy is undoubtedly an intellectual who constructs a fictional image of the west of Ireland, he is nevertheless a writer who has emerged from the locality which he represents in his plays, rather than an 'urban based' writer emerging from the metropolitan centre. This is not to argue for a simplistic notion of cultural authenticity but only to state that where Synge was a cultural tourist who spent only a relatively short amount of time in the west of Ireland, Murphy was born there (in Tuam) and spent the first twenty-five years of his life in that region.

The setting for *A Thief of a Christmas* is a 'pub-cum general store in a remote village.' (2:172) It is all *'quite primitive'*, and *'[w]e are dealing with a neglected, forgotten peasantry.'* (2: 175) The store is located in the town of Bochtán, which literally means the 'poor place,' and during the course of events poverty is revealed as the informing motif. The play centres on a 'laughing competition' (2:215) between the local hero, Seamus Costello, and the visiting Stranger, Seamus O'Toole. The competition begins as a harmless proposition which the two antagonists are prepared to ignore, then recognize as a mighty challenge. Matters become deadly serious when the competition takes on economic dimensions as Costello strikes a bet with the stuttering gombeen-man [usurer] John Mahony, who is also the proprietor of the store and holds the villagers to ransom through the amount of financial credit he has given them: 'COSTELLO. [...] I'm sick of being called a f-fool by you. The whole farm to you for nothing if I lose. [...] JOHN. F-f-f-if yeh don't lose?/COSTELLO. I keep the farm and you'll be givin' me a hundred pounds.' (2:212-13) When the other villagers start to bet their property and very livelihood on Costello, the competition escalates to an almost mythical scenario where Costello is re-presenting the impoverished peasantry in unarmed combat against Mahony, the parasitic mercantilist.

The Stranger is as much a catalyst as he is a competitor, and his motivation for the contest is more for a triumph against constant misfortune than for economic gain. As they enter the store, it is evident that he and his wife, Brigit [Mommo in the pendant play *Bailegangaire*), are in mourning, symbolized by '*a black diamond stitched on his sleeve.*' (2: 196) The couple are on their way home to their three grandchildren, and Brigit is anxious about their welfare, as they promised to be 'home before dark.' (2:198) The couple have endured years of hardship and personal catastrophe, and are further worried by the suggestion of troubles – 'misfortunes' – which they will have to face in the future, as the 'three sticks of rock' meant for their grandchildren 'that death left in [her] care' (2:207) are knocked out of Brigit's hand and 'trampled underfoot' in the 'jostling' for a better view of the laughing contest. This is the final insult, and she retorts against incessant misery by throwing down the gauntlet to Costello on her husband's behalf: 'You can decree! – (*To her husband.*) All others can decree! but I'll-bear-matters-no-longer! (*To* COSTELLO.) Och hona-ho 'gus hah-haa! He's challe'gin' yeh.' (2:207)

Brigit's explosive challenge is a manifestation of her repressed grief, sparking a psychic chain reaction in the Bochtán community which is in turn manifest as the guiding, incongruous topic of the laughing contest: grief, or 'misfortunes' (2:214). The grief is itself born of material circumstances, as much of the historical trauma is the result of economic hardship. We are told that some of Brigit's children died trying to reclaim livestock: 'I had nine sons [...] An' for the sake of an aul' ewe was stuck in the flood was how I lost Jimmy an' Michael [...] An' Pat who was my first born [...] Married the widdy against my wishes [...] An' when he came back for the two sheep (that) were his [...] You'll not have them, I told him, and sent him back, lame, to his strap of a widdy [...] An' he was dead within a six months.' (2:232-33) During the contest, Brigit's story becomes one of many symptoms of repressed historical trauma, as the villagers' woes build into a chorus of catastrophes, from 'those lost to America', through 'blighted crops', to mortal disease, 'the decline', to the unbaptized and the still-born, all invoked as laughable and blasphemously sent *'To the heavens'* (2:235-36).

Fintan O'Toole suggests that this narrative 'enacts the classic Nietzschean gesture of man's defiant laughter in the face of death but reverses its political and theatrical meaning. For Nietzsche, that God-defying laughter is a mark of tragedy and of the hero's division from the unworthy crowd. For Murphy, it is a theatrical move beyond tragedy into black comedy, and the moment at which the crowd, the great unwashed of history, becomes collectively heroic.'[10] If this gesture is Nietzschean, I would suggest that it is also Benjaminian, in that Costello is the metonymic representation of what Murphy calls 'the forgotten and neglected peasantry' (2:229) who 'blasts open the continuum of history,'[11] his audacious laughter demanding representation for the marginalized histories of a peasantry *shaped and formed by poverty and hardship.'* (2:215) Costello's roaring laugh blasts open de Valera's metanarrative which marginalizes the peasant's traumatic histories in favour of an idyllic totalizing History. As a result of his supreme effort Costello expires, but in his dying breath both he and the villagers are saved from Mahony's economic tyranny as the bet is won or lost depending on who laughs last. Costello's death is both cathartic and redemptive, as the villagers' historical trauma is represented and the forces of economic terror are momentarily vanquished.

In *Bailegangaire* Murphy performs a similar critique of the post-Lemass administration. The temporal setting for *Bailegangaire* is also the contemporary moment of its production: 'DOLLY. [...] 1984, and I read it – how long ago was it? – that by 1984 we'd all be going on our holidays to the moon in *Woman's Own.'* (2:141) Dolly's sardonic comment is indicative of the disillusionment with the epochalist dream of progress and economic expansion which fuelled Ireland's transformation from beleaguered colony to postcolonial nation state. The dream is further undermined by harsh economic reality, as the Japanese owned multinational company which supported the local economy is closing down. The economic hierarchies of the colonial past are as prevalent as ever in the postcolonial present with the change from British imperialism to global capitalism. 'The weekend-long meeting at the computer plant place. All the men, busy, locked outside the fence.' (2:142) Despite their protests, the workers are as powerless against the multinational company as their historical forebears were against the might of the colonial British army: Again, Dolly comments ironically on the 'funeral' of cars when the fruitless weekend-long meeting is over: 'Now are they travelling at the sound of speed.?' (2:161) Fintan O'Toole notes that during the 1980s, '[t]hree quarters of Irish manufactured exports are from foreign-owned multinationals which import most of their inputs and export most of their profits. The cost of components imported for assembly in Ireland is exaggerated, the extent of exports overstated and the profits invisibly exported through the Black Hole.'[12]

The economic difficulties represented in *Bailegangaire* are amplified by the ethical problems manifest in Dolly's sexual permissiveness: on coming in, the stage direction says, '*She stretches herself. (She has had her sex in ditch, doorway, old shed or wherever.)*' (2:128) Later, in act 2, she '*decides to take off her coat and see what effect flaunting her pregnancy will have.*' (2:136) Dolly's threat to illegally abort the pregnancy is a dramatic intervention in contemporary Irish cultural politics: 'The countryside produced a few sensations in the last couple of years, but my grand plan: I'll show them what can happen in the dark of night in a field. I'll come to grips with my life.' (2:152) The contemporary ethical crisis in the 1980s of buried children is the echo of an earlier trauma which is represented in Mommo's story: 'The unbaptised an' stillborn in shoeboxes planted, at the dead hour of night treading softly the Lisheen to make the regulation hole – not more, not less than two feet deep – too fearful of the field, haunted by infants to speak or to pray. [...] leaving their pagan parcels in isolation forever.'(2:164) Ireland may have modernized, but the old social and economic dilemmas come back to haunt the new social consciousness in spite of any progression from a politically backward looking sentimentalism.

The 1980s disillusionment with the epochalist dream of the 1960s is also poignantly manifest in the predicament in which Mommo's eldest granddaughter Mary finds herself. Mary left her home in Ireland in the 1960s to work successfully as a nurse in England (assistant matron at age thirty), a fact which causes tension between herself and her sister Dolly who stayed behind to look after

Mommo. However, Mary's experience in England was far from that of the exile delivered into the promised land, as her story undercuts the prevailing myth of economic prosperity: She admits to Dolly, 'I failed. It all failed. I'm as big a failure as you, and that's some failure.' (2:149) Mary's homecoming is equally disappointing as the epochalist bubble has burst at home as well as abroad. Consequently she is left in a state of utter confusion and desperation as to who she is and what she should do, *possibly near breaking point.* (2:91) This problem is compounded because the senile Mommo no longer recognizes her: 'Miss? ... Do I know you?' To which Mary replies: 'No, you don't know me. But I was here once, and I ran away to try and blot out here. I didn't have it easy. [...] So I came back, thinking I'd find – something – here, or, if I didn't I'd put everything right, Mommo?' (2:152-53)

In an attempt to overcome her *'increasing sense of loneliness and demoralization'* (2:92) Mary determines to help Mommo finish her never-ending story in order to resolve the emotional crisis which plagues her family and to reclaim her identity at the same time. She persists in her attempt to have Mommo finish her tale: 'you've nearly told it all tonight. Except for the last piece that you never tell.' (2:157) This persistence is fuelled by a desperate yearning to have Mommo recognize her as her grand-daughter: 'Please – who am I?' (2:157) The dramatic tension parallels *A Thief of a Christmas* as the emotional climax and eventual catharsis are achieved only when grief and historical trauma are acknowledged and represented. Mary prompts Mommo: 'and they took Tom away to Galway, where he died ... Two mornings later, and he had only just put the kettle on the hook, didn't grandad, the stranger, go down too, slow in a swoon ... Mommo?' The memory is released, as Mommo responds: 'It got him at last. [...] Poor Séamus.' (2:169) And as she allows her grief to surface at last Mommo acknowledges historical trauma and then contemporary joy as she acknowledges her grand-daughter: 'To thee do we cry. Yes? Poor banished children of Eve. [...] To thee do we send up our sighs ... For yere Mammy an' Daddy an' grandad is *(who are)* in heaven. [...] Mourning and weeping in this valley of tears. *(She is handing the cup back to* MARY.) And sure a tear isn't such a bad thing, Mary, and haven't we everything we need here, the two of us.' (2:169)

Thus, in *Bailegangaire* Murphy critiques the vision of modernizing Ireland, and in *A Thief of a Christmas* he critiques the nostalgic idyllicization of the Irish past. However, this critical process is not so much an end in itself as it is the necessary precursor to a further project of reconstructing and re-invigorating the historical past in the service of the present and the future. The main thematic connection and primary intertextual link between these two plays, embodied in Mommo's story, is the need to acknowledge the past, to dramatically enact a return of repressed historical trauma in order to open the possibility of reconstructing the present and negotiating possible futures.

The problem of representing the historical past, and particularly traumatic historical events, is the key issue in the later 1980s debate between nationalist and revisionist historians on the topic of Irish historiography. Arguing for the revisionist position, Roy Foster suggested that 'Irish cultural self-confidence should surely have reached the stage where this [political history] can be questioned. [...] And to say "revisionist" should just be another way of saying "historian".'[13] Similarly, Ronan Fanning claimed that, 'if the nation-state outgrew infancy in 1937-38, many of its self-appointed intellectual guardians have yet to shed the insecurities of adolescence.'[14] In stark contrast, Seamus Deane argued that:

> Revisionists are nationalists despite themselves; by refusing to be Irish nationalists, they simply become defenders of Ulster or British nationalism, thereby switching sides in the dispute while believing themselves to be switching the terms of it.[15]

Brendan Bradshaw also critiqued the notion of objectivity in historical discourse by suggesting that the revisionist or 'modern tradition actually developed in reaction against an earlier nationalist tradition of historical interpretation and aspired to produce "value-free"' history.[16]

Moving beyond this antagonistic binary opposition, Declan Kiberd suggested that 'If nationalism was the thesis, revisionism was the antithesis: of its nature it was not so much wrong as incomplete. The dialectic needed to be carried through to a synthesis.'[17] Kevin Whelan also recommended the movement to-wards a post-revisionist position by focusing on the hermeneutic nature of historical analysis, especially of the revolutionary period of 1798: 'The very instability of the narrative of '98 [...] is a salutary reminder that past and present are constantly imbricated and that the positivist reading of historical texts is no longer adequate to the enterprise of historical scholarship.'[18]

It can be argued that Murphy adopts a post-revisionist position in many of his plays. In *Famine*, Murphy quite literally puts the trauma back into Irish history by dramatizing the slow, inevitable death of a village community while its leader, John Connor, can only stand by and witness the decline despite his best efforts to save the lives of his friends and family. Similarly, in *A Thief of a Christmas*, Murphy describes the play as the 'actuality' of how Bailegangaire got its name, but the actuality, the events themselves, are part of a larger dramatic construction which heightens the traumatic effect of those events. The central issue in relation to both Irish historiography and particularly Tom Murphy's play *Bailegangaire*, is the notion that any historical discourse is, by definition and of necessity, a narrative or story which is itself produced in specific cultural and historical circumstances. Mommo's story involves a re-telling of events from the historical moment of *A Thief of a Christmas* in the 1950s, but this re-telling, the story itself, is constructed in the contemporary moment of 1984. The dialectic between past and present which is predicated on the void of temporal distance is fractured when one accepts that events or 'objective facts' from the past cannot exist outside of the narrative which reconstructs those events.

In *Bailegangaire* it is only when the traumatic past is acknow-ledged as intimately linked to the crisis-ridden present that the healing process can begin. Murphy contradicts a nostalgically essentialist vision of the past, and also contradicts the myth of modernity by focusing in both instances on the historical trauma revealed in Mommo's story. In parallel to this thematic engagement, Murphy also deals with the issue of national identity by dramatizing Mary's desperate desire to finally return 'home'. Her predicament is characteristic of the post-structuralist aporia which confounds any fixed notion of identity: '(*To herself:*) Give me my freedom, Mommo ... What freedom? No freedom without structure ... Where can I go? ... How can I go (*Looking up and around the rafters.*) with all this? [...] And it didn't work before for me, did it? ... I came back.' (2:120) Just as it is impossible to return to an essentialist origin in order to achieve ontological metastasis, the epochalist rush to abandon all essentialist notions of national identity is equally misleading as Mary's attempted escape to England resulted in her eventual return in order to find a 'home' and re-create a sense of self.

Mary says there is 'no freedom without structure', and a clichéd post-structuralist response may be to argue that the point is not to abandon essentialist notions of cultural identity, but to unfix that identity and thereby open up the possibility of re-inventing it. If it is necessary to deconstruct a cultural fiction at a moment of crisis then it is also necessary to subsequently reconstruct that fiction in a manner which will enact catharsis and promote renewal. What such a reading radically underestimates is the fundamental desire for structure or even for the illusion of structure in the first instance. Whether that desire is for the kind of economic structure which underpins *A Thief of a Christmas* or the ontological structure which underpins *Bailegangaire*, the desire is there before the fact of structuration and is the grounding principle on which that structuration is predicated. The processes of both construction and reconstruction are based on the same desire for structuration, which is itself radically contingent on material, historical contexts.

It is this desire for structuration which is rooted in the dialectical tension between essentialism and epochalism, between nationalism and revisionism, and manifest in *Bailegangaire* in Mary's situation which typifies the fraught tension of this dialectic in her plea for a synthesis: 'There must be *something*, some future for me, somewhere.' (2:160) What Murphy offers in *Bailegangaire* is not the kind of relativism which has become the hackneyed resort of post-structuralist thought, typified perhaps by Lyotard.[19] Instead we have a continual focus on the ontological trauma of three disenfranchized women which builds to a climactic synthesis between the past (Mommo), the present (Mary), and the future (Dolly's unborn child). The structural integrity of this synthesis or *modus vivendi* is ethical, comprising what Terry Eagleton, arguing that love is actually political, calls 'self-realization' and 'self-fulfilment'.[20]

It is at the intersection of the personal and the political that Murphy breaks new ground in the Irish context in terms of both thematic preoccupation and dramatic execution, specifically in moving through identitarian paradigms of national identity into the ethics of interpersonal relationships. Mary's future is dependent on Mommo's recollection of the past in order that the two of them can be re-united, so that the past and the present can finally acknowledge each other. Yet Mommo and her grand-daughters, the 'Poor banished children of Eve,' do not return from their banishment to an essentialist Eden of the Irish past, nor do they depart for an epochalist Utopia in the future. As the play moves towards its cathartic ending, Mommo, Mary and the pregnant Dolly, respectively representing the temporal stages of past, present and future, are shown to be intimately linked to each other through the recently renewed bond of familial affection. Through Mommo's intertextual link with the events of *A Thief of a Christmas*, marginalized discourses are represented in a narrative which reconnects the traumatic past, and in so doing provides an historical syntax in which the traumatic present can heal and renew itself. The historical syntax is itself predicated on the interpersonal syntax or working arrangement between the three women in *Bailegangaire*, in which personal self-fulfilment quite literally depends on the self-fulfilment of the others in the group. It is the reciprocal aspect of self-fulfilment in *Bailegangaire* which exemplifies the function of love as an ethic of life-affirming desire and constitutes a timely response to post-structuralist relativism.

---

[1] An earlier, abbreviated version of this article was first published as '"Pauvres enfants d'Eve en exil": Tom Murphy et la syntaxe de l'histoire', in *L'Annuaire Théâtral*, No. 40, 'Le théâtre irlandais: au carrefour des traditions', trans. Sarah Migneron Autumn 2006: 72-84.

[2] Tom Murphy, *On the Outside*, in *Plays:4* (London: Methuen, 1997):170. Subsequent quotations are from this edition and are referenced in the text as 4 plus a page number.

[3] Tom Garvin, *Preventing the Future: Why Was Ireland so Poor for So Long?* (Dublin: Gill and Macmillan, 2004): 27.

[4] Tom Murphy, *On the Inside*, in *Plays: 4* :195. Subsequent quotations are referenced in the text as 4 plus a page number.

[5] Tom Murphy, *A Crucial Week in the Life of a Grocer's Assistant*, in *Plays :4*:94. Subsequent quotations are referenced in the text as 4 plus a page number.

[6] Tom Murphy, *Bailegangaire*, in *Plays: Two* (London: Methuen, 1993):168-69. Subsequent quotations are referenced in the text as 2 plus a page number.

[7] The terms 'essentialist' and 'epochalist' are used in a deliberately dialectical relationship and are derived from Clifford Geertz's *The Interpretation of Cultures* (New York: Basic Books, 1973). According to Geertz, essentialism entails 'local mores, established institutions, and the unities of common experience – to "tradition," "culture," "national character," or even "race" – for the roots of a new identity', while epochalism involves an awareness of 'the general outlines of the history of our time, and in particular to what one takes to be the overall direction and significance of that history.'

[8] See Paul Murphy, 'J.M. Synge and the Pitfalls of National Consciousness', in *Theatre Research International*, 28, no. 2 (Summer 2003): 125-142

9 Luke Gibbons, *Transformations in Irish Culture* (Cork: Cork UP in association with Field Day, 1996): 85.

10 Fintan O'Toole, *Tom Murphy: The Politics of Magic* (Dublin: New Island Books: Nick Hern Books, 1994): 239.

11 Walter Benjamin, *Illuminations,* trans. Harry Zohn (London: Fontana, 1973): 254.

12 Fintan O'Toole, *Black Hole, Green Card: The Disappearance of Ireland* (Dublin: New Island, 1994): 11.

13 Roy Foster, 'We Are All Revisionists Now', *The Irish Review*, no. 1 (1986): 5.

14 Ronan Fanning, 'The Meaning of Revisionism', *Irish Review*, no. 4 (Spring 1988):18.

15 Seamus Deane, 'Wherever Green is Read', in Ciaran Brady (ed.), *Interpreting Irish History* (Dublin: Irish Academic Press, 1994): 242-44.

16 Brendan Bradshaw, 'Nationalism and Historical Scholarship in Modern Ireland', in Ciaran Brady (ed.), *Interpreting Irish History*: 191-201.

17 Declan Kiberd, *Inventing Ireland* (London: Jonathan Cape, 1995): 644.

18 Kevin Whelan, *The Tree of Liberty: Radicalism, Catholicism and the Construction of Irish Identity* (Cork: Cork UP, 1996): 175.

19 Jean-François Lyotard, *The Postmodern Condition* (Manchester: Manchester UP, 1997): 82.

20 Terry Eagleton, *The Ideology of the Aesthetic* (Oxford: Blackwell, 1990): 412-13.

Comparative Essays

6 | *A Crucial Week* and *The Glass Menagerie*

Helen Heusner Lojek

American playwright Lorraine Hansberry, recalling her 'accidental' attendance at a performance of *Juno and the Paycock* noted that 'the melody was one that I had known for a very long while. I was seventeen and I did not think then of *writing* the melody as *I* knew it ... in a different key; but I believe it entered my consciousness and stayed there.'[1] The recognition of O'Casey's 'melody' by a young African American woman signals the extent to which that melody transcends issues of culture, nationality, gender, race and age. O'Casey clearly influenced Hansberry, who later kept a photo of him in her work space,[2] but no one would confuse her 1959 *A Raisin in the Sun*[3] with O'Casey's 1922 *Juno and the Paycock*. Hansberry's play is neither an imitation nor the sort of direct 'translation' produced by Trinidad playwright Mustapha Matura when Synge's *Playboy of the Western World* (1907) became *Playboy of the West Indies* (1984). Connections between Hansberry's work and O'Casey's are melodic rather than narrative. Similar melodic connections exist between Tom Murphy's *A Crucial Week in the Life of a Grocer's Assistant* (1969)[4] and Tennessee Williams's *The Glass Menagerie* (1944).[5] Murphy and Williams evoke very specific but very different times and places, and they write their often common melodies in very different keys. As Fintan O'Toole so gracefully put it (speaking only of Murphy), in confronting their specific cultures Murphy and Williams have been able 'to confront an entire universe.'[6] Juxtaposing *Menagerie* and *A Crucial Week* allows us to discern the general melody and to expand our appreciation of Murphy by considering him in a context beyond that of Irish or even continental drama.[7]

I know of no place where Murphy mentions *The Glass Menagerie*, but he has repeatedly noted the influence of Eugene O'Neill, Arthur Miller and Tennessee Williams (the three major early twentieth-century American playwrights), declaring that he 'would infinitely prefer Tennessee Williams,'[8] and that he 'can't stand' Miller's moralizing.[9] He has also repeatedly mentioned Williams' Big Daddy as a father figure related to those in his own plays.[10] Murphy has described himself as 'searching for a Theatre of Emotionalism – without sentimentality,' which he contrasts with Theatre of Cruelty or Absurdist Theatre.[11] His insistence that his plays begin in emotion and that his 'first aim would be to re-create the feeling of life' suggest one reason for his preference for Williams, who also repeatedly mentioned the need to convey emotion effectively on stage. *A Crucial Week* is an early example of Murphy's willingness to break out of the strict conventions of fourth-wall realism, in this case to incorporate expressionistic devices often similar to those used by Williams. Murphy's early willingness to violate realistic conventions was followed by later, often surrealistic approaches, so that over thirty years later Ben Barnes (then artistic director of the Abbey) paid tribute to Murphy's 'startling originality' – that of a 'restless writer' who continued to experiment with form.[12]

Regardless of whether there was direct influence, either conscious or unconscious, *The Glass Menagerie* and *A Crucial Week in the Life of a Grocer's Assistant*, each rooted in the playwright's autobiography, share situations and concerns. Juxtaposing the plays illuminates the extent to which each is also rooted in a particular time and place – and the extent to which the playwrights have achieved Murphy's goal of 'finding out about the world through myself.'[13] Murphy may or may not be right that 'The human condition that is experienced [in Ireland] is the same as that experienced in Timbuktu in terms of man's sense of isolation and alienation.'[14] It is undeniable that the human condition as experienced by Tom Wingfield in 1930s St Louis and by John Joe Moran in 1950s Tuam are very similar.

Both characters are young men trapped in situations that both push them to leave and pull them to stay in households with diminished father figures. Williams has created a father whose absence typifies a common US cultural concern: he has long since deserted the family and is present now only in a photo on the wall. Murphy has created a father whose domestic and spiritual power has been usurped by the common Irish alliance of wife and priest,[15]

so that he is now given to '*trance-like staring at nothing*' (95), occasionally making incoherent sounds, and playing a role not significantly greater than that of a photo.

The sons are left to deal primarily with their mothers, who are
matriarchs to be reckoned with. The mothers too represent types
commonly associated with particular segments of US and Irish
society. Amanda Wingfield is a middle-aged 'belle' of the sort associated with the American south, a type portrayed in, among other
works, *Gone With the Wind* and *Steel Magnolias*. Mother Moran,
whose first name (Julia) is used only by her brother, is a type of
Mother Ireland, '*a product of Irish history*' (94). Both mothers are
representative products of vanishing worlds that (at least in lip
service) posited non-economic values that have been overwhelmed
by the materialistic focus of the worlds in which they now live. They
are also simultaneously nurturing and smothering, anxious for their
sons to succeed, terrified that their sons will leave, and aware that
the departure of the sons will result in both economic and personal
difficulties for the rest of the family. One has endured the trauma of
abandonment by her husband; the other has endured the trauma of
abandonment by her now disgraced older son. Both feel the full
burden of maintaining the family in the present and planning for
their children's futures – goals that are not always compatible. The
mothers are the alarms that rouse their sons in time for work in the
depressing, dead-end jobs on which the family depends. The
mothers pass along unsolicited advice about clothing and table
manners and drink. They worry that their sons do not eat enough.
Irish motherly advice and Southern belle motherly advice may not
always be the same, but the instinct to pass it on, to seek to maintain
control over an adult son, is directly parallel.

Southern belles and Irish mothers are stereotypical figures that
are easily, and often, parodied. Williams and Murphy provide scenes
in which these mothers are laughable as they give advice and
attempt to use their feminine wiles to charm both their sons and
others. Such scenes are intended to be humorous, and they are
frequently played for laughs. Both playwrights, however, insist in
their stage directions that the women receive more than a one-
dimensional presence on stage. Amanda's characterization,
Williams specifies,

> must be carefully created, not copied from type. She is not
> paranoiac, but her life is paranoia. There is much to admire in
> Amanda, and as much to love and pity as there is to laugh at.
> Certainly she has endurance and a kind of heroism, and though

her foolishness makes her unwittingly cruel at times, there is
tenderness in her slight person. (5)

Murphy describes Mother as 'slovenly [...] harsh in expression and
bitter; a product of Irish history – poverty and ignorance; but something great about her – one could say "heroic" if it were the nineteenth century we were dealing with' (94). His creation of Mother's
complex character is at least a partial refutation of the frequent
charge that only with *Bailegangaire* (1985) did he successfully
dramatize a woman. Amanda Wingfield had a more privileged background than Julia Moran, and Amanda retains social pretentions
Julia never had. The mothers nevertheless share a great deal.

Stage directions and dialogue make it clear that Amanda
Wingfield and Julia Moran fear the departure of their sons, feel they
are hopeless to cope if the sons do indeed depart, and exercise
emotional blackmail in order to prevent any departure. Julia reports
that John Joe was 'The favourite child I lavished with praise,' (94),
and Amanda continues to lavish Tom with praise. Julia charges that
John Joe does not 'think of others' (95), and Amanda declares that
'Self, self, self' is all that Tom ever thinks of (53). Both mothers
berate their sons for coming in at all hours and worry about their
drinking.[16] Amanda notes that humans must chew their food more
carefully than animals, because animal stomachs have secretions
humans lack (24) and is horrified when Tom suggests humans have
instincts, since (she declares) 'Instinct is something that people have
got away from!' (52). John Joe gets the message about the distinction between humans and animals when his mother enlists the
aid of Father Daly, who declares 'Man is made in the likeness of
God, not in the likeness of your kittens' (133). And both mothers
join in the common cultural stereotyping of their worlds, making
clear though perhaps unconscious links between class and ethnicity:
Amanda refers to domestic chores as work for a 'darky'; Julia wails
that John Joe's drunken rant makes him 'worse than the tinkers!'
(161).[17] Though each is more than a stereotype, both have (as Shaun
Richards puts it about Mommo) 'been scarred by physical poverty
and, more devastatingly, by emotional starvation' (472).

Responding to the tensions of worlds in which they are confined
by their mothers' religions, expected to remain children, denied the
right of any desires (sexual or otherwise) that might be deemed
'animal', and smothered by the obvious love of mothers whom they
obviously love, Tom and John Joe lash out in anger and create exag-

gerated parodies of their mothers' fears. Tom's exaggeration highlights typically American stereotypes:

> I'm going to opium dens! Yes, opium dens, dens of vice and criminals' hangouts, Mother. I've joined the Hogan Gang. I'm a hired assassin, I carry a tommy gun in a violin case! I run a string of cat houses in the Valley! (42)

John Joe's exaggeration is stereotypically Irish:

> You saw the priest here this evening. No, it wasn't about the job he's trying to get me. I spent all night in Fogarty's hay shed last night with a girl called 'streeleen' [...] I raped her. Out all night with her, what else could it be? (159-60)

And both sons direct ugly personal charges at their mothers. Tom: 'You ugly – babbling old – *witch*' (42); John Joe: 'The house is filled with your bitterness and venom. A person can hardly breathe' (159). Csilla Bertha's declaration that such moments represent John Joe's attempt 'to slay symbolically the mother'[18] perhaps overstates the situation, but Murphy himself opened the door for her conclusion, explaining in 1986 that

> I ran away from [Tuam] in the sense that one has to flee the nest of one's home, in the way that, when I was young, whoever explained the universality of the fairytale – that the witch is one's mother and the dragon is one's father and you have to slay them both to win the heroine, who becomes your wife or your sweetheart. And I think in the same way, that one has to slay one's own town by getting away from it ...[19]

Nevertheless, John Joe (like Tom) is a young man struggling with a common existential dilemma – how to locate himself as an independent being in a constricting world and family. The play is about the 'trauma of choosing between exile and the prospect of life in a small town in the West of Ireland: 'Forced to stay or forced to go. Never the freedom to decide and make the choice for ourselves. We're half-men here, and half-men away, and how can we hope ever to do anything?'[20] Murphy's Mr Brown asks, 'what should be our role in this unstable comuffle of affairs?' and answers that 'we can be and will be the anchor of this trembling universe' (124). Williams's Amanda finds Tom her 'right-hand bower' in 'these trying times' (48-49). Neither John Joe nor Tom accepts these formulations as sufficient.

The world of *The Glass Menagerie*, like the world of *A Crucial Week in the Life of a Grocer's Assistant*, is one in which conversations are so often repeated that they become set pieces that can be mimicked. Repetitions (of old happinesses, old complaints, old attitudes) both distract attention from a dismal present and undermine efforts to create a better future. Visitors from a wider world (Jim, the Gentleman Caller in *Glass Menagerie*, and Mona, the bank teller in *A Crucial Week*) bring whiffs of changing cultural dynamics, but for the most part these changes are merely unsettling, not liberating.[21] In *The Glass Menagerie* Jim's dogged pursuit of self-improvement seems unlikely to move him very far up the ladder of the commercial, materialistic society that is such a contrast to the world in which Amanda grew up. Laura is unable even to attempt pursuit of the dream of advancement, and Tom rejects it outright. Ironically, Amanda is the Wingfield who adapts most successfully, selling undergarments and magazine subscriptions, and seeking a career for her daughter. In *A Crucial Week*, John Joe is unable to bring himself to go to the city with Mona, whose career girl status and open sexuality make her an anomaly in his village community, and whose name allows for wonderful moans during John Joe's opening dream.[22] John Joe (like Tom) throws up his job in a rash gesture of frustration, and it is his mother who takes steps to secure an income for him (and to secure his presence at home) by talking to the priest and by betraying her own brother in hopes he will turn his shop over to John Joe. These mothers may be overbearing and often unattractive in their worry, but they are not passively awaiting developments – even though their present realities are radically different and more materialistic than the societies of their youths.

These sons may be very different than their parents, but they do not 'escape' into other situations without ambivalence and a kind of splitting of identity that suggests the fracture in their beings resulting from their efforts to become independent. Tom is split between identities as poet and warehouse employee, but a more radical split is revealed by the presence on stage of Tom present and Tom past (played by the same actor). His closing lines, summarizing his travels from city to city, yet focusing on his memories of Laura, reveal the radical tension that he can never resolve: 'Oh, Laura, Laura, I tried to leave you behind me, but I am more faithful than I intended to be!'(115).

John Joe's crisis of individual identity has a somewhat happier resolution, despite the fact he loses Mona and seems unlikely readily to find a substitute lover. Nevertheless, the tensions remain. John Joe says repeatedly that 'It's not just a case of staying or going' (152). The rich fantasy life revealed by his dreams is a stark contrast to the dullness of work in Mr Brown's grocery shop, the repressions indicated in his relationship with Mona, and the guilt-inducing sameness of his home life. His dreams also illustrate the difficulty he has separating staying and going. He dreams of living at a new address that is an amalgamation of English and American forms. He locates this dream address in America (apparently New York), but his description includes details that sound a great deal more like Tuam: 'Look at those fields, the first soft grass! Look at the bracken, the smell of the bog, and Gardenfield Wood whispering to Molloy!' (117).[23] The dream is neither of staying nor of going, echoing the complexity of *Philadelphia, Here I Come!* (Right back where I started from) in Brian Friel's adapted song. Moreover, the coupling of John Joe 'real' and John Joe 'dream' involves a stage doubling as powerful and suggestive as that embodied in the two Toms.

Commentators regularly link John Joe's crisis of individual identity with Ireland's post-colonial crisis of national identity, and the parallels are apt and suggestive.[24] Fintan O'Toole notes that John Joe's search for economic success is simultaneously a search for psychological independence.[25] Tom's search for psychological independence takes a precisely opposite tack: independence for Tom results from a rejection of the search for economic success in favour of artistic development. In the 1950s, independence came late for Irish children, and the identity crises for these young men come at times typical for their cultures: Tom is 22; John Joe is 33.[26] The split between generations in both plays, however, is stark and deeply informed by materialism and commercialism. Tom's fractured identity is seldom linked to any national identity issues – perhaps because residents of the United States are considerably less aware of their postcolonial status than are residents of Ireland – but the American world with which he struggles is as riven by class distinctions as the Irish world where John Joe must find his way, and the situation of each central male character is illuminated by contrast with other young men (Tom-Jim; John Joe-Pakey-Frank). John Joe's situation is also illuminated by contrast with Mona, and with Agnes, who – despite her own powerful mother, her prayer book, and her ringlets – manages to separate herself from both mother and Mother Ireland and depart for Boston.

Williams and Murphy present their often parallel themes and characters using dramatic techniques that are also often parallel. Some of the technical parallels are relatively minor. Both plays are divided into scenes but not acts. In both, characters who are extremely unlikely to move far from their present locations sing songs that are, ironically, about sailing away: Jim in *The Glass Menagerie* (91) and Father in *A Crucial Week* (134).[27] Both plays incorporate the sound of off-stage church bells as a sort of non-verbal commentary. Tom's situation is illuminated by contrast with the (stereotypical and mythic) description of life on Blue Mountain given by his mother; John Joe's mocking use of a 'stage-Irish brogue' in describing 'the mists that do be on the bog'(113) provides a similar mythic contrast to his situation.

More importantly, both Williams and Murphy use expressionistic techniques to reveal the emotional truths of their dramas. In the Production Notes to *The Glass Menagerie*, Williams dismissed the 'exhausted theatre of realistic conventions' in favour of unconventional, expressionistic techniques that allow for 'a closer approach to truth' (7).[28] Williams relies heavily on unrealistic lighting, which he notes is 'In keeping with the atmosphere of memory' (9), and he uses music 'to give emotional emphasis to suitable passages' (9). The text of *The Glass Menagerie* also pro-vides for the use of a screen on which images or titles may be projected to accent 'certain values in each scene' (8). Most productions eliminate the screen, but Williams' description of it indicates the general mood he wanted for the play.

Murphy too specifies the use of 'unusual lighting' to suggest 'the unreality of the dream scenes' (90), and the sound of a train whistle in the opening scene provides additional emotional emphasis. That opening dream scene signals the basic approach of *A Crucial Week*, which regularly violates the strict conventions of realistic drama in order to provide clear evidence of the ways in which John Joe's reality both informs and contrasts with his dreams. Like Brian Friel's *Philadelphia, Here I Come!* (1964), *A Crucial Week* allows us access to the main character's inner thoughts and yearnings not by anticipating that actors will develop sub-text through their actions and not by providing situations in which characters voice their dreams. Rather, Friel and Murphy embody inner feelings in 'characters' who actually appear on stage, but whom we recognize as manifestations of realities that cannot ordinarily be seen. Both Irish plays have elements that are considerably funnier than anything in *The Glass Menagerie* (unless we count the moment when Jim seeks Laura's favor by offering her a piece of chewing gum and linking gum with the Century of Progress, before wrapping his chewed gum in paper and depositing it in his pocket). *Glass* and *A Crucial Week*, though, share a willingness to violate realistic conventions in an effort to convey emotional realities.

In the programme for the Abbey Theatre's 2001 celebration of Murphy's work Fintan O'Toole described Murphy's terrain as 'the vast space that stretches between illusion and reality,' calling the playwright a 'great fabulist' who uses 'magic realism'. O'Toole described Murphy's plays as 'above all, European plays, profoundly engaged with the archetypes of western culture.'[29] With his usual astuteness, O'Toole has put his cursor on significant aspects of Murphy's themes and style. Balancing *A Crucial Week* against *The Glass Menagerie*, though, reveals that it is indeed engagement with 'western' rather than 'European' archetypes and styles that is the backbone of Murphy's play.

Particularly in the opening scene, Murphy uses details (Mona's medals, the train whistle, the hold-all) symbolically. *A Crucial Week*, though, does not share Williams's reliance on a heavy use of recurring symbols (the glass collection, the record collection, the fire escape, the candelabra, and so on). The antic disposition evident in Murphy's dream scenes, however, is close to that created when a drunken Tom describes the 'magic show' to Laura. Both plays have sets that make clear the families live in spaces that are identical to those inhabited by their neighbors, what Williams calls 'the cellular living-units...[of] overcrowded urban centers' (21) and Murphy describes more neutrally as 'two in a row of houses' (100). And both playwrights are willing to abandon the strict conventions of fourth-wall realism in favour of techniques that remind audiences that this is a play. Williams has Tom fill the role of Stage Manager, talking directly to the audience and directing lighting; in *The Glass Menagerie*, 'Eating is indicated by gestures without food or utensils' (24); in the closing scene past and present co-exist on stage and Amanda's gestures become 'almost dancelike' (114). In *A Crucial Week*, the grocery shop is represented when a shop-counter is pushed on stage; a bed of hay represents the hay shed.[30]

Writing several years after Murphy wrote *A Crucial Week*, Brian Friel defined Irish drama as 'written in Irish or English on Irish subjects and performed by Irishmen' and noted 'persistent' demands that Irish drama be 'relevant' to 'Ireland today.'[31] Commentators on Irish drama have continued to share that concern – as Karen Fricker and Brian Singleton have pointed out, in Ireland there is an 'unusually intimate relationship between theatre and nation-building.'[32] Murphy's plays are frequently analyzed from a nationalistic perspective in which post-colonial, sectarian, and border issues are key.[33] The plays are in fact illuminated by – just as they illuminate – the context of national situations and issues. Friel also, however, pointed out that 'the intensity of the emotion we all feel for our country (and in the present climate that emotion is heightened) is not of itself the surest foundation for the best drama.'[34] Irish issues *are* important in assessing Murphy's work. Equally important, though less often stated, is Richard's Kearney's awareness that Murphy's work 'transcend[s] its local or national setting' and assumes 'a stature of epic, international propositions' that allows it to 'travel well.'[35] Anne Kelly has accurately observed that 'There is no escaping the rootedness of Murphy's work in the Ireland in which he grew up and came to adulthood,'[36] and the same judgment can be accurately applied to Williams's plays, particularly to The *Glass Menagerie*. Nicholas Grene's equally accurate assessment that Murphy's dramas ultimately 'stand free of originating circumstances'[37] fits Williams's plays as well. In juxtaposing *Glass* and *A Crucial Week*, I have sought not to demonstrate that Murphy's play mimics or depends on Williams's, but that both are rooted in particulars from which they stand free to present very similar melodies to which very broad audiences respond.

Williams was American; Murphy is Irish; each is a major playwright whose achievements cannot be confined within a national label.

---

[1] Lorraine Hansberry, 'Take Away Our Hearts O' Stone,' in *To Be Young, Gifted and Black*, adapted by Robert Nemiroff (New York: Signet, 1970): 87. Emphasis and ellipsis are in the original.

[2] She also had a photo of Paul Robeson, a bust of Einstein, and Michelangelo's *David*. Hansberry further signalled her awareness of Irish literature by sketching a self-portrait that she entitled 'A Portrait of the Artist as a Young Woman Contemplating Christmas,' reproduced in *To Be Young, Gifted and Black*: 103.

[3] One indication of the enduring popularity of Hansberry's play is the number of major stage, screen, and television productions that have attracted big name stars: Sidney Poitier and Ruby Dee (1959 stage; 1961 screen); Danny Glover and Esther Rolle (1989 television); Phylicia Rashad and rapper Sean 'Diddy' Coombs (2008 stage and television).

4 All references are to the version of *A Crucial Week* included in Tom Murphy, *Plays 4* (London: Methuen, 1997).

5 All references are to the New Directions paperback edition (1945).

6 Fintan O'Toole, *Tom Murphy: The Politics of Magic* (Dublin: New Island Books, 1994): 19.

7 Shaun Richards's discussion of Murphy's plays in comparison with Eugene O'Neill, Arthur Miller, and a general US tendency to regard the west as a sort of paradise regained, provides a revealing non-European contextualization of the works. See '"There's No such Thing as the West Anymore": Tom Murphy and the Lost Ideal of the Land of the Free,' *Études Irlandaises* XV:2 (December 1990): 83-94.

8 Mária Kurdi, 'An Interview with Tom Murphy,' *Irish Studies Review* XII:2 (2004): 235.

9 James F. Clarity, 'Arts Abroad: Praise Doesn't Equal Fame, but Playwright Persists,' *New York Times*, 29 July 1999. http://query.nytimes.com (accessed 13 June 2008).

10 References to Williams also appear in 'Tom Murphy: In Conversation with Michael Billington,' in *Talking about Tom Murphy*, ed. Nicholas Grene (Dublin: Carysfort Press, 2002): 91-112; and in a June 2006 interview conducted as part of Theatre Forum Ireland. www.theatrevoice.com (accessed 16 June 2008).

11 Quoted in Joe Jackson, 'Murphy's Law,' *Hot Press* 11 October 2001. www.hotpress.com/archive/1536232.html (accessed 24 June 2008).

12 Ibid.

13 Theatre Forum Ireland interview, www.theatrevoice.com.

14 Mária Kurdi, *Irish Studies Review*: 240.

15 See Declan Kiberd's discussion in 'Fathers and Sons,' *Inventing Ireland: The Literature of the Modern Nation* (London: Jonathan Cape, 1995): 380-94.

16 Learning that the Gentleman Caller's full name is James Delaney O'Connor, Amanda exclaims 'Irish on *both* sides! *Gracious!* And doesn't drink?' (63). Emphasis in original.

17 In Murphy's earlier play *A Whistle in the Dark* (1961), Irish emigrants in London display a similar tendency to mingle class and ethnicity in evaluations of their world, recounting with pleasure their fights with blacks and Muslims. The characters might be unconscious of their assumptions about a link between class and ethnicity, but Murphy is not. In Tuam, which lacks the cultural diversity of London, 'tinkers' (an insult also used in *A Whistle*) fill the role of low class, marginalized ethnic minority.

18 'The House Image in Three Contemporary Irish Plays,' *New Hibernia Review* VIII:2 (2004): 15.

19 John Waters, 'The Frontiersman,' interview with Tom Murphy, *In Dublin* 15 May 1986: 27.

20 Ibid.

21 Murphy was writing shortly after Seán Lemass began (in 1958) a radical change in Irish economic policy that resulted in diminished emphasis on the Irish small farm and increased emphasis on international commerce and industrialization. Changing economic practices changed Irish culture.

22 The equally sexual woman in *The Gigli Concert* (1983) is also named Mona.

23 The reference is to *The Wood of the Whispering* (1953), by fellow-Galway playwright M.J.Molloy. Molloy's play is a comedy focusing on poverty, depopulation, and relationship difficulties in rural Ireland. The 'wood' was a meeting place for lovers who have left the area. I am grateful to Christopher Murray for identifying this reference for me.

24 Fintan O'Toole, for example, notes in *The Politics of Magic* that Mother conforms closely to 'the generalized picture of the Irish mother' (83) and that the play was written and takes place during a time of massive cultural shift in Ireland, concluding that the end is an 'endorsement of the Irish future (92). See as well Lionel Pilkington, '"The Superior Game": Colonialism and the Stereotype in Tom Murphy's *A Whistle in the Dark*,' in *Ritual Remembering: History, Myth and Politics in Anglo-Irish Drama*, eds C.C.Barfoot and Rias van den Doel (Amsterdam: Rodopi, 1995): 165-79.

25 *The Politics of Magic.*

26 In the 1978 Gallery Books edition of the play, John Joe is 29. Murphy's decision to adjust John Joe's age to match that of Christ does not add much to the play.

27 Earlier (p. 105), Father has sung a song 'presumably' called 'The Ship that Never Returned', which sounds suspiciously like the Kingston Trio's 1959 song 'M.T.A'.

28 Compare Eugene O'Neill's contention: 'The old "naturalism" – or "realism," if you prefer [...] no longer applies. It represents our Fathers' daring aspirations toward self-recognition by holding the family kodak up to ill-nature.' See 'Strindberg and Our Theatre,' Provincetown Playbill for *The Spook Sonata*, 3 January 1924, reprinted in Helen Deutsch and Stella Hanau, *The Provincetown: A Story of the Theatre*, (New York: Russell and Russell, 1931): 191.

29 Fintan O'Toole, programme note for 6 at the Abbey: A Celebration of the Work of Tom Murphy, 1-14 October 2001: 8.

30 Arthur Miller's *Death of a Salesman* (1949) uses similar devices of light and music. Miller's kitchen is represented by only the minimal fixtures necessary for the action, and a set change is indicated when a character wheels a typewriter on stage.

31 'Plays Peasant and Unpeasant' (1972), reprinted in *Brian Friel: Esssays, Diaries, Interviews: 1964-1999*, ed. Christopher Murray (London: Faber, 1999): 53.

32 'Irish Theatre: Conditions of Criticism,' *Modern Drama* 47:4 (Winter 2004): 562.

33 See, for examples, analyses by Fintan O'Toole, Lionel Pilkington, and Csilla Bertha.

34 'Plays Peasant and Unpeasant' in *Essays, Diaries, Interviews*: 53.

35 'Tom Murphy's Long Night's Journey into Night', *Studies LXXII* (Winter 1983): 331. Joseph S. O'Leary has a less positive judgment of Murphy's localism, concluding that the plays (particularly in their consideration of Christianity) never escape their 'engagement with the audience's most intimate woes' sufficiently to escape a 'datedness and provinciality' that are 'inimical to art.' See O'Leary, 'Looping the Loop with Tom Murphy: Anticlericalism as Double Bind,' *Studies* 81 (Spring 1992): 41, 46.

36 'A Feminist Reading of the Plays of Tom Murphy (Part One),' http://www.ucd.ie/irthfrm/akelly.htm (accessed 9 June 2008).

37 Nicholas Grene, 'Tom Murphy and the Children of Loss,' *Cambridge Companion to Twentieth-Century Irish Drama*, ed. Shaun Richards (Cambridge: Cambridge UP, 2004): 207.

7 | 'Camelot Lost': The Death of the American Dream

Patrick Burke

Three events dominate my memories of 1963: the death of the greatly loved Pope John XXIII, with his liberating emphasis on *aggiornamento* for Christian renewal, and two memories of President John F. Kennedy: his visit to Ireland in June and his assassination in November. The visit, the first by a USA President in office, came at a significant point in modern Irish history, in that a predominantly agricultural economy, an overwhelmingly Catholic society and a network of traditionally sanctioned social *mores,* were beginning to feel the winds of change: Ireland's President, Eamon de Valera, had stepped down as Taoiseach in 1959, T.J. Whitaker's *First Programme for Economic Expansion* was published in 1958, *Telefís Eireann* (Irish Television) had begun transmission on the very last day of 1961, and long experience of foreign travel, mainly by Catholic missionaries, was gradually being extended by new agencies (such as Joe Walshe's) into resolutely secular holidays abroad. A country opening up in such a context felt powerfully and palpably vindicated by the prospect of a USA president of doubly Irish descent – young, handsome, charming, impressively articulate – visiting in triumph, locations associated with his forebears and, in a brilliant speech to both houses of the Oireachtas, affirming Irish identity and boosting national *morale.* Kennedy's assassination, then, within less than six months, while undoubtedly a source of real grief in the USA and across most of the so-called 'free world' had, I recall, for many people in Ireland, much of the impact of a death in their own family. An iconic index of the impact of both events, unique to Ireland in its extensiveness, was the abundance of portraits and photographs of Kennedy which began to appear on the walls of houses, public and private, not to mention cathedrals!

With the passage of time, the Kennedy era was subject both to mythologization and harsh reassessment: one way, he and his beautiful wife Jacqueline had created and presided over a political order coded as 'Camelot' (from the Lerner and Loewe musical), patronizing the arts and encouraging the intellectual life.[1] Kennedy had courageously and wisely seen off the threat to his presidency posed by the Cuban crisis in 1962, and with his brother Robert inaugurated a programme of social reform likely to benefit, in particular, black citizens of the USA. On the other hand, in almost symmetrical balance to the above, there was growing evidence of Kennedy's extensive marital infidelity (including a sexual fling with Marilyn Monroe), of his poor judgement in the Bay of Pigs *débacle* in 1961, and of his and Robert's compromising association with leading Mafia figures. And for 'friend and foe alike,' there was the ongoing, divisive issue of USA intervention in Vietnam, which Kennedy had sponsored.

꙾꙾

In this essay I want to consider two plays – or, to be precise, one play (American) and two versions of another (Irish) – to which the Kennedy presidency supplies significant background as well as dramatic focus: these are *The White House* (1972)[2] by Tom Murphy – alongside the revised version, *Conversations on a Homecoming* (1985) – and *Kennedy's Children* (1973) by Robert Patrick.

On 20 March 1972 the Abbey Theatre, Dublin, premiered Murphy's *The White House*, a play in two acts. Contrary to some lazy impressions of him as a 'gut' writer guided essentially by the power of emotion, Murphy always takes trouble, when context demands, to read carefully and thoroughly around his topic, in this instance the life and times of J.F. Kennedy, in particular, as we learn from the Murphy papers in Trinity College, the monumental *A Thousand Days* (1965) by Arthur M. Schlesinger, Jr, who was a well-known admirer of Kennedy. Twenty-two hand-written quotations from that source in one of Murphy's notebooks (regrettably undated), reflect, one assumes, the scope of his interests in Kennedy and the Camelot years: key terms include 'courage', 'style', 'individuality', 'the arts [and] a healthy society'.[3]

The most striking dramatic feature of *The White House* text is that act one, entitled 'Conversations on a Homecoming', is set in time present, and act two, entitled 'Speeches of Farewell', takes place on 22 November, 1963, the date of Kennedy's assassination nine years earlier. The cart was firmly before the horse. Instead of conventional plot sequence, orientated to presenting action as some form of outcome from motivation and aspiration, or, in Francis Fergusson's well-known phrase, mirroring the dramatic rhythm of *passion, purpose and perception*,[4] *The White House* took to the stage in reverse, presenting first the consequences of action and, secondly, its impetus. After three weeks of a five-week run, when it was adjudged in performance that, in spite of some favourable reviews, especially of Dan O'Herlihy in the leading role, the play was asking too much of audiences, the sequencing was reversed, providing a seemingly more linear chronology. The cart was now put back behind the horse. This alteration had the approval of the play director, Vincent Dowling, and, it was claimed, of Tom Murphy.

Retaining my belief in what Murphy originally wrote, and focussing on form and structure, *The White House,* I would contend, represents an important experiment: that which is *recalled* in act one is *presented* in act two. That is to say, the plot describes the attempt by JJ Kilkelly, a young widower newly returned to the west of Ireland from England, where, according to himself, his wife had been killed in a road accident, to convert into an art gallery the unexceptional pub he has acquired by marrying his second wife, Della (its putative name, 'The White House', reflecting JJ's consuming obsession with President Kennedy). The basis of this obsession with Kennedy is JJ's his alleged physical resemblance to him, a feature to which both acts of the play draw attention (though JJ enters only in one). In the words of Tom, temporary teacher, speech-writer to JJ, co-founder of 'The White House', and, in the second act, caustically disillusioned interrogator of the whole lost enterprise, 'Kennedy is a personal matter with you.'[5]

Assisting JJ in what he himself terms a 'co-sponsorial job', are, in addition to Tom, Michael Ridge, an aspirant actor, Larry O'Kelly, a draughtsman and talented amateur painter, Junior, a rather callow youth, who works in his father's garage, thirty-year-old Peggy, who despite having a crush on JJ , is drawn to Tom by the ending of 'Speeches of Farewell', Johnny Quinn, a local handyman, and, of course, Della, nicknamed 'Missus', and titled, consistently with the Kennedy parallels, 'the first lady'. In *Speeches of Farewell* the visible manifestation of their support – painting, shifting furniture, stitching curtains, general 'business' – is natural preamble to the animated discussion between JJ and Father Connolly, the local parish priest, as to the appropriateness of displaying in the art gallery a nude, which Larry has painted. That exchange ends in stalemate: the priest, needing JJ's good offices to secure a job for a young member of an impecunious family, accordingly tries to behave more diplomatically than *clichéd* images of clerical dominance would require, while JJ's defence of the nude, though robust, forceful and politically astute, is deficient in aesthetic grounding. Moreover, Larry, in the interests of his own social survival, is less than emphatic as to the artistic imperatives of exhibiting the nude, a stance rendered ironic by later events, when a price is exacted for even mild rebellion, as we learn from the later version: 'Larry O'Kelly got transferred [...] and *Bridget Reclining* with him.' [6]

Because both versions of the Murphy play record the rapid failure of what was intended to be a life-enhancing gallery – a failure made visible in the contrast between the settings of 'Speeches of Farewell' ('in good taste'[7]) and *Conversations on a Homecoming* ('a run-down pub'[8]) – and because bringing it to reality was identified so singularly with JJ, it may be tempting to construe the play's action as not merely holding him responsible for that failure but as presenting him accurately through Tom's eyes – a straw man, lacking courage, emotionally dependent, pathetically bibulous and politically opportunist: 'JJ is a dangerous and weak slob who limped back here from England. England was finished for him: He couldn't face it again. And people here fell flat on their faces for him and he left them high-and-dry.' As to his admiration for JFK, Tom goes on, JJ simply jumped up on 'some American bandwagon of idealism [that] was passing at the time' and 'hopped up on that load of straw, and had so little going for himself that when that load of straw went up in smoke, JJ went with it. Hmm?'[9]

The fact that JJ 's sole defender is Michael – 'he had his own idealism' – is less than reassuring, given the extent of Michael's own failure, which is not confined to the art of acting. However, these antipathies, late in the act, lose their edge when 'Conversations', in clever irony, brings to the fore forms of failure in Tom's own stay-at-home life. His bitterness derives from disillusion. It is notable that, in revealing insecurity, Tom is also impressed to be told that JJ admired him in those far-off days in 1963.

In general, it is critically limiting to address Murphy's play, in whichever version, in terms of disillusioned memory of transitory liberation (the original sequencing of 'The White House') *or* as emancipation doomed to rancid failure (the later sequencing), mainly because 'Speeches of Farewell' is peculiarly resistant to such tidy categorization. JJ *is* affable, engaging, and a good talker; he is also, in spite of Tom's negative comments, genuinely aware of the 'place of the artist' in society and, as Peggy reminds us, of the value of classical music, of the naivety of non-ideological liberation and the mindlessness of what JJ terms 'the country-and-western system itself. Unyielding, uncompromising in its drive for total sentimentality! A sentimentality that would have us a gullible herd should the day ever arrive for a drive towards total domination.' At that stage, 'We, the sentimentalists, would be ready victims of ourselves, of any leader, any cause – Hitler fodder, Nazis, inqui-sitors, fascists.'[10] It can be noted that this speech is given almost verbatim to Tom in the 1985 *Conversations* (*Plays 2*: 67): ironically, Tom has not forgotten.

Further, JJ is actively sympathetic to the plight of a couple he has heard about who are reluctant to bear a child into a corrupted world to which, presumably, arts activity might make a political difference. Inhibiting of such transformative commitment, however, are, at one level, a hard-headed awareness that the gallery, though not priori-tized as profit-making, might be good 'for selling pints' as well as facilitating JJ's possible entry into local politics, and, at another, his deep debilitating insecurity, not invisible behind his apparent con-fidence, as the action of 'Speeches of Farewell' unfolds to the dramatic collapse of JJ. It is worth recalling that in an earlier draft 'Speeches of Farewell' was entitled 'Images', as this underlines how dependent JJ was on a heroic model. Following the death of his first wife, JJ 'doubts his own ability to manage another knock' (MS2: 2), while part of his motivation in proceeding as he does is so that '[the locals] won't put him wrong a second time' (MS2: 24). Hence the significance of his identification with Kennedy : inner emptiness in JJ, insecure *ego*, poor self-definition, the sense, in his own words, that '[he] was sentenced to life', that 'Life is unfair' (a known adage of Kennedy's) are all afforded protection by the charm and idealism of the Kennedy *persona*. (MS2: 12-13) Moreover, by calling, mantra-like, on the eloquent diction and rhythms of such speeches as Kennedy's presidential inaugural in 1961, 'Let the word go forth from this time and place to friend and foe alike', which he does with startling regularity, JJ can conceal deficiencies in his own thought or vocabulary. The risk he runs is obvious – when Kennedy is killed, part of JJ dies with him, and the slide to degradation, given partial impetus by self-hatred, is embarked on: JJ's last words (inconsolable, in tears) in the play are: 'I never liked him anyway. I never liked him' (MS2: 61). We do not see him again.

It seems to me that one of the first-night reviewers of *The White House,* David Nowlan, writing in *The Irish Times,* pinpointed the artistic problem with which Tom Murphy had presented himself with irrefutable accuracy:

> Something close to anti-drama spreads itself fatally over all the second act, after a first act that must rank as one of the best pieces of accurate drama reporting of a whole Irish generation [...] they don't gel. [...] The trouble ultimately is in the structure of the play.[11]

For Murphy such inherent structural problems were compounded, *vis-à-vis* the premiere performance, by what he strongly felt, against the reviewers' consensus, was a seriously self-indulgent inter-pretation of JJ by Dan O'Herlihy: in his notebooks he censures 'acting by rote, steam-rolling through speeches where changes of mood, attitude are required [...] stentorian. [...] JJ as presented is a great bore.'[12]

Acknowledging all the inherent difficulty of presenting theatri-cally a scenario of creative potential through a prism of disillusionment, I nonetheless believe that, despite many fine moments, 'Speeches of Farewell' is simply not as effective as 'Conversations on a Homecoming', as the many redrafts of the former probably serve to indicate. Considering that 'Speeches' theoretically celebrates creativity and new beginnings, its dialogue rarely carries the same *frisson* as 'Conversations', the more overtly melancholy second act. If we speak of characterization, Larry's, for example, is under-developed, given, not merely his artist role, but the fact that, in the past, he was a competitor with JJ, *à la* Othello and Cassio, for the affections of Missus. I suspect, too, that the very troubled young man we meet in Michael in *Conversations* is inadequately introduced in *Speeches.* The reduction, therefore, of the two-act *White House* to the extended one-act *Conversations on a Homecoming,* integrating all the salient elements of *Speeches,* seems wholly justified on grounds of an aesthetic rightness, having to do with a kind of intensified Ibsenite strategy where the pastness of the present and the presentness of the past, are interwoven. Fintan O'Toole puts it well:

> In *The White House,* the past and the present were appre-hended separately, invoking an overall irony at the end of the play in the contrast between one and the other. In *Con-*

versations on a Homecoming, the past and the present are on stage simultaneously, gnawing away at each other, making the ironies constant and infinitely more effective in dramatic terms. Real drama comes about when there is more than one world present on stage at the same time [...].[13]

Accordingly, later references to Murphy in this chapter will be on the basis of the definitiveness of the amended *Conversations on a Homecoming.*

ন্ন   ন্ন

The American play to be contrasted here with Murphy's is *Kennedy's Children* by Robert Patrick, which premiered at the Clark Center for the Performing Arts-Playwrights, New York, in 1973. On transferring to the King's Head, Islington, in October, 1974, and the Arts Theatre, London, in April 1975, it was more warmly received than in the USA, winning a notable number of awards. In the intervening thirty years, however, it has become something of a cult play on its native soil: tucked away in every dramatic season, either in commercial or, more likely, university campus theatres, will be at least one *Kennedy's Children.* In *that* regard, prescinding from its inherent artistic merits or flaws, the play resembles not so much Murphy's *Conversations* as Friel's *Translations* in the extent of its sociological relevance: just as Friel's genius was to give dramatic form to fundamental issues of language loss and acquisition, *Kennedy's Children* holds a mirror to the range of social, even epistemological forces at work at a determining time in the history of the USA. In an interesting departure from the norms of mainstream American drama (O'Neill to Mamet), the play communicates by means of the monologue format:

> At no time do the characters relate to one another, not even at the moments of greatest duress. Nor do they deliver their monologues directly to the audience. They are thinking to themselves, relishing phrases, suffering pain, reliving happy moments. [...] The actors move with complete freedom if they feel impelled to walk through a remembered scene.[14]

Patrick, however, seems more open than many twentieth-century playwrights were to directorial inventiveness with his script:

> The artists engaged in future productions will have to make their own decisions as to which [stage directions] to employ, which to ignore. In one production which took place in an enormous theatre, a brilliant director used a great deal of 1960's music and imaginative movement for the cast, actually

having them play roles in one another's memories. It worked beautifully whereas static staging as called for in the text might have been lost on the huge stage. (1)

Kennedy's Children, set like *Conversations on a Homecoming* in a bar, albeit less grotty, has a cast of five monologuists and a mute barman. It is in two acts, in the course of which we meet Wanda, mid-thirties, who had been captivated by the Camelot dream, Sparger, former drag queen, a cynical veteran of 'alternative' theatre, Rona, a disappointed hippy idealist, Mark, a traumatized survivor of Vietnam, and Carla, a beautiful would-be actress, whose icon is Marilyn Monroe. Their monologues invoke, sometimes very affectingly, a shared sense of communal *malaise,* given impetus, inferably, by the assassination of Kennedy, even if Wanda and Rona are the only ones to name him directly. It is detectable from her final monologue that Wanda has not yet completely despaired:

> [N]ow I have my temporary teaching certificate and can work as a substitute teacher. I just thought – if all of us who believed in him don't go out and try to do some good, then he died completely in vain. [...] If he had lived, he would have stopped the war. If he had lived, he would have solved the race problem. If he had lived, he would have found some way to bring us all together. (18)

The more politically astute Rona gives voice both to the first hopes of the hippy movement and to their failure: 'I printed pamphlets and made incense and washed dishes and marched.' Robbie, her lover, 'was deep into political reading, and he and a lot of the cats and an awful lot of the chicks, too, were for a violent revolution, but- American kids weren't raised for that. And besides, killing and fighting were the things we were trying to stop. 'Love' became a new word, it was everywhere, a bigger love than just two people, people were talking about the Aquarian Age.' (25) Within three years of Kennedy's death, that kind of aspiration had altered:

> [T]he streets were starting to be pretty full of these sort of insincere   kids ... they were television addicts, they were middle-class kids, they were just after fun and dope and sex and funny clothes ... [While travelling], we'd stop to see the universities, where they were – God – burning draft cards and starting on acid and getting heavy into Civil Rights. (27)

In any society, the use of drugs is bound up, in ways however perverse and self-deluding, with what is perceived as assuaging the pain of raw reality, 'very much' of which, in T.S. Eliot's dictum, 'human kind cannot bear.' That is why we are not surprised at the comment from Mark, traumatized as he may be, that 'it is the [US]

Government itself that is selling us drugs' (33), as a form of Orwellian sedation. For all five characters, if with varying emphases, the widespread use of dangerous drugs is an uncomplicated measure of the post-Kennedy decline. A more complicated, if related, version of the measure is the outcome of the struggle between manifestations, however tentative, of authentic theatre, itself a form of detachment from quotidian banality, and gross exploitation of the human body. In that regard, for the beautiful Carla, general moral degradation in the US predated the Kennedy era: 'I hate the Goddamn Sixties. I hate everything that happened in them, and I hate everything that didn't happen, and I hate what happened to me and what happened to other people.'

For her, significantly, 'the sixties started off with Marilyn Monroe dying.' Thus, Carla, presented, like Monroe herself in real life, as not devoid of true acting talent, found herself, on the death of the actress, in competition with 'fifty million little boys and girls [who wanted] to be the next Marilyn Monroe' (16). In her graphic, alliteratively emphatic account of the degradations required to fulfil that ambition, Carla is supplying, beyond the immediate context, frightening images 'out of Hieronymus Bosch', of a deeply depraved society:

> And every dirty old man, cross-eyed agent, horny hairdresser, finger-fucking photographer, plastic playwright, demented director, urgent acting teacher, many-handed manager, oral office boy, anal choreographer, phallic vocal coach, orgiastic dress designer, and every other form of unlaid, opportunistic, scaly, slimy, sleazy son-of-a-bitch in this nation's great metropolitan casting centers, suddenly, found him – or her – or themselves deluged under ten million tons of automated, undulating, available, eager, MEAT! (16)

Sparger, former drag queen, has observed and been a victim of the exploitation and degradation, including rape, that a so-called underground theatre may risk attracting. Later, in one of the more engaging sequences in the play, he outlines how the performers in the underground 'Opera Buffo', managed by Buffo, the clown, were accidentally discovered, in the middle of an improvised slapstick routine, by a critic from the *Village Voice* who 'wrote [them] up that week as the latest thing in Dray-mah' (28), as a consequence of which, for the next few years, they were enabled to function as something like a vibrant arts centre. Yet again, in the recurring pattern of the play, apparent success leads to failure, as summed up by Sparger in his penultimate monologue:

> The first success drove our old audience away, then the critics drove away the new audience. [...] And now more and more we attracted not the real rebels, or the real drop-outs, but failures and phonies from uptown who just wanted to do whatever had been original and daring the year before. The new phony audience read the reviews and *loved* us! But for us – the sanctity, the privacy, was gone. (32)

The ultimate manifestation of the failure of 'Opera Buffo' is the horrific suicide of Buffo, hacking at his limbs and stomach with a hatchet.

ޮ ޮ

I can find no evidence that Patrick or Murphy have read the other's work, though I suspect Murphy would not seriously demur from Patrick's 'Word from the Author', as given at the outset of his play: '*the theme of the play is the death of the idea of heroes as guides for our lives.*' (1) Superficial points of resemblance include the alleged interest in military service abroad of Junior in *Conversations* and Mark's lived-out service in *Kennedy's Children*. Of perhaps more relevance is the arguable similarity between the failure as actors, within the same late-'sixties American culture, of Michael and of Carla or even Sparger. *Kennedy's Children* interrogates the aspirations and disappointments directly associated with the Camelot years, with JFK defined or understood to be, literally, a presiding influence.

In Murphy's more localized, though transferable terms, the purpose of the 'White-House' art gallery, over which JJ would preside as a 'look-alike' Kennedy, was radical and transformative but was to be later ironized by the disillusioned Tom: 'His real purpose of course was to foster the arts, to give new life to broken dreams and the horn of immortality, nightly, to mortal men ... But then came the fall.' (*Plays 2*: 53) The atmosphere of the 'White House', as warmly recalled by Michael, quoting words originally penned by Tom, 'derive[d] from no attribute of wild wisdom, vestige of native cunning, or selfish motive. The day of the dinosaur [wa]s gone forever.' (*Plays 2*: 12) The failure of the enterprise is reflected in subsequent events and attitudes: a resurgence of local sectarian animosity at the outset of the Northern Ireland Troubles in 1969; the increased incidence of sexual prurience and joylessness as evidenced, variously, in the unhappiness of Peggy, Tom's *fiancée* of ten years, the projection of lewdness onto a local bank clerk ('they say she wear no knickers'), the affective anaesthesia of Tom –'I can't feel anything about anything, anymore' (*Plays 2*: 76) – and, in particular, the crass vulgarity of Liam, local opportunist business-man, whose plans include not only a takeover of the pub but marriage to JJ's daughter, seventeen-year old Anne.

In terms of design, Murphy was anxious from the outset to image the failure of 'The White House' by providing the description, '*a run-down hotel*' (or 'pub' in some drafts), later qualified by the more pointed '*A forgotten-looking place*' (*Plays 2*: 3). Given that decline, the unexpected alliance of Tom with Liam, the 'Mr successful-swinging-Ireland–In-The-Seventies!' (*Plays 2*: 70) Tom had earlier excoriated, continues to surprise audiences. Michael, who had been attracted to Anne, and she to him, had agreed to go for a walk the following day. When Liam orders him not to 'infringe', Tom supports him with a shrug: 'Liam's territory.' (*Plays 2*: 85) To Michael's horror, Liam is to arrange the sale of the pub secretly; his designs on Anne must be respected.

The future ruler of the town, Liam is a more ignorant, obtuse, insensitive and callously greedy version of Lopakhin in Chekhov's *The Cherry Orchard,* a play Murphy was to 'translate' for the Abbey centenary in 2004. Liam's warning to Michael, just prior to the exchange referred to above – 'I know a thing or two about you' (*Plays 2*: 84), with its sexual *frisson* – coupled with earlier accounts, during his time in the US, of Michael's stripping off his clothes, of trying to set himself on fire, of finding himself sexually impotent, is a telling reminder that all is not well with a character experiencing failure in the acting career he apparently needs to follow. It emerges in the play that, while his homecoming is, at one level, an attempt to resuscitate JJ's dream, of 'doing what we did before', at another level it represents a frightened pursuit of security, even a death wish, or what Tom harshly and irreverently describes as 'bringing his new suicidal fuckin' Christ with him! ' (*Plays 2*: 50)

I have argued above that a substantial portion of the explanation for the failure of the 'White House' dream was the debilitating presence in JJ himself of insecurity, ineptitude and venality, however they might be balanced. However, Tom's admittedly embittered re-ferences to the liberal optimism of the early sixties as 'the John F. Kennedy show' or 'that American-wrapped bandwagon of so-called idealism' or 'the load of American straw' (*Plays 2*: 52, 54), forces the issue as to the limitations of the Kennedy dream *itself,* the issue which, fundamentally, links our two plays. In that regard, *Kennedy's Children* is considerably the more pessimistic, depicting as the legacy of that era a society not merely disillusioned but also destroyed by drugs, morally adrift, especially in relation to sexuality, and lacking in hope.[15] The monologue format – this was, after all, pre-Brian Friel! – given Patrick's concern that 'the characters [do not] relate to one another' and given their deployment as, essentially, commentators on the *res Americana,* tends to make them one-dimensional: Sparger's is probably the most fully written in terms of character.

Conversations on a Homecoming, the revised version of the experimental 'White House', with relatively more pronounced positivity suggests in its totality that ambitious programmes of societal renewal, even when given local mediation, are ultimately dependent on personal and communal authenticity. The tokens of that authenticity, significantly associated with women characters, include JJ's beautiful daughter Anne, finally described as *'smiling her gentle hope out at the night'* (*Plays 2*: 87) and, in particular, the movement towards the realm of spirit, of redemptive otherness, represented by Peggy's moving singing of 'All in the April Evening'. The action of the play, its implicit concern with ownership of beauty, is realized in skilled dramatic shaping and securing of climax, deftly rounded characterization and some of the most electric dialogue Murphy has written.

---

[1] See, variously, Norman Mailer, *The Presidential Papers* (Harmondsworth: Penguin, 1963), A.M. Schlesinger and M.G. White, *Paths of American Thought* (Boston: Houghton Mifflin, 1963), and Gore Vidal, *Point to Point Navigation: A Memoir* (New York: Doubleday, 2006).

[2] 'The White House' has not been published. A number of versions, for the greater part bearing on the 'original' second act, 'Speeches of Farewell', form part of the Thomas Murphy Papers currently held at Trinity College, Dublin, MSS 11115/1/7. In alluding to 'Speeches', I refer to MS 11115/1/7/26.

[3] MS. 11115/1/7/17, Trinity College Dublin. Other sources from which Murphy took notes include James MacGregor Burns, *John Kennedy: A Political Profile* (New York: Harcourt, Brace, 1960), and William Manchester, *Death of a President* (New York: Harcourt and Row, 1967).

4 Francis Fergusson, *The Idea of a Theater* (Princeton: Princeton UP, 1949):13-41.

5 MS 11115/1/7/2.20, Trinity College Dublin.

6 *Conversations on a Homecoming* in *Murphy: Plays: Two* (London: Methuen, 1993): 19. All subsequent quotations from *Conversations* are from this edition, to which page numbers will refer.

7 MS 11115/1/7/2:31, Trinity College Dublin.

8 Murphy, *Conversations, Plays 2*: 3.

9 MS 1115/2/7a:33, Trinity College Dublin. Compare *Conversations, Plays 2:* 52.

10 MS 11115/1/7/2: 25, Trinity College Dublin. Hereafter, this source is referred to in the text as 'MS2' plus a page number.

11 David Nowlan, 'Small-Town Ireland is Theme of Abbey Play', *Irish Times* 21 March 1972: 12.

12 MS 11115/1/7/17, Trinity College Dublin.

13 Fintan O'Toole, *The Politics of Magic* , second edition (Dublin: New Island; London: Nick Hern, 1994): 171.

14 Robert Patrick, *Kennedy's Children: A Play in Two Acts* (London: French, n.d.): i. Subsequent quotations are from this edition, to which page numbers will refer.

15 It is beyond the scope of this paper, and would probably be impertinent, to attempt to evaluate some or all of the US presidencies since Kennedy as validations or otherwise of a fiction, *Kennedy's Children*. Memories, however, which the play inevitably compels – the enforced resignation of Richard Nixon, Ronald Reagan's campaigns against democratic governments in El Salvador and Nicaragua, George W. Bush's invasion of Iraq and sanctioning of Guantanamo internment prison – are disquieting. It is patently obvious, moreover, that part of the appeal (as I write) of the recently elected President Obama is the extent of his resemblance, in so many ways, to Kennedy.

8 | Murphy and Synge: Insiders and Outsiders

Riana M. O'Dwyer

Several commentators have drawn attention to the ways in which Tom Murphy is alert to the drama of Synge, whether by verbal echoes or plot parallels, or by his creation of evocative stage language based on the rhythms of rural Hiberno-English.[1] As a young man, he acted in Synge plays with the Tuam Theatre Guild. This at first seemed to produce a response of rejection rather than emulation, since he and the co-writer of his first play, Noel O'Donoghue, agreed that their play 'was not going to be set in a kitchen'.[2] It may, however, have been the formulaic plays written by successors of Synge that provoked this rejection. Subsequently, Tom Murphy scripted a short play about Synge, called 'Epitaph under Ether' which was performed at the Abbey in 1979 on the same bill as *The Well of the Saints* (which Murphy directed).[3] The title evokes an essay by Synge, 'Under Ether: Personal Experiences during an Operation' in which Synge described how ether, the anaesthetic used at the time, affected him in the course of his first surgery for swollen glands (later diagnosed as Hodgkins Disease) on 11 December, 1897.[4] Synge's account throws light on the practice of surgery in a private hospital at the time. For example, he was free to wander into the operating theatre the night before, and have a look at the preparations for his operation. It was not expected that he would do so, however, and a nurse who came in 'was horrified to find [him] on the scene of action.'[5] Synge remained semi-conscious during the operation, and remembered most of the proceedings, though they seemed phantasmic and visionary: 'I seemed to traverse whole epochs of desolation and bliss. All secrets were open before me, and simple as the universe to its God'.[6]

Murphy's sketch, for dramatically it is hardly more than that, represents Synge, played by two actors, during this operation, reliving important experiences of his life as it flashes before him. Quotes from 'Under Ether' and from Synge's 'Autobiography' fragment[7] become part of the script for 1st Synge, whose text provides a basic outline of his life. 2nd Synge's script generally quotes the plays, the poems, or the prose works, and is concerned with ideas and creativity. Occasionally, however, 2nd Synge also quotes 'Under Ether': 'I was received in the office by Nurse Smith'; 'you're not going to find it easy to keep me on that plank bed!'; 'What has happened?'; 'The ether apparatus is broken!'[8] Apart from the two actors playing Synge, the cast list further requires two men and four women, who are not named, but the first man appears to be Yeats, and the first woman Lady Gregory. Incidents from many of Synge's plays and quotations from his poetry and other writings make up the action, and at the end Synge appears near to death. In fact Synge recovered well from the surgery that he described in 'Under Ether', and remained relatively healthy for ten years. However, he required further surgery in 1907 and 1908, and died on 24 March 1909. His 1897 essay, however, concludes with him saying that 'the impression was very strong on me that I had died the preceding day and come to life again, and this impression has never changed'.[9] Indeed the twelve years that followed were the most productive of his life, as if the glimpse of mortality had galvanized his creativity.

Murphy's piece is a moving tribute to Synge, and an indication that Murphy accepted that, while at first he might have reacted against Synge, there was also a connection between them. The regular production of Synge plays by the amateur theatre groups of the fifties, including Tuam's Theatre Guild, indicates that they had resonance still, although literal imitation of sets and plots had run its course. The main focus of this paper, however, is the way in which the western plays of Tom Murphy share concerns with the plays of John Millington Synge, especially in two respects: first, their depiction of the psychology of traditional rural community cohesion and how it responds to challenge, including a consideration of violence in this context; second, the awareness of both of them, so lightly drawn as to be almost unconscious, of the economic dynamic that underlies so many interactions and close-knit relationships within these communities. In considering some plays of Synge and Murphy, I do not intend to develop a relationship of influence and reaction, although Tom Murphy was aware of Synge as a predecessor. Rather, I hope to explore areas of common interest, observations and concerns, that became part of the fabric of their plays, part of the lived experience that was being transferred to the stage; part also of the creative intensification that enables audiences to participate in the imaginary world that the play creates. Particular aspects that appear also in the drama of Tom Murphy are Synge's close observation of the dynamics of community relationships, and the impact of economic considerations on the lives of Irish people, decades after the direct impact of the population shifts and land agitation of the nineteenth century had waned.

Let me set the scene briefly for this discussion by placing the two writers side by side, as their experiences of Ireland were separated by sixty-four years, relative to year of birth. Synge was a member of a family that had been in Ireland since the seventeenth century, active in the ownership and administration of landed estates, and prominent in the Church of Ireland. John Millington Synge was the youngest of eight children, and his father died when he was only a year old. His mother was thus the dominant figure of his childhood and early manhood. The family lived in Dublin, but spent summers in Wicklow, where the more prosperous members of the family had comfortable houses and estates.[10] Tom Murphy, the youngest of ten children, was born in Tuam in 1935. During the Second World War, as the Irish building trade slumped into recession, his father Jack Murphy, a carpenter, went to Birmingham and worked there for the rest of his active life. Older brothers joined him and Birmingham 'became the centre of a family in exile: of which [Tom Murphy] was only occasionally a part'.[11] Many of the absent members of the family returned to Tuam for their annual holidays. They and others from the industrial workforce in England were free for a fortnight's holidays in August, when factories and building sites closed down, reluctantly complying with labour legislation. For the rest of the year, the mother was the dominant force in the life of the younger members of the family who remained in Tuam. She haunts many of Murphy's plays, by her presence in *A Crucial Week in the Life of a Grocer's Assistant*, and by her absence in *A Whistle in the Dark*. Is it too fanciful to imagine that the absence of the father from the childhoods of both Synge and Murphy resulted in a shared experience of loss and a longing for a more ideal existence represented for the Synge children by their relatives' castle at Glanmore and for Murphy by the filling of the family home with the returning brothers and father during the summer holidays, which provides a context for his play *The House* (2000).

Both young men expressed themselves at first through music. Synge was talented enough to contemplate a musical career, perhaps as a violinist, while Murphy has a fine tenor voice, although this was not seen as offering career possibilities in Tuam of the 1940s. Perhaps because of this aural sensitivity, both Synge and Murphy have been distinguished by the creation of a vivid colloquial stage language developed from the idioms of Hiberno-English. As Declan Kiberd has remarked: '[Synge's] language represents not the talk of the folk, but a colourful intensification of the peculiarly Irish elements of their idiom.'[12] The rich loquacity of the characters in Murphy's plays has also been noted. Nicholas Grene believes that 'Synge is Murphy's most obvious precursor in their common harnessing of ritual rhythms of action, their use of traditions of oral narrative, and their creation of a special style of enriched dialogue.'[13] Fintan O'Toole suggests that the work of folk dramatist M.J. Molloy, from the hinterland of Tuam, was an important example for Murphy, along with the plays of Federico García Lorca, but gives a special importance to Synge as a precursor: 'not only had Synge written of the West of Ireland, he had done so in a language charged with poetry, a non-naturalistic language imbued with a sense of scale and power.'[14]

It might be objected that the language of his characters was what Murphy himself spoke naturally, but this would be an over-simplification. The language of Tuam was distinct from the language of its rural hinterland in the fifties, and to some extent even today. Tom Murphy possesses a keen ear for nuances and variations, while the archaisms of speech in Tuam's surrounding villages: Caher-listrane or Kilconly or Milltown, are still distinctive, and underpin the flowing rhetoric of Mommo in *Bailegangaire*, or the more measured voice of Mark Dineen in *Famine*, who refers to 'my own childre ablow' [below, nearby], a form still in use locally.[15] Murphy has described a memory of his father, a carpenter, making coffins in his workshop: 'Sometimes he had to make one of a Sunday − an emer-gency, I suppose, or a work of mercy.'[16] The phrase 'of a Sunday', and similar phrases, are still current in local speech, derived from the syntax and expressions of Irish, which was still spoken in the countryside west of Tuam in the early twentieth century, in Belclare and Caherlistrane, the area from which his father's family came.

Murphy's dramatic language is, like Synge's, the product of careful listening and meticulous recording, followed by transformation in the crucible of dramatic creation, including the careful revisions of several drafts. The plays of both writers are rooted in the particularity of language and custom, but the magnification of specifics into a dramatic performance creates, at its best, universality.[17] As Nicholas Grene has argued: 'Murphy is closer to Synge than to Yeats in his development of drama out of a localised material of anecdote and folklore. *Bailegangaire* is akin to *Playboy* in the way a germ of supposed fact – the laughing-contest, the sheltered parricide – forms the basis for a dramatic fabulation which escapes altogether from a naturalistic/ representational mode.'[18] While the audience may believe, on the basis of set or costumes, that the play will represent its world realistically, these dramas move beyond, to explore the liminal area where human experience demands a divine explanation, as when the people of Bochtán face up to the reality of their destiny and defy the God who has put them in this position: 'Glintin' their defiance of Him – their defiance an' rejection, inviting of what else might come or *care* to come! – driving bellows of refusal at the sky through the roof. [...] 'Twas an insolence at heaven.'[19]

What exactly is taking place within such plays, and why do they have such resonance? Marvin Carlson, finds that 'performance is potentially one of the richest and most rewarding areas in the arts for exploring the interplay of art and culture.'[20] This is because it is such a material art, created not just from the texts, but also through the particularities of setting, costume, lighting and the performances of actors. Theatrical performance is at once very specific – a particular night at a particular play in a particular theatre – and very general. It is constructed out of the cultural materials available to a director at a particular time and place, but it also goes beyond that, as Stephen Greenblatt has suggested: 'Even if one begins to achieve a sophisticated historical sense of the cultural materials out of which a literary text is constructed, it remains essential to study the ways in which those materials are formally put together and articulated in order to understand the cultural work that the text or performance accomplishes.'[21] He goes on to say that:

> works of art are not neutral relay stations in the circulation of cultural materials. Something happens to objects, beliefs, and

practices when they are represented, reimagined and performed in literary texts or performances, something often
unpredictable and disturbing. That 'something' is the sign both
of the power of art and of the embeddedness of culture in the
contingencies of history.[22]

Both Synge and Murphy are gifted in representing this
conjunction of the 'contingencies of history': in reimagining or re-
arranging the 'cultural materials' so that they acquire a 'cultural
resonance.' Synge was aware that creativity involved both 'cultural
materials' (e.g. observations of lived life) and the unpredictable
element which is popularly called 'imagination'. He wrote that:
'what is highest in poetry is always reached where the dreamer is
leaning out to reality, or where the man of real life is lifted out of
it',[23] and also no drama 'can grow out of anything but the fundamental realities of life which are neither modern or unmodern, and,
as I see them, are rarely fantastic or spring-dayish.'[24] He had had
ample opportunities to observe the paradoxes of rural poverty in his
visits to Aran and the West. In his series of articles about the
congested districts, published as *Connemara*, he described the
contradictions implicit in admiring the exotic qualities of Irish
traditional life, while aware that it is based on real and continuing
hardship:

> One's first feeling as one comes back among these people and
> takes a place, so to speak, in this noisy procession of fishermen,
> farmers and women, where nearly everyone is interesting and
> attractive, is a dread of any reform that would tend to lessen
> their individuality rather than any very real hope of improving
> their well-being. One feels then, perhaps a little later, that it is
> part of the misfortune of Ireland that nearly all the charac-
> teristics which give colour and attractiveness to Irish life are
> bound up with a social condition that is near to penury, while
> in countries like Brittany the best external features of the local
> life – the rich embroidered dresses, for instance, or the carved
> furniture – are connected with a decent and comfortable social
> condition.[25]

The precise observations evident in Synge's prose writings about
Aran and Connemara indicate a nuanced awareness of the
implications of what he was observing, which extended to his
gatherings of folk-material. Éilis Ní Dhuibhne writing on Synge's
use of popular material, concludes that: 'he had an exceptional
sensitivity to folklore and an understanding of its character and
functions. [...] Certainly his understanding of tradition seems to
have been much better than that of his great contemporaries in the
Anglo-Irish revival. [...] From a folkloristic point of view, of that

particular set [W.B. Yeats and others] Synge was undoubtedly "the best labourer".'[26] The resonance of Synge's plays is based upon attention to the materiality of his representation, to the detail of clothes and utensils and speech and gesture. So also is the theatre of Tom Murphy.

What may complicate the matter, however, is the relationship between the plots and characters represented by these dramatists, and the ideology of community that was held by their first audiences. The gap between the dramatic representation and the audience's ideas of itself and its identity, may account both for the initial negative reactions to such plays as *Playboy of the Western World* and *A Whistle in the Dark,* and for the subsequent canonizing of them as classic texts when realization dawned that the plays have identified a site of conflict needing examination. Such dual reactions are to be expected at times of transition, such as the late nineteenth century when cultural nationalism was being politicized and prepared for military action, and the 1940s and 1950s when independence had failed to improve economic conditions or stem the flow of emigration, and national self-doubt had began to grow. In such times and circumstances, traditional values are challenged, the dominant ideology ceases to exercise its former control, and influence shifts in unexpected directions. Ferdinand Toennies, in his classic late-nineteenth-century study *Community and Society [Gemeinschaft und Gesellschaft]* (1887) developed a typological contrast between the small and cohesive agrarian society and the large and differentiated industrial society; a contrast also between a lifestyle that was essentially communal and traditional and one that incorporated swift change and social mobility. In the rural way of life, where the small village is the organized social unit, there are homogeneous values, a sense of common identity and strong ties of kinship.[27] However, towards the end of the nineteenth-century in Ireland, such traditional models of community were less common than might have been expected, as a result of the famine, agrarian unrest, emigration and related disruptive factors. Recent studies have explored many different kinds of community, and the attachments that underlie them: 'communities have been based on ethnicity, religion, class or politics ... they may be traditional, modern and even postmodern; re-actionary and progressive'.[28] The fundamental insight, articulated in particular by Anthony P. Cohen, is that 'people construct community symbolically, making it a resource and repository of meaning, and a referent of their identity.'[29] In other words, ideologies of community relate to a consensus existing in a particular group about what constitutes their aims and objectives, what is acceptable and what unacceptable behaviour, who is included within and who excluded from the community. The price of inclusion in communal protection is conformity to communal values, and so the possibility of exclusion, as well as inclusion, exists. Synge's account of his travels in Wicklow, Aran, west Kerry, Connemara or Mayo, as well as his plays, indicate his alertness to the dynamics of such communities, both positive and negative, at that turning of the century, when modernity was in the offing, and its consequences still unknown. Half a century later, in the plays of Tom Murphy, the pressures of this transition are more evident.

It would be possible to read all of Synge's dramatic works as interrogating the question of community, and he shows himself very closely tuned to the subtexts which underpin so many social arrangements. His plays cover the full spectrum of involvement, from integration to expulsion. *Riders to the Sea* represents the fullness of community participation, where the harshness of island life unites all the women in mutual mourning as the sea claims their menfolk. All who survive are included, and the ritual mourning, powerfully described by Synge in his Aran journals,[30] as well as represented in the play, assures the bereaved that they are part of an extended family, even while the nuclear one is being depleted.

In *The Shadow of the Glen* and *Playboy of the Western World*, Synge examines what happens when a stranger enters the closed community world, challenging its values and opening a door to another mode of existence. Both Nora and Pegeen are offered a life outside of the domestic. The tramp says to Nora: 'We'll be going now, and [...] you'll not be [...] making yourself old with looking on each day, and it passing you by'.[31] However, Nora is reminded by Dan that this will exclude her from the protection of community and reduce her to the status of an animal: 'It's lonesome roads she'll be going, and hiding herself away till the end will come, and they find her stretched like a dead sheep with the frost on her.' (24) She chooses to go in spite of this warning. In *Playboy*, Christy offers Pegeen the chance to go 'pacing Nephin in the dews of night' or wandering with him in Erris, 'drinking a sup from a well, and making mighty kisses with our wetted mouths'. (136) However, Pegeen has a lot more to lose than Nora; her father's pub, her status as most eligible woman in the area, her power over the men. She chooses to reinforce the community's judgement against Christy and not to go.

The Well of the Saints is also a very interesting study of the ebb and flow of community responsibility. As long as Martin and Mary Doul are sightless, they receive some measure of support from the local people, but among the revelations that sight brings is that the able-bodied have to work hard for a meagre living, as Martin complains: 'it's more I got a while since, and I sitting blinded in Grianan, than I get in this place, working hard, and destroying myself, the length of the day.' (73) In the end Mary says to the Saint: 'Let us be as we are, holy father, and then we'll be known again as the people is happy and blind, and we'll be having an easy time with no trouble to live, and we getting halfpence on the road.'(91) This resolution, however, is not to be. Martin and Mary, having defied the Saint, are driven from the church and the village by the people, lest they 'bring down a curse upon us, [...] from the heavens of God.' (93) Like Nora they become wanderers, while the villagers continue their lives as before, represented by the marriage of Timmy the blacksmith to Molly Byrne. This couple will maintain the responsibilities of kinship and property, sanctioned by the church and their neighbours, the community. The travelling family in *The Tinker's Wedding* are also outside the range of community, but try to join in by getting married formally in church. This desire is thwarted because they have no wedding offering for the priest, which underlines the economic nature of such formal alliances, involving property arrangements as much as a religious ceremony. The travelling couple are outside the regulation of custom, and are not bound by it. The priest is surprised at Sarah's tears when her request is denied and says: 'It's a queer woman you are to be crying at the like of that, and you your whole life walking the roads.' (35)

Deirdre of the Sorrows, though a version of a mythic tale, also exemplifies in an extreme form the sanctions of community against those who do not conform. Because she will have status as the future Queen of Ulster, Deirdre should behave in a certain way, be respectful of property, and not come back from the hills with 'a bag of nuts and twigs for our fires at the dawn of day.' She is reprimanded for this by King Conchubor, who has chosen her to be his bride: 'And it's that way you're picking up the manners will fit you to be Queen of Ulster.' (154) Because she will not conform and wishes to live by other values, she chooses exile with Naisi, and ultimately death. Her love story is also a study of community sanctions and the exercise of power against those who break them, in this case epitomized in the actions of the king and his comrades. As Alison Smith has pointed out: 'Synge's main characters all reject the communal, and by extension, the dramatic structures, leaving behind them a state of continuance that is clearly inadequate.'[32]

೯೦   ೯೦

Tom Murphy shares with John Millington Synge an interest in characters who find themselves in conflict with the norms of their community or outside its core group. This feature is epitomized by *On the Outside*, the title of his first play (in collaboration with Noel O'Donoghue). Its central characters, Joe and Frank, like the travellers in *The Tinker's Wedding*, are excluded from the communal socializing because they haven't enough money for admission to the local dance. They linger outside the dancehall, try all manner of devices to be admitted, and then watch the girl Frank fancied going home with his chief rival who happens to have a car. A central issue here is the economic nature of communal relations – the intricate way in which property and the power it gives is the hidden agenda of community adhesion. Within the hierarchy of community the myth of the new Ireland as a classless society does not hold. As Frank, standing outside the dancehall, says: 'The whole town is like a tank [...] And we're at the bottom [...] clawing at the sides all around. And the bosses – and the big shots – are up around the top, looking in, looking down. You know the look? Spitting. On top of us.'[33]

Property is not the only currency in this economy: Education also provided a route of advancement for those who had the brains to avail of it. Thus in *A Whistle*, the children of Pookey Flanagan, the road sweeper, become an engineer, a nun, and a university student, while Harry, the 'thick lad' derided at school, has nothing to fall back on but his physical strength and prowess in faction fights: 'I can make them afraid. What can you do? They notice me. Hah? Do they notice you?'[34]

As Fintan O'Toole has argued, in *A Whistle in the Dark* Tom Murphy 'dramatises the tensions of a society on the brink of industrialisation, about to become belatedly "civilised".'[35] However the legacy of Dada, the individual fighting his corner, defending his family against all comers, will not ensure material success for the next generation. The soaring emigration figures of the period, epitomized by the fate of Murphy's own family, had displaced the lives of Ireland's free citizens, so that they have become the labouring classes of the old colonial power, in a parodic continuation of the former colonial relationship. In nineteenth-century Ireland resistance took the form of maiming cattle and burning houses, as Pegeen Mike recalls in Act I of *Playboy*: 'Where now will you meet the like of Daneen Sullivan knocked the eye from a peeler, or Marcus Quin, God rest him, got six months for maiming ewes.'[36] In twentieth century Ireland resistance takes the form of gibes and insults and fisticuffs. *A Whistle in the Dark*, documenting the frustration of those who could not get ahead in the new Ireland, revealed the safety valve by which the problem was exported, and all the awkward people emigrated, the 'thick lads' with their aggressive tendencies, leaving the people of property, education and political status in possession of the land both literally and in terms of official self-image. Ireland could be pure and idealistic and rural because England was corrupt and materialistic and industrialized. Recognized or not, acknowledged or not, the validation of identity by physical force, or by narratives of physical force was still as powerful in Murphy's Ireland of the 1940s and 1950s as it had been during the agrarian agitations of the nineteenth century, during which the rift between peelers and people was driven deep by fundamental conflicts of interest. Succession, and success in the New Ireland, had to be fought for and won.

Famine situates the discussion about community in the past, but relates it, as Murphy has reiterated, to the present of 1960s Ireland.[37] As the community is depleted by the loss of its resources the related structures also begin to break down. John Connor, Chieftain of the Connor Clan of Glanconnor, finds himself unable to practise the chieftain's virtue of generosity, because he has nothing left to share. Gradually his view of what is right is superceded by necessity, his advice not to emigrate is ignored by his neighbours, his wife circumvents his authority by secret pilferings and concealments. At the end, like Michael in *A Whistle in the Dark*, John Connor's totally uncharacteristic violence against his own family dramatizes his impotence and the loss of his values, which no longer work in the face of disaster.

The identification of clashes of interest within communities is central to Murphy's western plays, and the focus of this discussion is economic, rather than social or religious, control. The new entrepreneurial activity is illustrated by the dancehall at the centre of *On the Inside* and *On the Outside,* the grocery shop in *A Crucial Week,* the pub in *Conversations on a Homecoming* and *A Thief of a Christmas,* the hotel in *The Wake,* the substantial residence in *The House.* Synge's description of village shopkeepers in County Mayo a hundred years ago might have been used by Murphy as the basis of *Thief,* so similar are they to John Mahony and his wife, who run the pub and general stores in which the action is set:

> Here, as in most of the congested districts, the shops are run on a vague system of credit that is not satisfactory, though one does not see at once what other method could be found to take its place. After the sale of whatever the summer season has produced – pigs, cattle, kelp, etc. – the bills are paid off, more or less fully, and all the ready money of a family is thus run away with. Then about Christmas time a new bill is begun, which runs on till the following autumn – or later in the harvesting districts – and quite small shopkeepers often put out relatively large sums in this way. The people keep no passbooks, so they have no check on the traders, and although direct fraud is probably rare it is likely that the prices charged are often exorbitant. What is worse, the shopkeeper in out-of-the-way places is usually the only buyer to be had for a number of home products, such as eggs, chickens, carragheen moss, and sometimes even kelp; so that he can control the prices both of what he buys and what he sells, while as a creditor he has an authority that makes bargaining impossible: another of the many complicated causes that keep the people near to pauperism![38]

At the opening of *A Thief of a Christmas,* John Mahony's wife is serving Bina, an old woman whose pension book provides the currency for her provisions from the shop. The publican's wife says to Bina: 'Your pension money now is for last week's and I have them articles down with the others that are outstanding.' Bina replies: 'That will do, ma'am, I understand.'[39] Later on we see Tomás Rua doing a deal with Mahony to get the money for medicine for his consumptive daughter, while other neighbours are also waiting their turn, to promise their fields to the publican as security for loans of ready cash. The setting of the play in the 'pub-cum-general stores'[40] in the week coming up to Christmas, emphasizes the economic dynamics of rural Ireland, as John Mahony controls his customers by giving them credit and free drinks, and by buying their land from them when times are hard. With the festive season close at hand, economic necessities are pressing, and are felt by everybody present. The crops were poor this year, the Christmas market in Tuam was full of provisions that nobody could afford to buy, and so the country people were unable to sell their produce. As a consequence they will be unable to afford the extra expenditure of Christmas themselves and will have to depend on credit from John Mahony, which will put them under an obligation to him. The denouement of *A Thief of a Christmas* relies on the defeat of the shopkeeper on his own economic terms. Mahony encouraged his customers to bet on the outcome of the laughing competition that is the centrepiece of the play. However, he is forced to pay out at the end, when he miscalculates, and the people's champion is successful.

The routine of the small-town shop, and its interactions with the minutiae of its customers' lives, is also central to *A Crucial Week in the Life of a Grocer's Assistant*, and is rejected by the protagonist John Joe when he says to his employer: 'And stick your job and your bags of rotten onions and your sugar and your stringy sausages!' (*Plays 4*: 125) There is no alternative job waiting for John Joe, but there is the liberation of speaking his mind. John Joe's mother is devastated by her son's loss of his job, and her bitterness provokes even further truth-telling, when John Joe reveals his family's secrets to the neighbours at the climax of the play. A similar release of tension occurs in *Bailegangaire* and *Thief* when 'misfortunes' is declared as the subject of the laughing competition, and the participants vie with each other to proclaim their troubles. The effect is like a communal psychotherapy session, which enables the participants to vent their anger and move on: 'Twas the best night ever! – the impoverished an' hungry, eyes big as saucers, howlin' their defiance at the heavens through the ceilin' [...] inviting of what else might come or care to come'.[41] In *The Wake*, the truth-telling consists of actions as well as words:

> Two and a half days every window in the hotel has been lit up, day and night, the middle of the town, with our sister, brother-in-law and one Mr Reilly parading themselves in all manners of drunkenness, undress, unseemly behaviour [...] for all or any outside who cared to stand in the Square and watch.[42]

Conversations on a Homecoming shares this perspective, dramatizing the defeat of various economic endeavours in a nineteen-seventies pub setting. The White House pub itself, in which so much hope had been invested by the characters, is about to be sold. Tom has not become a writer, nor Michael an actor, while Junior has settled for a job with his father, marriage and a family. The only character doing well is Liam the auctioneer, specialist in the disposal of rundown businesses.

In *The Wake*, in contrast, a family is torn apart by an obsession with property, inheritance and small-town status. Their acquisitiveness and arrogance is challenged when their sister Vera, who has been living as best she can in America, inherits the family hotel from her mother, the arch-manipulator of inheritances in the past.[43] The gesture appeals to Vera, who left her home town because she felt so much an outsider in her family. Perhaps there is still a possibility that she could belong? As she says herself: 'They [her siblings] mean an awful lot to me ... They keep me going. Life-long fear that I might be on my own'. (*Plays 5*: 117) However, when Vera thinks about it, she realizes that her mother's gesture may have been more revenge than affection: 'because [her other children] never came across with the money, she left this place to me'. (136) The denouement of the play seeks to neutralize the materialism of the characters, when Vera decides to sign over the hotel to her family. Her mercenary sister knows what Vera intends to do, but Murphy indicates, in the stage directions, that perhaps she will be troubled in the future by the gift: 'MARY JANE's smile: she has got what she wants; smile beginning to question itself: Has she got what she wants?' (178) This perhaps betrays the play's origin as a novel, *The Seduction of Morality*, because the subtlety of self-doubt is unlikely to be conveyed to a theatre audience by an actor's smile.[44] However, Murphy's later play, *The House*, makes the personal consequences of acquisitiveness the central theme. The focus shifts from the violent act that clears the way for the protagonist Christy to own the property that he craves, to the guilt and emotional loss that are the results. He achieves possession of the big house, but in the process destroys the relationship that meant the most to him, the maternal kindness and affection of his substitute mother, Mrs de Burca.[45]

It has often been remarked that Synge created a range of fully realized women's roles, and indeed that his plays address the limitation of the social position of women at the opening of the twentieth century, most notably in the opportunities his plays offer to break away from conventional life. Murphy's plays do not neglect consideration of this aspect either, especially as regards the limitations imposed by community expectations and economic conditions. *Conversations on a Homecoming* presents in miniature the situation prevailing in Murphy's time, sixty years after Synge. Missus is described in stage directions as '*a worried, slow-moving drudge of a woman, senses a bit numbed by life, but trying to keep the place together*'[46]: perhaps a Pegeen Mike to whom life has not been kind. This play has its own Peggy, who is forty, tries to act younger, and has been engaged to Tom for ten years. She, like Missus, is dedicated to keeping up a front, keeping things going, maintaining appearances, 'her life invested in Tom' who is making no return. (*Plays 2*: 80) Then there is Anne, aged seventeen, daughter of the house, 'smiling her gentle hope out at the night' at the end of the play. (87) But the boys already have her pinned down, though she is unaware of it. Tom warns Michael to leave Anne alone: 'Liam's territory. Right Liam, you nearly have [the pub] sold, right [...] better for everyone. Reality.' (85) In this situation Anne is part of the deal, part of the property, bartered already in spite of herself.

Bailegangaire puts the focus firmly on women as the persistent losers in the local traditional community. Mommo is an older version of Mother from *Crucial Week*, both making do in marriages of convenience, which have drained them of whatever powers of affection they once possessed. In *A Whistle*, while Mother is mentioned, she is in Ireland, not part of macho man's world. John Connor's wife is also called Mother. The namelessness of women, the substitution of their role as mother or carer for the individuality of themselves is almost taken for granted in these plays, until in *Bailegangaire* and *A Thief of a Christmas* the stranger's husband calls her by her name, Brigit. This results in a brief moment of tenderness, the first in years. In *Bailegangaire*, Mommo refuses to call Mary by her name, until her final apotheosis. When the roll-call of misfortunes takes place in *Bailegangaire* and *A Thief*, many of the disasters are the consequence of the hardening of the self which life has imposed on all of these women. This is especially true of Mommo, who blames herself for the deaths of all her sons: Pat, Jimmy, Michael, Willie: a catalogue of lost sons to equal that of Maurya in *Riders to the Sea*.[47] Mommo, however, does not take refuge in Maurya's resignation, she will not be satisfied.

One other aspect needs to be noted here. In Tom Murphy's plays, the hardening of the women is the consequence of their complicity in the status quo, in their acceptance of the requirements and standards of tradition. The girlfriends of *On the Outside* accept a lift home in the car that defines importance in material terms. The mother in *Crucial Week* is obsequious to priest and shopkeeper, both of whom insist that the price of a job for her son is conformity. She is a keeper of secrets, vulnerable to the scalding ache of shame, preferring an empty house to the gossip of her neighbours. The mother in *Famine* hides food lest she be forced to share it, and steals from the neighbours, shoring up her crumbling family. Vera, in *The Wake*, clings to an ideal of family for as long as she can, and only achieves peace when she relinquishes it and accepts her loneliness, but also her selfhood. In the world created in Murphy's early theatre the commitment of women to a form of community in which they are disadvantaged and victimized is represented rather than explained, but such theatre nonetheless exposed a fundamental area of cultural paradox. We can also observe, as his work developed, a move from passive and accepting women to the defiant and self-aware women of his later plays.

These are plays however, not merely social documents, and as Greenblatt has pointed out, what matters is not just the circulation of cultural materials, but what happens 'when they are represented, reimagined and performed'.[48] Relevant to this is Paul Ricoeur's account of narrative or myth in boundary situations:

> There are certain boundary situations such as war, suffering, guilt, death etc. in which the individual or community experiences a fundamental existential crisis. At such moments the whole community is put into question. For it is only when it is threatened with destruction from without or from within, that a society is compelled to return to the very roots of its identity: to that mythical nucleus which ultimately grounds and determines it. The solution to the immediate crisis [...] demands that we ask ourselves the ultimate questions concerning our origins and ends: where do we come from? Where do we go?[49]

The young Tom Murphy was familiar with the plays of Jean Anouilh, whose *Antigone* had been performed by the Tuam Theatre Guild before he left the town. When Anouilh wrote this play in 1942, France was experiencing just such a boundary situation, the German occupation during the Second World War. Antigone says: 'You know you're caught, caught at last like a rat in a trap, with all heaven against you. And the only thing left to do is shout – not moan, or whimper, but yell out at the top of your voice whatever it was you had to say. What you've never said before, what perhaps you didn't even know till now ... and to no purpose – just so as to tell it to yourself [...] to learn it yourself.'[50] This strategy of 'shouting' provides the climax of *A Crucial Week* when John Joe goes out to the road and shouts out the family secrets for all the neighbours to hear. It provides the climax to *A Thief of a Christmas* and *Baile-gangaire* when the catalogue of misfortunes was 'driving bellows of refusal at the sky through the roof'.[51] It is implicit in the aria at the end of *The Gigli Concert* when the tongue of JPW is loosened and he makes contact with an ecstatic release of song. It contrasts with the quieter acceptance of fate at the conclusion of *Riders to the Sea*.

Finally, if it be objected that Murphy and Synge did not provide social solutions, but only dissected the inadequacies of the community structures that existed, we might remember the words of Augusto Boal: 'It is not the place of the theatre to show the correct path, but only to offer the means by which all possible paths may be examined'.[52] This has certainly been the effect of the theatre of Synge and of Murphy.

[1] See, for example, Fintan O'Toole, *Tom Murphy: The Politics of Magic* (Dublin: New Island Books, 1994); Anthony Roche, *Contemporary Irish Drama: From Beckett to McGuinness* (Dublin: Gill & Macmillan, 1994); Nicholas Grene, *The Politics of Irish Drama* (Cambridge: Cambridge U P, 1999).

[2] Fintan O'Toole, *The Politics of Magic*: 22. *On the Outside* was written in 1958 and produced in 1962.

[3] Tom Murphy, 'Epitaph under Ether', 1979. The Abbey Theatre kindly gave me sight of the unpublished script, now deposited in the National Library, Dublin.

[4] John Millington Synge, 'Under Ether' in *J. M. Synge Collected Works: Volume II Prose*, ed. Alan Price (London: Oxford UP, 1966): 39-43.

[5] Synge, 'Under Ether': 40.

[6] Synge, 'Under Ether': 42.

[7] Synge, 'Autobiography' in J. M. Synge Collected Works: Volume II Prose): 3-15.

[8] Tom Murphy, 'Epitaph under Ether' typescript: 7, 8, 10.

[9] Synge, 'Under Ether': 43.

[10] W.J. McCormack has characterized the family origins of Synge succinctly in the *Field Day Anthology of Irish Writing* (Derry: Field Day Publications, 1991), II: 846-49. See also his *Fool of the Family: A Life of J. M. Synge* (London: Weidenfeld, 2000) and *The Silence of Barbara Synge* (Manchester: Manchester UP, 2003).

[11] O'Toole, *The Politics of Magic*: 26.

[12] Declan Kiberd, *Synge and the Irish Language*, 2nd edition (Dublin: Gill & Macmillan, 1993): 214-15.

[13] Grene, *The Politics of Irish Drama*: 241.

[14] O'Toole, *The Politics of Magic*: 34.

[15] Murphy, *Famine* , in *Plays: One* (London: Methuen, 1992): 76.

[16] Murphy, Introduction, *Plays: One* : xiii.

[17] See Christopher Murray's detailed discussion of this and related issues in 'Unlocking Synge Today' in *A Companion to Modern*

British and Irish Drama 1880-2005, ed. Mary Luckhurst (Oxford: Blackwell, 2006): 110-24.

[18] Grene, *The Politics of Irish Drama*: 241.

[19] Tom Murphy, *Bailegangaire* in *Plays Two* (London: Methuen, revised edition, 2005): 158. The 1993 edition of *Plays Two* has a longer passage, in which Mommo describes her father's philosophy of 'man and the earwig' and reiterates that 'God will not be mocked' (165).

[20] Marvin Carlson, *Theatre Semiotics: Signs of Life* (Bloomington, Indiana: Indiana UP, 1990): 121.

[21] Stephen Greenblatt, 'Culture', in *Critical Terms for Literary Study*, eds Frank Lentricchia and Thomas McLaughlin (Chicago: University of Chicago Press, 1990): 230.

[22] Greenblatt, 'Culture': 230-31.

[23] Synge, *Collected Works*: Volume II Prose: 347.

[24] David H. Greene and Edward M. Stephens. *J. M. Synge 1871-1909*. Revised Edition. (New York & London: New York UP, 1989): 169.

[25] Synge, 'In Connemara', *Collected Works*, Volume II, Prose: 286.

[26] Éilis Ní Dhuibhne, 'Synge's Use of Popular Material in *The Shadow of the Glen*', *Béaloideas* 58 (1990): 167.

[27] See discussion of the work of Frederick Toennies in James B. McKee, *An Introduction to Sociology* (New York: Holt, Rinehart & Winston, 1969), pp. 27-28, and the translation of Tonnies *Community and Society* by Charles P. Loomis (East Lansing: Michigan UP, 1957).

[28] Gerard Delanty, *Community* (London: Routledge, 2003): 2.

[29] Anthony P. Cohen, *The Symbolic Construction of Community* (London: Routledge, 1985): 118.

[30] See, for example, Synge, 'The Aran Islands', in *Collected Works,* II: 74-76, and 136-37.

[31] Synge, *The Playboy of the Western World and Other Plays,* ed. Ann Saddlemyer (Oxford: Oxford UP, World's Classics series, 1995): 25. Subsequent quotations from Synge's plays are from this edition, to which page references will refer.

[32] Alison Smith, Introduction, *J. M. Synge: Plays, Poems and Prose* (London: Everyman/ Dent, 1992): xvii.

[33] Tom Murphy and Noel O'Donoghue, *On the Outside* in *Plays: 4* (London: Methuen, 1997): 180.

[34] Tom Murphy, *A Whistle in the Dark* in *Plays:4*: 40, 44.

[35] O'Toole, *The Politics of Magic*: 58.

[36] Synge, *The Playboy of the Western World and Other Plays*, ed. Saddlemyer: 100.

[37] Tom Murphy, 'Introduction' to *Plays: One* (London: Methuen, 1992): xi.

38 Synge, 'The Inner Lands of Mayo: The Village Shop', *Collected Works,*
   II: 329-30.
39 Tom Murphy, *A Thief of a Christmas* in *Plays:Two* (London:
   Methuen, Revised edition, 2005): 170.
40 Ibid., p. 167.
41 Tom Murphy, *Bailegangaire* in *Plays Two* (London: Methuen, 1993):
   131. This passage was omitted in the later edition of *Plays: Two*
   (2005).
42 Tom Murphy, *The Wake* in *Plays: 5* (London: Methuen, 2006): 148.
43 Emilie Pine in 'The Homeward Journey: The Returning Emigrant in
   Recent Irish Theatre', *Irish University Review* 38.2
   (Autumn/Winter 2008): 310-24, discusses related aspects of *The
   Wake* and *The House*. See also Alexandra Poulain, *Homo famelicus:
   Le théâtre de Tom Murphy* (Caen: Presses universitaires de Caen,
   2008).
44 Tom Murphy, *The Seduction of Morality* (London: Abacus, 1994).
45 Tom Murphy, *The House* (London: Methuen, 2000).
46 Tom Murphy, *Conversations on a Homecoming,* in *Plays: Two*
   (London: Methuen, 1993): 6. Subsequent quotations are from this
   edition and are referenced by page numbers.
47 Nicholas Grene also discusses the relationship of *Riders to the Sea*
   and *Bailegangaire* in *The Politics of Irish Drama*: 227-35.
48 Greenblatt, 'Culture': 230-31.
49 Paul Ricoeur, 'Myth as the Bearer of Possible Worlds', in *The Crane
   Bag Book of Irish Studies* (Dublin: Blackwater Press, 1982): 261-62.
50 Jean Anouilh, *Antigone*, trans. Barbara Bray (London: Methuen,
   2000): 59.
51 Murphy, *Plays Two* (1993): 164-65.
52 Augusto Boal, *Theatre of the Oppressed,* trans. C. A. McBride and M-
   O. McBride (London: Pluto Press, 1979): 141.

9 | The Politics of Performance in *The Hostage* and *The Blue Macushla*

Alexandra Poulain

This paper is concerned with *The Blue Macushla* (1980), one of Murphy's most unfairly neglected plays, which I propose to read in relation to Brendan Behan's 1958 play *The Hostage*. Behan's play, itself inspired by Frank O'Connor's story 'Guests of the Nation', is a critique of Irish political nationalism which Behan, following O'Casey, sees as having degenerated into a purely destructive force when it became dissociated from its earlier aspiration to social justice. Behan's English language adaptation of his Irish play *An Giall*, which Behan translated for and in collaboration with Joan Littlewood's Theatre Workshop, preserves the tragic outcome but moves away from the original play's naturalistic frame towards a dramaturgy inspired from the English music hall, incorporating more songs as well as dances, bawdy humour, slapstick comedy, and topical jokes. While early commentators of the play tended to see it as a debased version of the Irish original, pandering to the taste and preconceptions of the English public, more recent readings have argued that the formal reshaping of the play is inherent in Behan's critical strategy as postcolonial writer, appropriating the codes of the English stage to write back to the English centre. Taking my cue from the latter, I will attempt to show that *The Hostage*, a play in its own right whose hybrid form (part Irish melodrama, part English music hall) is an expression of its politics, provides a thematic and aesthetic paradigm for *The Blue Macushla*. While both plays satirize Irish republicanism and expose the deleterious potential of identity politics, Murphy's play weaves in a paradoxical tale of homecoming as antidote to the morbid narcissistic fixation with identity which both plays target, and thus finds a way out of tragedy.

The transfer of Behan's play from Dublin's Damer Hall to London's West End entailed a double process of translation, linguistic and dramaturgic, in a movement of what John Brannigan, following Mary Louise Pratt, defines as one of 'transculturation': 'Behan did not just translate *An Giall* for a metropolitan audience, but re-invented *An Giall* within the terms of metropolitan culture itself.'[1] The resulting play, Brannigan argues, is a culturally hybrid form, combining the indigenous codes of Irish nationalist melo-drama (which *An Giall* parodies) with the metropolitan aesthetics of music hall which Behan appropriates to expose both Irish nationalism and English imperialism as theatrical posturing. The gesture of transculturation in fact works at two levels: on the one hand, the inherent meta-theatricality of music hall, deflating sentimentality with constant comic interruptions of the melo-dramatic plot, undermining the naturalistic ethos by inviting blatant contradictions in plot and character, allowing characters to step in and out of their roles, subverts all claims to ontological stability and reinterprets identity as performance; on the other hand, the formal hybridity of *The Hostage* both inscribes the play within the national tradition of nationalist melodrama and estranges that tradition from itself by combining it with the predominantly English aesthetics of music hall – thus pointing the way for the emergence of a hyphen-ated Irish modernity.

While Murphy wrote *The Blue Macushla* primarily for an Irish audience, he resorts to a similar sort of formal hybridity in order to question concepts of Irish nationalism, identity and modernity. As in *The Hostage*, the backdrop of the play is naturalistic and melodramatic: the story of Eddie's childhood, evoked in his liminary soliloquy, is one of social exclusion and deprivation in 1960s suburban Dublin, and Eddie's spectacular rise from the gutter to his current position as 'boss' of a trendy night-club follows – and parodies – the familiar pattern of rags-to-riches melodrama.[2] This naturalistic backdrop thus constructs a social reality which the character of Danny, Eddie's childhood friend and ex-pig-smuggling partner, still inhabits when he arrives at the Blue Macushla after spending five years in prison. There, however, he encounters the fantasy-world which Eddie has fashioned for himself, training his staff to ape the attitudes and speech-patterns of American gangster-films. While the character of Danny is played in the naturalistic style assumed to be the trademark of the Irish theatrical tradition, he evolves in a play whose dominant aesthetic code is cinematic rather than theatrical, American rather than Irish. This code informs the very structure of the play, which uses such cinematic devices as prolepsis and flashback, and resorts to split-staging in a dramatic approximation of cross-cutting in film. It also conditions the style of acting, since all characters except Danny ostensibly perform the parts which have been assigned to them out of the repository of gangster-film stereotypes. The discrepancy between the two aesthetic modes exposes the artificiality of the identities which are performed on the stage, so that, as in *The Hostage*, the play's critique of Irish republicanism is contained within a larger questioning of ontology. Like Behan, Murphy writes within a national tradition which he deliberately distorts to produce a (differently) hybridized form. As Fintan O'Toole has argued, 'the language of the play makes clear the extent to which the country has been colonized by American patterns of speech and thought'; yet the hybrid style also contributes to renew the Irish theatrical tradition by appropriating those patterns in a new gesture of transculturation.

The plotline of *The Blue Macushla* can be seen as a variation on *The Hostage*. In both plays, Irish republicans invade a disreputable house of entertainment (a brothel in *The Hostage*, the eponymous nightclub in *The Blue Macushla*) where they sequester a young man who is unrelated to their activities and has been randomly drawn into the picture. In *The Hostage*, the plot revolves around the English soldier Leslie's fate, which is held in suspense until the final scene, when he meets his death accidentally in a messy attempt by a group of improbable secret policemen to set him free. In *The Blue Macushla*, the execution of the 'kid-priest', dramatized in the proleptic first scene, is the foregone conclusion which only the final peripeteia revises. Unlike Leslie in *The Hostage*, the young priest is not the hero of the play. He is in fact hardly a character at all, being entirely passive, inarticulate (apart for one mumbled cue), anonymous and most of the time faceless (indeed in the *dramatis personae* he appears only as 'Hooded Figure'). While the victim's identity is thus erased, allowing the question of his fate to be displaced to the margins of the play, it is the pair of small-time criminals who claim ownership to the Blue Macushla (Eddie and Danny) who occupy centre stage. They are a characteristic pair of Murphy twins – both rival brothers and complementary figures –

and their individual quests for identity intersect with the nationalist theme, complicating the argument of *The Hostage*.

The structure of *The Blue Macushla* is similar to that of Murphy's 1989 play *Too Late for Logic*: an inaugural soliloquy culminates with a gunshot; it is followed by a long flashback at the end of which the first scene is replayed, but in a distinctly different tonality, revealing that our original understanding of it was in fact erroneous. The incipit or opening takes place in a characterless room, lit only by a desklamp: Eddie O'Hara, in a white tuxedo and carrying a gun, addresses a long soliloquy to a hooded figure slumped on a chair, and in the end shoots him coldly. The victim's identity is clarified, it seems, in the very first sentence: 'We become quite int'mates you'n'me, kid-priest, an' lot in common.'[3] Yet we only have Eddie's words to go by; the figure is inert and presumably unconscious during the whole scene: his voice will not be heard once, or his face seen, until Eddie shoots. Addressing the young priest, Eddie unravels a horror tale of growing up in suburban Dublin, in a district so deprived that the mere mention of the family's address (the antiphrastic Lady O'Perpetual Succour Mansions) was enough to stamp them with infamy. Recalling the programmatic diptych *On the Outside/On the Inside*, which provides the fundamental pattern of Murphy's plays (the sense of exclusion and the frustration this generates) a familiar sociological geography emerges, based on a divide between the city and its margins, towards which the outsiders who might be tempted to get inside are systematically rejected. In an oddly detached tone Eddie anatomizes the workings of a teratogenic social mechanism. While 1960s Ireland knew a time of unprecedented prosperity, proudly gaining its name as one of the modern nations of the world, it did so at the expense of a significant part of the population which remained cut off from the new opulence, stranded in a nightmare of ongoing famine:

> Most of my family's I would say, mainliners now: some's inside, some's has even had their legs sawed off. Two of them comes along oh sometimes back: Sure, I get rid o' them fast: "Go get rehabil'tated." For what they says an' was grinnin' kinda foolish. But understood what they meant. The only sane brother I got left is crazy. Washes his hair six times a day in every day 'n draws the dole, Fridays. Then has comp'titions with my ole man, I'm told, at relievin' theirselves through the broken pane to the winda-box was left behind by Mom. Oh but got a older sister. Now Susie was a looker an', so married this guy in reg'lar work an' she helped out Mom a lot. Only her husband – husband? Understand that word? – Only her husband's then got no job an' starts a-burglin', right? Only he's

su'prised one night, see? an', so, stabs this guy to death an', so, he's in for life. Now Susie's pregnant – pregnant? – with two twins while this comedy's goin' on an' has two other young uns too as well, an' one o' yours, a coonic (*Priest.*), comes up runnin' to her rescue with his ros'ry beads. Offer it up he tells her. Needn't tell yeh what our Susie says to him, because in Lady O'Perpetual Succour Mansions the rats had took a fancy to her babies bottles. But now she's makin' out, ole Susie is. I tell her once, "pack the pushin' game", but she's doin' fine she says an' the christian guys she's workin' for'll kill her if she does, an' fort'nately she don't want out. "Out where", she says. I 'gree. Bishopspricks. (*Takes out a silencer and fits it to the gun.*) Oh yeah: Like we wasn't all zombies: some was nat'ral retarded, like Mom's own favourite, Tim. He was blessin' in disguise, she said. But O'Hara's quite a name up there, cops in all hours hide-n-seek about the place, maybe that's what made him do it. Tim. A overdose o' somethin'. Rat poison? Could be. An' I figure that's the straw at last broke our Mom's back. Naaw, never went to see her. What for? Yeh, bishopspricks. But only part o' one family's history an' I'm feelin' kinda tired. (*P1*: 153-54)

In a parodic exaggeration of the cliché of the large Irish Catholic family ('can't remember 'xactly how many of us there was'), Eddie evokes the O'Hara clan as an indistinct horde of sociopaths, heroin-addicted 'zombies' crippled by gangrene ('their legs sawed off'), or imbeciles distorted by an endemic deprivation so familiar that it has become naturalized ('some of us were nat'rally retarded'). In this famine-ridden world the circulation of food is grotesquely unsettled, so that rats feed on baby food while children overdose on rat-poison. Even Eddie's language, disaffected as it is, suggests a form of emotional starvation. His logorrhoea turns horror into bleak comedy, leaving out the unspeakable grief of loss and guilt which can best be heard in the gaps of the text. The death of the mother is at first evoked tangentially in the pathetic tableau of the father and son's pissing contest as they target the now useless window-box ('was left behind by Mom'). It then re-emerges euphemistically – as the last straw that 'at last broke our Mom's back' – and elliptically ('never went to see her': in the mental home? the hospital? the cemetery?). Like James's 'Nickerdehpazzee' in *The Morning After Optimism*, the strange interjection 'bishopsricks', an obscene distortion of 'bishopric', represses surging pathos under the surface of the text, declaring feelings to be as superfluous as Episcopal genitalia. Having miraculously survived the familial disaster, Eddie depicts himself as an insider who has appropriated the discourse of the moral order ('Go get rehabil'tated', 'pack the pushin' game') and now perpetuates its mechanisms of exclusion ('Two of them comes along [...] I get rid o' them fast'). In this mock confession which brings together a priest and a native of the tenements, the traditional balance of power is reversed: the priest is not only anonymous and invisible (as in the confessional) but also, crucially, voiceless (the usual condition of the outcasts) while Eddie, in full light and brandishing the emblem of power (the gun), speaks at length without ever encountering contradiction, then shoots. Eddie's fatalistic musings ('Always knew somehow'd hafta use one o' these') and the anticipated catastrophe construct a pattern of tragic inescapability: Eddie's quest for social respectability (phrased in terms of identity: 'I just wantedta become a person') has led him to ultimate abjection. The long flashback which constitutes the bulk of the play negotiates a way out of this aporia.

Scene Two takes place three months earlier, on Christmas Day: Eddie is the owner of a flourishing Dublin night-club, a converging spot for the rich and beautiful. For all its apparent glamour, the Blue Macushla is clearly reminiscent of Behan's seedy brothel in *The Hostage*. The club's main attraction is the sexy singer Roscommon, whom Eddie, in her own words, encourages to 'perform in all sorts of ways'. Thus the whorehouse is also a playhouse, a liminary space of theatrical experimentation in which masks are donned and dropped. In *The Hostage* Behan makes no attempt to justify the play's theatricality realistically: there is no reason for the presence of the piano and piano-player in the brothel other than that they are needed to support the songs, and the queer trio who are entirely superfluous to the action but crucial to its carnivalesque exuberance celebrate the arbitrariness of their own parts in an acme of ineptitude ('we're here because we're queer because we're here because we're queer'). By turning the brothel into a night-club, Murphy, on the contrary, provides a realistic basis for the inclusion of songs – yet the play's theatricality by far exceeds and subverts the conventions of realism. The Blue Macushla is both the emblem and instrument of Eddie's social success, a theatrical machine which he uses to create a role for himself, modelling his speech and body language on the performance of the emblematic actors of American gangster films. He not only plays the lead (the feared and respected Boss) but also acts as director and set- and costume-designer, supervising every detail of an ongoing performance which is played out on and off the stage, during and between Roscommon's routines. The eerie, decidedly unrealistic atmosphere of the play comes from a series of discrepancies which foreground the artificiality of Eddie's fantasy world – between seventies' Ireland and interwar America, between the idiolects and syntax of Dublinese and the slang and intonations of American mob-speak, and between theatrical and cinematic acting styles. Theatre actors are deprived of the expressive subtleties offered by the close-up shot in the cinema, so that the transfer from screen to stage turns the characters who people the Blue Macushla into a series of caricatures – the husky-voiced femme fatale, the effeminate pianist, the aphasic bodyguard, all surrounding the boss and comforting him in his new status as a public figure. The Blue Macushla redirects Eddie's wish to 'become a person' by providing him with a persona, inspiring him with a morbidly regressive passion ('I love this place, I love it more'n anythin' an' I'll do anythin' for it!') (*P1:* 180) Indeed at one level, the whole play is like an extensive narcissistic fantasy of Eddie's which suddenly goes wrong.

Eddie's control of the Blue Macushla is compromised by two simultaneous events, both connected with long-forgotten unpaid debts. The money which bought the Blue Macushla came from a bank which Eddie robbed single-handed, leaving behind him the signature of a nationalist group, the Erin Go Brath [*sic*], to cover his tracks. When the Erin Go Braths [*sic*] pick up Eddie's lead and muscle their way into the Blue Macushla, Eddie finds out that he has unwittingly signed a kind of Faustian Pact: he now has his name in the group's 'little black book' of accounts ('debitors' section') and is given the choice of giving the money back or giving the group free access to the club's 'hospitality room'. As in *The Hostage*, the Yeatsian motif of the 'strangers in the house' is reversed, and both plays cast the nationalist activists as the illegitimate usurpers. Their first appearance creates an unspeakable malaise, although they seem to blend perfectly smoothly into the atmosphere of gangster films – so much so that the scene offers a hilarious parody of the genre's *scène à faire*, the godfather's visit to the petty criminal who has tried to double-cross him. All the clichés are there: the gang leader, hardly visible in the darkness, is flanked by two henchmen who form a well-known filmic pair: a short hothead with a gun and a tall quiet one who is biding his time. A sense of threat pervades the whole scene – Vic's weapon, N°2's mysterious package and above all N°1's exquisite politeness – and Eddie's authority is brought to nought within a few minutes. All this fits in perfectly with the style Eddie has imposed in the Blue Macushla, but this seamless continuity is precisely what makes the scene uncanny. Before the entrance of the Erin Go Braths [*sic*] everything that took place in the Blue Macushla had been carefully scripted and supervised by Eddie. They, however, were not part of his original plan, but seem to emanate from the Blue Macushla itself, which appears as a kind of mad matrix, escaping the control of its creator to generate its own monsters. Murphy subtly revisits the fantastic topos of the creator outwitted by his creature: 'You love this – club – of yours, only it don't appear to be yours no longer – does it?', Roscommon comments tersely. (*P1*: 179) The process of Eddie's dispossession is carried one step further when Danny, just out of prison, resurfaces on St Patrick's Day, claiming that 'half this place is mine'. (*P1*: 205) Again, Eddie finds himself indebted, and while he immediately offers to give Danny back his half of the few hundred pounds they had made together as pig-smugglers, he is in no position to pay back the moral debt he owes Danny for giving himself up to the police while Eddie escaped. Unlike Eddie, Danny is no performer – no dupe, that is, of the fiction of identity: 'Danny Mountjoy: I'm nobody' (*P1*: 207; the name is another homage to Behan), so that his naturalness foregrounds the artificiality of Eddie's social persona, and shakes its very foundations. Unpaid debts are symbolic of all that Eddie has compromised for the sake of a constructed identity – not so much authenticity, a fiction which the play consistently deflates, as an ethics of responsibility and solidarity such as the whole nation seems to have given up.

Indeed Eddie is 'a representation of the psychic history of a country in search of a new self-image'[4], which makes the nightclub, like Behan's rundown brothel, a metonym of 1970s Ireland – or rather of that part of Irish society which enjoys the new prosperity that emerged in the 1960s, while the economic crisis takes its toll on the more vulnerable, who have remained 'on the outside'. Subverting the conventional nationalist trope of the house-as-nation, both plays represent Ireland as a place in which affluence and pleasure depend on a system of exploitation of the weakest. That it becomes a hideout for republican activists is an acerbic comment on the irresponsibility of Irish political nationalism, which calls for a united Ireland but turns a blind eye to the country's social divide, a rent as deep as the partition which runs across the country's map. In *The Hostage*, Pat, the caretaker and ex-IRA member, pours contempt on de Valera for prioritizing the national question over social issues, and recalls that in 1925, he supported agricultural labourers who had seized 'five thousand acres of land from Lord

Tralee'[5] against the orders of the IRA, for which he was subsequently court-martialled.[6] The theme is taken up in lower-key tonality in *The Blue Macushla*, in which the display of riches and glamour points obstinately, though silently, to the deprived margins from which Eddie has walked away. Echoing Behan, Murphy contrasts the republicans' rhetorical obsession with unity with their inability to unite even their own movement, let alone Ireland. The Erin Go Braths [*sic*] are a splinter group of the Provisional IRA, which makes them, in Eddie's words, 'a splinter o' a splinter group'. (*P1*: 189) When Eddie is forced to take the oath and join the organization, he becomes 'N°19', the figure a sarcastic comment on the group's absurd smallness, though members are distributed into several 'divisions'. The oath itself is emptied of its meaning and of its performative dimension, since Eddie takes it under duress, with N°2 threatening to crush his fingers under a concrete block. The same N°2 later betrays the group and sells the little black book to a British agent – so that the myth of a united nation, bound together by its communal values and aspirations, is exposed as a political fiction destined to legitimize the republicans' gangsterism.

Thus the trope of the house-as-country is used for satirical purposes: just like the Blue Macushla, Ireland is being troubled by a group of fanatics akin to a criminal organization; it strives to present a façade of respectability, but its foundations are unsound. The play discloses a pattern of generalized corruption and exposes the collusion of the country's power-wielders. The little black book contains the list of all those business men and political figures who have supported the group financially, including the Minister to whom Pete speaks on the phone in the play's epilogue; the episode is reminiscent of the 1970 Arms Crisis, when two cabinet ministers were tried for illegally attempting to import arms for the IRA in Northern Ireland, and eventually acquitted. 'I knew that gangsterism in movies did not spring gratuitously out of the ground', Murphy writes, 'that it had come out of American culture; I don't remember when it was I realized I had discovered in it an apt metaphor for a play about Ireland in the 1970s.' (Introduction: *P1*: xxi) While the republicans behave like gangsters, the whole country is looking to America to create a borrowed 'identity' for itself, an Americanized version of Irishness epitomized by the imported ritual of the St Patrick's Day parade, which is glimpsed through the club's door, complete with majorettes and green Guinnesses. The Irishness which legitimizes the republican movement is an empty signifier:

that is the scandal which the play discloses, an unbearable void which a whole symbolic edifice attempts to palliate. Awakening from the colonial nightmare, a stranger to itself, Ireland constructs its Blue Macushla, its American dream or utopia which resonates in the play's songs: *Off to Philadelphia*, and also *Murteen* [*sic*] *Durkin*, which pictures California as a miraculous land of plenty ('sure's my name is Carney I'll be off –' Ta? – 'Cal'forny, an' 'stead o' diggin' praties I'll be diggin' lumps o' gold!') (*P1*: 185) The fairytale palace in Arline's famous song in *The Bohemian Girl* ('I dreamt I dwelt in marble halls', *P1*: 170) is just one more version of the nowhere land which invents itself night after night within the walls of the Blue Macushla.

Thus individual and national identities are shown to be theatrical constructs, a matter of performance rather than substance. Both Behan and Murphy recycle the devices and topoi of the baroque stage (the reign of illusions, the play within the play, the *theatrum mundi*) and deflate the rhetoric of identity with a carnivalesque aesthetics of masking and unmasking. In the course of *The Hostage*, the bigoted Irish Catholic Miss Gilchrist is revealed as a nympho-maniac with loyalist sympathies, while her admirer Mulleady is converted to homosexuality. The play ends with a parodic *coup de théâtre* when the Russian sailor proves to have been '*a police spy all along*', while Mulleady shouts out the wonderful line, 'I'm a secret policeman and I don't care who knows it' (Behan, *CP*: 232, 235) *The Blue Macushla*, itself a parody of *The Hostage*, takes this decon-struction of identity one step further, showing all the tenets of identity (nationality, political affiliation, occupation, sexual pre-ference and even gender) to be performative constructs. The leader of Murphy's Irish revolutionaries turns out to be an English lesbian, the gay pianist a straight Special Branch agent, and the Hungarian Countess (an absurd distortion of Countess Markiewicz, whose 'Battle Hymn' N°1 sings as she strangles the British agent, *P1*: 198) a Northern Irish republican activist. While Murphy adds the element of gender, N°1 is clearly modelled on Behan's Monsewer, England-born and public-school educated, who embraced the cause of Ire-land and became a hero in 1916 because his mother was Irish and he didn't get on well with his father. Monsewer's life is one long performance of (what he assumes to be) Irishness, consisting in wearing a kilt and playing Gaelic football in London, then taking 'a correspondence course in the Irish language' (*CP*: 143), and eventually playing the bagpipes in a brothel which he mistakes for an IRA headquarters. N°1's background is the same as Monsewer's, and her motives for electing Ireland as her '*chosen* native land' just as unrelated to politics: an uncaring family and 'the unhappiness that attends privilege' (*P1*: 199, emphasis added). In *The Hostage*, Leslie recognizes an uncanny similarity between Monsewer and his own Colonel ('Same face, same voice. Gorblimey, I reckon it is him', *CP*: 189). This note is echoed in *The Blue Macushla* when N°1 sees herself mirrored in the face of the British agent she is busy strangling: 'Oh dear! A British Intelligence Agent, an English Officer and a Gentleman, Victor. I know every jot and tittle of his background as I know my own. Public schools, boring summer hols, mother's stupid social calendar, father's tantrums, oh dear!' (*P1*: 198) Both passages implicitly indicate that class universals transcend national constructs of identity and thus undermine their relevance. With N°1 Murphy comically exaggerates another filmic stereotype, that of the lovesick butch lesbian, here a neurotic version of Simone Renant's Dora in Henri Georges Clouzot's *Quai des Orfèvres* (where Dora is in love with a music-hall singer, just as N°1 who sighs for Roscommon before sadistically burning her hand with her cigar when she is rejected). The profusion of queer characters in both plays, coupled with the element of cross-dressing (including the two IRA officers who try to escape dressed as nuns at the end of *The Hostage*), also contributes to destabilizing received re-presentations of gender-identities and to re-conceptualizing identity in terms of performance.

The emphasis on role-playing is essential to the plots of both *The Blue Macushla* and *The Hostage*. Both resort to what we might call, after Deleuze, an aesthetics of the 'empty space'. According to Deleuze, a system (in the structuralist sense) has a number of formal characteristics (he names six), one of which is the fact that it depends on a symbolic object which is in constant movement and allows the circulation of meaning within the whole system, like the empty space in a sliding puzzle. This paradoxical object, which 'has no place other than the 'hostage' himself in Behan's play, who is there only in his capacity as a British soldier, a marketable commodity to be exchanged for the boy who awaits execution in Belfast. When Leslie (referred to anonymously as 'SOLDIER' in the stage directions) arrives at the brothel he steps into his hostage's role and performs it to the bitter end, undeluded as to his actual value on the political market: 'You're as barmy as him if you think that what's happening to me is upsetting the British Government. I suppose you think they're all sitting around in the West End clubs with handkerchiefs over their eyes, dropping tears into their double whiskies. Yeah, I can just see the Secretary of State for War now waking up his missus in the night: "Oh Isabel-Cynthia love, I can hardly get a wink of sleep wondering what's happening to that poor bleeder Williams."' (*CP*: 217) Leslie is there only to fill the empty space left by the Belfast boy and symbolized by the chalk circle which Pat draws around him in Act III. As Declan Kiberd suggests, the finale of the play, when Leslie briefly resurrects to sing that 'The bells of hell/ Go ting-a-ling-a-ling/ For you but not for me', shows not only the actor meta-theatrically stepping out of his role but also conveys the more sinister sense that 'soldiers are dispensable, that willing canon-fodder comes easily, and that there are plenty more where he came from.'[7] Soldiers, like actors, are nonentities: who or what they are is literally cancelled out by the role they perform, a quality as cynically exploited by the British authorities as by the nationalists, whose mystique of identity is thus ironically deflated. *The Blue Macushla* again looks to *The Hostage* and complicates its system. The little black book which passes from hand to hand (from N°1 to N°2 to the British agent to Vic Camden to N°1 to Pete) sets in motion the whole system of exchange which takes place offstage, bringing together the Erin Go Brath [*sic*], British intelligence, the Irish Special Branch and Irish politicians, and resulting in the sequestration at the Blue Macushla of the British agent – at least according to N°1's initial plan. Indeed the hooded figure's identity is another empty space which gives rise to a series of substitutions off and on the stage: the young priest first stands in for the British agent out of Christian charity; then Danny frees the priest and ties up the false Countess in his place. Thus Eddie's initial soliloquy, as we discover at the end of the flashback, was in fact addressed to her, so that he really shoots the 'Countess' by order of her own organization.

In both plays, the brothel or club is thus primarily a theatrical space, where identities are floating signifiers which can be put on and taken off like masks; yet tragedy comes from those who cling to the rhetoric of identity and mistake the mask for the substance. Both plays target the nationalists' destructive fixation with identity, but *The Blue Macushla* also approaches the theme at the individual level. Eddie dies in the final 'showdown' for clinging too long to the club and his role as boss – which he plays to his dying breath: 'Oh God, don't let me die, I got a few more parties to throw.' (*P1*: 229)

The real hero is Danny, who learns to play with the codes that prevail at the Blue Macushla and speak 'the lingo', but remains aware that he is merely performing a role ('Danny Mountjoy: I'm nobody'). Danny's release from prison and arrival at the Blue Macushla is like a homecoming ('It's good to be home, partner'), a return from exile and a promise of stability and security. The club, of course, fails to fulfil that promise – in keeping with the song after which it is named, and which Roscommon sings, revisiting a universal story of fantasy and loss: 'Macushla, Macushla, your sweet voice is calling [...] My blue-eyed Macushla I hear it in vain." (*P1*: 155) Macushla, meaning 'my darling' or object of desire, is here a house of illusions, a liminary space which must eventually be left behind as Roscommon well knows: 'Just walk out that door', she suggests to Danny, 'and don't once look back.' (*P1*: 205) Danny's heroism resides in his capacity to leave the Blue Macushla behind him, to give up its false promise of identity and face the unknown. The very short final scene of the play, with its short, elliptical speeches, rewrites the end of *The Morning After Optimism*:

> **DANNY.** Where yiz goin'?
> **ROSCOMMON.** Dunno.
> **DANNY.** Will yiz give us a lift?
> **ROSCOMMON.** Where to?
> *He looks up and down.*
> We have no place to go.
> **DANNY.** Let's go there. (*P1*: 231)

Roscommon, whose name ironically points to the alleged purity of the Gaelic West, is another 'common rose' like *Optimism*'s Rosie; but in *The Blue Macushla* she follows the innocent, not the cynical pimp, on a trip to 'nowhere'. Like Synge's blind tramps in *The Well of the Saints*, Danny and Roscommon choose the freedom of the road (the danger and excitement of a fluctuating identity) and leave behind the trap of the house of self.

As I have tried to argue, *The Blue Macushla* is a rewriting of Behan's *The Hostage* which takes up both the political theme of the play (the critique of identity politics and of a purely destructive practice of nationalism) and its hybridized aesthetics which challenges the tradition of Irish naturalistic drama. However, the play should also be envisaged in the larger context of Murphy's theatrical corpus, in which Danny's mock-heroic journey of homecoming to the Blue Macushla constitutes an important landmark. Murphy had first experimented with the motif of homecoming in *The White*

House (1972), whose form did not satisfy him. *The Blue Macushla* was his first successful handling of the theme, and set a paradigm for a number of subsequent 'plays of homecoming': *Conversations on a Homecoming* (1985), the revised version of *The White House*, *The Wake* (1998), and *The House* (2000). In all these plays, the protagonist comes home to a house which exile has made him or her idealize, and endow with a sense of authenticity. The house always works as a metonym of Ireland and a metaphor of self: to come home is to regain an identity long lost to the estranged traveller. Homecoming, however, proves to be the beginning of a new journey of the soul, in the course of which the idealized construct of the house is confronted to reality, and exposed as an illusion. Most of these plays end when the hero leaves the house behind him/her and takes to the road again, giving up the lure of a stabilized identity and embracing a life of open possibility. In *The House*, however, the hero ironically named Christy like Synge's Playboy, refuses nomadism and clings to the house of his dreams, which closes in upon him like a tragic trap. *The Blue Macushla*, which initiates the series, is an important play not just in the Murphy canon, but in the counter-tradition of non-naturalistic Irish plays which uses meta-theatricality to reassess received concepts of personal and national identity.

---

[1] John Brannigan, *Brendan Behan : Cultural Nationalism and the Revisionist Writer* (Dublin, Four Courts Press, 2002): 114.

[2] See Fintan O'Toole, *Tom Murphy : The Politics of Magic* (revised, London: Nick Hern Books, 1994): 163.

[3] Tom Murphy, *The Blue Macushla*, in *Plays: 1* (London: Methuen, 1992): 153, hereafter cited in the text as *P1*.

[4] O'Toole, *The Politics of Magic*: 163.

[5] Brendan Behan, *The Hostage*, in *The Complete Plays* (London: Methuen, 1978): 160. Hereafter quoted as *CP*.

[6] See Declan Kiberd, *Inventing Ireland* (London: Jonathan Cape, 1995): 524-25.

[7] Kiberd, *Inventing Ireland*: 528.

Performance and Text

10 | 'A Better Form of Drama': Tom Murphy and the Claims of Music

Harry White

> Words, literature, writing drama is such a linear thing, whereas when I listen to music, I hear emotion, I hear mood; when I listen to the sound people are making, I hear emotion and character. 'All art aspires to the condition of music'. The aspiration is to get a simultaneity of things happening, not to confuse the situation or make it over complex, but to get the richness of music that is not just a linear point going from A to D or A to Z. In music you can be elated, deflated, happy, sad in a phrase of music. I try to write in a certain way, varying rhythms, or seeking to continue a certain rhythm or repeat a certain rhythm, as a composer would a phrase of music to get what I think is a better form of drama.
>
> [Tom Murphy in conversation with Michael Billington, 7 October 2001][1]

The pressures exerted by music on the Irish literary imagination have not always been acknowledged. The very trace of music as a formative presence in Irish fiction, poetry and drama has not, until recently, excited a commensurate level of critical discourse which might concede to music its constituent status as a preoccupation which endures in the minds of writers as otherwise diverse as Tom Moore, W.B. Yeats and J.M. Synge, even if this presence, once identi-fied, is comparatively easy to register. Moore's attempt to translate into verse the meaning of Irish music, Yeats's reliance on music as a symbol of the creative imagination (and his abiding sense of music as a rival presence to poetry) and Synge's explicit pro-gression from music to literature are all paradigmatic of a funda-mental engagement with music which dominates Irish writing to the present day. This does not mean that every Irish writer is a composer *manqué* (although that designation could justifiably be applied not only to Synge, but to Bernard Shaw, James Joyce and Samuel Beckett), but it does mean that a certain longing for music, which is all the more acutely felt because of Ireland's verbally dominated cultural matrix, has inflected the cultivation of literary genres which in some measure answer the need for music. I have argued elsewhere that such genres indeed satisfy this longing to the extent that Irish poetry, fiction and drama have often functioned as correlatives of musical discourse. The mere experience of European art music in particular, so strikingly dislocated in Irish cultural history until very recently, is rehabilitated and domesticated in the Irish literary imagination. [2]

The hospitality which Irish writing affords to music is perhaps most self-evidently apparent within the domain of the theatre. Even if we discount the peculiar conditions of Irish cultural history (above all with regard to music), the proximity of literary and musical genres in the history of European drama is a commonplace, and one which gains particular focus in an Irish context. Opera and drama are strikingly interdependent throughout the history of modern European theatre (although the ascendancy of opera over spoken drama is a prominent feature of conservative political hegemonies until after the French Revolution), but in Ireland, this conjunction is nevertheless problematic.[3] It is hard to escape the impression, conveyed by almost any model of cultural history, that in Ireland, the spoken drama is domestic, whereas opera belongs to a borrowed culture. Another way to approach this imbalance would be to suggest that in Ireland, opera remains an aspirational genre, whereas the spoken drama is an achieved form. In this distinction lies the difference between a musical culture and a verbal one, however much the latter may depend upon or even act for the former.[4]

In the recent history of the Irish theatre, this interdependence between musical aspiration and achieved form becomes cardinal. In another context, I have used the phrase 'operas of the Irish mind' to characterize this interdependence in the works of Brian Friel, partly because in Friel's plays a vast seam of musical experience becomes essential to his dramatization of Irish experience, and partly because Friel's own work depends explicitly on at least two pre-eminent generic prototypes drawn from music, of which opera is one (the other is the concerto). The interior history of musical ideas which his work constantly proposes and domesticates becomes an unmistakably Irish history of ideas. A borrowed musical culture (as in

Chopin, Mendelssohn, and Beethoven) becomes constituent of Friel's Irish drama.[5]

Although this tendency to absorb the expressive and formal resources of European art music is more far-reaching and more plural in Friel's work than in the work of any other Irish dramatist (I do not exclude Bernard Shaw from this assessment), it also obtains to a remarkable degree in the plays of Tom Murphy. In what follows here, I shall argue that in Murphy's case, the aspiration towards what he himself characterizes as 'a better form of drama' not only gains from a comparison with Friel in this regard, but also depends on a response to music in general and opera in particular which is radically distinct. It is a response which narrows the difference between words and music to a degree unknown in Friel. It is also a response which promotes a likening between Friel and Murphy as between a classical temperament and a romantic one.

ʠ ʠ

Oh the dreaming! The dreaming! The torturing, heart-scalding, never satisfying dreaming, dreaming, dreaming, dreaming!

[Larry Doyle in Shaw's *John Bull's Other Island*, 1904][6]

An explicit engagement with music is not often apparent in Murphy's plays, at least not to the extent that such an engagement might displace or even rival that preoccupation with distinct musical works that characterizes so many of Friel's plays. The sovereign exception to this observation, of course, is Murphy's masterpiece, *The Gigli Concert*, in which the claims of opera reach their keenest pitch in the Irish theatre, even if that work does not exhaust Murphy's recourse to individual arias in others of his plays. Nevertheless, it is useful to declare *The Gigli Concert* as a special case in relation to Murphy's more general approach to musical paradigms, if only because that play brilliantly explores the rival claims of music and drama through the agency of a theatrical engagement which is practically *sui generis*. I would argue that this engagement foregrounds music to a degree which throws into sharp relief the more pervasive tendency in Murphy's work to imbue his dialogue with a rhythmic and indeed melodic structure in which musical precedents (phrase, rhythm, sound and formal control) are instructive. These precedents produce a stylized and balletic sound-world in which the express intelligence of dialogue is constantly subordinated to the impressionism of rhetoric. In this respect, a constant in the plays prior to *The Gigli Concert* is to promote the set-piece either as a bravura exchange between characters or as an *arioso* indulgence in which this rhetoric defines 'the sound people are making' as a dramatization of character as well as situation. A passage from the opening of *A Crucial Week in the Life of a Grocer's Assistant* (1969) conveys this characteristically impressionist technique. A man in his late twenties (John Joe) is dreaming of escape and sex. In a scene more than faintly reminiscent of *opera buffa*, his girlfriend (Mona) enters his bedroom through the window. She urges him to abscond with her. As she is about to kiss him, the (religious) medals on the chain around her neck drop into his mouth:

> **JOHN JOE.** The medals are coming, the medals are coming! – Hail Mary, Holy Mary! – Jesus mercy, Mary help! [...]
> **MONA.** My suitcase is outside on wheels for away, on wheels for away on the puff-puff!

Still dreaming, John Joe tries to follow her through the window but is interrupted by his mother:

> **MOTHER.** Lord, Lord, Lord! Where is he going? [...] The hold-all in his hand, the good chair displaced, the poor windy open that's always been stuck! And dressed like that!
> *He sees that he is not wearing his trousers; he retreats to the bed.*
> **JOHN JOE.** I was on'y–
> **MOTHER.** Put down the good chair! –
> **JOHN JOE.** On'y playing –
> **MOTHER.** Replace the hold-all! –
> **JOHN JOE.** On'y –
> **MOTHER.** Cover your knees from the frost-bite!
> **JOHN JOE.** (*Getting into bed*) On'y playin', Mammy.
> **MOTHER.** Only playing was he? Now for ye! Disturbing the equilibrium, on'y playing! Off-to-America, that's where he was going! The liar, the rogue!
> **JOHN JOE.** No, Mammy.
> **MOTHER.** Leaving us here in the lurch. Deserting his mammy and daddy and uncle that's good to him. That's gratitudinous! That's the son I reared. The favourite child I lavished with praise, the plans I had for his economy: the spotless boy, in days of old, who was so nice and knew his place: now as bad, if not worse, than his brother before him.
> **JOHN JOE.** (*Groans*) Frank, oh Frank!
> **MOTHER.** I'd swear my oath that poverty is not good enough for him. Heeding that hussy of a clotty of a plótha of a streeleen of an

ownshook of a lebidjeh of a girleen that's working above in the
bank. And she putting nonsense talk on him. [7]

The dream in which these exchanges take place is itself an
impression: it also licenses Murphy's mesmeric high comedy and
the ebullient poeticisms with which this is achieved. It is the
dreaming condemned by Larry Doyle in *John Bull's Other Island*
refracted through the agency of a dramatic discourse which takes its
cue from a host of different sources: Synge's *Playboy*, the dream
sequences in *Ulysses*, Denis Johnston's *The Old Lady Says No!*, the
Irish kitchen-comedy, even *Philadelphia, Here I Come!* (to which *A
Crucial Week* bears a problematic affinity).[8] But the discourse
belongs to Murphy: its motivic cadences and modulating iterations,
its accumulation of neologisms and Anglicized transliterations from
the Irish speech to a sound-world in which the fabric of exchanges
and set-pieces (as in the pejorative hedonism which closes this
extract) takes precedence. This is because Murphy remains attentive
to the ambiguity of the moment, the 'simultaneity of things happening' which music more easily affords, but which his own insistence
on the drama of sound (as against the drama of event) also allows.
The drama of the dialogue, often provisional and frequently
parenthetic, amounts to an impressionism which the action
facilitates, rather than the other way around. In this specific sense,
Murphy's attachment to the sovereignty of an expressive moment
becomes increasingly important as the plays unfold, so that the
gusto of his dialogue, whether tight-lipped ('How yeh!' [the opening
phrase of this play]), grandiloquent ('Disturbing the equilibrium') or
lyric ('The favourite child I lavished with praise, the plans I had for
his economy: the spotless boy, in days of old, who was so nice and
knew his place') tends to subvert the 'linear thing' which Murphy
would avoid throughout his dramaturgy. The plays linger in this
kind of lyric consciousness. *A Crucial Week* may present all kinds of
problems with regard to its sense of rural Ireland, its hybrid
idealism and its divided loyalties in respect of narrative and
character, but the tonality of its diction is, I would suggest, as distinctive and memorable as that of Synge or O'Casey, to cite two
pertinent exemplars. Whereas a dramatist like Friel will re-invent
this diction from the ground up as each new dramatic situation
requires, Murphy's greatest plays are bound to each other by a
recurrent and unmistakable voice.

It is this quality of voice – instinctive, lyric, formal and rhetorical
– which, I would suppose, brings Murphy close to Pinter in

contemporary theatre, as against those thematic affinities (as between *A Whistle in the Dark* (1961) and Pinter's *The Homecoming* (1965), for example) which critics rightly identify in the work of both writers.[9] No matter how strikingly diverse Pinter's settings – from the slums of West London, through the elegance of Hampstead to an unspecified prison camp in South America – the consistent quality and identity of his diction remain paramount. It is (it was) his principal resource as a dramatist. A similar consistency obtains in Murphy's work, so that the anti-pastoral subversions of the fairytale in *The Morning after Optimism* (1971) and the heroic realism of *The Sanctuary Lamp* (1975)[10] present vitally different surroundings which nevertheless are subsumed by what Gerard Stembridge many years ago described as Murphy's 'theatrical language of empathy'.[11] The nimble quartet of personages which inhabits *Optimism* and the anguished trio at the heart of *The Sanctuary Lamp* have this much in common with Murphy's earlier work. In both of these plays, the visual setting promotes a sense of space waiting to be filled with a corresponding grandeur of sound: the tall tree-trunks of the forest in *Optimism* and the great columns of the church in *The Sanctuary Lamp* which 'dwarf the human form,' condition the scale of the drama which is to take place.

It is difficult to resist the suggestiveness of these settings in relation to nineteenth-century opera, to a received idea of opera, especially in relation to the domestic realism of kitchen comedies, dance halls, village shops, and so on. In *The Sanctuary Lamp*, this suggestiveness is fortified by the use of 'introductory' music – Tchaikovsky's score for the ballet *The Sleeping Beauty* – and the 'vaguely balletic' movements of Harry outside the church before the play begins in earnest. Taken together, such elements comprise an overture to the play itself, a progression which is marked (in the first version of *The Sanctuary Lamp*) by a gradual declension from the orchestral assurance and power of the Tchaikovsky to Harry's fragmentary rendition of 'When the red, red robin' and the church congregation's 'pathetic' singing of 'Michael rowed the boat ashore'.[12] In such pitiful transitions the stage is set (literally) for the gradual recovery of spoken language, in which a distinction (endemic to opera) between recitative (dialogue) and aria (set piece, speech or monologue) becomes essential to Murphy's theatrical discourse. This is a distinction which is more emphatic in the revised version of the play (1984), so that Francisco's sermon in Act II ('The Story of the Critics Ball'), deprived of its parodic counterpart in Act I (an actual sermon, delivered by a Young Priest cut from the revised version), engages thematically and more directly with Harry's corresponding monologue in Act I.[13] In both acts (and in both versions of the play), the movement towards and away from these heroic set-pieces is mimetic of the crescendo and diminuendo of musical discourse to such an extent that it is difficult to escape the impression that the possibility of opera hovers in the wings of *The Sanctuary Lamp*. It is a possibility that Murphy promotes with uncanny results in *The Gigli Concert*.

∾   ∾

> As the old gifts of recital and storytelling pass out of everyday life, they make a compelling reappearance on Stage. [Declan Kiberd, *The Irish Writer and the World*][14]

I have already suggested that it may be useful to contrast the explicit romanticism of Murphy's dramatic imagination with the narrative composure of Friel's work, expressly in relation to music. The formal poise which musical prototypes (notably the concerto) bring to Friel's plays is largely absent from the Murphy canon, which draws on the available power of music not formally but expressively. Although Murphy himself occasionally characterizes his plays as 'symphonies' and 'chamber music', it is not the classical availability of form which such genres suggest in his work, but rather their romantic intensity of expression. This intensity is attested in Murphy's reliance on those paradigms of recitative and aria which pervade his dialogue (as I have tried to indicate here), but it gains prominence in a special way in *The Gigli Concert*. This play is haunted by the expressive possibilities of opera, and of nineteenth-century Italian opera in particular. There is no other work in the Irish theatre which so painfully explores music as the true domain of emotional intelligence, or which so poignantly verses this conviction as a Faustian pact between the author's imagination and the medium in which he is working. Unlike Synge and Friel, Murphy confronts the possibility of being undone by the expressive power of music as an end in itself. If Friel's verbal operas and concertos are tempered by classicism, Murphy's plays, and *The Gigli Concert* in particular, dispense with that restraint and draw all the more dangerously close to music itself. In this proximity, Irish theatre in the twentieth century revisits the expressive power of nineteenth-century opera.

The Gigli Concert resigns itself to music: it proposes that there are no 'gifts of recital and storytelling' (Kiberd) which are supervened by the emotional intelligence and narrative power of opera. That is its most dangerous and audacious argument, all the more potent because of Murphy's astonishing juxtaposition of opera and spoken drama, an adjacency which not only domesticates opera (the Italian aria as an apotheosis of Irish drama), but which also drives home the sovereignty of music as the fundamental language of dramatic discourse. The claims of music are absolute: when King leaves his office, he knows that Gigli will 'sing on forever'. The only credible redemption which the theatre affords comes through the agency of music, and the only redemption which opera affords to the spoken drama is that it too engages with language. But there is no turning back: this is a play in which the spoken word, for all its lyric and dramatic prowess, defers to the triumph of *dramma per musica*. In that ascendancy, the story of what happens to Irish Man and King through the course of the play achieves an aesthetic of music which is not only plausible but, I would argue, essential. No less essential is Murphy's strategic location of the spoken drama on the borders of musical discourse, so that the bravura encounters of the dialogue invariably lead, over and again, to the transcendent terminus of music. In this plural and complex trajectory, Murphy not only advances the case for opera ('a simultaneity of things happening') as against the linear progressions of the spoken drama: he also invokes the orphic enchantment of the genre itself – its sheer auditory power – as the only satisfactory resolution available to him. In this invocation, the Faustian allegiances to music as 'the supreme mystery in the science of man' (Claude Lévi-Strauss), which the play constantly promotes, are decisive. 'Like, you can talk forever, but singing. Singing, d'yeh know? The only possible way to tell people', is the [Irish] Man's tentative formula for this imperative.[15] It is an imperative which governs the play from the outset.

In a masterly reading of *The Gigli Concert* (which nevertheless avoids any real consideration of its encounter with music), Fintan O'Toole remarks of the setting that 'As a peculiar kind of church, JPW [King]'s office is a theatrical space analogous to the church of *The Sanctuary Lamp* or the forest of *The Morning After Optimism*, half-real, half a place in which anything could happen, in which dreams or nightmares can be tested against reality. But once the second protagonist of the play, The Irish Man, enters, he brings with him a crisp and clearly defined view of what the outside world is like.'[16]

I'm not sure that I would agree with that last observation – Irish Man seems anything but 'clearly defined' in his bluster and dissimulations – but the persuasive affinities between the setting of *The Gigli Concert* and its predecessors which O'Toole identifies can help to explain the hermetic condition of King's office as a sacred space in which the action will unfold. These affinities also encourage us to regard the setting of *The Gigli Concert* and its urban ambience (a loft which looks 'over the roofs of the city') as elements not immediately vulnerable to the intrusions of natural representation. The world is indeed outside. Within, we hear the sound of Gigli's singing which not only introduces the play but which bridges the scenes. It even continues 'through the intermission' and indefinitely into the future as the play comes to a close. The ultimate sound-world of *The Gigli Concert* is the sound which opera makes, even if Murphy ingeniously contrives a counterpoint between this sound and his own (verbal) imaginings, a contrast which is brilliantly sustained up to the point where music alone can answer the demands of the plot. We hear Gigli singing at the outset, just as we hear Tchaikovsky at the outset of *The Sanctuary Lamp*, but it is not until the second act of *The Gigli Concert* that this auditory presence becomes diegetic, when Irish Man produces his record player in King's office. Thereafter, the ineffable impact of Meyerbeer, Verdi, Boito, Giordano and of course Donizetti is variously grounded in the movement and action of the play.[17] We cannot explain what the music means, but we can account for its presence. This strategic (and partial) realism – the record player is switched on and off as the action requires – serves to integrate the music into the fabric of the play and prepares the ground for King's unnerving absorption of Irish Man's obsession, but it does not weaken the centrifugal force of that music to which King triumphantly aspires. In what is perhaps one of the two most remarkable *coups-de-theâtre* in contemporary Irish drama, Murphy takes care that the record player is unplugged before King performs Gigli's rendition of 'Tu che al Dio spiegasti l'ali'.[18] The music is finally imagined, and therefore real. In that respect, it partakes of the same fictive subversion which the play maintains throughout. Irish Man is a builder who physically resembles Gigli and wants to sing like him, who represents his Italian childhood based on Gigli's biography, who modulates from this representation to a brutal family life in rural Ireland (as he warms to his theme, an Italian sibling becomes Irish again), who seeks an impossible cure for an uncertain malady. King's practice of 'dynamatology', his erstwhile membership of a loosely-defined sect led by 'Steve' and his pronounced sense of dislocation (in exile, in Ireland) likewise enhance the play's subversive ambiguities as it slips in and out of realistic representation. Only the archival past-ness of Gigli's voice, heard through the scratch and blur of imperfect recordings, seems to assent to a verisimilitude which in any case is the implacable truth of music itself.

It is this implacable quality – to which everything else in the play aspires – which guarantees *The Gigli Concert* its aesthetic plausi-bility. By the time the physician (King) heals himself through the agency of an operatic aria, the Faustian pact between Murphy's imagination and the power of music is irreversible. Were it anything less than that, it would be impossible to concede the author's genius in gambling the whole enterprise of spoken drama as a prelude (however complex, however brilliant) to the musical utterances of Gaetano Donizetti, especially when these have been helplessly rehearsed by King himself within minutes of his (proverbially) operatic catharsis. When the music deliberately silhouettes the action, as in the mimetic relationship between the trio from Verdi's *Attila* which follows a disclosure of mortal illness and heralds the final encounter between King and Irish Man (one operatic *scena* amplifying another, as it were)[19], Murphy prepares his audience for that decisive modulation in which music is no longer suggestive or ancillary, but 'triumphant' (this is Murphy's adjective) in its impera-tive address. To surrender words to music in this way is a daring astonishment.

চ   চ

But there can be no gainsayin' it, Costello clear had the quality laugh. 'Wo ho ho, ho ho ho' (in) the barrel of his chest would great rumbles start risin', the rich rolls of round sound out of his mouth, to explode in the air an' echo back rev'berations. The next time demonstratin' the range of his skill, go flyin' aloft (to) the heights of registration – 'Hickle-ickle-ickle-ickle!' – like a hen runnin' demented from the ardent attentions, over-persistent, of a cock in the yard after his business. Now!

[Tom Murphy, *Bailegangaire* (1984)][20]

Anezka, my dear, you'd learn so much more by just listening to the music.

[Brian Friel, *Performances* (2003)][21]

The longing for music which *The Gigli Concert* dramatizes has an abiding presence in the Irish literary imagination (much of *Ulysses*, for example, is driven by it), but the redemption of musical drama which Murphy advances in this play is another matter. In other of his works before and after *The Gigli Concert* there are characters who take refuge in music, to say nothing of the stylized balladry and Brechtian panache of the music in a play such as *The Blue Macushla* (1980). But these contrivances and resources are absolutely removed from that magisterial resignation to music which is represented in *The Gigli Concert*, to such an extent that the claims of music which abide in that play uniquely overwhelm the enterprise of spoken drama. It is scarcely surprising that Murphy's reaction to this state of affairs was to ingather his response to the claims of music by writing *Bailegangaire*, a play in which Murphy's apprehension of 'a better form of drama' is once more internalized in the rhythm and pitch of Mommo's diction. The trio of women's voices in *Bailegangaire* represents a recovery of verbal music saturated with sounds (including the sound of Irish) invented or reshaped by Murphy and decisively removed from those sirens of Italian opera which dominate *The Gigli Concert*. The sound of Schubert (which closes the play) is a faint intimation of catharsis by comparison with the demented rhetoric and movement of Mommo's story, so often repeated that Dolly can prompt her mother in the same idiom when she falters in the narrative. It is hard not to conclude that the sheer extremism of Mommo's diction comprises a harsh rebuff to the soaring optimism and grace of music in the earlier play, but in any case the verbal music of the laughing competition in the later work is redeemed by another kind of compassion. In *Bailegangaire*, it is the music of language and not the language of music which prevails. Muted allusions to the earlier play ('The Sunday Concert,' Dolly's remark that her mother *goes on like a gramophone* and the faint promise of hope invested in the Schubert) subtly underscore the fundamental difference between these two great works. The abiding auditory impression left by *Bailegangaire* is a harrowing verbal music of Murphy's own invention.

But Gigli sings on forever. Exactly twenty years after *The Gigli Concert*, Brian Friel's *Performances* revisited the question of music and its ascendancy over language in the theatre with such compelling deliberation and grace that it can be regarded (at least in part) as a classically-tempered response to Murphy's play.

Performances also ends in music: a performance of the last two movements of Janáček's Second String Quartet, entitled 'Intimate Letters'. In this instance, the music is not imagined or recorded: it is given in live performance by four musicians, a string quartet which interacts throughout the play with Janáček and a PhD student in musicology, Anezka, who is writing a dissertation on the composer's late works. The play is set in Janáček's work-room in Brno in 1928, a few months before he died, but the time is 'the present'. The affinities with *The Gigli Concert* are compelling; in both plays music is the sovereign intelligencer of feeling, of authentic discourse, of complex expression. *The Gigli Concert* exposes the spoken drama to the rival claims of opera. *Performances* affirms the greater powers of music through the medium of a string quartet, in which the distance between biography and art is deliberately widened. Anezka and Janáček debate the significance of the composer's 700 letters written to the woman who undoubtedly inspired the quartet, Kamila Stösslová (hence the work's title – 'Intimate Letters'). Anezka would affirm this correspondence as something which 'enriches our intimacy' with the 'great amplitude' of the music itself. Janáček disavows this necessity: 'But finally, Anezka, finally – all this petty agitation aside – [...] the work's the thing. That must be insisted on. Everything has got to be ancillary to the work. And for all her naiveté in these matters even Kamila acknowledged the primacy of the work. She understood that from the very beginning: the work came first'.[22] In dramatizing this tension between the claims of an autonomous artwork and the claims of biography as a *combattimento* between language and music, Friel ends as Murphy ends, with spoken drama made silent in the presence of music.

Janáček's calm insistence on the autonomy of art in *Performances* makes of this silence a composure. Beyond the immediate circumstances of the play, this composure summons JPW King's remark at the end of *The Gigli Concert* that 'mankind still has a delicate ear'.[23] In either case, the autonomy of art, of *play*, guarantees to the spoken drama a degree of discourse and representation which endures against the implacable claims of 'a better form of drama'. The romanticism of Murphy's encounter with these claims is qualified by the serene deliberation of Friel's meditation on 'perfection of the work,' if only because Friel engages with the abstract condition of instrumental music, as against that intimacy between the singing voice and spoken utterance (opera and drama) which lies at the heart of *The Gigli Concert*. Not only is the distance between biography and art widened in *Performances*, but also the gulf that lies between music and language. This widening affords Janáček a better perspective on the difference between one art and the other, but it also speaks to the difference between Friel's classical temperament with regard to music itself and Murphy's romantic quest for a music inside language. To explore that difference would be another day's work, but in the meantime, these plays affirm not only a longing for music in the Irish theatre but a sovereign acknowledgement of its dramatic intelligence. In these enterprises, it seems characteristic that Murphy's decisive encounter with music should be vested in a single masterpiece, even as his other works pursue a verbal music which music itself both inspires and delimits.

---

[1] In Nicholas Grene (ed.), *Talking About Tom Murphy* (Dublin: Carysfort Press, 2002):108

[2] See Harry White, *Music and the Irish Literary Imagination* (Oxford: OUP, 2008).

[3] A prominent instance of this ascendancy is represented by the almost complete absence of spoken drama in Vienna during the period 1660-1740, during which time *opera seria* was assiduously cultivated as a means of imperial propaganda. It is not too much to add that the recovery of spoken drama in Europe after the *ancien régime* signifies an emancipation from the dictates of *opera seria*, and that opera itself was strikingly liberated from these dictates partly through the agency of a rejuvenated and politically mature spoken drama.

[4] It remains the case even today that opera belongs to a borrowed culture in Ireland, at least to judge by the tiny handful of works in this genre which originate in this country. By contrast, a significant number of Irish writers have deliberately situated their work against the immediate background of Italian or German opera: James Joyce and Bernard Shaw are obvious examples of this tendency. For an extended consideration of this relationship, see the introduction to *Music and the Irish Literary Imagination* (as note 2): 12-18.

[5] See White, *Music and the Irish Literary Imagination*, chapter 7, 'Operas of the Irish Mind: Brian Friel and Music': 206-27.

[6] *The Bodley Head Bernard Shaw, Collected Plays with Prefaces*, ed. Dan H. Laurence, vol 2 (London: Bodley Head, 1971): 909.

[7] Thomas Murphy, *A Crucial Week in the Life of a Grocer's Assistant* (Dublin: Gallery Press, 1978): 12-13.

[8] What I have described below as the 'pejorative hedonism' of Mother's speech-song in this play re-imagines the virtuoso bitterness of Pegeen Mike in late middle-age. In the excerpt cited here, Mona's exhortations summon the rhythmic patterns of The Speaker in *The Old Lady Says 'No!'* (1929), which in turn reflect the influence of dramatic diction in the 'Night-town' sequences of *Ulysses* (1922). Mr. Brown's interrogation of John Joe in Scene Eight of *A Crucial Week* also stems in part from Joyce (and from the 'Cyclops' episode in *Ulysses* in particular), to judge by the querulous litany of questions which John Joe will never satisfactorily answer, although the comic surrealism of this episode is no less suggestive of the interrogation sequences in Pinter's *The Birthday Party* (1958). By contrast, the affinities between *A Crucial Week* and *Philadelphia* are thematically obvious, but the expressionism of Murphy's language in this play, for all its musicality of invention, has very little (if anything) in common with Friel's dialogue or musical strategies.

[9] See the discussion between Billington and Murphy on the potential influence of Murphy's *A Whistle in the Dark* on Pinter's *The Homecoming* in 'Conversation at the Abbey Theatre' (as n.1): 98-99.

[10] Throughout this essay, I have given the date of first performance as the date of each play in question, although with regard to this question of influence, it may be pertinent to add that *The Morning after Optimism* was written c.1963. See Fintan O'Toole, *Tom Murphy: the Politics of Magic*, revised edition (Dublin and London: New Island Books and Nick Herne Books, 1994): 12.

[11] See Gerard Stembridge, 'Murphy's Language of Theatrical Empathy' in Christopher Murray (ed.), *Thomas Murphy Special Issue, Irish University Review* 17. 1 (Spring, 1987): 51-61.

[12] With the exception of the Tchaikovsky, these preliminaries are removed from the revised version of the play, first published in 1984.

[13] The disappearance of Francisco from the revised version of the first act of *The Sanctuary Lamp* (he makes one fleeting appearance as the first act closes), intensifies the impact of Harry's monologue in the first act of the revised version. This monologue is itself considerably re-written and expanded in the newer version, so that its function as a set piece is all the more prominent stylistically as well as thematically.

[14] Declan Kiberd, *The Irish Writer and the World* (Cambridge: CUP, 2005): 4-5.

[15] Thomas Murphy, *The Gigli Concert* (Dublin: Gallery Press, 1984): 23. When King presses him on the meaning of this formula ('to tell people'), the Man [*sic*, in this edition] half-explains it as a means of identification (i.e. to tell people 'who you are').

[16] O'Toole, *The Politics of Magic* (as n.10): 210. O'Toole's analysis of *The Gigli Concert* as an inversion of the Faust myth (above all in Goethe's drama) is, in my view, especially enlightening. *The Gigli Concert* represents a significant addition to the presence of Faust in European music and literature to the extent that Murphy joins Goethe, Gounod and Thomas Mann (among others) in this enterprise.

[17] The rhetoric of longing which this music achieves through these Gigli recordings is rarely conceded in explicit terms, with the sovereign exception of the trio from Verdi's *Attila* (see below) and the aria from *Lucia di Lammermoor* ('Tu che a Dio spiegasti l'ali'), which (all but) closes both Donizetti's opera and Murphy's play. But even here, the actual dramatic circumstances of Donizetti's aria remain irrelevant to the action of *The Gigli Concert*. Edgardo (in the opera) will lament Lucia's death and then kill himself. No such trajectory applies to King's performance, even if he is mortally frightened in its immediate aftermath.

[18] It is impossible in this context not to reference the other one, which is of course Friel's conveyance of Irish through the medium of English in *Translations*.

[19] The proximity of *Attila* to what is happening in the course of *The Gigli Concert* on this (one) occasion is remarkable: the three characters in Verdi's trio (Odabella [soprano], Foresto [tenor] and Ezio [bass]) correspond closely to Mona, King and the Irish Man, at least insofar as King's emotional devastation in the wake of Mona's disclosure that she is dying compares closely to Foresto's outburst against the pleading Odabella in Verdi's music. Murphy, moreover, calls for the Irish Man's entrance in this scene to coincide with the entrance of Ezio into the musical texture, because Ezio's attempts to remonstrate with Odabella and Foresto and his efforts to restore some degree of calm adumbrate the Irish Man's new-found composure as he makes his 'beaming' way into King's office. See *The Gigli Concert* (as n.15): 70-71.

[20] *After Tragedy. Three Irish Plays by Tom Murphy* (London: Methuen, 1986): 71.

[21] Brian Friel, *Performances* (Oldcastle, Co. Meath: Gallery Press, 2003): 30-31.

[22] Friel, *Performances*: 38.

[23] Murphy, *The Gigli Concert* (as n.15): 75.

11 | The Fell of Dark: *The Gigli Concert*

Ben Barnes

Approaching a production of *The Gigli Concert*, as I did in 2001 and again in 2004 at the Abbey Theatre, you become quickly aware that it operates on many levels – most accessibly as a dissection of middle-aged men in crisis but also on the level of myth as a Faustian fable which goes through several iterations and reversals.

It is in the figure of Irish Man that this juxtaposition of the familiar and the mythical is best exemplified and both must be adverted to in any attempt to grapple with the play's multi-layered complexities. This is so for the urgent reasons that it is from the local that the actor must, perforce, construct his performance and it is out of the mythical that the director assembles the architecture of his/her production.

The bleak hinterland from which Irish Man emerges seeking deliverance is the venal world of construction in the Ireland of the 1970s and its murky interface with politics, local and national. By his own admission his fortune is built on 'corruption, brutality, backhanding, fronthanding, backstabbing, lump labour and a bit of technology'[1], and he corrects the initially slow-to-understand, JPW King's designation of him as a builder with the more accurate soubriquet of 'operator'.

Rising above less than promising beginnings this Irishman has built an empire and a fortune which is veritably unassailable, and when, like a conquering hero, he steps from his car with 'beautiful nature' all around him, he can only see 'fine sites for development', fresh citadels to be toppled, he thinks:

> Will I build a thousand more? No, I've made my mind up on that one. There's more to life than working myself to death or

wheeling and dealing with that criminal band of would-be present-day little pigmy Napoleons we've got at the top. (224)

No longer driven (or distracted?) by the need to make more money, and disillusioned by the dishonesty and criminality he has had to rub shoulders with to reach a place of wealth and influence, Irish Man becomes acutely aware, not only of his isolation from those around him, but of a kind of spiritual emptiness. If there is, as he attests, more to life than 'working myself to death' what shape might that fulfilment take and how might he access it?

Here is a man washed up on the beach of middle age without a compass. He cannot begin to know the answers to his longings because he cannot even recognize the shape of the questions. In his alienation he lashes out not only at those who aggravate him but at those by whom he is loved. This sense of embattlement and barely repressed fury is spectacularly fixated on the itinerants who have camped themselves on his property, and explaining to the Englishman, JPW, what a slash hook is, he describes how he takes it up to deal with the intruders:

> The place is a shit house. It's everywhere. Why did they choose me, my territory? [...] So. *Went* out. To kill them. But someone – the wife – called the police, and they stopped me. I would've killed them otherwise. No question about that. Jail – hospital mean nothing to me. Jail – hospital have a certain appeal. (174)

And this process of alienation then turns on those he loves: his wife and young son. In one of the most moving and haunting passages of the play (perhaps of any play) Irish Man describes how his wife is near nervous breakdown and how she has become bewildered by his increasingly erratic and violent behaviour, the latest manifestation of which is directed against his young son:

> And I burned all his toys last night. I rooted them out of every corner. And I'm so proud of him. I see him watching me sometimes. He's almost nine. I watch him sometimes too, secretly, and wonder will I write him a letter. Or take him for a little walk, my arm around his shoulders. Because, though he's nearly nine, and a boy, he would still allow me to put my arm around his shoulders. My son. And explain to him that I don't matter. That it would be better if I disappeared. (185)

His wife makes one last attempt to get through to him, at first tenderly but with increasing frustration. His impotence in the face of her appeal has all the resignation of a fatally wounded animal and the intensity of emotion he finds in the quiet telling to JPW of this nocturnal scene requires enormous skill and delicacy on the part of the actor. The technical key to its successful delivery depends – as Murphy explained to me in rehearsal once – on the repeated use of the conjunction 'and' and its alternate signifier as a musical rest and as a device to bridge and contain the emotion which wells up in the telling:

> My wife come down last night. Nightdress, long hair. I pretended I didn't hear her come in or that she was watching me. And I kept listening to the music. Then she come and stood beside my chair. Smiling. What are you listening to. I use the headphones at night. Elgar, I said. I don't know why I said that because the only thing I listen to is him. *And.* You off I said. To bed. And she said yes, it's ten past one heighho. *And.* You coming up she said. And I said, in a little, I said. *And.* Then she knelt down and put her head on my knees. And then she said talk to me, talk to me, please love talk to me. And I couldn't think of a single thing to say. And then she said I love you so much. And I said I love you too ... but not out loud. *And.* Then she got up. And then she said pull yourself together, what's the matter with you, for God's sake get a grip on yourself, pull yourself together. She was trembling. She'd let go for a moment. And then she said goodnight. When she left I stood up. Out of respect. I knew she would've stopped in the hall. She usually does. Just stands there for a few moments. Before going up. *And.* Then it come out. My roar. Fuck you, fuck you ... fuck you. (*Though delivered quietly and the intense emotion contained, tears have started down the* IRISH MAN's *face during the speech.*) (185-86, italics added for 'And')

Of course, it is not Elgar he is listening to. It is the great Italian tenor, Beniamino Gigli and all that sense of loss and longing which Irish Man feels, the utter absence of beauty in his comfortable but brutalized world, a life as loveless as a 1970s Irish bungalow, is crystallized through those dark nights of the soul spent listening to that record over and over again. It is as if this man, so powerfully present in the commercial transactions of his life, so corporeally solid, has been otherwise invisible to himself and to those around him. He might be Beckett's Hamm in the nadir of his despair:

> **HAMM.** Clov.
> **CLOV.** (*Absorbed*) Mmm.
> **HAMM.** Do you know what it is?
> **CLOV.** (As before) Mmm.
> **HAMM.** I was never there. [...]
> **CLOV.** Lucky for you.
> (*He looks out window*)
> **HAMM.** Absent always. It all happened without me. I don't know what's happened.[2]

In this vortex of depression and longing Murphy's Irish Man arrives at the rooms of the similarly afflicted JPW King with the impossible quest to inhabit the world of the tenor and to sing like Gigli. It is here the Faustian pact is made and the mythical architecture of the drama becomes manifest: 'I'd give my life for one short sweet hour to be able to sing like that.' (210)

Not that in JPW King we have what could be described as a cool Mephistophelian genius; he is no genie waiting to grant three wishes for the price of a soul. He would find no obvious place in the pages of Goethe or the score of Gounod. By a different route he has washed up at the same place of despair as the man he is hired to help. In words directly echoed by Irish Man later in the play, JPW opens with the line, 'Christ, how am I going to get through today?' (166), a sentiment distinctly at odds with the self-help business he advertises with the mantra 'anything is possible'. (168)

If Irish Man has alienated himself from his society, JPW King is a *de facto* alien, hailing from the neighbouring island. In an era when the country was racked by the dark deeds perpetrated in the name of Irish republicanism, King represents that most ambivalent of figures, the upper middle-class, educated Englishman in Ireland. He scans as a vestigial remnant of a type so gloriously alive in the pages of Molly Keane or Elizabeth Bowen or J.G. Farrell, and in that end-of-the-line inability to make something of himself he recalls the endearing, but hopeless, Casimir from the *Aristocrats* of Brian Friel: an association made all the more vivid for me by virtue of the fact that the same actor, Mark Lambert, played both Casimir and JPW King in productions which I directed at The Gate and the Abbey respectively.

Echoing a prejudice as old as the Song of Dermot and the Earl, Irish Man notes 'you're a stranger here, Mr King?', to which JPW (understanding) replies: 'Well I have been here for nearly – five years? I mean to say.' And Irish Man persists: 'But you're a stranger, you're English?' (170) This diffident Englishman, JPW King, presides in the eyrie of his adopted city as the lone representative of a defunct consciousness expanding the 'organization' whose leader, one 'Steve', has long since fled the country under some unnamed cloud of scandal which is never specified but clearly implied when JPW recoils from the depth of Irish Man's despair:

> Ah, Mr ... I'm out of my depth. This organization, Steve, our founder, leader, came over to set up this office. Though I have always wanted to achieve something, I couldn't do even that much on my own. They sent me over here. But even they have

forgotten me. And I have forgotten them. I think it is likely they shipped Steve back to the States. I do not even know if we are still in existence. (186)

JPW on the promise of a generous fee, and out of the depths of his own loneliness and despair, gamely takes Irish Man on and with the assistance of a set of utterly confusing charts, and a blitz of incomprehensible gobbledegook jargon delivered with increasingly manic energy, he explains the processes of 'de-stratification' which must be undergone to arrive at a state of 'nihil' out of which a new persona can be created. In parallel with this he researches the chemical cocktail that might enable Irish Man to achieve his mad goal: to sing like Gigli. Either that or it will kill him.

It is not a promising scenario, but Irish Man keeps returning, partly because he recognizes in JPW a fellow traveller, unlikely as that may on first sight seem, and partly because he has nowhere else to go. Slapping the money down on the table he warns JPW:

IRISH MAN. Noon tomorrow! And you had better be here! Do you understand that? [...]
JPW. You bring the pistols! I shall bring the booze! (189)

Instead of pistols Irish Man comes armed with his record and his record player and the soaring incandescence of Gigli's rendition of 'Dai campi, dai prati', tellingly from the opera *Mefistofele*, succeeds, in that one playing, in sweeping all JPW's *faux* psycho-babble to one side and the two men, all pretence gone, huddle around the record player as if around a two-bar electric fire, lay waste the bottle of vodka which JPW has supplied and open their hearts to one another.

It is in this sequence we learn that JPW has his own unattained and unattainable dream, his love and pursuit of his 'Helen' over four bleak and fruitless years. Here, as with the Faustian leitmotif, the classical parallels echoing Homer and Virgil abound – 'a present of a locket was not going to be of much use in this case' (206), but what becomes quickly apparent is that JPW's longing is not for a Helen of Troy but for that heady combination of sexual fulfilment and domestic security that has always eluded him: 'Yes. Beauty: a shy, simple, comely, virtuous, sheltered, married maiden.' (205)

But – the history continues – it was not to be: 'This simple married maiden was proving to be a combination of flirtatious se-ductive behaviour which, having aroused me, instantly turned to resistance and rejection.' (206) His pursuit, however, was nothing if not ardent and persistent, though it ended in the bathos and comedy of a final encounter in a car park:

> A hurried meeting: she had even forgotten to take off her apron which I glimpsed beneath her overcoat and which tugged strangely at my heart-strings. She said you are a remarkable man and goodbye. Do not regret it, she said, but you must, you *must* forget me. (207)

Irish Man counters with his fictionalized account of his pursuit of a telephonist in the guise of his hero Gigli. His prose aria, 'Her name was Ida', perfectly scored to the music of Toselli's Serenade, is a masterpiece of conflation and the comic highlight of the play. The fact that JPW's pursuit of his Helen is every bit as impossible as Irish Man's determination to sing like Gigli is not lost on us, even though JPW fails to appreciate the irony when he retorts, 'my story is about a real live living person, your story is bullshit.' (210)

Whatever about that, we have arrived by act's end (we decided on an interval after the third movement[3] in our 2001 production) with the frank acknowledgement of longing and unfulfilment from two middle-aged men with the wreckage of the years behind them and the desolation of their mortality staring them in the face. And the Faustian pact driving them on to some half-remembered or half-glimpsed notion of perfection or fulfilment. In a religious sense it might be given as 'grace'. Grace, that is, as the great American novelist Joyce Carol Oates describes it: 'a moment of insight. A moment of beauty, and purity [...] a sudden swift aerial view. We're lifted up out of ourselves, like out of clay pots and we see. In an instant, we know.'[4] What does Yeats say ? 'Before I am old/ I shall have written him one/ Poem maybe as cold/ And passionate as the dawn.'[5] And here from Irish Man: 'One short sweet hour with her, you said, and you'd give your life: I'd give my life for one short sweet hour to be able to sing like that.' (210)

This new-found camaraderie and sense of common purpose sets the play up for the emotional climax of the fourth movement. Wild with anguish Irish Man bursts through the door next morning with the declaration, 'She's gone, gone, gone, left me!' (212) But JPW is in no mood for these 'bull in a china shop' tactics:

> Now it is Sunday morning and you arrived – what? – three hours early and, great lapsed church-going people that we are, half of this city is still sensibly in its bed. But you have got me up and double-time or not, I want something more for my endeavours, so ... Yes! Sex, if you please. (214)

There follows Irish Man's comical account of his first sexual encounter but it is in the reporting of this back to his brother Danny that we discover the brutality of his upbringing and the mindless thuggery of his elder brother, Mick, who in loco parentis decided that Danny was the one to 'be put through school, educated'. But, he tells us, 'I don't think school suited our Danny' (215), and the domestic tension resulting from this failure led to many a savage beating of the hapless but hardened Danny. To Irish Man, who was younger, Danny offered the advice that 'when I got big, if I was ever in a fight with Mick, to watch out, that Mick would use a poker. I suppose he knew he'd never be able for Mick, unless he shot him, or knifed him.' And on foot of this revelation, 'He used to tell me never trust anyone, and that everything is based on hate.' (216)

So, it happened on this particular occasion, following a particularly savage beating, that Danny was indoors crying and Irish Man was aimlessly picking buttercups off a patch of grass outside in the garden. He goes indoors:

> I still had this little bunch of flowers. In my hand. I don't think I gave a fuck about the flowers. A few – daisies, and the – yellow ones. But Danny – he was eighteen! – and he was inside, crying. And it was the only thing I could think of (*He is only just managing to hold back his tears*) And. And. I took the fuckin' flowers to our Danny ... wherever he is now ... and I said, which do you think is nicest? The most beautiful, yeh know? And Danny said 'Nicest?', like a knife. 'Nicest? Are you stupid? What use is nicest?' Of what use is beauty, Mr King? (216-17)

I have given an account of rehearsing this scene with the actors and Tom Murphy in my book *Plays and Controversies*[6] but even now, battle-scarred old dog for the hard road that I am, I cannot read that passage with any kind of equanimity. The breakdown in Irish Man which follows these revelations is shocking in its ferocity and after he falls asleep with exhaustion, JPW watches over him tenderly throughout the day as the music segues from the *Agnus Dei* to '*Cangia, cangia tu voglie*', by Fasola.

≈   ≈

We feel by now in our journey through the play that a trust has built up between the two men and that Irish Man, in going back to the source of his pain and suffering, will finally free himself to reach out again to his wife and child and begin to see and feel the simple beauty in the world as exemplified so agonizingly for him, in his destitution, by the pure sound of the tenor's voice. And then something extraordinary happens.

Irish Man comes to his desensitized senses again and as his depression lifts he disowns his earlier revelations and rather pathetically (not to mention hilariously) makes a case for having had a happy childhood, blaming JPW for tricking him into saying things which he now regrets. When JPW expresses his scepticism at this return to the macho tactics of the earlier scenes, Irish Man rounds on him claiming that JPW's ministrations have had little to do with his 'recovery', that these bouts of depression are recurrent and on previous occasions he has cured himself:

> Last time I just went away and hid in a corner – you learn a lot from animals – like a dog in a corner, you couldn't prise me out of it, and stayed there licking my wounds till I cured myself. [...] The time before, boy, I went into your territory, debauchery, Mr King: got a dose of the clap in the course of the treatment, but I cured myself. (224-25)

Not content with reasserting his own image as a solid family man, an Irish Man, a man of the community he, with a brutality worthy of his hated brother Mick, must demolish the fragile ego of his erstwhile friend and saviour – the Stranger, the one who can't keep a woman, the man without a house, the man without substance and into the bargain a 'Charlatan, quack, parasite! And, yeh know, there's a stink in this pig-sty: you'd be better off cleaning it up.' (225)

So, it is left to JPW to complete the journey alone and to slay all his own dragons single-handedly. Once the illusion of his Helen begins to evaporate he latterly comes to appreciate that his occasional lover Mona, whom he has dismissed as 'someone I met in a supermarket' (208) is, in fact, the love of his life only to discover that she is suffering from an illness from which there is no recovery. In not flinching from that, or from his other shortcomings, it is JPW who finally achieves that transformative moment. It is he, and not Irish Man, who finally – in a Catholic sense – is transfigured by his suffering and freed to sing like Gigli.

Returning the play to its governing mythology, however, it is Mephistopheles, in the absence of Faust, who becomes Faust himself and sees his pact through to its conclusion. Looking for help in his quest to sing JPW looks first to the heavens, to God, and then has a change of mind: 'Rather not. You cut your losses on this little utopia of greed and carnage some time ago, my not so very clever

friend. (*To the floor.*) You, down there! Assist please. In exchange – '
(239)

And after that catharsis he looks forward to a 'rebirth of ideals,
return of self-esteem, future known' (239), and this resolution in
turn allows him to finally leave that garret and engage again with the
world, in the sober words of the poet Thomas Kinsella, 'not young
and not renewable, but man'.[7]

But before he goes he sets the record on repeat and opens the
windows to the rooftops and the sky and delares his faith anew: 'Do
not mind the pig-sty, Benimillo ... mankind still has a delicate ear ...
That's it ... that's it ... sing on forever ... that's it.' (240)

The ambition of *The Gigli Concert* which takes inspiration from,
and measures itself against, the operatic and sacred music of the
nineteenth century, its baroque structure and its mythical echoes
and sub-structure, locates it in a great European tradition stretching
back to Goethe and beyond. At the same time its 'domestic' locus as
a thrilling drama of middle-aged men in crisis makes a compelling
case for its inclusion as one of the corner-stone Irish dramas of the
twentieth century. Those pillars also include *The Playboy of the
Western World*, *The Plough and the Stars* and *Translations,* but for
the ambition of its structure, the beauty of its writing and the sheer
breadth of its compassion, *The Gigli Concert* is, arguably, the
greatest of these.

---

[1] Tom Murphy, *The Gigli Concert*, in *Plays: Three* (London: Methuen,
    1994): 173. Subsequent quotations are from this edition, to which
    page numbers in parentheses will refer.
[2] Samuel Beckett, *Endgame*, in *The Complete Dramatic Works*
    (London: Faber, 1990): 128.
[3] I say 'movement' rather than scene in order to reinforce the idea of
    The Gigli Concert as a play which approximates to music and,
    indeed, annexes it throughout. In the text (212), Murphy suggests an
    'intermission, if required' at the end of scene 4. With his approval I
    decided to have the interval after scene 3 because it was a natural
    break in the action about half-way through the evening. I felt that an
    interval after scene 4 would make the second half seem too thin and
    keep us close to an hour and forty minutes in act 1, which is simply
    too long for modern audiences.
[4] Joyce Carol Oates, *Middle Age: A Romance* (London: Fourth Estate
    Fiction, 2002): 476-77.
[5] W.B. Yeats, 'The Fisherman', in *Collected Poems* (London: Macmillan,
    1950): 167.

6 Ben Barnes, *Plays and Controversies: Abbey Theatre Diaries 2000-2005* (Dublin: Carysfort Press, 2008): 153-55.

7 Thomas Kinsella, 'Mirror in February', in *Selected Poems 1956-1968* (Dublin: Dolmen Press, 1973): 61.

12 | New Mind over Old Matter: The Evolution of *Too Late for Logic*

José Lanters

Tom Murphy's approach to playwriting is instinctive rather than intellectual. Early on in his career, he told an interviewer that he usually begins the first draft of a play 'in a state of high panic,' with no more than a first sentence, a vague idea, and no particular plan. 'Then I re-write for months, redrafting the play anything up to ten times, until I know the whys and wherefores of every comma.'[1] Plays often have their genesis in 'something autobiographical, usually a mood or an emotion,'[2] and writing takes the form of 'discovering the process of doing ... which isn't a method at all.'[3] To Fintan O'Toole, Murphy described this process as a form of madness: 'You start with a certain degree of good health and you move into lunacy and you arrive back at good health. [...] The shadow moves and you start to pursue it. A lot of that is nightmare but eventually you come out of it and you feel you have done something.'[4] That 'something,' however, is only a beginning. 'I can't really finalise the script until I see it in rehearsal,' Murphy confessed in another interview, and even then, 'I'm writing my own final version of the play, not for this production, but for the next one.'[5] Each revised version or production reflects the play's, and the playwright's, 'personality' at that particular moment in time.[6]

To illustrate Murphy's 'non-method' of continuous, open-ended (re-)creation, there are few better examples than the evolution of the text of *Too Late for Logic*, first performed at the Abbey Theatre in October 1989 under the direction of Patrick Mason. The play was written in between the staging, in 1985, of one of Murphy's most successful plays, *Bailegangaire*, and his venture into new territory, the writing of a novel, which appeared in 1994 under the title *The Seduction of Morality*, and which was the basis for his 1997 play *The Wake*. The protagonist of *Too Late for Logic* is a philosopher named Christopher. In the opening moments of the play, we see him holding a gun with which he has, possibly, shot himself in the head. He, or his ghost, then introduces the main action of the play, which shows the events of the previous three days leading up to the present, in order to explain how this crucial life-or-death moment was arrived at. At the beginning of the retrospective action, Christopher is composing a lecture on Schopenhauer's *The World as Will and Idea*. It will be televised and should increase his chance of being appointed to the coveted chair of philosophy at Trinity College, whose current holder, Dr Wuzzler, has just been run over by a bus. Six months earlier, Christopher had left his wife and teenage children to devote himself entirely to his scholarship. Now, however, his work is interrupted by the arrival of his son, Jack, and his daughter, Petra, with whom he has not been on good terms; they have been sent by their mother, Patricia, to enlist Christopher's help in locating his brother Michael. The latter's wife, Cornelia, who is also Patricia's sister, died in hospital the day before; it is now Wednesday, the funeral is planned for Friday, but no final arrangements can be made because Michael is suicidal and has disappeared. Reluctantly, Christopher joins his children in the search for his elusive brother.

The 'autobiographical mood' out of which *Too Late for Logic* emerged was Murphy's general sense of guilt at having neglected his immediate family for the sake of his art. While the conflict between necessary selfishness and the need for love and family forms a recurring theme in Murphy's work, it has a particularly poignant presence in his plays of the 1980s, starting with *The Gigli Concert*, because they were written during the period when his children were growing up and conscious of the effect of the writing process on their father. Murphy recalls:

> There was ... all the Daddy the Bear stuff – children not knowing what sort of mood I'd be coming out of the room in, and me carrying the play that was trying to emerge with me to the dinner table. You've got a child sitting down and you've got a silent father.[7]

Too Late for Logic can, in many respects, be seen as a dramatization of the private emotions that followed the writing of

Bailegangaire, emotions that were, eventually, exorcized to some degree in *The Seduction of Morality* and *The Wake*.

In a 1986 interview, Murphy expressed the opinion that 'A family is a bloodknot – it's also a trap.'[8] For Schopenhauer, the subject of Christopher's lecture in *Too Late for Logic*, our greatest anxieties and fears are caused by other people, particularly those close to us; peace of mind can come only when we sever those ties, 'thus extracting from our flesh this thorn that is always causing us pain. Yet this is very difficult, for we are concerned with a natural and innate perversity.'[9] Christopher borrows Schopenhauer's metaphor to refuse involvement with his relatives: 'So, no Michaels thank you, or those complicated thorns of kindred in my side.'[10] But towards the end of the play he changes this to '*Beloved* thorns? Yes. Beloved' (*TLFL*1, p. 41). As an offer of reconciliation, Christopher presents his daughter with a rose. According to Schopenhauer, there is 'No rose without a thorn. But many a thorn without a rose.'[11] *Too Late for Logic* suggests that the moderate pain of a beloved thorn, a thorn with a rose, may be the best one can hope for.

About the character of Vera in *The Seduction of Morality* and *The Wake*, Murphy says: 'Vera ... is in pursuit of her family ... I could be Vera.'[12] He finds that writing about a female character can help him conceal the privacies of his life: 'I write autobiographically and prefer the mask, even though it is more difficult.'[13] In *Too Late for Logic*, the mask often appears to be off. Murphy's struggle to distance himself from the material, to wrestle feeling into form, shows in the play's numerous working titles and endless revisions. In 2000, Murphy described in detail to Mike Murphy the physical process of how he writes a play – always in longhand:

> I love rewriting and with every draft I try to create the most immaculate script with very good calligraphy. I would have three notebooks and as one begins to get dirty I'd transfer to the next one ... There are little things that keep me going. I use an ordinary biro for early drafts but then as I feel I'm nearing home, which might mean three or four more drafts, I go out and buy a certain type of biro that costs about twenty-five bob or something like that.[14]

The manuscripts of *Too Late for Logic* held in Trinity College, Dublin,[15] comprise seven such notebooks or notepads containing various handwritten outlines and drafts, dated between February 1987 and April 1989; a typescript with handwritten corrections dated April-May 1989; a draft in longhand dated July 1989; a draft dated 1 August 1989; and two more versions dated, respectively,

August-September 1990 and September 1990 (marked 'Final'). The text of the play was published by Methuen in 1990. Further revisions were made for the 2001 production at the King's Theatre, Edinburgh, again directed by Patrick Mason, and for the 2006 inclusion of the text in *Plays: 5*.

The first notebook of the manuscripts in TCD relating to *Too Late for Logic* (MS 11115, box 21, file 271), covering the period from February 1987 to January 1988, reflects what Murphy has called 'the period of incubation which really is the triggering action, the false starts, the honeymoon period, where the writer, self-delighted, indulges in all sorts of nonsense and goes to extremes.'[16] It begins with two separate, brief outlines of a possible plot: both involve two men, brothers or friends, one whose marriage is in trouble, the other whose beloved has died and who is going to kill himself.

In the first outline, entitled 'Trying to Give up Drink,' Tom loves Jean. He is trying to stop drinking but loving Jean 'requires' drink. Jimmy, Tom's brother-in-law, is undergoing ridiculous grief: 'Grief is his profession.' He is declaring that he is going to kill himself: his beloved has died, and her house ('the shrine'), in which he lived with her, now belongs to her son, a common-sensical businessman who is giving him six days to vacate the place. 'So, the deadline for Jimmy's suicide is 6 days from now.' Tom enlists the help of Bernard, his son, an 'observer' with his own set of problems with alcohol and girls, to protect Jimmy. Jean, meanwhile, is getting depressed: 'what am I doing among these people?' Some of the nonsensical 'indulgences' associated with the 'honeymoon period' of a play's gestation are evident in this draft, as Murphy makes Tom '210 years older than Jean,' while 'Jimmy's late beloved was 200 years older than him.'

In the second outline, entitled 'Revenge,' on the next page of the notebook, the names have changed. Michael, depressed and full of self-pity, 'has got himself in a rut.' His friend Christopher, while ostensibly very successful, is privately going crazy under the burden of self-loathing: '(Why?),' Murphy's note to himself asks. The two men are a variation on the recurring motif in Murphy's oeuvre of two complementary characters, and he suggests in this sketch that 'Michael is possibly Christopher's "mask-let-down?"' Christopher is pretending to help Michael while pushing him towards destruction, in the form of drink or sex: '(Michael recklessly manifesting an incestuous interest in a young niece, perhaps),' or possibly 'fuelling a thought about murdering someone.' Murphy notes here that 'The appalling deed – if extreme enough – was to the Greeks something to be celebrated just as much as the great heroic deed.' It is clear that, at this stage, Murphy is casting around for his characters' motivation. 'Perhaps Christopher is a university lecturer – a Professor of Greek or Philosophy who is going crazy. Philosophy driving him crazy? The heroics of the Greeks – in contrast with his domestic and secure life – is driving him crazy.' The question of whom Michael might want to murder – 'And of what importance the target' – is followed in the notebook by a draft scene in which Michael tells Christopher about being bullied in school for three months.

A third outline in the same notebook, dated 16 February 1987, is preceded by a set of notes taken by Murphy from his reading of H.D.F. Kitto's *Greek Tragedy*. The subject that preoccupies Christopher here is forgery, a topic taken straight from the opening pages of the third edition of Kitto's book.[17] Murphy places a slight variation of Kitto's words in Christopher's mouth: 'A forger has every reason to be careful over detail: a forger may well know what he's talking about.'[18] In this outline for the play, Murphy makes his protagonist about forty years old, married to a professional woman, possibly also a lecturer, with a young daughter and an infant son. Michael in this version has just lost his beloved to someone else: 'His ex-mistress and her new young lover are going to find him dead in the apartment when they return in six days time.' Here, Murphy contemplates making the two men brothers, and English. The outline of this plot is followed in the notebook by the draft of a scene in which Christopher and Jack arrive at a nightclub owned by a woman named Veronica – later to become Monica in *Too Late for Logic*.

At this point in the manuscript, there appear two versions of a kind of 'meditation,' which captures the crux of the problem Murphy is wrestling with in all these early try-outs: his characters are suffering under a burden of grief and guilt, but its cause seems to be greater than the death or loss that ostensibly triggered it, and lies rather in some source buried deep within the self.

> The unconscious wanders, troubled, vigilant, wary, vulnerable,
> Searching for the answer to some grave and crucially significant thing. . . .
> The problem does not have a name;
> No more than innocence once lost can ever be discovered, the cause of all this sorrowing grief and guilt can never be discovered.

The meditation also appears to signal some kind of breakthrough for Murphy in the writing process, because it is followed by a draft of the opening scene, where Christopher is giving a lecture in which he invokes a broad range of writers and philosophers, before turning, at length, to the topic of suicide: 'The insidious appeal of suicide to the Romantic mind is a startling phenomenon.' A synopsis of the plot of what will become *Too Late for Logic* follows this scene, dated 22 January 1988, but called, at this point, 'Trying to Give up Smoking.' In a further draft of the scene composed four days later Murphy suggests that Christopher has arrived 'at a nightmare time of life,' and has him turn, in his lecture, to Schopenhauer. With the basics of his new play now in place, Murphy turns to a new notepad to start composing the first draft of the script.

In that draft (MS 11115, box 21, file 272), written in the first two months of 1988, Christopher's focus is on the post-revolutionary age of depression, and Schopenhauer was 'the man who was there, to reap – not with pessimism, I think cynicism – the harvest of it all.' Here, suicide is the topic Christopher has decided to set for an essay contest: 'The subject shall be, Self-destruction, Then and Now, its causes, its curses.' Murphy continues this train of thought in a new draft entitled 'Schopenhauer, Isn't It?' contained in a notebook dated 16 March 1988 (MS 11115, box 21, file 273), in which Christopher and Michael have become twin brothers, before moving on to a new notebook (MS 11115, box 21, file 274), undated, bound and with a stiff red cover, of superior quality to the previously employed notepads, in which he writes a draft version of the play entitled *Too Late for Logic*.

For Murphy, getting to the first draft of a play is, by his own admission, 'a huge nightmare,' a process of trial and error, starts and stops, 'and then the pressure of decision, the frustration of indecision, and onto the infinite number of endings.'[19] All evidence suggests that Murphy struggled most with the ending of *Too Late for Logic* and, to a lesser degree, with the opening scene. It was in these scenes that the play as it was first produced at the Abbey differed most significantly from the 1990 printed text, which was again considerably altered for the 2006 republication. The revisions Murphy made to these scenes in the course of a period of over a decade and a half veer back and forth between more positive and more pessimistic interpretations of Christopher's final deed.

It is instructive to compare three different incarnations of the opening and closing scenes of the play, beginning with a draft from an untitled notepad probably dating from early 1988 (MS 11115, box 21, file 275) of what would eventually become the play's closing scene. In this version, the notion of suicide is introduced almost accidentally as Christopher toys with the gun:

> Tight pool of light. He sits there alone. Takes out the gun, puts it to his head, pulls trigger: just a click. He knows nothing about guns. He sets to examining it, adjusting it, pulling the trigger, sometimes pointing it at himself; cocks it, fortunately it's pointed away from him this time, pulls the trigger: Bang.
>
> His first reaction is fright; his second, concern that someone will have heard; third gets to hell out of it, getting rid of gun (perhaps like someone throwing it or dropping it into a river).

Murphy's notes in the manuscript indicate that this scene is to be followed by the play's actual conclusion, in which Christopher delivers his lecture on Schopenhauer.

It appears from the manuscripts that Murphy did not work on the script for almost a year, for the next draft is dated 1 February 1989 (MS 11115, box 21, file 276). In it, the action of the final scene is more deliberate:

> A shot from a gun. ... Christopher is featured, a gun in his hand. ... He points the gun away from him and tries it: there is just a click. He dumps the gun on the floor; it lands noiselessly. ... He ... picks up the gun, adjusts it to his satisfaction so that it will work. He is trying the gun against his head in the manner of someone wondering if he has just shot himself.

In a subsequent version, in a new notepad entitled 'Too Late for Logic' and not dated, but written between February and April 1989 (MS 11115, box 21, file 278), Murphy clarifies in a note that 'Christopher's starting place, the one that he constantly returns to, is called Limbo for simplicity's sake: It can be interpreted geographically or as a mental state or as both by Director and Actor.' That starting position is elaborated on in the opening scene that follows the note, which ties the beginning of the play more firmly to its conclusion. Shadowy figures are seen on stage (Petra, Jack, Patricia, others); a gunshot sounds, Christopher has a revolver, the figures look confused or upset. They arrange themselves as around a graveside – is this Cornelia's funeral, 'Or?' Christopher speaks:

> Wait a minute, what's this, what has happened here, hold on! ... I mean, I never thought I was a great guy, I even sometimes thought that I was in the wrong, but – Yes, but: This is pretty desperate stuff ... Hold on! A replay. Back-track, step by step? And if findings should decree this drastic course of action – the

taking of the always open door – then I'll take it. (Do we have)
A deal?

The foregoing scene is also incorporated in a new draft of the
play written in a spiral-bound notebook dated April-May 1989 (MS
11115, box 21, file 281), now called 'Impossible Man or Cordelia's
[*sic*] Wake.' In this version, Murphy creates a more inconclusive
ending by suggesting that the play's circular action will allow for
infinite repetition of the events. Christopher concludes by weighing
his suicidal despair against his love for his family:

> Yes, but, this is pretty desperate stuff. My love for them is –
> boundless; my pride – great, pleasure unspeakable when I look
> at them, so – Hmm? And though I cannot understand how they
> can possibly love me, I know they do. So? ... I know we made a
> deal, and the findings seem to decree that the taking of the-
> always-open door would be understandable – but unnecessary.
> Do you see the distinction? ... Play back. This time I think I'll
> come up trumps. Okay? A deal? (He gets rid of his coat and
> gun). And we'll keep it on repeat until we get it right . ...

Further revisions indicate that Murphy was still not happy with the
play's ending. The spiral notebook containing the above draft of the
final scene also includes the draft of a confidential letter to Martin
Fahy, the general manager of the Abbey Theatre, in which Murphy
refers to 'Impossible Man or Cordelia's Wake' as the 'penultimate
draft' of the play and asks for a rehearsed reading of the script
before embarking on the final draft. Murphy had used this method
with *Bailegangaire*, and hoped that in this case it would help him
work out the play's conclusion: 'I would like more of an up-beat
ending,' he told Fahy, 'but the animal will not yield further to me
right now. Perhaps after a reading.'

Three more drafts follow the version of the play quoted above – a
handwritten draft of 'Impossible Man' in February-April 1989 (MS
11115, box 21, file 282), a typescript of 'Impossible Man or Cordelia's
Wake,' with corrections in pen, dated April-May 1989 (MS 11115,
box 21, file 283), and a draft in longhand of 'Too Late for Logic'
dated July 1989 (MS 11115, box 21, file 285) – before Murphy creates
a more positive ending on 1 August 1989 (MS 11115, box 22, file
286):

> **CHRISTOPHER.** I *know* I made a deal ... And though I
> cannot understand how they can possibly love me, now I know
> they do.
>
> *The figures are converging on him. He raises the gun slowly to
> his head. He is smiling – a little foolishly. Then he points the
> gun in the air – grins broadly – pulls the trigger: Nothing*

happens.
The figures are around him: they are all moving off together.

Subsequent adjustments to the scene indicate that Murphy felt he still had not struck the right note with this rather too up-beat conclusion.

The above is the final draft of the play in the TCD archive with a composition date before the play's production in October 1989. However, from reviewers' responses to that production (Jennifer Johnston and Richard Kearney among them) it is clear that this was not the ending that appeared on stage. In fact, the ending presented there suggested unambiguously that Christopher had killed himself. Monica Frawley, who designed the set for the Abbey production, makes no bones about the fact that Christopher is dead:

> There are enormous pointers in what Tom has written: a man has shot himself and he is in 'Limbo' ... The action in this play might be taking place in one day, or in the three minutes he takes to die, a strange juxtaposition. The events are real but they exist through recall. Because the man is dead, the situation is unreal.[20]

The reference to 'Limbo' recalls the note in the version of the script Murphy wrote in the first months of 1989. Fintan O'Toole also confirms that 'we know that Christopher is dead – and what remains is a sense, not of possibility but of irony, the irony that Christopher concludes that suicide is unnecessary but has done it anyway.'[21]

Before the publication of the text of *Too Late for Logic* Murphy revisited the text again, in August-September 1990 (MS 11115, box 22, file 289), when he wrote the opening scene as it appears in print in the 1990 edition, and changed the ending by having Christopher reconsider his suicide and by adding the parable of the porcupines from Schopenhauer's *Paralipomena* to his lecture. In September 1990 he marked a further revision as 'Final' (MS 11115, box 22, file 290). This did not, however, signal the end of his revisions to the play, for it was substantially altered for the Edinburgh production in 2001, and again for the inclusion of the text in the 2006 collection *Plays: 5*.[22]

There are numerous differences between the printed texts of 1990 and 2006, although most of the changes are minor and aesthetic rather than substantial. Their main function is to remedy the slightly awkward quality of the earlier text that has to do with the order in which the dialogue is rendered on the page, and the nature and placing of the stage directions. Murphy himself is aware that his scripts can be difficult to read. As he became immersed in the form and discipline of theatre, he found himself becoming '"extraordinarily self-conscious" about writing prose, even of the simple kind needed for stage directions ... "Like mental dyslexia if there can be such a thing. I couldn't put the thing in its proper order to make a simple sentence. I would end up saying 'exits'."'[23] The 2006 revisions expand some of the cryptic shorthand in the earlier stage directions, and present the information in a more relaxed prose. In general, the text is arranged more logically on the page, and the dialogue sounds more naturalistic.

The most important revisions once more occur in the opening and closing scenes of the play. Murphy has decided at this point that Christopher does not kill himself with the gun, but instead 'rejoined the persecuted minority of smokers, in slow death' (*TLFL2*: 54). The gun and the cigarette are therefore important props throughout the course of the play. The 2006 version uses these indicators of the shift in Christopher's mindset in a more logical fashion than does the 1990 text, which presents the progression from suicidal thoughts to smoking in an unnecessarily complicated manner. At the beginning of the 1990 text, Christopher is seen '*in overcoat, smoking; a gun in the other hand. A man contemplating an action, timing it against the cigarette.*' Shadowy figures move around him, sometimes obscuring him; a report from a gun is heard, after which Christopher emerges, '*smiling, bemused, denying that he has done anything*' (*TLFL1*: 1). The situation is clearly meant to be ambiguous: 'What? What has happened here? Not at all ... Wait a minute, hold on, this is pretty desperate stuff. ... Nothing is what's happened here. Hold on ...! Okay, let's see' (*TLFL1*: 1). At the con-clusion of this version of the play, the stage direction indicates that '*We are back in the situation which prevailed at the top of the play*' (*TLFL1*: 53). Not everything, however, is the same in the end as it was in the opening scene: Christopher has no gun, and the cigarette he was smoking at the beginning is now unlit. The audience is meant to ask certain questions at this point, indicated by a note in the text: '*But what about the gun-shot, where is the gun, the cigarette should be lit. He'll explain that*' (*TLFL1*: 53). These are relatively minor details for audience members to be asked to remember, especially since there is little in the way of dialogue to clear up any confusion:

> ... *the figures move again, he is among them, pointing a gun to his head* –

It probably doesn't work anyway –
Throws the gun away; it fires on impact with the floor: he hardly
reacts, if at all: he is lighting the cigarette.

Instead, after long, penitential abstinence, he rejoined the
persecuted minority of smokers, in slow death. (TLFL1: 53-54)

In the 2006 printed text, Murphy has rearranged the order of the
above events and added more explanatory dialogue, to clarify the
intention behind the scenes and disambiguate the action depicted
on stage. The opening scene of this version shows Christopher
'isolated,' looking '*bedraggled in his overcoat, an unlit cigarette in
one hand and, now from his pocket, a gun in the other hand: a man
with a problem*' (*TLFL2*: 5). A gunshot is heard and Christopher
emerges from among the shadowy figures, minus cigarette and gun,
'*smiling, denying that he has done anything.*' The revised monologue that follows specifically draws attention to the cigarette, in
addition to clarifying the transition to the retrospective action:

CHRISTOPHER. Wait a minute – Hold on! ... I mean, this is
pretty desperate stuff. Oho! ... I am very well thank you. Hold on –
hold on! – We can work this one out! All I was doing was – what
was I doing? – was trying to write something – a speech for God's
sake, that's all! While trying to give up – ('*smoking': he holds up
his cigarette hand*). That's all. I'm very well thank you. I'll prove it!
Let's go back a few days, backtrack a little, and I bet you I will. OK?
OK. O-righty!

*He removes his overcoat to become his former self of a few days
ago.* (*TLFL2*: 5)

In the final scene of the 1990 text of the play, Petra leaves with
the rose she has received from her father before the action returns to
'*the situation which prevailed at the top of the play.*' Figures move
about, a gunshot is heard, and there is confusion ('*where is the gun,
the cigarette should be lit*'). Christopher emerges '*pointing a gun to
his head*' before discarding the weapon, which fires on impact with
the floor, and lighting a cigarette. He then launches into the anecdote about the porcupines, which ends the play (*TLFL1*: 53-54). The
action of this final scene is presented more logically as well as more
economically in the 2006 version. To demonstrate the diffe-rence
the final page of the later text is here quoted in full:

Lights changing. CHRISTOPHER, *alone, isolated, feels his
pockets. He finds the gun and the cigarette. He has a choice to
make. But he has no light.*

CHRISTOPHER. (*whispers*) Help ... Help.
PETRA. *returns, ostensibly to collect her hat.* (*He holds the gun behind his back.*)
PETRA. My bloodywell hat. Oh, I thought everyone had gone. (*Then, the flower:*) Is this for me? (*He nods.*) An olive branch?
CHRISTOPHER. No, it's a rose.
She takes the rose, smiles to herself, dumps a box of matches (JACK's) on the table and leaves, putting on her hat.
Nothing is what's happened here.
He lights the cigarette and draws deeply on it.

Instead, after long and penitential abstinence, he rejoined the persecuted minority of smokers in slow death. Draft two. President, fellow acolytes of IASA, ladies and –

The phone is ringing. He lifts it and replaces it on the cradle.

But, here, before giving my paper, it might be appropriate to take a preamble from the Paralipomena. A group of porcupines – hedgehogs – on a winter's day crowded close together to save themselves from the cold by their mutual warmth. Soon, however, they felt each other's spines and this drove them apart again. Whenever their need brought them back together, this discomfort intervened until, thrown this way and that between the cold and the spines, they found a moderate distance from one another at which they could survive best.

The figures have returned, music comes up, the figures are circling him. He looks at the gun.

It probably didn't work anyway.

As the figures close on him, he appears to be tossing the gun away and there is a bang. (*TLFL2:* 74)

The reordering of the text in this latest version has a number of advantages. The porcupine speech is tied more directly to Christopher's reconciliation scene with Petra; the lighting of the cigarette and the rejection of the gun show Christopher making a clear decision against killing himself; and the play literally ends with a bang rather than with the comparative whimper of Schopenhauer's parable.

The above revisions to the text of *Too Late for Logic* do much to streamline and clarify aspects of the play's language and action that were confusing in the earlier versions. There remain, however, two scenes in particular that evoked expressions of puzzlement, confusion, and even hostility from commentators on both the 1989 and 2001 productions of the play. The first is Christopher's confrontation with Walter, the old school bully, and Maud, his wife. Christopher threatens Wally with the gun to make him apologize for his deeds of the past, after which he breaks down in tears; meanwhile, Maud narrates the tragic love story of Rusalka and her handsome prince, while listening to Dvorak's opera on the record player. The second is the scene in which Christopher gives his televised lecture on Schopenhauer, which immediately follows his visit to Wally and Maud, and which, too, ends in breakdown and failure.

In a review responding to the 1989 production, Richard Kearney considered the lecture scene pivotal to the play's theme and action:

> Christopher's TV lecture – surely the most dramatic moment of this comic-tragic play – seeks to demonstrate logically why Schopenhauer didn't commit suicide, given his view of reality as a wilful striving for impossible unity. But when it comes to it, Christopher's prepared performance collapses before the cameras; his minutely rehearsed script about Schopenhauer's impersonal philosophy of life and death turns into a personal psychodrama of life or death. The ultimate question of all philosophy – what does it mean to be? – explodes onto the stage, as the academic breaks down and the truth of his questioning breaks through the mask of mere performance. He touches ground. But this return to earth (humus) is experienced as humiliation rather than humour by Christopher. And so he chooses the tragic solution of suicide rather than the comic one of laughter.[24]

Rhoda Koenig, who reviewed the 2001 production and hated the play – 'now revised and revived (why? why? why?)' – also read the lecture scene as realism but found it completely unconvincing:

> When Christopher gives his lecture, he is meant to be so frayed that he self-destructs . ... He refers to the Ding an Sich as the 'ding-a-dong,' then rambles on in an even less believable fashion until someone pulls the plug. Nobody approaches him with rage or concern, and at lunch he says nothing about it to the others – who appear not to have seen the speech, and aren't curious.[25]

The criticism might be valid if the scene were indeed a representation of Christopher's actual lecture, but both Kearney and Koenig misinterpret the nature and purpose of the scene. As Fintan O'Toole has pointed out, the action of the play, barring the opening and closing scenes, 'loosely preserves a classical unity of time, everything happening within the space of a few days. In this narrow sense, the idea of time is very specific and obvious.'[26] Since the lecture is immediately followed in the play by the *'post-funeral feast at MICHAEL's place'* (*TLFL2*: 58), and since the conversation at the end of that scene indicates that Christopher's lecture is still in the future, what we see on stage in the previous scene is unlikely, given the strict chronology of the events depicted, to be a representation of the actual event.

The stage directions of the 1990 text provide an important clue to the scene's function. Christopher is '*attempting to feign casualness. He is quite simply terrified. It's a nightmare ...*' (*TLFL1*: 39). This is not the actual lecture but a bad dream, which, on one level, represents an expressionistic 'what-if' scenario – an enactment of Christopher's anxiety about the imminent televised event, on which, in his mind, his whole future career as Dr Wuzzler's successor to the chair at Trinity College rests. On another level, however, it represents Christopher's confrontation with his own inner despair – a moment of transcendence in which the old self falls apart and a new, more positive self can emerge. Towards the end of his nightmare lecture, Christopher discusses Schopenhauer's refusal to kill himself, in spite of the many reasons he provided for doing so. While increasingly confusing the philosopher's life with his own – 'His father was a suicide! ... Need I mention his brother?' (*TLFL2*: 56-57) – Christopher produces various items from his pockets and puts them on the desk in front of him. As he begins to move his thinking into a more positive direction, away from thoughts of suicide and towards taking up smoking, the nightmarish quality of the scene recedes:

> He [Schopenhauer] must have found something to keep him going, some harmony. Sorry, President? (He *holds up the book.*) This? (*The earphones.*) These? (*The gun.*) This? (*The cigarette.*) This? (*Nods, puts the cigarette away.*) And because we have to push on.
>
> *The bright lights, in turn, go out on him during the following and his voice, if miked, is unmiked, until he becomes a man, lost, alone in a room, talking to himself.* (*TLFL2*: 57)

In the course of his nightmare, Christopher has faced and overcome his despair. Logically, the next scene is Cornelia's funeral, which similarly allows Michael to emerge, regenerated, from his breakdown in a deserted parking lot after leaving Monica's nightclub earlier in the play.

For the interpretation of the lecture scene as an expressionistic projection of Christopher's fears and desires, much depends on the play's production, as the nightmarish effect may be conveyed or enhanced by appropriate lighting and other dramatic means. The misinterpretation of the scene as reality by so many reviewers (Fintan O'Toole and Victoria White among them), however, is largely due to the fact that *Too Late for Logic* in its entirety has a 'dream-like structure.'[27] Monica Frawley's set design for the 1989 Abbey production, moreover, which started from the premise that Christopher kills himself at the beginning of the play, emphasized the unreal quality of the 'Limbo' in which the protagonist subsequently finds himself: 'Constantly you see the sky over the side of a couch, people are isolated on the stage, with sky, or nothingness, behind them all the time, to denote a surreal landscape.'[28] Murphy's creation of a nightmare within the already dream-like structure and design of *Too Late for Logic* turned out to be too subtle a device for theatre audiences, including the sophisticated reviewers quoted above, to register successfully.

While Michael Billington did understand and appreciate the 'dream-like structure' of *Too Late for Logic*, he confessed to being puzzled by the 'particularly odd scene' in which Christopher confronts 'an old playground tormentor and his Rusalka-like wife.'[29] Fintan O'Toole, on the other hand, who appears to have taken Christopher's 'demented lecture' for realism,[30] considers his confrontation with Wally 'a blackly comic nightmare from Schopenhauer' in which Christopher is trying to face head-on the hurts and insults of his past:

> But Wally and his wife Maud are not in Christopher's ordinary time-frame at all. They are like ghosts, trapped in an eternal present, embodiments of Schopenhauer's terrifying timelessness. Maud's record goes round and round again, maddened old schoolfriends like Christopher come again and again to shoot Wally. They are sealed off in a kind of Hell, reminiscent of Beckett's characters who are doomed to repeat every day what happened the day before. Chr[is]topher can no more affect them than he can affect his own past.[31]

Logically, it makes sense to read Christopher's meeting with Walter and Maud and his nightmarish lecture in the next scene as a sequence of self-confrontations in which Christopher first attempts to put paid to his past (by killing the old school bully) and then to create his future (by gaining the Trinity chair with a brilliant lecture). Both these efforts fail ludicrously, because Christopher is using them to avoid a confrontation with the real issues of his personal past and future: the break-up of his marriage and his relationship with his children, particularly his daughter Petra.

Murphy's note accompanying the draft of the scene with Walter and Maud in the manuscript of the play dated January-February

1988 (MS 11115, box 21, file 272) clarifies the idea from which these characters emerged. The note reads:

> Catalani composer of La Wally
> Operas show affinity with German Romantics
> La Wally by Catalini [sic]   W von Hillern's novel
> Die Geyer-Wally

The reference is to Alfredo Catalani's best known opera *La Wally* (1892), whose libretto is based on Wilhelmina von Hillern's 'Heimatroman' *Die Geyer-Wally* (1876), subtitled 'Eine Geschichte aus den Tyroler Alpen.' The music on Maud's record player at the opening of the scene, however, is 'O Silver Moon,' an aria from *Rusalka* by Antonin Dvorak. Walter cannot tell the two composers apart:

> **WALLY.** Oh, put on the bloody Catalani again, I know that's all yer itching for.
> **MAUD.** Dvorak, Walter.
> **WALLY.** Dvorak, Catalani, elephant's brain but I keep mixing the twisters up. (*TLFL2*: 51)

If Christopher's plan to murder Walter represents his misguided attempt to come to terms with the pain of his past, the operatic theme introduced by Maud draws Christopher back to the issue from his much more recent past which he is still not willing to face: the desertion of his wife and family.

Within that thematic strand, it could be argued that Walter and Maud are nightmarish versions of Christopher himself and his wife Patricia, in the form of projections from the depths of his unconscious. When we hear Patricia on the phone early on in the play, she '*is a woman so exhausted and unhappy that she is unaware of her own confusion – has she phoned* CHRISTOPHER *or* MICHAEL? *– or that she is at times talking to herself*' (*TLFL2*: 14). The death of her sister has come on top of the breakdown of her marriage, and Michael's unwillingness to face his bereavement is as frustrating to her as Christopher's refusal to face his own responsibilities. 'I thought love was stronger than death. Doesn't he want to kiss her? ... And there are papers to be signed. Always bloody papers ... when someone dies, walks out. Dies ... (*TLFL2*: 15). Like Patricia, Maud is a woman disappointed with marriage and locked in grief about the need for love, and its impossibility, expressed in the words of the aria from *Rusalka* on her record player. At the top of the scene, Maud is

> *seated, posed, watching her reflection in a cheval mirror. She's
> about sixty; a sad, elegant anachronism in dress and lost dreams.
> (Apart from once, at the end of the scene when she looks at*
> CHRISTOPHER *directly, she looks at the mirror; the pitch at
> which she holds her head acknowledges the person she is
> addressing. And it does not appear to matter that*
> CHRISTOPHER *does not answer her questions; it's as if she
> knows the answers.) (TLFL2: 47)*

While Maud represents Christopher's repressed acknowledgement
of the grief and anger he has caused Patricia, Walter is, like
Christopher, a man haunted by a guilty conscience and by figures
demanding that he recognize how he mistreated them in the past.
Wally's use of a wheelchair, which he does not need, to evoke
sympathy while he is warding off callers with hostile intentions, is a
concretization of Christopher's fake 'paralysis' in the face of his
family's demands, and his use of the lecture and the academic career
as an excuse for his failure to deal with the pressing issues in his
personal life.

Walter's confusion of *Rusalka* with *La Wally* reflects Christopher's confusion over the choices he faces in his own life, a
connection implied by some of the revisions to the 2006 text. In the
1990 version, the final words of Patricia's telephone message to
Christopher/Michael are, 'Where are you my beloved. Where are
you O where are you my beloved ...' (*TLFL1*: 10). These words are
cut from the revised text, where, however, they reappear in lines
added to Wally's dialogue with Christopher:

> **WALLY.** Dvorak, Catalani, elephant's brain but I keep mixing the
> twisters up.
> **MAUD.** Do you mind hearing it again?
> **CHRISTOPHER.** (*absently*) No.
> **WALLY.** Where are you, oh where are you my beloved – same old
> thing.
> CHRISTOPHER *looks at him; fixes on him.*
> **WALLY.** Eh? ... Music man yourself, Christopher? ... (*TLFL2: 51*)

Both *Rusalka* and *La Wally* are sweeping tales of love, betrayal,
revenge, and death. In Catalani's opera, the eponymous heroine is
initially spurned by the man she loves. After many tribulations, he
finally declares his love for her, but shortly thereafter is swept away
by an avalanche, whereupon Wally throws herself down a precipice

to be united with him in death. Suicide is her response to personal tragedy.

The opera foregrounded in *Too Late for Logic* is not, however, *La Wally*, but *Rusalka*, whose story is related by Maud as she and Christopher listen to 'O Silver Moon.' The changes to the 2006 text make the connection between the opera and Christopher's life more overt than it is in the 1990 version by having Maud interject poignant questions. Maud explains to her visitor:

> **MAUD.** She is singing to the moon ... because she has fallen in love with the handsome prince, who came to bathe in the limpid pool, her home ... she longs for a mortal body in order that she might know the warmth of union with him ... to share the wonder of life with a human being ... Are you married?
> **CHRISTOPHER.** Is that you? (*'Singing'*)
> **MAUD.** No. Because then, for very good reason, I stopped. ... And her wish is granted. But there is a condition. If he proves false, both she and he will be damned for ever ...The decision is irrevocably taken ... Do you love her? (*TLFL2*: 47)

The conclusion of the scene in this later version also makes it clearer that the emotional confrontation in which Christopher points a gun at Wally is triggered by the story of Rusalka:

> **MAUD.** But the prince is unable to learn ... He is unkind to her ... He betrays her trust ... She wants to die.
> **CHRISTOPHER.** (*emotionally, to himself*) ... What's her name?
> **WALLY.** You interested in? (*'this kind of music?'*) He's interested in (*'this kind of music'*) – Speak up!
> **MAUD.** Rusalka ... And she returns to the limpid pool, to sink alone back into the water ... But she knows that he, too, will never be free of her. And she waits for him to follow, to die, in understanding at last, in her arms. (*She rises.*)
> **WALLY.** Eh? ... Sit!
> *She remains standing. She looks at* CHRISTOPHER.
> **MAUD.** Would you like me to leave?
> **WALLY.** What's that?
> CHRISTOPHER *rises. He is trembling, highly agitated, the gun pointed directly at* WALLY. (*TLFL2*: 52-53)

Christopher does not shoot Wally, although Maud encourages him to, because the past cannot be killed; for it to 'die,' for its ghost to be laid, it must be embraced, just as, for his marriage to end properly, he first has to make peace with Patricia.

In the nightmare lecture that follows the scene with Wally and Maud, Christopher rejects the gun in favour of the cigarette and, as

he becomes a man 'talking to himself,' begins to relate Schopenhauer's reasons for rejecting suicide to his own. Although the
philosopher expressed hostility towards women and children, he
had 'casual amours' of sufficient duration to produce offspring –
'thorns of kindred': 'And though he could not see how they could
possibly love him, could it be possible that they did?' (*TLFL2*: 57).
Through his two nightmarish experiences, Christopher learns what
Schopenhauer also realized: that his callous attitude towards his
wife and children is caused by an underlying fear of losing them.
Michael's apparent lack of interest in the death of Cornelia, and
Christopher's seeming indifference towards his family, are actually
strategies of avoiding pain. Tom Murphy stated in a 1986 interview
that 'Physically and mentally, one cannot stand the pressure of
constant love.'[32] This is also the reason Christopher gives for
sending his wife divorce papers to sign: 'For what? To escape, *ease*
the pain of boundless love. For what? In order, in isolation, to
achieve that other state, the terror of memories and guilt mocking
the impotence and failure of a jumble of words' (*TLFL2*: 59). The
possibility of a middle ground between the pain of love and the
terror of isolation does not strike Christopher until the very end of
the play, when he relates Schopenhauer's parable of the porcupines:
'they found a moderate distance from one another at which they
could survive best' (*TLFL2:* 74).

In *Too Late for Logic*, as in so many of Murphy's plays, music,
particularly opera, as well as references to classical mythology, are
used to underscore the work's major themes. For Murphy, the voice
is a conduit between the innermost self and the transcendence of
that self; he has likened great singing to prayer. The music that
opens *Too Late for Logic* in both printed versions is the aria 'J'ai
Perdu Mon Eurydice,' sung by Maria Callas, from Gluck's opera
Orpheus et Eurydice. This myth of love and loss, expressed through
song (not least by Orpheus himself), captures the psychological
journey both Christopher and Michael have to undertake in order to
return from their own versions of 'hell.' Each man, like Orpheus, is
in denial about the 'death' – literally or metaphorically – of his beloved until each has confronted the underworld of his own psyche,
from where the reborn self can then resurface and go out into the
world.

Murphy used more operatic references in the 1990 version of the
play, notably the aria 'Porgi Amor' from Mozart's *Le Nozze di
Figaro*; he also suggested that, should the play have an interval after

the nightclub scene, the aria 'Casta Diva' from Bellini's *Norma* might be used as a bridging device. More informal song complements these classical pieces. Jack improvises psychedelic lyrics to his own music, which can be read as referring both to Christopher's mental crisis and his eventual overcoming of it. In the 1989 production of the play, moreover, the taped operatic arias punctuating the play eventually gave way 'to the reality of the voices of Patricia and Petra, on stage, gently singing, unaccompanied, the folk song, *Down by the Sally Gardens.*' The reviewer was not entirely convinced by the performance: 'They did not sing quite in tune. Was this deliberate, in which case a further meaning is embedded there; or was it simply another unfortunate instance of the doctrine of the approximate?'[33]

Derek West felt that the use of music in the 1989 production was appropriate: 'Music serves to underpin the emotional density of Murphy's text, to suggest the operatic scale of life.'[34] What Alexandra Poulain says about *The Gigli Concert* is also true of *Too Late for Logic*: 'the words of the arias, and the contexts in which they are sung in the original operas, match the play's dramatic situations very precisely.' At the same time, as when Christopher and Maud listen to 'O Silver Moon,' singing often 'expresses whatever remains unsaid in the dialogue: all the feelings and emotions that the characters are reluctant or simply unable to verbalize.'[35] Poulain regards this use of music as a dangerous game by Murphy, however, 'as the contrapuntal effect of the arias partly depends on their referential value: the reasonably cultured spectator ... will necessarily miss out on at least some of the implications of the songs.'[36]

When Murphy revised *Too Late for Logic* in 2006, he reduced the operatic and mythological effects to a minimum. That scaling down may well indicate that Murphy has come to terms with the issues of the play. He told Marianne McDonald in 1992:

> I find that in writing a play, I come to the numerous full stops which are also areas of great despair. I feel, you know, I can't go on. I think, 'This is ridiculous, this means nothing to me, and what could it possibly mean to anybody else?' And then I start to look for some sort of precedent in mythology on which I can hang it to make it work, and I usually reject that and say, well, am I trying to make this play work? Or am I trying to write some mood, feeling, attitude, that I feel within myself? I don't comprehend it, but I feel it within myself.[37]

The stripping down of *Too Late for Logic* to its essentials signals that Murphy himself, like his protagonist, is ready to face the play's emotional essentials without the crutches of myth and music. We are left with a single reference to the myth of Orpheus and Eurydice, the stories of Rusalka and La Wally, and the song sung by Jack, who, O'Toole suggests, 'is the re-born Orpheus'[38] – although some new lines Monica addresses to Christopher in the 2006 version suggest more strongly that he, too, might be reborn as an artist rather than a philosopher: 'But *you* should be able to write a book – or a play? Have you ever tried?' (*TLFL2*: 72). At the end of *Too Late for Logic*, Michael, Patricia, and Christopher are ready to go back to work, having transcended the pain and denial of the past year: Michael's sabbatical is over, Patricia is opening a shop, and Christopher has a lecture to give and possibly a play to write.

'Writing,' Tom Murphy has stated, 'in one sense is turning one's back to real living, and I find that I can't cope with real life.'[39] There is a cost to being an artist, but, he adds, 'I'm very happy that I did it. I'm sorry for the neglect of my nearest and dearest, but had I done anything else I think I would have been an unkinder person.'[40] The evolution of the text of *Too Late for Logic* over a period of almost two decades reflects Murphy's struggles to come to grips with the 'real life' issues that formed the emotional starting point of the play, while it also captures the essence of his artistic method. Declan Kiberd has argued that Murphy cannot afford to resolve his own painful psychological complexes because they provide him with his art: he knows intuitively 'that it will not serve an artist to become overly self-analytical. That kind of analysis might sterilize the impulses which it investigates.'[41] Although some of the numerous versions of *Too Late for Logic* also show that elements of Murphy's 'own painful psychological complexes' at times stand in the way of the art they generate, the multiple revisions to the play are, in the final reckoning, a refusal of finality. Both the self and the art keep evolving: 'Murphy's theatre as a whole ... aims at leaving the pre-written text of the old world for a new world in the making, a world of endless, as yet undefined possibilities.'[42] Logic does not enter into this process of remaking: it is rather, in the words of *The Gigli Concert*, a case of 'new mind over old matter.'[43] In other words, the stuff of magic.

[1] Kay Kent, 'Festival Faces: Thomas Murphy and Dan O'Herlihy,' *Irish Times* 20 March 1972: 10.

[2] 'Tom Murphy,' in *Reading the Future: Irish Writers in Conversation with Mike Murphy*, ed. Clíodhna Ní Anluain (Dublin: Lilliput Press, 2000): 174.

[3] *Reading the Future*, ed. Ní Anluain: 181.

[4] Fintan O'Toole, 'Tribune Portrait: Tom Murphy,' *Sunday Tribune* 1 May 1983: 6.

[5] Kent, 'Festival Faces' : 10.

[6] Victoria White, 'Drama of Music and Madness,' *Irish Times* 16 March 1991, Weekend: 5.

[7] Fintan O'Toole, 'Off Stage and onto the Page,' interview with Tom Murphy, *Irish Times* 22 June 1994: 8.

[8] Deirdre Purcell, 'Into the Dark,' interview with Tom Murphy, *Sunday Tribune* 19 October 1986: 17.

[9] Arthur Schopenhauer, *Parerga and Paralipomena*, trans. E.F.J. Payne, 2 vols (Oxford: Clarendon Press, 1974) 1: 358. For more about Murphy's use of Schopenhauer, see José Lanters, 'Schopenhauer with Hindsight: Tom Murphy's *Too Late for Logic*,' *Hungarian Journal of English and American Studies* 2. 2 (1996): 87-95.

[10] Tom Murphy, *Too Late for Logic* (London: Methuen, 1990): 8. All further page references to this edition (henceforth *TLFL1*) will be given parenthetically in the text.

[11] Schopenhauer, *Parerga*, vol. 2: 648.

[12] 'Delving into the Dark,' part 1, *Irish Times* 15 January 1998. http://www.irishtimes.com (archive). Accessed 4 July 2008.

[13] Philip Fisher, 'Tom Murphy's Belated Fringe Debut,' interview with Tom Murphy. http://www.britishtheatreguide.info/otherresources/interviews/-Tom Murphy.htm. 14 January 2009.

[14] *Reading the Future*, ed. Ní Anluain: 182

[15] TCD MS 11115, Box 21 and Box 22. I am grateful to the staff of the Manuscripts Library at Trinity College for granting me access to the drafts of *Too Late for Logic* in their collection while the cataloguing process was still ongoing.http://www.irishtimes.com/

[16] *Reading the Future*, ed. Ní Anluain: 181.

[17] H.D.F. Kitto, *Greek Tragedy: A Literary Study*, 3rd ed., rpt (London: Routledge, 1990).

[18] Cf. Kitto, 'Yet a forger has every reason to be careful over detail: this one may have known what he was talking about': 2.

[19] *Reading the Future*, ed. Ní Anluain: 182.

[20] Derek West, interview with Monica Frawley, *Theatre Ireland* 21 (December 1989): 32.

21 Fintan O'Toole, 'Murphy in the Underworld,' *Irish Times* 7 October 1989 Weekend: 5.

22 Tom Murphy, *Too Late for Logic*, in *Plays: 5* (London: Methuen, 2006): 3-74. All page references to this edition (henceforth *TLFL2*) will be given parenthetically in the text.

23 Fintan O'Toole, 'Off Stage': 8.

24 Richard Kearney, review of Tom Murphy, *Too Late for Logic*, *Theatre Ireland* 21 (December 1989) : 54.

25 Rhoda Koenig, 'An Evening of Sterile Condescension,' review of Tom Murphy, *Too Late for Logic*, *Independent* 16 August 2001. http://www.independent.co.uk (archive). 25 December 2008.

26 Fintan O'Toole, *Tom Murphy: The Politics of Magic*, rev. ed. (Dublin: New Island, 1994): 262.

27 Michael Billington, review of Tom Murphy, *Too Late for Logic*, *Guardian* 16 August 2001. http://www.guardian.co.uk (archive). 10 January 2002.

28 West, interview with Frawley: 32.

29 Billington, review, *Guardian* 16 August 2001.

30 O'Toole, *Politics of Magic*: 260.

31 O'Toole, *Politics of Magic*: 263.

32 Purcell, 'Into the Dark' : 17.

33 Lynda Henderson, review of Tom Murphy, *Too Late for Logic*, *Theatre Ireland* 21 (December 1989): 56.

34 Derek West, review of Tom Murphy, *Too Late for Logic*, *Theatre Ireland* 21 (December 1989): 55.

35 Alexandra Poulain, ' "A Voice and Little Else": Talking, Writing and Singing in *The Gigli Concert*', in *Echoes Down the Corridor: Irish Theatre – Past, Present and Future*, ed. Patrick Lonergan and Riana O'Dwyer (Dublin: Carysfort Press): 111.

36 Poulain, 'A Voice and Little Else': 112.

37 Marianne McDonald, interview with Tom Murphy, *Ancient Sun, Modern Light: Greek Drama on the Modern Stage* (New York: Columbia UP, 1992): 199-200.

38 O'Toole, *Politics of Magic*: 264.

39 *Reading the Future*, ed. Ní Anluain: 174.

40 *Reading the Future*, ed. Ní Anluain: 186.

41 Declan Kiberd, 'Theatre as Opera: *The Gigli Concert*,' in *Theatre Stuff: Critical Essays on Contemporary Irish Theatre*, ed. Eamonn Jordan (Dublin: Carysfort Press, 2000): 152.

42 Poulain, 'A Voice and Little Else': 113.

43 Tom Murphy, *The Gigli Concert*, in *Plays: 3* (London: Methuen, 1994): 238.

13 | *Alice Trilogy*: Seen through the Looking-Glass of the London Critics[1]

Peter James Harris

Nobody could ever accuse Tom Murphy of being unduly optimistic about the human condition. His plays depict the outcasts of society with a relentless bleakness and, although there is humour in his writing, it is not generally the laughs that remain in the mind after having watched a Tom Murphy play. In his essay entitled 'Tom Murphy and the children of loss', in *The Cambridge Companion to Twentieth-Century Irish Drama*, Nicholas Grene states that 'messed-up lives, dead-end states, the extremes of dereliction and despair – these provide the staples of Murphy's drama, whatever the form and milieu'.[2] Nonetheless, plays such as *The Gigli Concert* (1983) and *Bailegangaire* (1985) hold out the redeeming possibility of transcendence of grim circumstances, grotesque though the means may be. Christopher Morash describes *The Gigli Concert* as being 'part of a theatre of exorcism that emerged in the 1980s, where the past is conjured up, neither to be mocked nor to open old wounds, but so that it might be accepted and healed.'[3] In his survey of twentieth-century Irish drama Christopher Murray registers the reaction of audiences to the play's 'combination of compassion and an ethic derived from music', and notes that 'it was [quack sciento-logist] King's triumph over tragic circumstance which had Irish audiences on their feet in a standing ovation when *The Gigli Concert* had its premiere at the Abbey.'[4] However, besides the notable hits, Murphy has also had a few misses. In her overview of his *oeuvre* José Lanters recognizes that 'the extreme reactions evoked by his plays are reflected in the many ups and downs of his career', and concludes her essay by quoting from a 1991 *Irish Times* interview in which Murphy stated 'the risks have sometimes left me with injured legs, but sometimes they've paid off. My motto is, "If you can do it, why bother?"'[5] That is, as writer, Murphy never takes the easy way.

∾ ∾

Alice Trilogy, which opened at London's Royal Court Theatre on 16 November 2005, was Murphy's first new play in five years, and once again it was an exercise in risk-taking. Like another new Irish play, which followed it onto the Royal Court stage in January 2006, Stella Feehily's *O Go My Man*, the focus was upon the well-heeled middle class in the heady days of the Celtic Tiger economy. It should have been a surprise to no one that, although Murphy had celebrated his seventieth birthday earlier in the year, neither his advancing years nor the transformations brought about by Ireland's Euro-wealth had mellowed his perception of the human predicament.

The play depicts its eponymous central character at three moments in her life, in the 1980s, in 1995 and in the present. The title suggests that we should perhaps respond to what we see on stage as a series of three one-act plays, rather than as three acts in a single drama. What Murphy offers us is essentially a triptych, three juxtaposed images bound into a single unifying structure. The name of the central character provides the optic through which to view the three pictures, for Alice is an inescapable reference to the heroine of Lewis Carroll's classic tales *Alice's Adventures in Wonderland* (1865) and its sequel *Through the Looking-Glass and What Alice Found There* (1872), as is made clear by a quotation from the latter work in the third play in the trilogy.

In the second of Carroll's books Alice passes through the looking-glass on the chimney-piece in her drawing-room and finds herself in Looking-glass House, in which the normality of her own world is inverted so that 'the things go the other way' and 'the books are something like our books, only the words go the wrong way'.[6] She soon discovers that she is caught up as a pawn in a giant chess game, in which the characters she meets on her journey to the eighth square are *dramatis personae* of increasing grotesquerie in the same game. As in the previous book Alice wakes at the end to find that the whole adventure has been no more than a particularly vivid dream. Carroll (i.e. Charles Lutwidge Dodgson) describes his book as a fairy-tale, and the story of its creation, improvised to entertain the young Alice Liddell and her two sisters in a rowing-boat on a summer's afternoon, has already acquired a legendary quality of its own. Both books are prefaced with a dedicatory poem, in the first case addressed to all three sisters, but in the second to Alice alone. Carroll was forty years old when the second book was published and, although he was to live for another twenty-six years, the poems, which frame *Through the Looking-Glass* are tinged with a melancholy recognition of life's ephemerality:

> Come, hearken then, ere voice of dread,
> With bitter tidings laden,
> Shall summon to unwelcome bed
> A melancholy maiden!
> We are but older children, dear,
> Who fret to find our bedtime near.[7]

The book's epigraph closes with the rhetorical question, 'Life, what is it but a dream?'

In Tom Murphy's play, although Alice is no longer a little girl, she is nonetheless trapped in a looking-glass world. In her case, the proportions of this world are no longer those of a dream but of a nightmare. The first play in the trilogy is set in 1981 and it introduces us to an over-stressed, twenty-five-year-old Alice seeking respite from the daily routine of her married life in the solace of her retreat in an attic room. Here, amidst the family's discarded broken furniture, reminded of the mundane reality from which she is trying to escape by the remote thump-thump, thump-thump of the washing machine in the house below, she washes down her Valium with coffee strongly laced with whisky and smokes a cigarette before rushing off to collect her three children from school. (One has a strong sense of having travelled back to the mid-'sixties and an encounter with the middle-class housewife of the Rolling Stones' 'Mother's Little Helper'.) It is here too that Alice communes with her alter ego Al. The black and white contrasts of Jeremy Herbert's set for the Royal Court production were redolent of Carroll's chessboard and, when Derbhle Crotty's Al steps out from the frame of a cheval mirror to join Alice in her looking-glass world, she too is dressed in black, wearing whiteface makeup. Juliet Stevenson's blonde Alice wears blue jeans and a light-blue blouse, reminding us of the image created, for better or worse, by Walt Disney's cartoon version of Carroll's character.

The dialogue between alter ego and ego is conducted in the interrogatory form of an inane television quiz-show, opening with, 'Your name, age and profession, please?'.[8] However, from this very first question there is an ironic sub-text underlying the banality of the questions and answers, for Alice has no profession. Despite the promise of her top-of-the-class results at the Loreto school for girls, her skills in mental arithmetic, her general knowledge and her command of French, Alice is now restricted to the mundane role of a housewife, a fact underlined by the music-hall misogyny of the later question, 'Why do women have small feet?' (15), to which Al herself provides the answer 'So that they can stand close to the sink' (22). Of course, the ludic-interrogatory mode is also that employed by Alice's interlocutors in *Through the Looking-Glass*, particularly in the case of her meeting with Humpty Dumpty:

> 'In that case we may start fresh,' said Humpty Dumpty, 'and it's my turn to choose a subject – ' ('He talks about it just as if it was a game!' thought Alice.) 'So here's a question for you. How old did you say you were?'[9]

Although it is Humpty Dumpty and Al who are, respectively, the quizmaster and -mistress, Tom Murphy's Alice shares Humpty Dumpty's playful attitude to language itself. Just outside the attic room is the wire-mesh-and-timber aviary where Alice's husband Bill keeps the budgerigars which serve as his relaxation in the odd moments between his work as an up-and-coming young banker and his four nights a week of evening classes. Alice, however, describes it as an apiary, no doubt, in recognition of the alliterative qualities of Big Bill the banker's interest in 'breeding budgies and babies and suchlike' (19):

> **ALICE.** I know that it's an aviary –
> **AL.** But ask her, go on, ask her and she'll tell you.
> **ALICE.** I prefer to call it an apiary.
> **AL.** She calls things what she likes.
> **ALICE.** Should I call things by what other people have decided for me?
> **AL.** Her mind, her life.
> **ALICE.** My mind, my life. (12)

Humpty Dumpty likewise sees his relationship with language as a question of control:

> 'I don't know what you mean by "glory",' Alice said.
> Humpty Dumpty smiled contemptuously. 'Of course you don't – till I tell you. I meant "there's a nice knockdown argument for you!"'
> 'But "glory" doesn't mean "a nice knockdown argument",' Alice objected.
> 'When *I* use a word,' Humpty Dumpty said in rather a scornful

tone, 'it means just what I choose it to mean – neither more nor less.'

'The question is,' said Alice, 'whether you *can* make words mean different things.'

'The question is,' said Humpty Dumpty, 'which is to be master – that's all.'[10]

For Tom Murphy's Alice, however, her interlocutor is no nursery-rhyme character: her alter ego is a dark presence seeding her mind with the appalling thought that, if she is to commit suicide by driving her car into the docks, she should take her three beautiful children, aged six, five and four-and-a-half, with her. The budgies also acquire a sinister force in Alice's topsy-turvy looking-glass world. As in Alfred Hitchcock's film *The Birds* (1963), Bill's pets constitute a nightmarish threat. Twice Al refers to the impenetrable rationale of their daily routine, their occasional outbursts of chirping 'for reasons best known or unknown to themselves' (13, 24), an echo of the leitmotif, repeated eleven times, in Lucky's monologue in *Waiting for Godot*, that rambling catalogue of divine and human irrationality.[11] The first play in the trilogy closes as Alice rushes off to collect her children from school and the theatre is filled with waves of head-splitting sound from the budgies, 'singing all together like a hacksaw cutting through wire' (24), reminding us of the shrieking violin in another Hitchcock film.

Notwithstanding the irrational shrillness of the budgies there is no murder in the shower for Alice or for her children. The second play in the trilogy takes place thirteen or fourteen years later. It is no longer in her attic hideaway that Alice seeks escape from her humdrum quotidian round. A serious car crash some ten years previously has frightened her off both driving and drinking. It is now her husband who has turned to drink, even though he is the high-flying 'area manager for half the banks in the country' (37). Meanwhile Alice seeks what she describes as her 'opium for the housewife' (35) in a fortnightly book-club meeting and a creative writing class every Tuesday night. We meet her on one such night walking through a badly lit lane by the gasworks wall. Out of the shadows a voice calls her name and emerges cautiously into the light. The voice is that of the famous television newsreader James Godwin, Jimmy, her former flame of twenty-one years ago, to whom she has written on the off-chance of a meeting. Dressed in black, like Al in the first play, Jimmy likewise serves as a mirror to Alice – they both have three children, for instance, 'nearly *touché* there' (34).

Like Al too Jimmy reveals an undercurrent of violence beneath his
slick surface. To begin with, their meeting, after a separation of
more than two decades, seems to hold out the possibility of a return
to the halcyon days of adolescent innocence. They hold hands in
silence and Alice asks, 'Which of us is dreaming this?' (36), the very
question that Lewis Carroll's Alice raises at the end of *Through the
Looking-Glass*:

> Now, Kitty, let's consider who it was that dreamed it all. This is
> a serious question, my dear [...] You see, Kitty, it *must* have
> been either me or the Red King. He was part of my dream, of
> course – but then I was part of his dream, too![12]

For Tom Murphy's Alice, however, the dream quickly sours and
becomes a nightmare as her 'Red King' surrenders to his paranoia
about his colleagues in the television studios. This quickly extends to
Alice herself as Jimmy conceives of the possibility that she may have
set up their meeting in order to obtain compromising photographs
for the purposes of blackmail. The second play in the trilogy ends as
he threatens her with violence:

> **JIMMY.** Do you realize, because of your 'fantasizing', that I could
> hurt you now. I could? I could?
> **ALICE.** You could.
> **JIMMY.** And I would like to. Would that 'reality' suit you? Fear of
> consequences are [*sic*] not stopping me. I could kill you right now?
> I could?
> **ALICE.** You could, Jimmy, but you won't. (47)

Much to the relief both of Alice and of the theatre audience Jimmy
fails to put his threat into action and takes his black-coated male-
volence off into the night.

The final play in the trilogy is set in the present. Alice, now
nearing fifty, is sitting in an airport lounge with her husband.
Although she eats nothing herself he steadily munches his way
through a plate of fish and chips during the course of the play. In the
final scene of *Through the Looking-Glass* Alice is also sitting down
to a meal. At the head of a table of fifty guests, sandwiched between
the Red Queen and the White Queen, Alice does not manage to eat
anything at all, for the Queens order the waiters to remove every
dish before she can make a start on it. In the case of Tom Murphy's
Alice there is a very plausible reason for her lack of appetite, for she
and her husband are at the airport in order to receive the body of
their son, which is being flown home after his premature death in an
accident abroad. While her pragmatic husband eats his meal we

hear Alice's interior monologue. In the first play in the trilogy Alice's alter ego referred to her ego in the third person: now Alice refers to herself in the third person. Bereft of her favourite son, her 'gallant escort' (34) of ten years previously, Alice refers to God as 'the Almighty Terrorist' (61). Like Lewis Carroll's Alice, she is unable to provide a rational explanation for the disorientating world in which she exists:

> There is no explanation for what cannot be explained, no comfort for what cannot be comforted. [...] But she accepted the explanations and the religious platitudes for the sake of those who offered them. (61)

Trapped in 'a nightmare that is pretending to be a dream' (53) she recalls her self of 'twenty-five, no, thirty years ago when everything seemed possible' (56):

> Dreaming. She was a great dreamer. Back then she was a fool to any kind of suggestion: suggestion did not take no for an answer. 'It's no use trying,' said Alice, 'one cannot believe in impossible things.' 'You haven't been practising,' said the White Queen. (56-57)

This, of course, is almost an exact quotation from the conversation that Lewis Carroll's Alice has with the White Queen on the occasion of their first meeting:

> 'Now I'll give *you* something to believe. I'm just one hundred and one, five months and a day.'
> 'I can't believe *that*!' said Alice.
> 'Can't you?' the Queen said in a pitying tone. 'Try again: draw a long breath, and shut your eyes.'
> Alice laughed. 'There's no use trying,' she said: 'one *can't* believe impossible things.'
> 'I dare say you haven't had much practice,' said the Queen. 'When I was your age, I always did it for half an hour a day.'[13]

However, it is not the White Queen who enables Alice finally to escape from her depressed introspection but the Waitress in the airport restaurant, who unburdens herself of her own nightmare, confiding to Alice that, having lovingly fostered her sister-in-law's baby for over a year, she and her husband had recently returned the baby to its mother, who, Medea-like, had killed the child just two days previously. Finally, at the very end of the play, Alice is jolted out of her solipsism to extend the hand of empathy to the Waitress, embracing her and, speaking of herself in the third person still, admits that 'she loves the waitress, Stella, and clings to her for a moment in sympathy and in gratitude for releasing this power within her.' (66) Although this transcendent moment was insufficient to unlock the 'strange, savage, beautiful and mysterious country' (23) that Alice had sensed within herself at the end of the first play, the final image in the London production, of tears running down Juliet Stevenson's equine face, was an indisputably powerful theatrical moment.

Curiously, the London critics failed to detect any intertextuality between Tom Murphy's play and Lewis Carroll's *Through the Looking-Glass*. Of nineteen reviews published in daily and weekly papers in the ten days following the play's opening on 16 November 2005, only three even so much as mentioned the nineteenth-century precursor of Murphy's stage character. In the *Times*, Benedict Nightingale mentioned Alice only in terms of frustrated expectations:

> The title of Tom Murphy's new play suggests that we should expect a three-parter along the lines of Shakespeare's *Henry VI*, but with Lewis Carroll's flaxen-haired princess rather than a doomed king. However, it lasts just over two hours and is called a trilogy because it observes an Irish woman in a doleful 1980, a wretched 1995 and a 2005 somewhere the other side of despair. (*The Times* 17.11.05).

Elsewhere, Ruth Leon described Murphy's Alice as emerging 'through the looking-glass of her thoughts' (*Daily Express* 17.11.05), while Susannah Clapp referred to Juliet Stevenson's portrayal of Alice as being 'a woman trapped behind her own face like Alice behind the looking-glass' (*Observer* 20.11.05).

On the other hand, two-thirds of the critics pointed out parallels between Murphy's writing and that of Samuel Beckett and, in some cases, that of Virginia Woolf. Most of the eleven critics who detected evidence of Beckettian influence saw this as having been inadequately absorbed. Thus, the *Times* reviewer described the play as 'a short trilogy as might have been penned by Samuel Beckett in collaboration with a dozen depressed housewives' (*The Times* 17.11.05). A few days later, another reviewer echoed this analogy:

> Imagine Desperate Housewives written by a wannabe Samuel Beckett and an exceptionally depressed Virginia Woolf and you'll have the flavour of Tom Murphy's *Alice Trilogy*. (*Mail on Sunday* 20.11.05)

Carole Woddis, in the *Herald*, asked why Murphy's play sounds 'disturbingly like a thin amalgam of Samuel Beckett and Virginia Woolf?' (*Herald*, 25.11.05) In the *Independent on Sunday*, Kate Bassett felt that the play was 'too obviously indebted to Samuel

Beckett' (*Independent on Sunday*, 20.11.05), while the *International Herald Tribune* stated that 'the show nods in the direction of the greatest Irish playwright of them all – Samuel Beckett – without beginning to approximate his power' (*International Herald Tribune*, 23.11.05). Probably the most seriously pondered view of the question of Beckettian influence, however, was voiced by Michael Billington, the elder statesman amongst the London critics, who has been reviewing plays for the *Guardian* since 1971:

> Dramatists, as they get older, often do away with the impedimenta of realism. Tom Murphy here focuses with Beckettian directness on the decline of his eponymous Irish heroine over a quarter of a century. The result is a strange, poetic, poignant study of a life half lived, and of suffering stubbornly endured. (*Guardian* 17.11.05)

It is regrettable that very few of Michael Billington's colleagues in the press corps were prepared to extend the same level of tolerance towards Murphy's work. The management of the Royal Court would certainly not have wished to adorn the theatre's billboards with such damning comments as:

> '... fuddled, feeble ... drama-lite ... emptily verbose ... glowering lack of dramatic purpose' (*Evening Standard* 17.11.05);
>
> '... both precious and thin' (*Financial Times* 18.11.05);
>
> '... two hours of relentless misery ... theatrical masochism' (*Daily Telegraph* 18.11.05);
>
> '... badly engineered' (*Independent* 18.11.05);
>
> '... irritating ... pretentious ... tiresome' (*Daily Mail* 17.11.05);
>
> '... very disappointing' (*Independent on Sunday* 20.11.05);
>
> '... exasperating' (*International Herald Tribune* 23.11.05);
>
> '... rather tedious' (*Jewish Chronicle* 25.11.05);
>
> '... often dreary' (*Sunday Telegraph* 27.11.05).

Although several of the critics referred to Tom Murphy's status as one of Ireland's leading contemporary playwrights, very few saw fit to comment on the play's actual Irishness. Thus, Murphy's focus on a sector of Irish society that has rarely featured in the work of Irish dramatists was not mentioned by any of the nineteen critics. Only Michael Billington ventured to argue that the virtue of the play is that it 'implies some malaise in Irish society not confined to women', although later in his review, rather than attempting to specify what this malaise might be, he fell back on generalities. Thus, for Billington, the second play in the trilogy 'beautifully brings out both the wan despair of middle-age and some baffled affliction within the Irish temper', concluding his review with the affirmation that, although the play's 'final meaning is elusive [...] it admits us to the solitude and despair within the Irish soul.' (*Guardian* 17.11.05)

Of more interest to the critics were Juliet Stevenson's struggles with her Irish accent. The reviewers were unanimous in declaring that Juliet Stevenson's performance as Alice was the great strength of the production. They referred to her:

'... mesmerising performance' (*Guardian* 17.11.05);

'... lyrical self-pity' (*Evening Standard* 17.11.05);

'... virtuosic performance' (*Daily Telegraph* 18.11.05);

'... talent for sadness' (*Daily Mail*, 17.11.05);

'... wrenching intensity' (*Sunday Express* 20.11.05);

'... tour-de-force of virtually solo acting' (*What's On* 23.11.05);

'... mixture of suppressed fury and almost inaudible restraint' (*Herald* 25.11.05).

On the other hand, her unsuccessful attempts to produce a convincing Irish accent were the object of general reprobation. The critic of *The Times* described Juliet Stevenson's accent as 'iffy', while Michael Billington wrote that her 'Irish roots were only fitfully suggested'. Alastair Macaulay said that an Irish accent that 'comes and goes' was her only obvious fault (*Financial Times* 18.11.05). The *Daily Mail* described her accent as 'dim to non-existent', while Martina Shawn, writing in *What's On*, said that her accent was 'forced to tour all over the place'. Given that most critics did not believe the play's Irishness to be of particular significance, Juliet Stevenson's difficulties with her accent were considered to be a blemish on her otherwise outstanding performance, but not a problem as far as the production as a whole was concerned.

Curiously, given their evident dislike for Tom Murphy's text, the critics seemed to think that the production itself was successful, largely due to the positive qualities of Ian Rickson's direction. Here the praise was indeed fulsome: the critics described the production as:

'... expertly judged' (*The Times* 17.11.05);

'... wonderfully spare' (*Daily Express* 17.11.05);

'... sensitive' (*Time Out London* 23.11.05);

'... characteristically meticulous' (*Mail on Sunday* 20.11.05);

'... spare, eerie and gripping' (*Independent on Sunday* 20.11.05);

'... a superb study in claustrophobic detail' (*Herald* 25.11.05).

Personally, I feel that the London critics were unduly harsh. I went to see the Royal Court production with my son, then twelve years old, not long after we had both enjoyed an excellent revival of Joe Orton's *What the Butler Saw*. The two plays make an interesting pairing since they offer two very different perspectives on the theme of mental health. In the case of my son, a young adolescent can certainly be forgiven for finding the neuroses of a fifty-year-old woman less entertaining than the farcical mayhem of Dr Prentice's clinic. For my own part, although I was enthralled by Juliet Stevenson's portrayal of the central character, neither she nor Tom Murphy was able to make me *care* very much about her angst. Like many of the London critics, I found myself siding with Alice's long-suffering husband who, dull though he may be, is more sinned against than sinning. Perhaps this was the risk that Murphy took with this play, for he must have known that it would be difficult to write the tragedy of a wealthy married woman whose principal problem throughout the major part of the play is that she has no problems. In this sense, Tom Murphy's Alice is much like her nineteenth-century namesake – both characters are lost in a labyrinth of irrationality, but this does not earn them the right to the theatre-goer or reader's empathy: one observes the plight of both Alices with dispassionate detachment.

By way of a post-script, it is worth noting that, on 6 October 2006, almost a year after its world premiere in London, *Alice Trilogy* opened at the Abbey's Peacock Theatre in Dublin. The production, directed by Tom Murphy himself, and starring Jane Brennan as Alice and Mary Murray as Al, was a sell-out success. There can be no doubt that the Abbey's audience holds Tom Murphy dear to its heart – in 2001, for instance, his work was celebrated with the six-play season *Tom Murphy at the Abbey* – but it is interesting to conjecture that his *Alice Trilogy* may have struck a chord with the Irish audience that failed to resonate with London's theatregoers.

Two months later, on 5 December, I was fortunate enough to be present at the play's first performance in Brazil. In a sensitive translation by Domingos Nunez, who also directed the play, the presentation took place in a small studio theatre high above the Avenida Paulista in São Paulo. Curiously, I found Alice to be considerably more likeable as a character in Brazil than I had found her in London. This may have been because Marcia Nunes, who played the role, and Sylvia Jatobá as Al, achieved a playful, almost sisterly, empathy between ego and alter ego that was very different from the sinister darkness pervading their dialogue in the London production. Similarly, both Jimmy and Bill were played with an aura of warmth by, respectively, Marco Antônio Pâmio and Walter Granieri, which lent a humanity to the characters that was somewhat lacking at the Royal Court. Granieri's Lear-like stage persona in particular brought a tragic intensity to Alice's long-suffering husband. Perhaps the Brazilian cast was responding to a glimmer in Tom Murphy's text that Ian Rickson and the London critics failed to spot in the corner of their looking-glass.

---

[1] A version of this text was previously published in *ABEI Journal – The Brazilian Journal of Irish Studies* (Number 9, June 2007). Grateful acknowledgement is hereby made to the editors for permission to republish.

[2] Nicholas Grene, 'Tom Murphy and the Children of Loss', *The Cambridge Companion to Twentieth-Century Irish Drama*, ed. Shaun Richards (Cambridge: Cambridge UP, 2004): 212.

[3] Christopher Morash, *A History of Irish Theatre 1601-2000* (Cambridge: Cambridge UP, 2002): 259.

[4] Christopher Murray, *Twentieth-century Irish Drama: Mirror up to Nation* (Manchester: Manchester UP, 1997): 226.

[5] Tom Murphy, quoted in José Lanters, 'Thomas Murphy,' *Irish Playwrights, 1880-1995: A Research and Production Sourcebook*, ed. Bernice Schrank and William W. Demastes (Westport, CT: Greenwood Press, 1997): 231-42.

[6] Lewis Carroll, *Through the Looking-Glass and What Alice Found There* (London: The Folio Society, 1962): 7.

[7] Ibid.: ix.

[8] Tom Murphy, *Alice Trilogy* (London: Methuen, 2005): 4. All subsequent quotations from *Alice Trilogy* refer to this edition, as it is relevant to the London production. Murphy revised the text for the Dublin production at the Peacock, and published the revised text in *Plays 5* (2006).

[9] Carroll, *Through the Looking-Glass* and *What Alice Found There*: 71.

[10] Ibid.: 74-75.

[11] Samuel Beckett, *Waiting for Godot* (London: Faber and Faber, 1965): 42-45.

[12] Carroll, *Through the Looking-Glass* and *What Alice Found There*: 131.

[13] Ibid.: 62.

14 | Recreating the Front of the Tapestry: Murphy's Version of *The Cherry Orchard*

Zsuzsa Csikai

Discussing the achievement of Tom Murphy's early plays, Nicholas Grene offers the conclusion that Tom Murphy 'did not write the "Irish" plays that an Irish playwright should'[1]. Similarly, it is arguable that when Murphy reworked Chekhov's *The Cherry Orchard* (1904) in 2004, adding a new piece to the list of numerous, already existing Irish Chekhov rewritings, he did not quite produce an Irish Chekhov expected of an Irish playwright. Murphy's adaptation, though undoubtedly an Irish-English version, is one that represents a move away from the Chekhov rewritings in the 1980s and 1990s Irish trend set by Thomas Kilroy and Brian Friel to thoroughly acculturate and domesticate the original texts of European classics. In contrast, it allows space to the Russianness, the otherness of Chekhov's play.

Indeed, Murphy's dramatization of Ireland refuses some modes of representation that might be seen as characteristically Irish. Considering the question why lasting international success seems to elude some writers, Grene explores the traits that show how atypical an Irish playwright Murphy is on many different counts. In plays like *A Crucial Week in the Life of a Grocer's Assistant* (1969), or *Conversations on a Homecoming* (1985), he resists the pastoral mode in his creation of images of Ireland, and what he presents is the grim reality of Ireland in the second half of the twentieth century without redeeming features. His dramatic language, often rooted in a strongly localized vernacular, or his experimental style to achieve a fusion of words and music, and even going beyond the conventions of stage language, as Grene argues, would be likely to hinder his plays' appeal to a wider macrocosm of international audiences.[2] In his treatment of subject matters such as emigration, provincialism, or even love, reassurance, or positive resolution are hardly ever offered. Instead, the features of dark comedy and black pastoral prevail, where there is no chance for liberating laughter. His lyrical masterpiece, *Bailegangaire* (1985), is also seen as different from the conventional Irish endeavour to use history to shed light on the present, as the play's 'traumas have little or nothing to do with the colonial matrix of national and sectarian identity which underlies all the other retrospective history plays of the time'.[3] Instead, it is a play that critically comments on the Irish preoccupation with history, its maniacal and senile retelling of the past.

Murphy is also somewhat atypical in his treatment of Chekhov. His version *of The Cherry Orchard* is the latest addition to a long list of Chekhov rewritings produced since the early 1980s by Tom Kilroy, Brian Friel and Frank McGuinness. Murphy's Russian play, however, dissents in significant ways from what can be seen as the established mode of Irish rewriting of Chekhov, as well as other Russian authors, exemplified by Kilroy's and Friel's seminal Chekhov adaptations. Justified by the perceived and often discussed similarites and affinities between the two nations' histories, the earlier adaptors of Chekhov tend to represent the Russian experience as an analogy to the Irish one. To emphasize the analogy, they carry out in the rewriting process a conspicuous Hibernicization of the plays. There is either a complete translocation of the original Russian play into an Irish milieu, as in the case of Kilroy's adaptation of *The Seagull* (1981), or there is a thorough domestication of the original through translation and adaptation techniques that downplay the cultural origins of the works, as in Friel's *Three Sisters* (1981) and *Uncle Vanya* (1998). Friel's rewriting techniques, manifest in omitting the culture specific vocabulary and specific Russian literary and cultural references approximate the plays to the receiving culture. More importantly, his method of adding lines and speeches with allusions to nineteenth-century Irish, and even contemporary Northern Irish reality, further contribute to the Russian plays' successfully resonating with Irish audiences.

It is not merely the observed similarities and affinities between the two cultures that underlie the choice of the domesticating/-Hibernicizing approaches to the translation and adaptation of Chekhov's works. There seems to be a wider concern with the intellectual decolonization project as the first re-translations and adaptations by Friel and Kilroy function partly to challenge the Anglicization of Irish culture through their aim to replace the existing Standard English, Anglicized translations. When situating Hiberno-English above Standard English as a language used for translating classics, these playwrights consciously attempt to bring about greater cultural assertion.

What the groundbreaking reworkings of Chekhov by Irish playwrights in the early 1980s challenged was the cultural influences stemming from the fact that the Russian author's works had been transmitted for the Irish audiences through English culture in the form of Standard English translations. Reappropriating world classics, Irish playwrights staged resistance to and challenged the idea that 'truth speaks received Standard English'.[4] By rendering the Chekhov plays in a distinctively Irish idiom, and adjusting them in a way that they reflect on Irish experiences, these retranslations and adaptations effect a displacement of the earlier Anglicized translations. This, consequently, contributes to the dismantling of the English cultural influence extended even to the representation of foreign literature for Irish readers and audiences. In other words, the Irish reworkings further a literary severance from the colonial legacy and at the same time enable independent cultural self-assertion. Creating Hibernicized versions of Chekhov, therefore, involves similar concerns to the typical Irish retrospective history plays that attempt 'to refashion the past'[5].

Murphy's *The Cherry Orchard* demonstrates a move away from the particular approach to re-translation, described above, that underpins the earlier Chekhov versions where post-colonial concerns were served by the most fitting translation technique, domestication[6] in the form of Hibernicization. In contrast to its predecessors, Murphy's *The Cherry Orchard* is characterized by a less politically loaded approach to rewriting, and signals resistance to such expectations. Instead of emphatic Hibernicization, his Chekhov version is marked out by its turning away from the trend to significantly adjust the original play so that it expresses Irish experience. Although his rewriting of the play slants it towards the target audience and its needs[7], it does not lose sight of its cultural origins either, which is conspicuous due to a certain measure of 'foreignization'[8] he infused into the otherwise domesticated base of Irish-English. If the Hibernicized rewritings of Chekhov gave the Russian works new relevance for Irish audiences, replacing the stale and alien Anglicized translations in Standard English, Murphy's Chekhov in turn represents a different way of endowing the play with freshness of perception and vitality of language. With less emphasis on Hibernicization, his version can allow Irish audiences to rediscover the Russian playwright once again, this time more on his own terms and with a greater awareness of his foreignness.

Before exploring in detail the ways in which Murphy's version represents a new approach to rewriting Chekhov, some consideration should be given to the place *The Cherry Orchard* has in Murphy's oeuvre. Although Chekhov's influence in Murphy's career is not generally noted as significant, two of his plays have Chekhovian echoes. Fintan O'Toole argues that in *The Orphans* (1968), for example, 'Chekhovian air comes from its setting in an English country house, a place which has the same relationship to London as a Chekhovian country house has to Moscow, and from the general paucity of outward action, the sense of a group of people frozen in time and space, hovering on the edge of some great catastrophic event in the outside world'[9]. He goes on to describe *The Orphans* as a play 'which considers the dialectics of change, and the consequences for the people concerned in it' (134). A similar summation would be relevant not only for Chekhov's *The Cherry Orchard* but also another of Murphy's plays, *The House* (2000), which has strong, exciting echoes of Chekhov's *The Cherry Orchard* in terms of plot, characters and subject matter.

The House, with its focus on the decline of the old land-owning classes and its concern with changes in lives arrested in the past, contains obvious parallels with Chekhov's *The Cherry Orchard*. As Csilla Bertha notes, 'at the beginning of the play one can almost hear Chekhov's axes felling the trees in the orchard and see the quietly decaying world of the three (de Burca) sisters'[10]. It is true, however, as Bertha also remarks, that Murphy's world is different from Chekhov's, in that *The House* 'dramatises mid-twentieth-century Irish historical and social reality' (215), and especially an emotional condition Murphy describes as 'a most curious guilt'[11] typical of Irish emigrants, which easily spills over into violence. Nonetheless, there are certainly strong resemblances between Chekhov's and Murphy's plays. The protagonist of *The House*, Christy, is from the underclass like Lopakhin, and his obsessive bond to Mrs de Burca, owner of a Big House, and a mother substitute for him, strongly recalls Lopakhin's devotion to Ranyevskaya, similarly rooted in emotionally charged childhood experience. When hit as a young boy by his drunken peasant father, Lopakhin was comforted by Ranyevskaya, which makes him grateful and emotionally attached to her. Likewise, Christy used to come to the Big House as a child in search of a home begging Mrs de Burca once: 'I'd like to be in this family, please'[12]. Also, Christy's adoration of Mrs de Burca and his relationship to one of her daughters, that is, the unrealized attraction between him and Marie, resembles very closely the emotional tensions of the trio of Lophakhin, Ranyevskaya, and her step-daughter, Varya. When the Big House is for sale, Christy, like Lopakhin, is determined to buy it, which entails a series of destructive acts affecting not the estate, as in the Russian play, but human lives.

What makes *The Cherry Orchard* conveniently fit in with Murphy's oeuvre is that it can function as a site for the playwright's intense exploration of the meaning of home, a preoccupation central to his original plays. The playwright identifies the theme of finding and losing home as a central theme in Irish literature in general, but with regard to his own works he says: 'In recent times I noticed that the recurring theme seems to be the search for home. What that 'home' means, I am not sure. [...] Now, I see it more as a search for the self, for peace, for harmony.'[13] Elsewhere Murphy says: 'I seem to be coming at the subject of the search for home, doing different takes on it, sometimes more sophisticated, sometimes more complex'.[14] His version of *The Cherry Orchard* is another such take on that haunting topic, with a focus on the characters' losing a home, their past, and the way they are trapped by that past.

Murphy's treatment of the Russian play, as I have argued earlier, points to a new direction for the role of adaptations and translations of classics by Irish playwrights. The rewriting techniques that signal this new approach, however, are more subtle than obvious, and not easily perceivable due to the tradition established by the earlier, Hibernicizing, mode of reworking classics by Irish playwrights. Interestingly, the trend of domesticating Chekhov into an Irish context has become so established in public perception that if an Irish playwright deals with Chekhov, the presumption, or even the expectation, is that he/she will produce a version in which the original is adjusted so that it reflects Irish historical, social or cultural issues. Only at first glance, and mostly due to the above mentioned conditioning, does Murphy's *The Cherry Orchard* seem to conform to the by now somewhat conventionalized approach of complete appropriation of the original. The back cover of the published version of Murphy's *The Cherry Orchard* advertises it as a 'fine adaptation with its Irish vernacular [which] allows us to re-imagine the events of the play in the last days of Anglo-Irish colonialism, giving *The Cherry Orchard* vivid new life within our own history and social consciousness.'[15] However, having looked closely at the two texts involved, i.e. the Russian original and its version by Murphy, and having made a thorough analysis of the rewriting techniques[16] Murphy employed, one finds that this description is not the most appropriate summing up of the nature and effects of Murphy's reworking of the play. The words 'adaptation' and 'Irish vernacular' suggest much wider implications than the textual reality of the version allows.

As for Murphy's use of the Irish vernacular, it must be noted that given an already well established trend of 'Irishing' Chekhov's plays, around 2004 when the play was staged, for an Irish writer to rework a classic in Irish-English as opposed to Standard English already seems to be more of a natural choice than a politically loaded one. In any case, Murphy's language use is not even conspicuously Hibernicized: there is no sense of deliberate Irishing, no emphatic or overwhelming use of Irish-English. It is not marked by a multitude of explicitly Irish phrases or idioms like Friel's or Kilroy's pioneering adaptations of Chekhov, where Irish-English idiomatic language lends a conspicuous characteristic to the plays. Indeed, the sentence 'have you no fear of God, are you ever going to bed?!' (27) stands out as one of those few exceptions that are strikingly Irish on the ears.

Regarding the Irish vernacular Richard York points out (in his discussion of another Chekhov version, Friel's *Three Sisters*) that there is a whole range of Irish-Englishes, from the readily recognizable Hiberno-English idiomatic constructions through obviously Irish-English words and phrases to a more pervasive

> range of rhythms that is more elusive to define but which most people would recognize as characteristically Irish, rhythms of accumulation and emphasis which are quite different from English brusqueness and self-effacement.[17]

York refers to the latter as a 'common Irish tone' (157), and if there is indeed such a thing then this is what characterizes Murphy's version of *The Cherry Orchard*, in that it does not display a pronouncedly Hiberno-English idiomatic language, but features the natural ease of everyday language that is English as it is spoken in Ireland. Therefore, although inevitably written in a language that has Irish rhythms and cadences, Murphy makes no discernible attempt at acculturating the Russian original; in fact, through various foreignizing techniques his translation ensures that the play is not completely deprived of its roots in the Russian culture.

It is noteworthy that the main feature of Murphy's Chekhov that tends to be singled out is that it allows the Irish to re-imagine the events of the play in the context of Anglo-Irish colonialism. This approach to his version is symptomatic of the extent to which Irish readers and audiences are conditioned by the earlier adaptations to see Russia automatically as a counterpart for Ireland, and to place all Chekhov adaptations within a distinctive Irish context. Beyond doubt, Murphy's *The Cherry Orchard* does allow a re-imagining of the events in terms of the Anglo-Irish colonial past, but only inasmuch as a close translation would. The reason for this is that the parallels between Chekhov's world and the world of the Irish audiences of Murphy's version are not perceivable because they are enhanced by any specific intervention on the part of the writer. They simply stem from the long recognized similarity between realities of Chekhov's Russia and nineteenth-century Ireland. Murphy's rendering of Petya's famous 'All of Russia is our orchard' speech can serve as an illustration of this point. The speech ends with the following lines in Murphy's version:

> We haven't come very far. We have nothing yet. No *conscious* attitude towards the past. Theories, melancholy and vodka. And to live in the present the past has to be consciously acknowledged, and atoned for by suffering and work. (43)

Even an Irish audience not conditioned, as much as it is, to search for Irish relevance in Chekhov's works may easily interpret these lines within their social consciousness as a reference perhaps to the stagnation of the Northern Irish situation, or in a wider sense as an allusion to Ireland's obsession with her past and the acknowledged need to come to terms with its legacy. Compare, however, a possible literal translation of Petya's speech:

> We are at least twenty years behind our times, we don't have anything yet, no clear attitude to the past, we can only philosophize, complain about despondency or drink vodka. But it is so obvious that in order to start living in the present we have to start to atone for our past, to get over it, but it is only through suffering, only through working ceaselessly and especially hard that we can atone for it. [present author's translation]

Murphy's, in fact, is a very close rendering of the original speech as far as the meaning of the words is concerned, so the sense conveyed in these lines derives strictly from the literal translations of *The Cherry Orchard* Murphy worked from. The playwright changed an important aspect of the speech, however, and this is its syntactic structure. Chekhov's fully grammatical, long sentences are broken up into shorter, elliptic ones, which is one means of successfully updating the language and a general tendency notice-able in Murphy's version, a feature to which I shall return.

It is not only the similarities between Russian and Irish historical and social phenomena that can result in the preconception that the creator of the version significantly adjusted it in order to approximate the original play to its target audience's cultural milieu. Certain typical, culture-specific elements are after all not that speci-fic to one single culture, and the preservation of such features in a version may also give the mistaken impression to the audience that they are actually the receiving culture's own features, added by the adaptor. The abundance of religious expletives is a typical culture-specific feature of the original Russian play preserved in Murphy's version that might, quite paradoxically, be mistakenly considered to be a consequence of Hibernicizing the text, if one did not have access to the original. Chekhov's play is full of various, typical Russian expressions featuring God and other religious figures, which Murphy neither cuts out, nor translates literally. The former would make the text sound like transparent, smooth Standard English, the latter too outlandishly foreign. (Translating them literally, and thus often distorting meaning and character, was one of the weaknesses of some earlier British English translations.)[18] Murphy consistently keeps these invocations and provides the corresponding English phrases appropriate to the given context: '*bog s nim sovsem*'[19] is translated as 'Bless him' (12); '*Gospod s toboi*' as 'God bless you' (15); '*Tsarstvo ei nebesnoie*' as 'God rest her' (16), and '*Gospod s vami, mamochka*' as 'Bless us mamochka, don't!' (23). Although the regular occurrence of such phrases in the play surely has a potential to produce an Irish feel to it, since the frequent use of religious expressions is a familiar element of Irish speech, it is, again, merely a characteristic of the original text, rendered 'faithfully' in translation. Thus, many of the features in Murphy's version that might superficially be judged as a consequence of his enhancing the Irishness of the play are, in fact, the result of his following the text relatively closely.

Although the above mentioned features of Murphy's *The Cherry Orchard*, that is the abundance of religious expletives, and the thematic concerns similar to those of Irish drama in general, stem from the original and not from a Hibernicizing approach, they nevertheless contribute to the Irish feel of the play. This is enhanced not only by audience expectation, but also by the fact that an Irish reader or viewer of the play will inevitably hear the dialogue in an Irish-English accent whether it is the stage version or its mental representation in the process of reading the play. However, the expectation that a translated play's language is a transparent, fluent Irish-English is hindered at least to some extent by the foreignizing measures Murphy employed in his version.

Foreignizing techniques used by Murphy include his treatment of the culture-specific elements in the original text, through which Russianness, or otherness, is allowed a strong presence in his version. As a general feature of his *The Cherry Orchard*, the Russian elements are emphasized instead of being omitted. A typical feature of Chekhov's texts is that they abound in Russian terms of endearments. This linguistic feature seems to support the stereo-typical view that the Russians are more emotionally explicit than speakers of English. Unlike English speakers, a Russian audience would not find anything amiss in hearing servants addressing their masters with such phrases as 'little lamb' and 'my loved one', not even when an old servant woman addresses a professor this way (as in Chekhov's *Uncle Vanya*). Therefore, a domesticating translation, in an attempt to ensure a natural-sounding language for their target audience, would likely omit these elements foreign to English (including Hiberno-English) ears and customs. To carry these features over into the translation is a very different choice as by doing so the translator challenges the illusion of fluency, and creates a foreignizing effect. It is the latter that Murphy opted for when he kept all the diminutive forms of address and terms of endearments, even adding a few of his own creation. One of the many instances of Murphy's preserving such phrases is when Dunyasha, a young housemaid, calls Anya, the daughter of her employer, '*milaia maia, radost' maia, svetik*' (literally: my dear, my pleasure, little light), which Murphy gives accordingly as 'my *little* [sic] darling,' 'Pet,' 'my *little* [sic] flower' (9).

Instead of toning down this Russian speech characteristic Murphy emphasizes it by adding more than there is in the original: the single word '*rodnaia*' is expanded in his translation into 'my pet, my love, my darling little sister' (28); Pishchik addresses Lopakhin 'Dearest heart' (70) instead of the emotionally less charged phrase in the original that means 'man of the greatest intellect', and Gayev, the landowner parts with the peasants with the words: 'Thank you, my brothers, my little brothers!' (62), which is the direct translation of the Russian phrase. What is more, Murphy even coins a phrase of endearment, which is a fusion of English and Russian when Anya calls Ranyevskaya 'mamochkamine' (24). This general preservation and even enhancement of the strong emotionality of the play's language is again detected in Murphy's rendering the line '*milaia maja, prekrasnaia komnata*' (literally: my darling, beautiful room') as 'sweet, darling, beautiful, *angel* of a room' (9, emphasis in original). Another typical Russian linguistic feature, the use of diminutive forms of first names falls into the same league as endearments and is treated similarly: all the numerous instances of the girls calling Ranyevskaya 'Mamochka' are preserved, just like the diminutives 'Petya' or 'Anyechka.'

A similar approach is employed in the case of the Russian custom of addressing people by both first name and patronym, which traditionally was rendered invisible by domesticating British English translations, as well as the domesticating Hibernicizing translations. Murphy's characters address each other as Lyubov Andreyevna (16), Peter Sergeich, (10), Boris Borisovich (20), Leonid Andreich (27) or Avdotya Fyodorovna (31), which will definitely convey a sense of foreignness for Irish audiences, and this in turn works towards preventing an automatic identification of the Russian reality with the Irish one.

In his subjective treatment of the original to give it a new life that is just as vibrant as in the original Murphy carries out numerous alterations by way of changing statements into questions and turning grammatically complete sentences into elliptical ones. These changes have the effect of updating, modernizing the play by approximating its language to the potential expectations of twenty-first century audiences, for whom a straightforward translation of Chekhov's full grammatical sentences in the characters' conversations may very well sound outdated. The fragmentation resulting from Murphy's turning of statements into hypothetical questions makes the characters and their way of speaking sound more realistic in a modern sense. Lophakhin, before Ranyevskaya's arrival, says in the Russian text: 'Lyubov Andreyevna has lived for five years abroad, I don't know what she has become like ... She is a good person,' etc. In Murphy, he is wondering: 'What will she be like after her five years abroad? She won't have changed ... The eyes, you know: the kindness in them. Always ...' (5). More questions, more gaps, more suggestiveness. Also, when in the original Pishchik says: 'my daughter, Dashenyka sends her regards', Murphy has him say: 'Dashenka? My daughter? ... Sends her regards' (16), which, too, suggests a subtext of humbly asking whether Ranyevskaya remembers her.

In addition to the above examples there is a host of other instances of breaking down complete grammatical sentences into shorter, elliptical ones. This is a way of avoiding the often too explicit spelling out of facts, already known for the characters, but necessary for the audience. The very first utterance in Murphy's play is: 'Well, it's in' (5), the referent of which becomes clarified only with a delay in the subsequent exchange: 'What time is it?' 'Nearly two'. 'So how late does that make the train?' (5). In Chekhov the first line clearly states 'the train has arrived.' Elliptical sentences become a salient feature: the characters in Murphy's play regularly converse in half sentences while the rest of the meaning is indicated in the stage directions, left to be expressed by the actors' gestures, non-verbal language, on stage. For instance, the complete Russian sentence, 'Esli bi ia magla zabyt' maio proshloe' (literally: If only I could forget my past, is rendered as 'If only I too could forget [*If only, I, too, could forget my past*]' (22, italics in Murphy); or the sentence 'Eto tak poshlo, prostite' (Literally: this is so vulgar!) turns into 'But cottages, "bungalows". (*The vulgarity of the idea.*)' (34), and finally Lopakhin, 'I'm going to! [*scream*]' (34) and Anya, clearly gesturing towards her brooch: 'Mama. (*Meaning "Mama bought it". Going off to her room.*) I went up in a balloon in Paris.' (12)

Another retranslator of *The Cherry Orchard*, Trevor Griffiths, convincingly argues for the need for such alterations of the original text when keeping in mind that the translation's aim is to create functional equivalence between the original and the target text. Noting that this type of expository method of introducing information to the audience is outdated, Griffiths observes that

> There is a history of realism that spans some eighty years beyond Chekhov: a realism of the stage, but also a realism of film. The craft of realism, of shaping realist texts, has advanced in some ways beyond what Chekhov was able to achieve – particularly in levels of obliqueness[20].

Similar motives and intentions are discernible behind Murphy's frequent alterations of the syntactic structure of the original text, the result of which is a vibrant dramatic language that conveys the same sense of immediacy, of being in the present that Chekhov's language had in its own time.

The first Irish adaptations and retranslations of Chekhov's works are very much part of Ireland's engagement with its own history: in them, Hibernicization served as a resistant translation strategy that gave a fresh insight into Chekhov after the long influence of Anglicized translations. But Murphy's more recent version, produced in the Ireland of the twenty-first century, demonstrates that the time has come when an alternative approach can ensure a different kind of freshness of perception. In contemporary Ireland, where the presence of foreigners in large numbers due to reverse migration is a significant new phenomenon, it is especially important to challenge audiences to react on more levels to foreign classics, and the foreign element in them, instead of almost exclusively on the level of Irish affinities and analogies.

In his introduction to *The Cherry Orchard*, Murphy discusses the distinction between translation and version. Having acknowledged the two literal translations he worked from, he describes the difference between the roles, as he sees them, of a literal translation and a version:

> The objective of a literal translation – to render in another language the exact contextual meaning of the original – differs from the purpose of a version. A version, as I see it, is more subjective and more interpretively open; it is speculative in its considerations of the "spirit" of the original and seeks to translate that "spirit" into a language and movement that have their own dynamic; the ordering in the version attempts to recreate what was alive, musical and vibrant in the original. A version, of itself, wants to avoid looking like the back of the tapestry. (n.p.)

The metaphor for translation he uses here comes from the comment Cervantes' Don Quixote made on literary translation: 'It seems to me that translation from one language to another, as long as it is not from the queens of languages, Greek and Latin, is like looking at Flemish tapestries from the back side, because even though you can see the figures, they are covered by threads that hide them, and you can't see the smooth texture of the front side.'[21]

Murphy's achievement is that he created a version that not only avoids looking like the back of the tapestry where the threads hide the original figures but equally avoids introducing new threads in his reconstruction of the tapestry that would colour the figures in completely new hues. He manages to make the original figures and colours alive and vibrant through his superb rendering of the play in contemporary Irish-English with an ease and naturalness. The language of his *Cherry Orchard* both allows the audience to enjoy a play that shows functional equality to the original, and to be exposed to a measure of Russianness, that is, to experience and be more open to the cultural climate of the original. With its attention to and preservation of the foreign elements, Murphy's version of this European classic reflects to some extent the need to cope with alterity for Irish society, which has been greatly influenced and challenged by the cultural and economic effects of its own success in a globalized world.

------

[1] Nicholas Grene, *The Politics of Irish Drama. Plays in Context from Boucicault to Friel* (Cambridge: Cambridge UP, 2000): 218.

[2] Grene, *Politics*: 217.

[3] Grene, *Politics*: 236.

[4] Richard York, 'Friel's Russia', *The Achievement of Brian Friel*, ed. Alan Peacock (Gerrards Cross: Smythe, 1994): 165.

[5] Grene, *Politics*: 235.

[6] Domestication (or fluent translation) as a method of translation means that in the translation process the original text is acculturated to such an extent that it becomes perceived not as a translation of a foreign text from a foreign language and culture but as one that sounds familiar for its new audience in terms of culture-specific elements, and fluent in terms of language. As the translation scholar Lawrence Venuti observes in *The Translator's Invisibility* (London: Routledge, 1995), 'by producing the illusion of transparency, a fluent translation masquerades as true semantic equivalence when it in fact inscribes the foreign text with a partial interpretation, partial to English-language values, reducing if not simply excluding the very difference that translation is called on to convey' (21).

[7] Because its aim is to make the foreign intelligible, translation, by definition, needs a domesticated base. The language of Murphy's Chekhov play is, of course, that of the dominant discourse of his country, English as it is spoken in Ireland. Even if it is important for the translator to register the otherness of the source text, as Venuti argues in *The Translator's Invisibility*, 'otherness can never be manifested in its own terms, only in those of the target language' (20). The specific target language discourse constructed by a translator can, however, function as a site of refusing complete domestication, and become infused, to varying degrees, with foreign effects.

[8] In an opposition to domestication, one of the most favoured modes of translation is neoliteralism, or foreignization, one of the first advocates of which was Friedrich Schleiermacher. In his lecture titled 'On the Different Methods of Translating', Schleiermacher argued that the best method of translation is when 'the translator leaves the writer alone as much as possible and moves the reader toward the writer.' The translator should do this by seeking 'to communicate to his reader the same image [...] he himself has gained [...] of the work as it stands, and therefore to move the readers to his viewpoint, which is actually foreign to them' (Schleiermacher, in *Theories of Translation: An Anthology of Essays from Dryden to Derrida*, eds Rainer Schulte and John Biguenet, Chicago: U of Chicago P, 1992 :42). Drawing on Schleiermacher's description of the two different methods, it was Lawrence Venuti who introduced the distinction between domesticating and foreignizing translation methods into translation studies. The foreignizing translation strategy follows the contours of the source text closely, retaining as much of its textual and lexical features as is possible. Foreignization can offer the target audience an exposure to difference; therefore, it prevents an imperialistic, assimilating view of other cultures.

[9] Fintan O'Toole, *Tom Murphy: The Politics of Magic* (Dublin: New Island, 1994): 132.

[10] Bertha Csilla, 'Poetically Dwelling: The Mythic and the Historical in Tom Murphy's *The House*', *Hungarian Journal of English and American Studies* 8. 1 (Spring, 2002): 216.

[11] Nicholas Grene, ed., *Talking about Tom Murphy* (Dublin: Carysfort Press, 2002): 96.

[12] Tom Murphy, *The House*, in *Plays: 5* (London: Methuen, 2006): 211.

[13] Mária Kurdi, 'An Interview with Tom Murphy', *Irish Studies Review* 12. 2 (August 2004): 234.

[14] Anne Fogarty, 'Tom Murphy in Conversation with Anne Fogarty', *Theatre Talk: Voices of Irish Theatre Practitioners*, eds Lilian Chambers, Ger FitzGibbon and Eamonn Jordan (Dublin: Carysfort, 2001): 362.

[15] Tom Murphy, *The Cherry Orchard* (London: Methuen, 2004), back cover. Subsequent references to Murphy's text are cited in the essay by page number.

[16] In this article I am following Gideon Toury's very broad definition of translation: 'a translation will be any target language text which is presented or regarded as such within the target system itself, on whatever grounds', as cited by Maria Tymocko, *Translation in a Postcolonial Context* (Manchester: St. Jerome, 1999): 35. In literary critics' discussions of the contemporary translations and adaptations

of Chekhov by Irish playwrights there is also a prevailing
terminological uncertainty.

17 Richard York, 'Centre and Periphery', in *The Internationalism of
Irish Literature and Drama*, ed. Joseph McMinn (Gerrards Cross:
Smythe, 1992): 156.

18 As Valentina Ryapolova notes, Trevor Griffiths, for instance, 'has
Varya down on her knees, kiss the crucifix she is wearing (!), and
pronounce "God is with you, Mama"', making her sound far too
outlandish, since Varya simply warns her stepmother Ranyevskaya
not to say foolish things. In the original, Varya's words, '*Gospod s
vami, mamochka*', are 'her reaction to Ranyevskaya "seeing" her
dead mother in the orchard, and mean "what are you saying
mother", "come to your senses", "it's impossible", "you're seeing
things", and so forth'. See Ryapolova, 'English Translations of
Chekhov's Plays: A Russian View', in Patrick Miles, ed., *Chekhov on
the British Stage* (Cambridge: Cambridge UP, 1993): 226.

19 The source of this and subsequent references to the Russian original
text is Чехов, Антон Павлович. *Вишневый сад. Комедия в 4-х
действиях*. Интернет-библиотека Алексея Комарова
<http://ilibrary.ru/author/chekhov/index.html>

20 Quoted in David Allen, ' *The Cherry Orchard*: A New English Version
by Trevor Griffiths', in *Chekhov on the British Stage*, ed. Patrick
Miles (Cambridge: Cambridge UP, 1993): 161.

21 Quoted in Howard Mancing, *Cervantes' Don Quixote: A Reference
Guide* (Westport, CT: Greenwood Press, 2006): xi.

Identity, Family, Religion

15 | Gender, Violence and Identity in *A Whistle in the Dark*

Aidan Arrowsmith

Although Tom Murphy's drama is rated by several influential critics amongst Irish theatre's greatest achievements, it is also, as Michael Billington has remarked, one of Ireland's 'least known exports'.[1] By comparison with contemporaries such as Brian Friel, Murphy's drama has received surprisingly little critical attention. In 2001, however, the Abbey Theatre devoted a season to Murphy's plays, beginning, appropriately enough, with his 1961 debut *A Whistle in the Dark*. This is a play that in many ways crystallizes the paradox surrounding this playwright. *Whistle* is rated by Billington as 'one of the great postwar Irish plays'.[2] Murphy himself, attending the Abbey event, was 'astonished', upon seeing Garry Hynes's production, at 'how extraordinarily well-structured the play is. I wish I could now structure a play as well as *A Whistle in the Dark*.'[3] And yet this play has enjoyed far less critical attention than it deserves. In later works such as *Bailegangaire* (1985) and *Conversations on a Homecoming* (1985), audiences (and critics) can clearly see the concerns that have become key to Murphy's oeuvre – the possibility of redemption via the past, for example. In *Whistle,* these familiar themes are certainly rehearsed, but in ways that are complex and less than obvious. This essay will discuss the complexity of this early play by focusing on the entangled issues of nation, migration, gender, and class which appear there.

My contention is that Murphy's concern with redemption in *Whistle* is centrally concerned with the problems and obstacles thrown up by working-class migration, specifically around notions of masculinity and national identity. According to Murphy, *Whistle* springs from his own experience of migrant Irish workers in England:

> When I started to go to England [...] whether to work on the buses or on the buildings or in pubs, I of course gravitated to places where my brothers were including areas which had become predominantly Irish ghettoes. There was an extraordinary cult of violence in those places that I still don't understand. Some of the reasons for the violence were that the men had money for perhaps the first time in their lives, and they did drink too; but much more importantly perhaps, they had a sense of being betrayed by the country of their origin here, and they also felt that they had betrayed that country. They were carrying a most curious guilt that they were very much inferior to the people they had left behind, and they were people who didn't belong in England. When they came back for the summer sojourn, they found they didn't quite belong here either. Strange dichotomies had grown up in them, and they didn't know what to do with themselves, with their freedom, with their money, with this fragmented, fractured identity.[4]

A Whistle is an exploration of the complex interpenetration of various discourses of identity, specifically class and gender, and of the effect of this over-determination upon ideas of the nation at a particular moment in the history of the (postcolonial) Irish State. In many ways, Murphy's concern anticipates that of postcolonial theory since Frantz Fanon, where light is cast upon the replication of colonialism's social and political structures and oppressions in the anti-colonial, national revolution. These archaic power relations are shown to shape the post-imperial nation, manifesting themselves with increasing strength in discourses of gender, class, ethnicity, and sexuality.[5] Thus the Subaltern Studies group of critics has identified nationalism and the new Nation-State as 'ideological products'[6] of colonial rule, and placed a critical emphasis upon the multifaceted over-determination of subjectivities in the new nation. These subjectivities, as Robert Young argues, are the product of the interplay of discourses of class, ethnicity, gendering, all of which have their own specificities:

> The conflictual structures generated by [the] imbalances of power [in culture] are consistently articulated through points of tension and forms of difference that are then superimposed upon each other: class, gender and race are circulated promiscuously and crossed with each other, transformed into mutually defining metaphors that mutate within intricate webs of surreptitious cultural values that are then internalized by those whom they define.[7]

The struggle into agency of groups 'othered' in these complex ways within the new nation constitutes what Gramsci calls a 'fragmented and episodic' history, and it is this disruption that has been the key focal point for postcolonial studies, as David Lloyd points out: 'Where subaltern historians like Ranajit Guha have been largely concerned with the problem of the *consciousness* of subaltern groups, with the historian's attempt to reconstruct their own understanding of their actions, postcolonial cultural studies have been more concerned with how the unrepresentable can be said to have subjectivity and, by logical extension, agency at all.'[8] Gayatri Spivak's famous question, 'Can the subaltern speak?'[9] is usually focused on the socially subordinate, female subject of colonization. But in Murphy's play questions of othering and of agency are explored in relation to male economic migrants, who move from a particular kind of 'postcolonial' Ireland to a particular kind of 'post-imperial' England.

A Whistle is set in the late-1950s and focuses upon the working-class Carney family from County Mayo. The economy of Mayo in the pre-Lemass late 1950s is shown to have offered little for men such as the Carneys – and even less for women such as their mother, whose absence from the play is marked. If, as Des Carney suggests in the play, Ireland presents no hope for the future, there of course remains Irish society's eternal safety-valve of emigration. Thus Des contrasts Ireland's 'postcolonial' poverty with the plethora of opportunities anticipated in England: 'There's too many bosses in that factory job. Slave-drivers. You don't have to lick no one's shoes over here.'[10] With their oldest brother having already emigrated to Coventry in the English midlands, the Carney brothers, along with Dada, follow.

Where Dada and the Carney brothers could be seen to symbolize an older value system of clannish loyalty and tough justice, Michael, in Fintan O'Toole's words, 'to his fingertips, is the new Ireland labouring to be born'.[11] The play thus locates itself on the cusp of a radical change in Ireland, the end of an era in several respects. Christopher Morash has argued that the Republic of Ireland Act of 1948 put paid to the last remnant of a 'forward-looking republicanism' that anticipated reunification: with the disputed twenty-six county Republic officially accepted, the decades of the 1940s and 1950s were characterized by an Irish culture that Morash calls 'post-utopian' – 'a culture which no longer trusts the utopian, which in some respects believes itself to have passed beyond utopia'.[12] The end of this political utopianism coincides with the end of the economic idealism of de Valera's nationalist protectionism. And the emigration of the Carneys certainly demonstrates a perceived poverty of future opportunity, one linked by Mush to the end of that particular form of nationalism: 'the economy [is] destroyed since the demand for St. Patrick's day badges fell.' (*Plays 4*: 26)

In place of romantic, protectionist nationalism, T. K. Whitaker's economic report of 1958 demanded 'post-nationalist' modernity. With Sean Lemass's installation as Taoiseach under de Valera's presidency in 1959 Whitaker's recommendation that Ireland should become an export-based and dollar-earning economy seemed the only way forward. As Terence Brown says, the future apparently depended upon modernization, liberalism, and globalization:

> An Ireland that had espoused nationalism for a quarter of a century and employed manifold tariffs in the interests of native industry was to open its economy to as much foreign invest-ment as could be attracted by governmental inducement. Furthermore, an Ireland that had sought to define its identity since independence principally in terms of social patterns rooted in the country's past was to seek to adapt itself to the prevailing capitalist values of the developed world. Within three years of this economic *volte face* Ireland had made a first application for membership of the EEC. In 1965 an Anglo-Irish Free Trade Agreement was arrived at with Great Britain and duly entered upon. [...] Economic growth was to become the new national imperative, in place of the language and the protection of native values and traditions.[13]

Michael's bid to escape his past thus parallels the attempt by post-Whitaker Ireland to move into capitalist modernity, an era whose rationalism contrasts sharply with the violence and tribalism symbolized by Dada. His aim is to transcend the mythological Ireland of the 'rural idyll' which, in Declan Kiberd's words, has now become a 'downright oppression'.[14] Where the rural peasantry of the West had once symbolized the national ideal, now 'social advance-ment and upward mobility' became the watchwords of the new nation-state; now, as Shaun Richards has shown, 'the mark of success [was] the acquisition of a professional position'.[15] In this new world order Michael's version of the attempt by Stephen Dedalus to 'fly by the nets' of his nation is a bid to wriggle free from his class identity – his status as the formerly-idealized Western peasant. He seeks an education and a professional position as a teacher. He wants to be a homeowner and the head of a 'civilized' (that is, middle-class) family. Like the newly constituted State, he wants to carve out a liberated, truly independent future. From the point of view of Dada and the boys, Michael's aspiration to the values of bourgeois modernity might well appear to be an aspiration to Englishness – his move to England and his marriage to Betty, an Englishwoman, merely reinforcing the impression of an attempt to become English. However, the growing antipathy felt by Dada and the family towards this 'new' Michael/new Ireland is more fundamentally about class. It is the frustrated cry of the Irish working class, left behind by the post-Whitaker 'new Ireland'. Just as the national revolution of 1916-22 was like a wheel, to use David Fitzpatrick's description, with the social and political institutions of colonial Ireland merely turning full circle to continue unchanged, the modernizing revolution of the 1960s served simply to reinforce the economic inequalities of the Free State.[16]

At the beginning of the century, as Cairns and Richards note, the 'sectional claims of women, political radicals, and organized labour', were subordinated 'to the struggle for independence'.[17] Now, mid-century, with the discourses of modernization and egalitarianism having much the same effect, it is the profound disillusionment amongst marginalized sectors of Irish society that emerges as a key concern in the work of writers such as Patrick Kavanagh and playwrights such as Murphy and John B. Keane. Keane's 1962 play *Hut 42*, like *A Whistle*, focuses on the western, working class male in England – specifically on a group of construction workers. As in Murphy's play, these migrant Irishmen are conflicted characters, torn between England and Ireland, two places they both love and hate. The relationship to Ireland of men such as these is, in Murphy's words, 'a lengthening chain'.[18] And, like Murphy, Keane has them voicing some frank assessments of Ireland's ignorance of their plight: 'a country is like a father, too. It should be judged by the provision it makes for its sons. If Ireland is to be judged like a parent, it must be convicted on every count.'[19] The desperation of these 'Irish buck-navvies' is highlighted in *Hut 42*, which ends with a plea directed home:

> We're the hopeless ones, the God-forsaken ones. [...] we're always lonely here. We're not Jack or Tom or Mick. We're Paddy! Tell them we want a place at home and they needn't think they're doing us a favour, because it's us, the Irish buck-navvies that's been keeping your poor in bread and butter over the bad years. It's us that sent home the dough when the politicians were barking like the Deacon's elephants. Every time, boy, you see a sad-faced woman at home handing an English pound to an Irish shopkeeper, bow your head. Let you

pray then for the soul of old Root and men like him who fell for the love of a small home in Ireland. (40)

Working-class men like Skylight in *Hut 42* and the Carneys in *A Whistle* are forced from their homes in Ireland not by the English, as nationalist rhetoric may have had it, but by economic decisions made by Irishmen. As Lionel Pilkington argues:

> A calcified class hierarchy [was] coupled with a broader sense of the hollowness of a public rhetoric of opportunity and the absence of a responsive national political authority. The nationalist, egalitarian and meritocratic rhetoric that dominated Ireland in the 1960s, that is, is diagnosed by these plays as a subterfuge for a rigidly hierarchical and socially oppressive society. Ireland's public discourse of democratic politics, of freedom of choice and equality, then, is an artificial carapace: something that is only half-believed in and that cloaks and worsens the psychological impression of inferiority that characters experience on a daily basis.[20]

In *A Whistle,* Murphy presents the Carneys as the inevitable product of Lemass's post-nationalist, capitalist modernity and the embodiment of its contradictions. Once, perhaps, these Mayo men might have qualified as the lifeblood of 'authentic' Western Irishness. Now, however, the Carneys of Co. Mayo are an embarrassment to the 'new' Ireland. Murphy clearly shows the intense frustration and the inferiority complexes that emerge amongst these working-class men. Harry, for example, burns with the memory of humiliations at school:

> (HARRY *takes a knife off the table and lifts locks of* MUSH'S *hair with it.*)
> **HARRY**. He [the schoolteacher] ever do that to you? [...] To see if they was any lice, fleas, on you, hah? [...] Why do they only have to do it to some? You'd imagine – They're teachers! – Polite! – Polite to do it to everyone. Any time I got pox or crabs, wasn't off the ones I thought I'd get it off. Lifting your hair like that. [...] And asking you what you had for your dinner – Not because he cared. And person'l questions. (*Releases* MUSH. *To* MICHAEL.) He never asked you I suppose?
> **MICHAEL**. Yes.
> **HARRY**. Yeh – yeh – yes. (42-43).

Harry moves on to another narrative about the teacher's attitude: 'He asked all the class one day' about their ambitions. The double sense of 'class' here indicates that Harry's resentment of Michael lies in a perception of betrayal by his own: Michael now represents the dominant culture which increasingly oppresses his brothers and himself. With the resentment comes anger, hatred, and violence:

> **HARRY.** Yes, we're so thick, stupid, twisted, thick! Oh, Michael, you are such a bright boy. [...] You worry about me, don't you? And then you apologize to them with the lovely white collars for me, don't you? And to them with the lovely white collars you say, "Yes, sir, I'm a pig, sir, if you say so, sir!" [...]
> **DES.** Oh, I don't know. I'm not a fool around here. All this talk is inferiority –
> **HARRY.** Aaa, inferior complex. I know about that one too. That's a very handy one always when any of us, the thick lads, says anything about the big nobs – crap faces.
> **DES.** Not inferior complex; it's an inferiority complex. (77-80).

The burgeoning eloquence of Des here reinforces the Carneys' sense of marginalization. As the youngest brother, and therefore the future, Des becomes the focus of the conflict between old and new, Dada and Michael. Fintan O'Toole declares that Dada 'embodies the dream of nationalist Ireland, the dream of a country in which the common name of Irishman would serve to diminish differences of class and status.'[21] Michael's post-nationalist aspirations might seem distant, but in fact echo closely Dada's own desire, now disappointed, for acceptance by the professional classes with whom he once shared drinks and conversation at his local golf club. Acceptance of sorts was, indeed, granted. But when he is offered a job as a caretaker by 'a little pip-squeak of an architect' (*Plays 4*: 60-61) Dada realizes that his belonging is approved only on the basis of his acceptance of inferiority. These rejected aspirations recur throughout the play both in Dada's protestations of intellectuality and in his bitterness and anger towards Michael, whose ambitions are so uncomfortably familiar to him. When, during an argument, Dada taunts his eldest son – 'Are you grown up over us?' (31) – the tense, Oedipal mirroring of the two is shot through with social significance. Michael's attempt to socialize himself and Des into a new identity is a kind of 'civilizing mission' in which he overthrows Dada to become father figure to his youngest brother. The new ethic of Lemass's Ireland is seeking to drag (or educate) 'the old West' into the twentieth century. When Michael sends money home for his brother to buy schoolbooks, however, Dada and the brothers – defiant to the last and ultimately taking refuge in self-parody – encourage Des to spend this on beer instead. As Harry declares: 'Our intelligent brother is warning him [Des] to keep away from us trash.' (53)

The Carneys thus exist at the complex crossroads of postcolonial identity. Their resentment emerges from their subjection, as working-class Irish men, to a complicated entanglement of discourses of nation, class and gender. Lionel Pilkington sees the Carneys' resentment as directed against a vaguely defined 'bourgeois "them"'[22] which presupposes, or produces, an 'us' around which a sense of identity might, in response, form. But when Dada attempts clumsily to explain his violence by linking it with pride – 'No man can do more than [his] best. I tried. Must have some kind of pride' (87) – it merely begs the question: pride in what? This is an historical moment in which the security of traditional, nationalist mythologies of Irishness is under challenge. The changing economy and unemployment are disrupting traditional notions of both class identity and masculinity, and any sense of nobility attached to the older set of values symbolized by Dada and the boys has evaporated entirely. The attempt by the family to locate a sense of identity – something in which to have pride – seems thwarted. Rather than stability, the subject positions offered to these 'subalterns' in Ireland result only in marginalization, and their subsequent migration to the (ex-) imperial centre merely exacerbates the struggle, multiplying the complexity of this postcolonial aporia of identity as the weight of a history of colonial stereotyping in England is brought into play. In this English context, the identity category of 'Irishness', in which the Carneys find themselves crudely placed, is revealed as a complex compound of residual stereotypes. As L.P. Curtis has argued, the Irish have, since the nineteenth century, been stereotypically identified as a 'race' of natural workers, as essentially or racially working class:

> The intimate relationship between class and race consciousness is borne out by the fact that the word race was also used throughout the [nineteenth] century as a synonym for class. The "double dose of original sin" with which some Englishmen discredited the Irish referred as much to their inferior social position as to their racial and cultural inferiority. [...] The lowly social and occupational status of the mass of Irish immigrants in Britain served to enhance their reputation of inferiority among respectable Englishmen.[23]

Pseudo-scientific racial studies of the time 'proved' the Irish to be 'deficient in reasoning power and in application to deep study'. Unsuitable, therefore, for self-government, they were, however, highly suitable for English labour requirements, as D. Mackintosh's contemporary 'scientific' study suggested: '[they possess] great concentration in monotonous or purely mechanical occupations, such as hop-picking, reaping, weaving, etc.'[24] The Irish are placed at the 'far end of the chain of being' according to various criteria. In *The Condition of the Working-Class in England* Friedrich Engels distinguishes the Irish from the English working class, suggesting that they constitute a fourth and lowest category within the proletariat, and thus pose a threat of contamination:

> The habits and the intellectual and moral attitudes – indeed the whole character – of the working class, have been strongly influenced by the Irish immigrants. So it is not surprising that a social class already degraded by industrialisation and its immediate consequences should be still further degraded by having to live alongside and compete with the uncivilised Irish.[25]

Liam Greenslade, in studies of migrants conducted from the 1970s onwards, has shown that the real effect upon the Irish in Britain of this history of discursive positioning has been to produce rates of mental ill-health which are 'the highest [...] of any migrant or ethnic/racial group'.[26] Greenslade argues that these trends cannot be divorced from a history of colonialism and colonial discourse:

> To be adrift from home and family, and away from the environment in which one's personal identity and sense of self is formed and sustained, pushes the individual further towards the extreme of colonized experience, that of being through others, towards an ontological alienation of the self. This characteristic of the colonized experience is encountered by all Irish people in Britain from time to time. It causes them to wonder who they are, what they are doing and where they are going. [...] The health of Irish people in Britain is not simply an issue of medical and/or psychiatric concern. It goes beyond that and requires a consideration of the fundamental con-struction of Irish identities and Irish culture as social and historical facts. [...] The psycho-physical health experiences of the Irish in Britain are inextricably related to a basic socio-historical relationship.[27]

The Carneys' experience in England is thus permeated by the rhetoric of imperialism and also that of nationalism. Michael's attempt to transcend his 'old' class identity is a sell-out both to the class enemy and to the old imperial enemy which it appears to mimic. When, out of both principle and fear, Michael refuses to support his brothers in a fight with the rival immigrant 'Muslims' he is seen to be disowning his own in familial, class, and ethnic terms. The presence of such rival groups is crucial in the dog-eat-dog context of life amidst England's underclass: 'Blacks, Muslims. [...] And if they weren't here, like, our Irish blue blood would turn a shade darker, wouldn't it?' (*Plays 4*: 10) The issue of respect here is less about 'race' in terms of skin colour than about social status. Tribalism and loyalty rule these streets and the prize of respect is achieved only through a violence that is equated with proper masculinity. As Anthony Roche comments:

> [The Carneys'] loyalties are organised around the family, with Dada as the hitherto undisputed head or chief from whom they take both direction and orders. This is virtually an all-male society, the men making up the warriors of the tribe, while the women are relegated to the background (as with Betty and the absent Carney mother, back home in Ireland). The society defines itself constantly by measuring itself against other tribes, settling scores and feuds in a way that is violent but which also has a personal integrity since it is delegated to no one else and has the authenticity of action.[28]

It is an awkward, void position to be in. Murphy himself has commented on the working class Irish in England as 'limbo people'. 'It is difficult to succeed,' Murphy continues, 'if you are caught astride the Irish Channel. Wrongs, real and imaginary, take a fantasy form in the mind. There is a great confusion'. And it is this confused 'freedom' from the anchors of home that, for Murphy, 'can produce explosions of violence'.[29] Greenslade and others have also linked the psychological impacts of migration to violence that has its roots in a longer history. Ashis Nandy, for example, shows that anti-colonial nationalism is often characterized by an exaggeration of gendering. A history of feminization in colonial discourse, Nandy argues, often results in a performance of 'hypermasculinity' by colonized males: '[A] second-order legitimacy [is given] to what in the dominant culture of the colony had already become the final differentiae of manliness: aggression, achievement, control, competition and power.'[30] Notions of masculinity and, usually as a consequence, femininity become intensified and dichotomized. Violence becomes the means of asserting a strong, 'authentic' identity, the basis of integrity and pride, as Harry shows: 'Them shams!' he says to Michael. 'You suck up to them, I fight them. Who do they think most of, me or you? [...] I can make them afraid. What can you do?' (*Plays 4*: 44)

The models for these exaggerated performances of masculinity so associated with Irish working-class men in England are readily available in Celtic mythology, particularly the tropes of Irish heroism associated with Cuchulain.[31] These, as Declan Kiberd has noted, offered Irish nationalists an important symbol of masculinity with which to identify during the revival period.[32] In many ways, the battle for identity that characterized the revival is repeated in the pressurized locations of the diaspora, and the writing of the Irish in England is full of these belated Cuchulains. In J.B. Keane's autobiography, *Self Portrait,* for example, he recalls meeting many of them during his time as a publican in Northampton. These men, with their 'mighty brown hands', lived to work, reports Keane, 'boasted about great feats of tunnel-digging, block-laying and masonry', and on one occasion at least, helped him eject a group of drunks from the pub: 'I got the back gate opened for him and he stormed in. He is a farmer's son, weighs about fifteen stone and stands about six feet two inches in his socks. It reminded me of Cuchulain breaking his bonds.'[33] In plays like *A Whistle* and *Hut 42,* such myths are a further discourse threaded into the weave of these men's complex identities. It is in ballads that this diasporic self-dramatization is given form. In Keane's play, for example, we hear offstage voices singing of 'The Paddy' who 'breaks his back by day, and fills his gut by night/The Paddy knows the good old pro's and the Paddy he can fight.' (*Hut*: 21) The plot of Keane's play revolves around the death of the renowned fighter Willie Canafaun, killed in heroic circumstances:

> **SKYLIGHT.** The fate of all fair fighters and Irish buck-navvies. A bottle on the head or a boot in the breast. (*Sings*):

> 'Come all ye brave buck-navvies, now, and listen to my lay;
> All of young Willie Canafaun, who died Saint Patrick's Day.
> 'Twas in the Crown at Cricklewood, his life he did lay down
> (IDRIS *and* DEACON *join in at last line.*)
> Our darling Willie Canafaun, the pride of Camden Town.

> They struck him down with bottles and they kicked him in the head;
> They kicked young Willie Canafaun, until that boy lay dead.
> So when the glass is lifted, lads, remember well to pray
> (*All join in last line*)
> For the soul of Willie Canafaun, who died Saint Patrick's Day.

> So all ye gentle Irish lads, who cross the Irish Sea,
> Who leave your loving mothers, this direction take from me:
> Beware, my lads, of Cricklewood; from Camden stay away
> (*All join in last line*)
> For 'twas there that Willie Canafaun died on Saint Patrick's Day.'
> (*Hut*: 12)

In *A Whistle* it is the link between class identity and the violence of masculinity that dominates, and so Michael's gender identity becomes another dimension in the social tensions between him and Dada. Once again, Des is the focal point. When Michael comments on the difficulty of keeping a lad as big as Des well fed, Dada bristles. Coming from this 'outsider', excommunicated now from the tribe, Dada takes this remark as a slight upon his role as provider. His reply, after a 'slight pause', that 'We want for nothing at home' (*Plays* 4:21), indicates clearly that Michael is no longer part of that 'home', however defined. Similarly, Michael's enquiry about Mama's health is met with equal suspicion: 'Slight pause. DADA feels there is an accusation in such questions.' (20) Though Mama never appears in the play, let alone speaks, the implication of domestic violence is clear. In fact, she has remained in Ireland where, in Claire Gleitman's words, 'she scrubs floors to support her windbag husband.' Gleitman continues: 'Women exist for the Carneys as economic instruments (that is, as prostitutes: Harry is a pimp) and as mothers. [...] Genuine Irish women, like the Carneys' Mama, disappear in the shadow of the Warrior-Queen or Sainted Mother. [...] Like the old crone in the first chapter of Ulysses who delivers milk to Buck Mulligan's tower, Mama is the poor old woman of Ireland shrivelled to insignificance.'[34]

Michael's wife Betty is another 'prominent victim of exclusion' in the play. Real women are obscured by the myths of femininity central to the masculine identity pursued by the 'boys', just as their own mythical self-image veils an inglorious reality.[35] Dada's violent defensiveness towards Michael is a denial of his violence against Mama, and his rejection of his son is also a rejection of his own (former) desires, now re-emerging in Michael's 'effeminate', bourgeois objection to such masculine authority. Thus social aspiration marks Michael both as a snob, and (as such), as less masculine than his brothers. His valuation of the cerebral over the physical, of education over manual labour, and in particular his pacifism, are a 'betrayal' of his class and national identity, which translates into a doubtful masculinity. We even hear that Harry climbs into bed with Betty, his brother's wife, at one point, presumably with the belief that she might prefer a 'real man'. Dada mocks Michael in this vein: 'But he's our educated boy. [...] He wants to live with men, and he hasn't a gut in his body. Worse, he wants to give the orders.' (30)

Whilst Michael's otherness in terms of class and gender mark him as a 'West Briton' in the eyes of Dada and the boys, the effect Murphy achieves is simply to highlight the ambivalence of any assertion of an Irish national identity in this context. Ireland's inexorable graduation into capitalist modernity offers few adequate identity categories for the Carneys, the new 'post-nationalist' nation being far from a postcolonial liberation. The Western, working-class masculinity of the Carneys, once so central to the mythology of the nationalist nation, is now excluded as the Free State becomes a Republic whose new ethic of 'meritocratic' Irishness serves merely, in Pilkington's words, as 'a mask for enduring class inequalities'.[36] Where once the utopian ideology of an Ireland-to-come might have won out, in the post-utopian context the Carneys' struggle with identity categories culminates in a marked absence of pride in, or declared loyalty to, the Irish nation state. Instead, their identification or affiliation, and any emigrant nostalgia for 'home' they may feel, is focused locally, upon County Mayo: their 'West'. Mush's comical ballad again draws on Celtic mythologies of masculinity to establish historical and geographical connectedness – Iggy being compared favourably to Brian Boru – but that connectedness is about a specifically Mayo identity and the 'proud' masculinity which they see as central to it:

> When Iggy crossed the Atlantic foam
> To England's foggy dew,
> His name had swam before him
> And all the tough-uns drew; [...]
>
> Oh, Iron Man, Oh Iron Man, we proudly sing thy name;
> If Brian Boru let us down, thou kept up Erin's fame;
> Thou beat and blackened men galore for the sake of liberty,
> From the dear old glens in sweet Mayo
> To the shores round Coventry. (68)

Similarly, Dada sings 'The Boys from the County Mayo' to celebrate his sons' victory in the street battle with the rival Irish gang, the Mulryans. On top of the class prejudices at home in Ireland, their move to England brings subjection to a further set of crude stereotypes. Their response is to assert their archaic, parochial tribalism – a working-class brotherhood based upon violence. Once again, declarations of loyalty to the nation state are significantly missing:

> Far away from the land of the shamrock and heather,
> In search of a living as exiles we roam,

And whenever we chance to assemble together,
We think of the land where we once had a home.

But those homes are destroyed and our land confiscated,
The hand of the tyrant brought plunder and woe;
The fires are now dead and our hearths desolated,
In our once happy homes in the County Mayo.

(*Chorus*)
So, boys, stick together in all kinds of weather,
Don't show the white feather whenever you go;
Be each as a brother and love one another,
Like stout-hearted men from the County Mayo. (69)

For Pilkington, 'Michael's father Dada and his brothers and friend behave like Irish stereotypes lifted from a British tabloid newspaper: that is, they behave like drunken and belligerent thugs.'[37] This is certainly true. However, Pilkington underplays the extent to which this is a conscious performance – and deconstruction – of the stereotype of an Irishness towards which they are in any case deeply ambivalent. Thus Harry's resistance to the 'scopic drive' of the 'British boys', 'smil[ing], looking sideways, and spitting over their left shoulders' is to play the role of 'Paddy', the stereotypical working-class Irishman. His is a performance of otherness – a grotesque and exaggerated caricature of stereotypical Irishness, working-class identity and masculinity.

> **HARRY.** You're not a Paddy?
> **MICHAEL.** We're all Paddies and the British boys know it.
> **HARRY.** So we can't disappoint them if that's what they think. Person'lly, I wouldn't disappoint them. (14)

Harry's position appears defeatist to Michael, who argues that 'You won't fit into a place that way'. Yet, in echo of his father's experience at the golf club, Michael's own life in England attests to the power and all-consuming nature of the stereotype:

> **HARRY.** Who wants to [fit in]?
> **MICHAEL.** I do.
> **HARRY.** You want to be a British Paddy?
> **MICHAEL.** No. But a lot of it is up to a man himself to fit into a place. Otherwise he might as well stay at home. (14)

Even as Michael rejects Harry's attitude, his attempt to transcend the stereotype and assimilate fails. For Pilkington, the 'irrevocable' social fate within which Murphy imprisons the Carneys is the 'disjunction between the people and the state, and the way that the natural ethical hunger of the people tends to be mocked and exacerbated by the available vocabulary of politics and of public and social life.'[38] Such a disjunction is merely compounded by emigration to England. As Murphy says, the play explores a sense of betrayal 'by the country of their origin', and equally a sense of not 'belong[ing] in England'.[39] Thus, in England, the ubiquitous stereotype of the Irish 'Paddy' becomes an insurmountable barrier to Michael's aims of assimilation – his intention to cross from blue-collar to white-collar, and from green-white-and-gold to red-white-and-blue. As in the new Ireland of Lemass, the envisaged utopia of undivided meritocracy proves to be far from the reality of England. A protean and apparently all-consuming stereotype automatically fixes him triply, in terms of ethnicity, class, and gender. Able to gain only factory work in Coventry, Michael gradually relinquishes his dream of becoming a teacher.

For Michael and his family, as for the Irish nation-state, any bid for independence or attempt to assert a liberated identity seems inevitably to repeat the structures it seeks to escape. Just as nationalist and anti-nationalist identities ape what they try to counter, and Lemass's 'postnationalist' modernity maintains and indeed reinforces old hierarchies, Michael's quest for independence in various senses ends up simply replicating Dada. What O'Toole calls 'the tribe, the dark past of history, the whole baggage of sentiment and romance which is merely the other side of violence'[40] prove inescapable for Michael. The sins of the fathers are visited upon the sons and Michael's Oedipal quest for independence from Dada (also named Michael) and all he represents turns out to be a futile attempt to deny the 'Dada' within himself. Michael's dream of education is merely a retracing of Dada's abortive footsteps, and his violence towards Mama is replicated when he finally decides to submit to his brothers' demands that he play his proper masculine role by hitting Betty. Further, at the play's devastating climax, Dada's violence towards his sons is repeated when Michael unwillingly fights Des – his surrogate son – and kills him. With Dada *isolated in a corner of the stage* at the end of the play, Michael adopts Dada's central position.

When Dada voices his bitter disillusionment with his unemployed life – 'Oh I wish to God I was out of it all. I wish I had something, anything. Away, away, some place. ... No. No! I'm proud. I did all right by my family. Didn't I? [...] Yah – yah – yah! I hate!' – Betty responds: 'Michael talks like that sometimes.' (61) The latter's own sense of failure in England, similarly, takes the form of an on-going wish to escape the confinements of the identity categories which restrict and trap him within social, ethnic, and gendered identities:

> **MICHAEL.** I want to get out of this kind of life. I want Des – I want us all to be – I don't want to be what I am. I want to read. I don't want to say, 'Yes, sir' to anyone. But I can't get out of all this. I could have had a good job. I could have been well fixed. I could have *run* years ago. Away from them. I could have been a teacher. I had the ability. (57)

By the end, Michael is back at the beginning, moving in circles in his attempt to fly by these discursive nets. Murphy shows the profound disillusionment of Irish working-class men who observe a 'new dawn' of Irish modernity but feel neither light nor warmth emanating from that rising sun.

---

1 Michael Billington, 'Which Side Are You On, Boys?', *The Guardian* 13 October 2001.
(www.guardian.co.uk/Archive/Article/0,4273,4275896,00.html) To coincide with the Abbey season, Trinity College Dublin hosted a symposium on Murphy; the proceedings were edited by Nicholas Grene, *Talking About Tom Murphy* (Dublin: Carysfort Press): 2002.

2 Billington, 'Which Side Are You On, Boys?'

3 'Tom Murphy: In Conversation with Michael Billington', in *Talking About Tom Murphy*: 95.

4 'Tom Murphy: In Conversation with Michael Billington', in *Talking About Tom Murphy*: 95-96.

5 See in particular Frantz Fanon, 'On the Pitfalls of National Consciousness', in *The Wretched of the Earth*, trans. Constance Farrington (Harmondsworth: Penguin, 1990): 119-65.

6 Ranajit Guha, 'On Some Aspects of the Historiography of Colonial India', in *Subaltern Studies: Writings on South Asian History and Society*, ed. Ranajit Guha, Vol. 1 (New Delhi & Oxford: Oxford UP, 1982): 1.

7 Robert J. C. Young, *Colonial Desire: Hybridity in Theory, Race and Culture* (London: Routledge, 1995): xi – xii.

8 David Lloyd, *Anomalous States: Ireland and the Postcolonial Moment* (Dublin: Lilliput, 1993): 9-10. See also Colin Graham, who advocates a postcolonial critique of Irish culture which might 'disrupt the dominance of the discourse of nationality in Ireland, reinvigorating the dissidences of gender and subalternity, undermining the complacencies of historiography, and moving towards a notion of Irish culture which views the dialogic hybridity of "Irishness" in empowered ways.' Colin Graham, 'Post-

Nationalism/Postcolonialism: Reading Irish Culture', *Irish Studies Review* 8 (1994): 37.

9 Gayatri C. Spivak, 'Can the Subaltern Speak?', in *Marxism and the Interpretation of Culture*, eds Cary Nelson and Lawrence Grossberg (London: Macmillan, 1988): 271 – 313.

10 Tom Murphy, *A Whistle in the Dark*, in *Plays: 4* (London: Methuen, 1997): 27. All subsequent references will be to this edition.

11 Fintan O'Toole, 'Introduction' to Tom Murphy, *Plays 4* : xii.

12 Chris Morash, '"Something's Missing": Theatre and the Republic of Ireland Act', in *Writing in the Irish Republic: Literature, Culture, Politics 1949 – 1999*, ed. Ray Ryan (Houndmills: Macmillan; New York: St Martin's Press, 2000): 71.

13 Terence Brown, *Ireland: A Social and Cultural History 1922 – 1985* (London: HarperCollins, 1985): 214.

14 Declan Kiberd, 'Inventing Irelands', *The Crane Bag* 8. 1 (1984): 13.

15 Shaun Richards, 'Refiguring Lost Narratives': 88.

16 See David Fitzpatrick, *Politics and Irish Life 1913-21: Provincial Experience of War and Revolution* (Dublin: Gill & Macmillan, 1977): 232.

17 David Cairns and Shaun Richards, *Writing Ireland: Nationalism, Colonialism and Culture* (Manchester: Manchester UP, 1988): 114.

18 Tom Murphy, interview in *A Paler Shade of Green*, eds Des Hickey and Gus Smith (London: Leslie Frewin, 1972): 227.

19 J.B. Keane, *Hut 42* (Dixon, CA: Proscenium, 1968): 19. Subsequent references will appear in parentheses in the main text.

20 Lionel Pilkington, 'Response To Chris Morash', in *Talking About Tom Murphy*: 35.

21 Fintan O'Toole, *Tom Murphy: The Politics of Magic* (Dublin: New Island Books, 1994): 67.

22 Pilkington, 'Response', in *Talking About Tom Murphy*: 38.

23 L. P. Curtis, *Anglo-Saxons and Celts: A Study of Anti-Irish Prejudice in Victorian England* (Bridgeport, CT: Conference on British Studies, 1968): 24.

24 D. Mackintosh, writing in the *Anthropological Review and Journal* in 1866, quoted in L. P. Curtis, *Anglo-Saxons and Celts*: 17.

25 Friedrich Engels, *The Condition of the Working-Class in England* (1844), trans. and edited by W.O. Henderson & W.H. Chaloner (Oxford: Basil Blackwell, 1958): 90.

26 Liam Greenslade, 'White Skin, White Masks: Psychological Distress among the Irish in Britain', in *The Irish in the New Communities*, ed. Patrick O'Sullivan (Leicester: Leicester UP, 1992): 201.

27 Liam Greenslade, 'The Blackbird Calls in Grief: Colonialism, Health and Identity among Irish Immigrants in Britain', in *Location and*

Dislocation in Contemporary Irish Society: Emigration and Irish Identities, ed. Jim Mac Laughlin (Cork: Cork UP, 1997): 51, 49.

28 Anthony Roche, *Contemporary Irish Drama: Second Edition* (Basingstoke: Palgrave Macmillan, 2009): 91.

29 Tom Murphy, in *A Paler Shade of Green*: 227.

30 Ashis Nandy, 'The Psychology of Colonialism: Sex, Age and Ideology in British India', *The Intimate Enemy: Loss and Recovery of Self Under Colonialism* (New Delhi & Oxford: Oxford UP, 1983): 8-9.

31 On navvy narratives, see Tony Murray 'Navvy Narratives: Interactions between Fictional and Autobiographical Accounts of Irish Construction Workers in Britain', in *Ireland: Space, Text, Time,* eds Liam Harte and Yvonne Whelan (Dublin: Liffey Press, 2005).

32 Declan Kiberd, *Inventing Ireland: The Literature of the Modern Nation* (London: Vintage, 1996): 25.

33 John B. Keane, *Self-Portrait* (Cork: Mercier Press, 1964): 64, 82.

34 Claire Gleitman, 'Clever Blokes and Thick Lads: The Collapsing Tribe in Tom Murphy's *A Whistle in the Dark*', *Modern Drama* 42 (Fall 1999): 318.

35 In this vein, Claire Gleitman argues convincingly that 'Murphy emphasizes the grotesque self-delusion that allows men like Dada to view themselves as great warriors fighting for a cause that in fact has done nothing to improve their own existence.' Gleitman, 'Clever Blokes': 324, n.7.

36 Pilkington, 'Response', *Talking About Tom Murphy*: 38.

37 Pilkington, 'Response' : 32.

38 Pilkington, 'Response': 35 – 36.

39 'Tom Murphy: In Conversation with Michael Billington', *Talking About Tom Murphy*: 96.

40 O'Toole, 'Introduction', Tom Murphy, *Plays 4*: xii.

16 | 'Complicated Thorns of Kindred': Murphy's Interrogations of Family[1]

Shaun Richards

In *The Politics of Magic*, Fintan O'Toole commented that Tom Murphy's work 'appears to have reached a destination with the exorcism of sorrow, grief and guilt that is *Bailegangaire*, presenting a body of work which moves from ferocious conflict to some kind of resolution.'[2] This judgement was made in 1987, only two years after the production of *Bailegangaire* had established Murphy as the most significant contemporary Irish playwright; this achievement being all the greater when seen in the context of his two other major plays of the early-1980s: *The Gigli Concert* (1983) and *Conversations on a Homecoming* (1985). Despite their differences of setting and style, what unites all three plays is their progression to a resolution of discord and discontent. In *The Gigli Concert*, while Irish Man retreats back into materialism, JPW not only sings like Gigli but releases the promise of 'O Paradiso' out into the sleeping city of Dublin, and in *Conversations* Michael's bleak 'They've probably cut down the rest of the wood by now' is countered by Ann's 'There's still the stream', and the play closes on her 'smiling her gentle hope out at the night.'[3] *Bailegangaire* is the summation of this impulse, with the final image of harmony as 'Mary gets into bed beside Mommo. Dolly is asleep on the other side',[4] healing the divisions which have scarred three generations of the family and, in the adoption of 'Tom' as the name of Dolly's yet-to-be born child, providing a quietus to the dead of a desolate history. Given this progression it was all the more striking that Murphy's next original play, *Too Late for Logic* (1989), dramatized family breakdown and the suicide of the protagonist; the initiation of a troubling series of plays in which 'family' was interrogated as the site of a seemingly irremediable series of traumas.

Murphy's work has always significantly focused on the family unit, specifically as it was both the initial point of impact for socio-historical change and the source for the reproduction of the crippling consequences of those changes across centuries. This is clearly expressed in *A Crucial Week in the Life of a Grocer's Assistant* (1969) where John Joe's mother is described as 'harsh in expression and bitter; a product of Irish history – poverty and ignorance'.[5] However it is his first play, *A Whistle in the Dark* (1961), which forged the template for his dramas of dysfunctional families.

Set in the Coventry home of Michael, an upwardly-mobile Irish emigrant whose aspirations for respectability are first tested and then shattered by the incursion of his violent brothers and father, the play is one of the earliest investigations of the effect of socio-economic changes on the rapidly-eroding cornerstone of Irish society – the family. Coming only a few years after the watershed *Report on Economic Development* (1958) the play takes on the full import of its opinion that 'It would be well to shut the door on the past and to move forward'[6], investigating the fates of those who, like Michael, pass willingly into the rootlessness of modernity or, like Dada, are left floundering in a now alien environment. Despite Dada's boast that 'Many's the conversation I have at home with John Quinlan [...] the doctor. And Anthony Heneghan – he's an architect. At the club',[7] the reality is that this 'little pip-squeak of an architect can come along and offer [him] the job as caretaker' (60-1), to which offer his impotent response is to steal Heneghan's overcoat. Underlying this bravado is a desperate realization that his social role and meaning has been eroded, confessing to Michael's wife, Betty: 'Oh, I wish to God I was out of it all. I wish I had some-thing, anything. Away, away, some place ...' (61). Her response that 'Michael talks like that sometimes' (61) illustrates that both father and son are caught in the consequences of 'detraditionalization' which 'entails the decline of the belief in pre-given or natural orders of things. Individual subjects are themselves called upon to exercise authority in the face of the disorder and contingency which is thereby generated.'[8] In such a changing environment

> people lose faith in what has been traditionally sustained by a way of socialization within a closed environment. The choices afforded by multivocal culture serve to confuse. Differentiation serves to undermine the exclusivistic claims and credibility of

what was homogeneous and therefore unquestioned. In sum, 'plausibility structures' lose their credibility – even collapse.[9]

The specifically Irish expression of this phenomenon is captured in Bord na Gaeilge's *The Irish Language in a Changing Society: Shaping the Future* (1986) which described Ireland as 'a fractious and individualised society, riven by inter-group conflicts and with few mobilising values for collective endeavour.' The result was 'a certain emptiness in the way Irish people now assert a sense of separate peoplehood, and a lack of consensus whether this is something worth asserting at all.'[10]

Fintan O'Toole has powerfully made the case that Murphy's work 'forms a kind of inner history of Ireland since the momentous changes which were set in motion in 1959' with the implementation of the *Report on Economic Development*,[11] and across his early drama it is clear that the condition of his characters is rooted in these precise socio-historical causes. However, with the developing interrogation of the values on which Irish society had been based, and in which meaning had been socially sanctioned rather than individually determined, an existential anxiety is generated. Michael's 'You don't know how to live either' (86), is a social condemnation of his brother Des but can progressively be seen as the initiation of a questioning of the extent to which individual lives and meaningful relationships can survive the removal of the rituals which once sustained them. In *Goodbye to Catholic Ireland* Mary Kenny wrote that 'Catholic Ireland of memory is for many people inextricably linked with the nest, the home, the mother taking out her Rosary beads, the votive lamp before the Sacred Heart.'[12] With the demise of these mutually reinforcing 'plausibility structures' the search for meaning becomes, literally, a matter of life or death played out on the fraught site of 'family'.

Christopher, the protagonist of *Too Late for Logic*, has deliberately abandoned his family and the 'Frightening, fossilising years of domesticity',[13] only to have their demands intrude into his life 'Just when I'm finding some meaning, some answers' (12). The play is a striking departure for Murphy, as Christopher is a university Philosophy lecturer, and while clearly set in the contemporary world of middle-class Dublin the drama is less specifically social than psychological. As is clear from the earliest drafts of the play the starting point of the drama was the fact that Christopher 'is going crazy. He is possibly bitter, soused, evil in a perverse fashion; filled with self loathing. (Why?).'[14] And rather in the way that Chekhov used the Russian landed-aristocracy, Christopher's preparation of a major lecture allows Murphy to investigate the answer to that question at a level which transcends the socially specific and, in the early drafts especially, becomes a meditation on existence:

> The place is that vast space, desolate; of the conscious mind asleep, the unconscious troubled, trying for the solution to a problem of grave and crucial significance. The solution to the problem lies in what the problem is, but what is the problem? That will never be discovered no more than lost innocence will be recovered. But something must be done. An act, a deed, a supposed relief that will bring back wide-eyed consciousness – Where was I? Where am I? [15]

Such extended musings are largely absent from the published texts,[16] but what remains is a discontent which permeates the play, especially with regard to a collapse of values on a European scale: 'An age begun in hope, an age of reason: for nothing' (7). A sense of malaise whose depth is underlined by reference to early drafts: 'The death of ideals, dreams, passions; Birth of sorrows, futility ... The esteem in which civilization was held had sunk too low this time.'[17] This is the context of Christopher's lecture in which he proposes to 'go for the reality principle, all-embracing life and what it means' (9); a quest in which Schopenhauer is central. For although Christopher claims that the philosopher's world in which 'Man had lost himself again' (8) and 'Suicide went rampant' is 'so unlike our own times' (55), his daughter, Petra's reference to the girls from her school, 'children', who attempted suicide and are now 'permanently damaged' (37), coupled with that of the five girls she knew who 'have done the trip to London for *that* little operation' (38), suggests that both moments are lost in a world whose God, in the words of an early draft, 'If God there was, he was an idiot, blind – Evil.'[18] That the discontent spreads wider than that of Christopher alone is evidenced by the suicidal intentions of Michael, his brother/alter-ego, and the case of Big Dennis who is 'a little depressed. He can't bask in himself, he can't bask in his family' (19). In such a world Schopenhauer's verdict appears to be vindicated: 'nothing whatever is worth our exertions, our efforts, and our struggles, that all good things are empty and fleeting, and that the world on all sides is bankrupt, and that life is a business that does not cover its cost.'[19] In such a context, the suicide 'wills life [but] is dissatisfied merely with the conditions on which it has come to him.'[20] This is the issue with which Murphy is grappling. As he observed in his notes to drafts of the play, Christopher's thoughts are 'Always back to suicide.'[21]

The 'will' which drives humanity to reproduce – and create families – is then the source of what Christopher refers to as the 'complicated thorns of kindred' (13) which he wishes to repel. However, in rejecting the pain of such attachments he drives himself to the other extreme of the solipsistic isolation of 'intellect' which results in breakdown and suicide. The play's structure is circular, opening at the moment of Christopher's death, after which he retraces the moments which led to his action in order to answer the question 'What has happened here?' (5), and closing when he arrives at an understanding. It is the ambiguous nature of that understanding and its implications for the trajectory of Murphy's subsequent work which lies at the heart of this most elusive of his plays and, as the many preparatory drafts and two published versions indicate, the understanding was not arrived at without profound authorial struggle.

Christopher progressively comes to understand that his flight from family 'to achieve that right of man to be left alone' (58) was not because he did not love them, rather because the 'the pain of boundless love' (58) made him agonize over the violent, or suicidal, fates that may lay in store for them. The thorns of kindred produce pain but, as he stresses, they are still '*Beloved*' (58). Finally he seemingly wishes to delay, or even halt his divorce, saying to Patricia 'there's no hurry ... Is there?' (73), and admitting to her that even though their children were produced by 'Blind will' (73) he 'didn't know how great' (73) they were until now. Earlier he had wondered 'Does it have to be suicide? Reconciliation: Too late?' (58), with the ever-present possibility of reconciliation being signalled most strongly as, in his penultimate action, he gives Petra a rose. As José Lanters notes, 'According to Schopenhauer, there is "No rose without a thorn. But many a thorn without a rose"' and in having Christopher make this gift Murphy suggests that 'the moderate happiness – that is, the relative painlessness – of a beloved thorn, a thorn with a rose, may be the best one can hope for.'[22]

The harsh truth of this fact is captured in Christopher's final recollection of Schopenhauer's parable from *Parrega und Paralipomena* of the porcupines in winter, who try to escape the cold by huddling together, only for the pain of being pricked by the quills of others to drive them apart, until finally 'they found a moderate distance from one another at which they could survive best' (74).

This is the 'bitter-sweet truth'[23] which allows Lanters to read the play positively in terms of those that preceded it, arguing that 'The method by which despair is transcended in *Too Late for Logic* is similar to that in *The Gigli Concert*[24] in that both Christopher and JPW pass through the abyss of despair into a form of resurrection. Similarly, Fintan O'Toole suggests that with this conclusion 'The broken families of his plays, the inadequate, monstrous, gapped scarred families of almost every play of his from *A Whistle in the Dark* onwards are given a kind of ambivalent blessing.'[25] Murphy's own struggle with the conclusion is expressed in a letter sent to Martin Fahy, General Manager of the Abbey Theatre, a matter of months before the play's premiere there: 'I would like more of an up-beat ending but the animal will not yield further to me right now';[26] clearly seeing the negative dimensions of the parable looming large. For, as one can conclude from Monica's image, embracing the family is a result of failure to function individually, the return really a retreat to mediocrity: 'You try to cut yourself off from the herd but you always come back to us' (23); itself a crystallization of Schopenhauer's view that the need for society 'springs from the emptiness and monotony of men's lives [which] drives them together.'[27] As Murphy noted in an early draft, Christopher 'does not know what he believes in'[28] and so 'has arrived at a nightmare time of life.'[29] In other words it is his lack of belief, indeed the absence of any belief system in the world of 'detraditionalization', which makes the family a means of hiding from that harshness; its 'warmth' being that of the cocoon rather than necessarily a place of reciprocal affection. Read in this context Christopher's reconciliation with his family is because he lacks the quality of the 'hero' in Schopenhauer's parable of the porcupines: 'Yet whoever has a great deal of internal warmth of his own will prefer to keep away from society in order to avoid giving or receiving trouble and annoyance.'[30] While this conclusion to the parable is excluded from *Too Late for Logic,* an interrogation of its implications informs Murphy's next play, *The Wake* (1998).

The play is a reworking of Murphy's novel, *The Seduction of Morality* (1994), whose conclusion reprises the optimism of *Bailegangaire* as the pregnant Vera greets the future: 'She would do up Mom's house and, before the new year was out, she would go home to live there with her child.'[31] Although the work closes on regeneration and the establishment of a home it is strikingly lacking in any desire for more than the biological unit of mother and child.

However, the opening of the novel is clear in its establishment of the conventional idea of family as a place of sustenance and sanctuary:

> She often thought of her family as the perfect place or state of happiness; even though the secret guilt of her unworthiness was important to her; through her mother and her father, her brother Tom, and now she had two younger sisters, she would be saved, she would belong.[32]

The drive of the novel, which is developed fully in *The Wake*, is that, as Murphy established from the earliest drafts of the play, 'The "flaw" in her character is her need to belong, and there is nothing to belong to except her family.'[33] But the family is staged as the locus of greed and rapaciousness in which even the closest ties of blood are denied in the rush for self-advancement and wealth. The drama is then a study of the process by which Vera, having cherished the idea that in her family 'she would be saved, she would belong', comes to see it as the location of an emotional contamination.

The play also echoes *Bailegangaire*, not least in Vera's verbalization of that play's final redemptive image: 'My grandmother. We shared the same big bed [...] Her bed. Sometimes I didn't have to go to school at all. "Ah stay there, child, it's too cold to get up." The two of us – I ask you! – My grandmother and myself, sitting up in bed for half the day – singing!'[34] However the joy of such moments as expressive of general familial harmony is undermined by the realization that 'the reason why I was sent to live with my grandmother was – has-to-be: She had a farm. They wanted her to sign it over. [...] And because my beloved grandmother wouldn't sign the farm over to them, to punish her they brought me home' (138). The same callousness expressed by Vera's parents is repeated by her adult siblings who have clearly conspired to deprive the now blind grandmother of sustenance, telling a neighbour 'I'm sure you have more things to be doing than visiting old women. And tell your mother the same' (83), so that while 'she'd have lasted another ten years if someone got to her' (82) the result is that she dies alone, having fallen into the fire and, despite having crawled out, could not get up and lay undiscovered for days.

The play opens as Vera returns home from New York, where she works as a call-girl, believing that her grandmother has only recently died, only to discover that the death occurred months previously and her family simply failed to inform her; as a stage direction notes, '*A dream is about to move into a nightmare*' (82). And the name of this nightmare is 'family'.

The Wake has resonances of earlier plays in that Vera's family, and Finbar, her one-time teenage sweetheart, are socially determined in the sense used by Zola. The stage directions are characteristically: '*He* [Finbar] *is a product of a culture*' (85); '*The culture has defeated him* [Henry]' (97); while Tom's behavioural traits are '*ingrained in him, adopted from the culture*' (102). Here the family failings are frequently attributable to what Murphy referred to as the 'racial memory' of famine as a result of which 'Love, tenderness, loyalty, generosity go out the door in the struggle for survival'[35] and in which the weaknesses of 'family' are socially and historically specific rather than generic. However this is essentially a residual concern in his plays and the new focus, established in *Too Late for Logic* where the family lacks any of the characteristics of greed and rapaciousness, is with the relationship between the individual and their family, irrespective of the nature of the latter, and it is that which provides the thematic spine through *The Wake* and subsequent plays.

What Vera comes to realize is that her concern with belonging to a family is a distraction from the more positive goal of self-realization: 'All my life the feeling of belonging has eluded me: Why should I go on thinking I'll find it? The thought of here *hasn't* kept me going: the thought of here cripples me' (124). And finally she resolves to sign over her inherited hotel to her family, not so much acquiescing in their collective acquisitiveness as sloughing off the ties which have bound her to this illusory ideal of belonging: 'Oh, I just want to – (*she shrugs*) simply – sign over a place to my family. Clean. Final. (*Smiles*) And begin again in a clean elsewhere' (179). The play closes as she prepares to leave for New York and starts to cry: '*Grief for her grandmother, for the family that she perhaps never had, and for herself and her fear at this, her first acceptance of her isolation*' (180). 'Isolated' was the first word used in describing Christopher in *Too Late for Logic* (5) and it is repeated again at the end of Scene One of that play (17), in the opening of Scene Four (44) and in the play's final moments (74). The critical question is as to the values Murphy is ascribing to that condition in *The Wake* which, in the earlier play, was one which Christopher was unable to sustain without the collapse into suicide and the too-late lament for the family he shunned.

The statement that Vera has moved to '*her first acceptance of her isolation*', coupled with her earlier desire for 'a clean elsewhere', suggests that this is a better state than that experienced by

Christopher for whom the first word linked to 'isolation' is 'bedraggled' (5). Vera's isolation can be seen as a more positive condition, especially when the play is read as the culmination of the early drafts where her desire for family was noted as her 'flaw'. In that context Murphy's draft comment on the plot progression and Vera's final state of mind is informative: 'the line of progression is a movement from the scarred self to become someone who is healed, someone who is to become her own woman. Eventually she admits to being totally alone in the world and she is a stronger woman.'[36] It is this idea of the desire to belong to a family as a 'flaw', even a pathological condition, which informs *The House* (2000).

Murphy worked on the play from 1997, but its origins are in a series of film treatments of the same basic story which date from 1990 and, as suggested by a working title for play, *Emigrants/The Golondrina*,[37] the subject is the seasonal return to Ireland of economic migrants, and their interaction with the communities they have left. The setting of the play is the 1950s when Ireland's economy was moribund and the society distinguished by an all pervading conservatism in which the returnees can be regarded as 'Paddies back from England [...] holding up pub counters every year here, day and night' (206). The class disdain directed towards the play's protagonist, Christy, by Kerrigan, the *parvenu* lawyer, has echoes of the humiliation of Dada in *A Whistle in the Dark*, just as Christy's livelihood as a pimp in England repeats that of Harry in the same play. Indeed Harry's savage indictment of 'they – they – they – they THEM! Them shams! [...] I fight them' (*Plays 4*: 44) could be projected forward as a rationale for Christy's determination to buy the house of the Anglo-Norman de Burca family as a demonstration of a changed power structure in which a conservative establishment had to recognize new economic realities. To this extent *The House* can be read as a reprise of Chekhov's *The Cherry Orchard* (which Murphy was soon to 'translate') where Lopakhin's bourgeois dynamism displaces the effete aristocracy from the Ranevsky estate. This, however, is to ignore the fact that in *The House* Christy's drive is based, as signalled in a working title for the play, on *The Pursuit of Love*,[38] and this takes its implications beyond the specific historical moment by which it is informed, and onto a psychoanalytic terrain in which the desire for 'family' is seen as a pathological condition.

For Christy, the de Burca house *is "home" to him – at least subconsciously* (187) and his shocked reaction to its disrepair is a determination to restore it to the ideal carried in his memory. However, the darker side of his concern is signalled by Susanne's speculative 'What does he *want* of us all these years?', and her question to Louise: 'Has he been sniffing around you since he came home?' (212). The animalistic sex suggested by 'sniffing' is echoed in her questions to Christy, 'and how far have you got with Marie? [...] What naughty things have you been doing to our Marie?' (244), followed, in the ultimate progression towards the object of desire, by 'Tell me, how far have you *got* with Mrs de Burca?' (245), for while the purchase of the house is Christy's nominal objective that is to enable him to possess rather than displace the family of four women. Christy has already had a relationship with Louise, '*now unsatisfactory to him*' (192), develops one with Susanne, and proposes that Marie remain with him in the house which his purchase seemingly forces her to leave. However, in that Marie rejects the offer, his sequential possession of the three sisters is halted. But, as he tells her, he is 'Eternally fond of you all' (292) – and that includes the mother.

In his notes for the first draft of the play, Murphy recorded Terry Eagleton's observations on Heathcliff of *Wuthering Heights* as 'the eternal child, [whose] adult wheeler-dealing is ironically driven by this implacable infant demand.'[39] Susanne refers to Christy as Heathcliff (212), but the fact that this occurs in the context of her questioning the sexual obsession informing his interest in the family suggests that Murphy's conception of Christy is informed by the 'infantile demand' rather than by ideas of class-informed economic aggression. Nicholas Grene noted that among the possible readings of the play is that of 'Freudian interpreters' for whom Christy's desire for an ideal family in place of his own brutal one 'derive(s) from disruptions of the ego originating in the infantile un-conscious'.[40] In his notes for the play Murphy recorded the names of both Freud and Lacan,[41] and it is this dimension which appears to have influenced the play's development, establishing a psycho-analytic 'deep-structure' to Christy's motivation in which the all-devouring desire for the 'family' is a destructive impossibility.

The play opens on Christy's arrival at the de Burca house where the mother repeats his childhood plea: 'I'd like to be this family please' (185). This crucial moment occurred after the death of Christy's mother, who worked for the family, at which point 'he started to come down here on his own, a little soul. And he arrived one day with his *bundle*. "I'd like to be this family please"' (212). The displacement of love for the dead mother onto the de Burcas is clear, but in wishing to 'be', rather than be 'in' the family, Christy expresses his all-consuming passion; as Susanne says to him 'I think you would possess us all' (244). Although the specific social conditions which led to the infant Christy's request are clear, as are those of a desire for home in nineteen-fifties' Ireland where the emigrants are displaced persons – 'Lads, ye belong nowhere, ye belong to nobody' (203) – the play's engagement is primarily with a psychological state whose origins, while social, are finally independent on historical causation and correction. As Murphy recorded in his notes for the play: 'because of childhood attachment to his mother. 1st she carried him down there (baby-fulfilled – stage), then they walked hand in hand down there (& out of the sight of the Father ...) Then Mother died and he transferred his longing/desire on to the de Burcas – the Object.'[42] In this nexus of desire Christy sexually possesses two of the daughters, and purchases the house but, in killing Susanne and confessing his crime to the mother, this comes at the cost of his ultimate objective – to 'be' the family. At the end of the play he stands alone: '*He chokes back a sob*' (293).

In closing on an isolated protagonist for whom belonging to 'family' has been the central concern, *The Wake* and *The House* have a degree of commonality. The difference is in the final response to the separation from the desired ideal; Christy's isolation is desolate while Vera's is the beginning of a journey to a self-realization. Both plays, however, have a specificity of Irish social moment recognizable from earlier works and in which that setting can be read, at least in part, as causal of the characters' condition. What is striking about *Alice Trilogy* (2005) is that, like *Two Late for Logic*, it occupies a middle-class world with limited references to an Irish specificity. However, its setting from the 1980s through to the immediate contemporaneity of 2005 suggests how far Alice's condition can be seen as illustrative of the full impact of 'detraditionalization' which strips away that national context; a historically-determined Irish society is no longer presented as the cause of family trauma, rather it is the site within which it is experienced.

The play's first sequence, 'In the Apiary', opens in '*an attic room*' furnished with '*a few objects of broken furniture*',[43] the exteriorization of Alice's disturbed state of mind, for this sequence is essentially a self-interrogatory monologue in which she speaks of family life as a 'slow death' (319) and, like Christopher in *Too Late for Logic*, seeks solace in drugs and drink, muses on the possibility of suicide and later (in sequence two) considers taking up 'Philosophy. I'd like to make sense of – well, myself for a start' (330-31). Her fundamental question, 'What's the complaint?' (309), echoes down the following two sequences in which Alice, aged firstly 'in her twenties' (299), then 'late thirties' (324) and finally 'somewhat younger' than her husband's 'mid-fifties' (348), attempts to comprehend a malaise whose origins lie in the void of material prosperity rather than in poverty.

That the condition is cultural rather than individual is captured in the second sequence, 'By the Gasworks Wall', when Alice engineers a meeting with Jimmy, her sweetheart of twenty-one years previously. His life, too, is one of material comfort but also distinguished by the sense that 'There is something missing. [...] Something has been lost' (334-35). And it is that same imprecision as to the precise nature of 'something' which marks Alice's reveries. Indeed, an almost inexpressible desire for 'otherness' characterizes her for most of the first two sequences of the play: *'She wants to breathe; she wants the freedom to develop/discover/explore her mind and spirit'* (319), and as time progressively proves this an impossibility she faces an emotional void: 'To get away. And away from what? Because if anything, there's increasingly nothing to get away from. [...] Things are getting emptier' (333). Time past is not so much a land of lost content as one of ungrasped, but ill-defined, potential, for which her family, and a husband distinguished by 'His *blindness*, his *mental deafness!*' (315), and suffering his own despair and incipient alcoholism, provides no consolation. And when she says to Jimmy, 'Your family', *'a simple brush of his hand deals with that'* (340).

The fact that Alice's intensifying despair covers decades, highlights the extent to which this condition has deeply pervaded the culture, for unlike the three previous plays whose plots cover days or weeks, there is no rapid progression to a clarifying climactic moment. Rather there is the monotonous repetition of the dull ache of dissatisfaction for which there is no defined social cause and therefore no clear correction. Only when faced with Jimmy's clear, and suicidal, mental instability does she declare that it is time she abandoned 'fantasising' and accepted her 'limitations': 'All I am looking for from here on in – I promise – is reality' (342-3). This, however, as she expresses it in the final sequence, 'At the Airport', is a life which is 'inescapably harsh, cruel, self-centred, ugly, sordid, mean. It is tediously suffocating and stubbornly bearable' (352).

In selecting an airport as the final location of a play centred on Alice's anomie Murphy makes the clearest possible visual expression of the condition whose nature he has been progressively divining since *Too Late for Logic*. As with the attic in 'In the Apiary', the airport is an expression of Alice's '*odd mental state*' (348) but also the locus of globalization's time-space compression and the attendant erasure of national 'plausibility structures'. While the social and financial status for which Alice's husband was working has now been achieved, they have 'so much money they don't know what to do' (350), her discontent is absolute, and this is exacerbated, rather than caused by the fact that she and her husband are waiting for the return of the body of their dead son. As in sequence two, Alice is plagued by an ill-defined sense of lost opportunities as her querulous 'And wasn't there a time' opens up speculations on the felt promise of the past and the poverty of a present which 'leaves a lot to be desired' (359). Alice's bourgeois affluence is a world away from Dolly's boast in *Bailgangaire* of having 'rubber-backed lino in all the bedrooms now' (*Plays* 2:107), but their shared discontent is of a piece.

As signalled by the off-stage sounds of the helicopter going to the Japanese computer plant, *Bailegangaire* is set in Ireland's historically-belated engagement with modernity which, as argued by Marshall Berman, 'promises us adventure, power, joy, growth, transformation of ourselves and the world – and, at the same time, that threatens to destroy everything we have, everything we know, everything we are.'[44] This is the context explored by Tom Murphy as he charts the fate of characters grappling with the loss of the once-sustaining 'plausibility structures' but, as argued above, the reconciliation of a fractured family in *Bailegangaire* is problematized, as subsequent plays interrogate the fraught relationship between families and individuals as family itself is, variously, the locus of the negative aspects of modernity or poor compensation for the loss and loneliness experienced in the aftermath of 'detraditionalization'. This is especially true for the protagonists of *Too Late for Logic* and *Alice Trilogy*, plays set in an Ireland which has entered what Seamus Deane termed a state of 'genial depthlessness'[45] which, as argued by Aijaz Ahmad, is created by a global economic change which 'subordinates cultures, consumers and critics alike to a form of untethering and moral loneliness.'[46]

This is the condition suffered by Alice as, condemned and abandoned by her daughters, and ignored by her husband in their moment of absolute loss, she reflects on the failure of her belief that 'What she was giving herself to had a purpose' and, in acknowledgement of that apparent impossibility, '*she laughs her hollow laugh*' (*Plays 5*: 359). In this lowest of moments the waitress confesses to Alice the recent traumatic loss of her grandson, who was killed by his own mother, and Alice '*inhales a long silent "O".* [...] *perhaps it is the first satisfactory breath she has taken in a long, long time*' (362). At this moment she declares that 'She loves her husband dearly. And she loves the waitress, Stella, and clings to her for a moment in sympathy and in gratitude for releasing this power within her' (362). However, while there is the declaration of love for the husband it is to the waitress that she turns: '*They take each other's hand, then embrace for a couple of moments*' (362).

Having reached 'some kind of resolution' with *Bailegangaire* which gave 'that – fambly ... of strangers another chance' (*Plays 2*: 170), Tom Murphy has ruthlessly dissected the ideal of the united family, exploring the pain of belonging as well as the agony of isolation. As Mary observed in *Bailegangaire*, there was 'no freedom without structure' (*Plays 2*: 120), but it no longer has to be provided by the family. *Bailegangaire* closed on the image of family unity, but in the closed and private world of the shared bed set in a world whose certainties are over. *Alice Trilogy* ends on an acknowledgement of the wider claims of human sympathy which provide a 'plausibility structure' in which Alice can find meaning in the 'savage reality of being alive, sharing humanity' (*Plays 5*: 359). While Alice's despair is clearly as profound as that of Christopher in *Too Late for Logic*, the Schopenhauerian pessimism is dispelled in the final confirmation of her belief that 'All would come well. She too, would you believe, was the world' (359).

---

[1] I wish to thank Dr Bernard Meehan, Estelle Gittens and Meadbh Murphy of the Manuscripts Department, Trinity College Library, Dublin, for their help in giving me access to the Tom Murphy papers.

[2] Fintan O'Toole, *The Politics of Magic: The Work and Times of Tom Murphy* (London: Nick Hern Books, 1994): 18.

[3] Tom Murphy, *Conversations on a Homecoming* , *Plays: 2* (London: Methuen, 1993): 87.

[4] Tom Murphy, *Bailegangaire* , *Plays: 2* (London: Methuen, 1993): 168. All subsequent references are set in the main body of the text.

[5] Tom Murphy, *A Crucial Week in the Life of a Grocer's Assistant, Plays: 4* (London: Methuen, 1997): 4.

[6] T.K. Whitaker, *Report on Economic Development, Pr 408* (Dublin: Official Government Publications, 1958): 9.

[7] Tom Murphy, *A Whistle in the Dark, Plays: 4* (London: Methuen, 1997): 26. All subsequent references are set in the main body of the text.

[8] Paul Heelas, Scott Lash and Paul Morris (eds), *Detraditionalization* (Oxford: Blackwell, 1996): 2.

[9] Ibid.: 4.

[10] In Terence Brown, *Ireland, A Social and Cultural History 1922-2002* (London: Harper Perennial, 2004): 344.

[11] O'Toole, *The Politics of Magic*: 19.

[12] Mary Kenny, *Goodbye to Catholic Ireland* (London: Sinclair-Stevenson, 1997): 394.

[13] Tom Murphy, *Too Late for Logic* , *Plays: 5* (London: Methuen, 2006): 13. All subsequent references are set in the main body of the text.

[14] Tom Murphy Papers, Trinity College Library, Dublin, TCD MS 1115/1/19/1.

[15] TCD MS1115/1/19/1.

[16] The play was first published by Methuen in 1990 and then in a revised version in *Plays: 5* in 2006.

[17] TCD MS1115/1/19/1.

[18] TCD MS1115/1/19/1.

[19] Arthur Schopenhauer, *The World as Will and Representation*, vol. II, trans. E.F.J. Payne (New York: Dover Publishing, 1966): 574.

[20] ibid, vol. I: 398.

[21] TCD MS 11115/1/19/14.

[22] José Lanters, 'Schopenhauer With Hindsight: Tom Murphy's *Too Late for Logic*', *Hungarian Journal of English Studies* 2 No. 2 (1996): 92.

[23] Lanters: 92.

[24] Lanters: 91.

[25] O'Toole, *The Politics of Magic*: 265.

[26] TCD MS 11115/1/19/13.

[27] Arthur Schopenhauer, *Parega and Paralipanena: Short Philosophical Essays*, vol. II, trans. E.F.K. Payne (Oxford: Clarendon Press, 1974): 625.

[28] TCD MS1115/1/19/1.

[29] TCD MS1115/1/19/1.

[30] Schopenhauer, *Parrega and Paralipomena*: 652.

31 Tom Murphy, *The Seduction of Morality* (London: Little, Brown and Company, 1994): 216.

32 *The Seduction of Morality*: 2-3.

33 TCD MSS11115/1/23/5.

34 Tom Murphy, *The Wake*, *Plays: 5* (London: Methuen, 2006): 91. All subsequent references are set in the main body of the text.

35 Tom Murphy, Introduction, *Plays: 1* (London: Methuen, 1992): xi.

36 TCD MSS 11115/1/23/10.

37 *Golodrina*: Spanish for swallow. The edition of *The House* cited in this section is from *Plays : 5* (London: Methuen, 2006), to which page numbers refer.

38 TCD MSS 11115/2/25/3.

39 Terry Eagleton, *Heathcliff and the Great Hunger* (London: Verso, 1995): 21. TCD MSS 11115/2/25/8.

40 Nicholas Grene, 'Tom Murphy and the Children of Loss', in Shaun Richards (ed.), *The Cambridge Companion to Twentieth-Century Irish Drama* (Cambridge: Cambridge UP, 2004): 217.

41 TCD MSS11115/1/23/12.

42 TCD MSS11115/1/23/12.

43 Tom Murphy, *Alice Trilogy*, *Plays: 5* (London: Methuen, 2006): 299. All subsequent references are set in the main body of the text.

44 Marshall Berman, *All That is Solid Melts Into Air* (New York: Simon and Schuster, 1982): 15.

45 Seamus Deane, 'Introduction', Terry Eagleton, Fredric Jameson and Edward Said, *Nationalism, Colonialism and Culture* (Minneapolis: University of Minneapolis Press, 1990): 19.

46 Aijaz Ahmad, 'The Politics of Literary Postcoloniality', *Race and Class* 36:3 (January-March 1995): 17.

17 | 'Of things that no longer matter': Alienation and Self-Understanding in *The Orphans*

Bernard McKenna

Tom Murphy's *The Orphans* explores issues of alienation and despair in the face of a changing world. Murphy's characters vocalize both a recognition of the issues and changes that confront them and their reactions to those changes in what is, essentially, a 'psychological melodrama'[1] set during the intense media coverage of the Apollo missions. The play, Christopher Griffin notes, 'portrays a group of "limbo" people who, at a time when people can reach the moon, still cannot reach each other.'[2] Griffin's observations suggest an intellectually challenging play, but he also calls *The Orphans* 'tedious.'[3] Similarly, Fintan O'Toole describes it as 'a well-made play about the homelessness of man in the world and the result is predictably cramped and static.'[4] He also notes that it is 'undoubtedly a weak play'[5] that 'collapses under its own weight.'[6] Robert Hogan is a bit more gracious in his response, describing it as 'a rather cold tragi-melodrama of a family, and I do not think that anyone connected with it has felt more than respect and interest, for it is not a piece to call forth enthusiasm or to generate warmth.'[7] Murphy, himself, was 'not satisfied' with the first production, staged at the Dublin Theatre Festival in October 1968. He nonetheless 'hoped the play will have improved very much by the end of the week,'[8] crediting only three weeks rehearsal time for the weak performance. As a result of its poor theatrical qualities, critics often bypass the play, preferring instead to focus on Murphy's more successful dramatic productions. Nonetheless, in 1974 Robert Hogan approached Murphy about publishing *The Orphans* as the second volume in the Proscenium Press's Contemporary Drama series, resulting in the availability of a play that perhaps reads better than it performs. On the textual level (as opposed to the performance level) the play does indeed present intellectually challenging scenarios that are both compelling and topical. Indeed, the text 'is concerned with a change which is very pertinent to what is happening in Ireland in the late sixties, the decline of religion and the rise of a new religion of technology.'[9] The text also presents complex associations between intimacy and avoidance, self-recognition and discovery, the new world and the old.

Very early in the play, Murphy sets up a confrontation between the old world and the emerging world, using the language of 'natural selection' to characterize the situation. Speaking to her cynical brother, Roddy, Kate asks him, with a touch of irony, 'how we poor earth-bound provincials should equate our home-preserves with the brave new world of ideas you would bring home'[10] In her reference to Aldous Huxley, Kate reveals her contempt and fear for the dystopian values of the new age; she soon mocks her brother's apocryphal perspective by calling 1969 the 'age of ages' (14). She contrasts the old with the new by reminding Roddy that 'the roof of my inheritance is still here,' where abides the 'same early Victorian roof with its turrets and cupolas and what-nots.' Roddy answers by reminding her that she had said that the 'family needed a mutation [...] if we were to survive' (10). The opening scene sets up a juxtaposition between those two worlds. The contemporary is a frightening world that displaces human volition with the scientific, with mutation, and with selection. The old world still stands. Sometimes, it is a quaint world of 'preserves', and, at other times, a world of careful artisanship, of the architectural flourishes of the Victorian Age. The play soon makes clear, however, that the new will prevail over the old, resulting in alienation and the loss of personal engagement. A component of that loss gives the play its title. As Christopher Murray observes, *The Orphans* 'thematically voices his [Murphy's] frequent assessment of our dislocation: if God is dead man is painfully orphaned.'[11] The characters understand the circumstances, but they prefer the values of the old world, of personal contact and of individuality. Kate articulates an analogy for their situation, relating Dan's story of the Ecumenical Council being like 'an attempt to amalgamate the branches of village smithies all over the world. You know: the futility of trying to reorganize something that no longer matters' (23). Likewise, the characters still have a need to come together, still have an instinct for contact with the divine, but that contact no longer 'matters.'

Kate elaborates on their predicament in two speeches in which she uses the phrase, 'not among the select.' In Act Two, she asks, 'What if we are not among the select? A body without the instinctual urges that have held good for millions of years; a mind, cluttered in a nostalgic daze of things that no longer matter' (32). Here, Kate plays into a popular notion of evolution (that man descended from apes), using the metaphor of a mountain gorilla in a zoo to stand for humanity: The gorilla 'just lies there, waiting, in a bed of his own excrement, watching himself, laughing at the sounds he is making. Hoping for something positive' (32). Kate's metaphor erases the Christian distinction between the human and the animal, representing both as creatures with an instinct for something meaningful but in circumstances that prevent the realization of meaning. The fair-copy typescript of the play reveals that Murphy structured the passage around a quest for the spiritual. In the typescript, Murphy inserts speculation on God and science immediately following the story of the mountain gorilla, writing that 'God was common property' but was 'exchan<g>[ed][12] for Science.' Murphy later expunges the explicit reference to God from the published text, making his message subtle but nonetheless clear. God is absent, especially in direct speculation about the human plight in the modern world; by excluding the reference to the divine, Murphy emphasizes humanity's orphaned state. The fair-copy typescript also reveals that Murphy chose to broaden the application of Kate's musings on the 'select.' In Act One, Kate asks of Moggie, 'What if *she* [my emphasis] were not among the select? Would she have no choice but to accept her lot and die out so passively?' (18) The fair-copy typescript inserts the following between Kate's two questions: '*Her* body without the instinctual urges that have held good for millions of years; *her* mind, cluttered in a nostalgic daze of things that no longer matter.'[13] Murphy's original intent had Moggie's circumstances stand for humanity's contemporary predicament. By changing the emphasis from Moggie to the gorilla, Murphy makes his speculations more universal and, ironically, values Moggie as an individual. He consciously chooses not to use her circumstances as a metaphor for all humanity early in the play. In doing so, he allows an audience to sympathize with Moggie as an individual character and not as an allegorical representation. Murphy then uses the change in emphasis to characterize the human plight. The characters are individuals but live in an age that places no value on the individual. In just the same way, Moggie's circumstances elicit an audience's sympathy; they are drawn to her. However, Murphy makes it difficult for an audience to draw a universal meaning from her suffering. Essentially, Murphy, if he had kept the passage in the published version of the play as it stands in the fair-copy typescript, would have enabled an audience to make an immediate connection between Moggie and the human predicament. By deferring that identification, Murphy forces readers to engage directly with Moggie and to feel her frustration before seeing her stand as a metaphor for individual stagnation in a changing world; humanity exists in a netherworld between the old and new. In her early conversation with Roddy about Moggie, Kate echoes such a reading by singing a children's song about The Grand Old Duke of York who 'marched his men to the top of the hill,/And he marched them down again.' Kate's rendition of the song at first seems a curious non sequitur, until she reaches the final lines: 'And when they were only half way up/They were neither up nor down' (19). Kate articulates the human predicament in the final words of the song. Humanity is 'neither up nor down.' Further, as frustrating and alienating as the circumstances seem, it does not matter if they are up or down.

As the play's action moves towards a climax, late in Act Two and in Act Three, characters express their dissatisfaction and sense of separation. Dan, in an angry exchange with Roddy, gives voice to feelings of futility and disaffection. He describes 'a rotting old Empire house,' contrasting his view of a decaying vestige of power with Kate's image of an enduring monument of artistry and personal expression. He then turns on himself, raving about 'prayers in case you'd go in the night' and 'love for the big baby in the big belly' (34). In retrospect Dan sees his faith based in fear of death and in the ridiculous; significantly, he chooses to characterize the conception and gestation of Jesus Christ in ludicrous terms. It is as if he unconsciously gives voice to his frustration with the creation and development of life. Further, he articulates his guilt at leaving the priesthood: 'Daddy [...] worked all his life for me. And the neighbours lit bonfires. Cause 'tis the finesht job in the world you might be afther sayin', though tishn't right to call it a job' (34). He references the hopes and dreams of his family and community, in connection with the priesthood: he understands that they, and he, saw a divine role in his choice, saw God's direct hand in the human world. His choice bound family and community together in work, hope and ritual; the neighbours lit bonfires to celebrate and to sanctify his choice. Recalling their actions, he demeans them by representing their use of language in a way that could be characterized as stage Irish. By demeaning them, he also reduces the value of their sacrifice and the hopes they vested in his vocation. He devalues their choices in order to dismiss the guilt associated with abandoning his vocation. He left the priesthood, in part, for love of Kate, and she, in Act Three, gives voice to her alienation from self and from Dan. She argues that she 'could become a cow with udders. In this age of ages, the beginning or the end, could that be some kind of answer? To flaunt a ridiculous bulge and bring forth a baby. What a ridiculous word, baby' (42-43). Just as she earlier described humanity in terms of an animal's experiences, Kate imagines herself as a grotesque, a human with animal parts. In a passage contained in the fair-copy typescript (later excluded from the published text), she goes further, asking, 'could the mere fact of an animal encumbrance help?'[14] In addition to reinforcing the animal nature of existence, the excluded passage reveals Kate's unconscious attitude towards maternity; she sees udders as an encumbrance, a burden. She also characterizes a baby as a 'ridiculous word' rather than an individual. Moreover, use of the phrase, 'bring forth a baby' is an unusual choice of words to describe giving birth and recalls the phrase of the gospel of Luke: 1:31: 'Behold thou shalt conceive in thy womb, and shalt bring forth a son.' Kate's use of language carries a biblical connotation. In addition, it is an echo of Dan's choice to describe Jesus' conception and gestation in ridiculous terms. Kate then has internalized something of Dan's attitude, not just towards Christianity, but also regarding the value of human life. Shortly afterwards, Kate asks Dan, 'Do you love me?' (43) He does not answer. In the typescript, she does not ask but rather states, 'I love you.'[15] Murphy's change reinforces a reading that highlights the effects of Kate's frustration. Rather than confidently articulate her feelings, she must ask if Dan loves her to determine if she has the ability to elicit love and affection. Declaring her love for him suggests an openness to pain, suggests a willingness to be vulnerable. In replacing the statement with an interrogative, Murphy emphasizes her insecurity. For Kate and Dan, their frustration and sense of alienation lead to feelings of vulnerability and isolation.

Fintan O'Toole notes similar thoughts of vulnerability and isolation for the characters, writing that the play 'has a purgatorial feeling of souls deprived of the vision of God.'[16] The play, to be more precise, has a feeling of limbo rather than purgatory, to borrow the Catholic characterizations of the afterlife. For the souls in purgatory, at least according to Catholic doctrine, there is the hope of seeing God's face. For the characters in the play, there is no hope of salvation. Life lingers, but it is a life of meaninglessness. Beryl, the housekeeper begins the play with a story: 'But here, this poor man died. And whereas he died, the cancer in his body was still alive. And now an eminent clergyman from the Midlands has made a statement. Yes. That it is wrong to bury the body, because the soul might still be alive in it. ... Wasting away like that for years' (7). Beryl's story, as O'Toole observes, is 'not just a parody of theological absurdity. [...] It also defines the atmosphere of the house in which there is no distinction or purpose, but signs of life persist.'[17] The story relates a world in which a cancer has replaced an individual as the house of a 'soul', a repository of the sacred in life. For the play, as for the story, a mutation lingers after the body perishes, and it is that mutation in which portions of society vest the eternal. Even theological speculation becomes not a source of reassurance but rather a source of anger and frustration. Moggie, in a rage, blurts out that she feels 'saturated' with the same old conversations: '"Do you believe Jesus Christ committed suicide?" Yes-I-Do-Now-shut-up! "Why are we here?" Because! Now shut up! [...] Let me lie down somewhere quiet, for God's sake, will you' (13). Moggie's rage centres on scholastic arguments concerning Christ's volitional death and on the purpose of life. She finds no comfort in an endless discussion, but, even more revealing, she chooses topics related to individual value and choice, themes with which the other characters also grapple. Moggie's emphasis on death and endless invective reveals that the truth, if there is any behind the answers to these stories, lies obscured by an invective born not of a pursuit of truth but rather of a pursuit of argument. The scholastic discussion then resembles a cancer that lives on after the body perishes and that remains and replaces the soul. If there is an anagnorisis in the play, it is that the characters realize their plight.

Thus in spite of her need to quell argument, Moggie realizes her situation. Her anagnorisis comes after an abortion placed her in a coma:

> I remember coming-to. It was dark; I didn't know where I was.
> But then I saw the light. Hah-haa! In a corner. And in this
> patch of light was a sort of man doing whirlings, and tubes
> sticking out of him all over the place. And I thought, if you can

catch one of his tubes you can pull yourself up to heaven.
Otherwise, you'll sink, Baby. And then I realised what it was.
And do you know what it was? The telly! You could see it had
been left on for days. You could see that. And a great big bloody
astronaut chirping away for himself in space. And the announcer talking about the strides the modern world was taking.
Christ, I said! But, Christ! (13)

Her reflections start with a common motif in 'after-death'
experiences: she sees a light and believes it will lead her to paradise.
However, her light turns out to be a television that has been left on
too long, and her Christ is an image of an astronaut. Not only does
Moggie's story relay a disappointed vision. It also speaks to a
saturation in technology. A man 'with tubes' fused in Moggie's
subconscious with a television news announcer as the new Christ.
Pulling on his tubes will lead 'to heaven.' Ultimately though, the new
Christ chirps in isolation, and 'Christ' becomes not a source of
salvation but rather an expletive, expressing anger and disillusionment. Moggie's anagnorisis reveals a troubled soul, willing to believe
but living in a limbo world of feints and illusions. Once again, the
instinct, the impulse for meaning exists but remains unfulfilled.

The moon landings become a motif in the play, providing for an
expression of the characters' anxiety with an emerging technological
age. Just as Moggie, in her vision, fused the technological and the
spiritual, the moon landings become confused in other characters'
minds with heaven and the divine. Beryl, concerned about the
problems with the astronauts' fuel system, asks if '[t]hey fixed up
that fuel pump' and if 'they're going up today' and, ultimately,
"[w]hat is the meaning of up there?' (39). Beryl's questions begin
simply enough. She focuses on technological problems, and the
questions, at least initially, betray no mistaken notions of the
astronauts and God. However, Beryl abruptly switches the focus by
asking about the nature of 'up there' or the heavens to which
technology has allowed the astronauts to ascend. Kate expresses
anger and frustration with Beryl's conflation, telling her that 'there's
no necessity for that alarm – Unless the fridge explodes!' (39) Kate
comically deflates Beryl's concerns by focusing on their immediate
surroundings; Beryl has been so preoccupied with the Apollo
missions that she had not defrosted the refrigerator and had been
neglecting her other household duties. Beryl's obsession and her
unconscious conflation of the astronauts with metaphysical
speculations certainly indicates that she lacks a spiritual component
in her work-a-day life, but it also reveals a mind that functions

through association rather than through reason. The play suggests that television, specifically, and technology in general serve such an intellectual life. Television offers ready-made forms of entertainment (no reflection required) and offers technological advancement as an end in and of itself: the moon landings become the focus of the technological age and the focus of the technology of that age that disseminates the news of the Apollo missions to the public. However, because the technology serves only to answer an immediate impulse and does not encourage reflection, and because of the nature of feeding and encouraging an impulsive (non-reflective) life, the characters remain dissatisfied. Ironically, the play, in the dissatisfaction, offers evidence of a spirituality. If the characters were content with the satiation of their impulses, they would not suffer anxiety. Anxiety, for Beryl, is a symptom of her lack of fulfilment, both in the moon landings and in her everyday life. She yearns for something more. Her conflation of the metaphysical and the technological suggests that 'something more' has a spiritual component. She never does find fulfilment although she approaches reflection.

In conversation with Kate and Mr Kyne (Dan's father) in Act Two, Beryl blurts out what she sees as a flaw in technological advancement, but she does not reflect on her observation. She tells Mr Kyne that 'automation is not an end in itself', reflecting her dead husband's '[r]eplacing his biological components with this – thing he drove on the building sites. Because he gave up his gardening too. [...] A dumper driver! That's right' (30). Beryl realizes both the limits of technology and its temptations; her husband abandoned his garden, his link to creativity. She also reflects on a particular aspect of her husband's relationship with the machine: "[H]e pulled this lever. (LAUGHING.) And this funny thing like a neck going up and down. And the funny noise, like laughing out of its mouth [...] A modern dinosaur.' She was 'ever so frightened' (30). Beryl's recall of her husband's laughter, regarding what is an obviously sexual motion of the machine reinforces her earlier observation about the dumper replacing her husband's biological components, but it also reinforces the play's attitude towards technology. The sexual motion of the machine produces fear and not life. Beryl's husband turns himself into a grotesque fusion of the mechanical and the human and gives expression to that fusion through the sexual motions of a machine. His transformation is consistent with the other characters' relationship with sexuality and reproduction. Dan's humour reveals an unconscious frustration with the creation and development of life. Kate offers a vision of her pregnant self that is a grotesque fusion of animal and human parts, and Moggie has multiple abortions. Certainly, Beryl comes close to reflecting on, what the play presents as, a central consequence of life in 1969. However, rather than encourage her reflection, Kate humiliates Beryl, saying that she's 'becoming most ridiculous' (30). Kate's response reveals her unwillingness to encourage reflection regarding technology and its consequences for creation. Interestingly, Kate attempts to help other characters live more self-conscious lives. Immediately before Beryl's reflections, Kate tells Mr Kyne 'to be sensible' and 'to be firm' with himself, yet she mocks rather than encourages Beryl. Kate's behaviour reveals that she cannot come to terms with a central problem in her life and that she cannot even discern the central issues that limit her growth. She unconsciously discourages the growth and development of those close to her in acts of avoidance. Kate's act of discouragement marks the turning point in the play. It occurs at about two-thirds of the way through the play. Prior to Kate's mockery, the characters had been discussing their circumstances. Their discussions could have led to reflection but rather deteriorate into avoidance, with the help of technology.

Mr Kyne's relation to the television typifies such a deterioration. He becomes childlike in his interaction with it, avoiding reflective conversation. Before Kate mocks Beryl, Mr Kyne had actively engaged in conversation with them, confessing that he works nights so that he will 'have someone to talk to night and day' (30), but after Kate's confrontation with Beryl he shuts down. He retreats. He now says to Kate that 'I-I was asking Moggie earlier about the telly' (31). His stutter betrays nervousness. He lacks the confidence he had only moments earlier, when he spoke of his 'nightforeman' who is 'a terrible bast – He's shockin'.' He commanded the room with his story so much so that those gathered 'laugh [with him] at his near slip' (30). However, after Kate mocks Beryl, he can only think of the television. When Kate ignores his request, he turns again to Moggie: 'I was saying earlier about watching it. [...] They're great men! I like the cowboys' (31). When Dan subsequently attempts to engage his father by asking if he 'remembers that piece of con-acre we got one year down near Gurrauns? We used to get mushrooms in the turfs of grass on the sides of the ridges', Mr Kyne does not look up and begins to run off: 'I'll just watch it for a small while' (31). The television provides Mr Kyne with an opportunity for immediate gratification, a numbing forgetfulness engrossed in cowboy shows. He avoids Kate's hostile mockery and even his son's attempt to reflect on their lives in favour of an interaction with technology. The impulse shelters him from pain but also from growth. He retains a simple disposition but does not reflect on his life, nor does he engage with others. He avoids anxiety by avoiding conflict but, as a consequence, also avoids meaningful interaction.

As the play moves towards its conclusion, the characters continue to speak at, rather than with, one another, while the disembodied voice of a radio announcer carries the unspoken anxiety and tension in news updates concerning the Apollo missions. Moggie wonders, 'Why me? Why always me? Why me already?' Her questions betray that she sees herself as a victim, as someone to whom things happen. She has no sense that she made choices which had consequences that shape who she has become. Because she does not take responsibility for her decisions, she feels that she cannot control her fate. She has no agency, yet, even as she says this, she is about to take control of her life. Kate lashes out with skepticism, speaking about '[i]sms', 'statistics', and '[p]hilosophical whims contradicting each other' (47). She deconstructs meaning, putting cynicism in place of understanding. By abandoning the potential for a reasoned self-analysis, Kate too defers responsibility for her actions. Her experiences become something that happen to her but are not controlled by her and lie beyond her ability to comprehend them. Dan also abdicates volition. He simply 'stands in the shed, face aghast' (where he has just been trying to seduce Moggie). He is mute in the face of his responsibilities and decisions. Just as his father retreats into an oblivion of television serials, Dan retreats into his shed, escaping responsibility and running away from his ability to control or reflect on his life. The characters' avoidance corresponds to the disembodied radio announcer's commentary, which raises the level of tension for the spectators. The voice speaks of a 'hail of meteorites, exposure to lethal radiation' and 'cosmic rays, excessive degrees of heat and cold' (46-47). All these 'hazards' lie beyond human control; there are things that simply happen. The juxtaposition between the characters' lives and ordinary (yet lethal) cosmic events explains why the Apollo missions attract the characters' attention. Not only are the moon landings the epitome of technological advance, they are also reduced, in the radio announcer's voice, to chance. The drama becomes a necessity to find out what happens rather than to discover how to shape what happens.

☙   ☙

Murphy's characters do, however, make certain attempts to control their lives through self-discovery and social interaction. Unfortunately, their attempts meet with frustration either at the hands of hostility or repression. Illustrating this point, Murphy begins his play, unusually for him, relating art and life inter-rogatively as if re-writing Virginia Woolf's *To the Lighthouse* for a new, confused age. Murphy's juxtaposition of Kate's painting with the characters' lives within the house reinforces the insularity of the group within the house, distanced from the harsh realities of the world. They are distanced also from themselves and from each other, apparently ill-equipped to deal either with the own struggles or the rapid societal changes that surround them. Like Lily Briscoe, Kate responds to disorder with painting and, like Briscoe, attempts to impose an aesthetic unity onto those in her home. Through creativity, Kate attempts to come to terms with her environment and with her circumstances, but her attempt does not catalyze introspection but rather deteriorates into trivial conversation. Kate's behaviour reveals the distinction between human relations and aesthetic relations.

The play opens in tableau, a balanced and ordered aesthetic, with Kate 'painting the group on the verandah', while her brother Roddy is asleep, Beryl is posing, and Moggie, Roddy's wife, heavily pregnant, is standing, 'Self-conscious at the moment; uncom-fortable' (7). Kate has hopes for the painting, insisting that 'we must finish it for Moggie's sake' (8). Kate, using the words '*we* [my emphasis] must', sees the painting as a collective project, as something that will pull each individual from his/her separate life and invest each in the lives of one another. Her focus on Moggie reveals that Kate perceives Moggie's troubled state and sees the painting as a way to help her. Painting, for Kate, offers the potential to imaginatively transform individuals' reactions to stressful circumstances. Unfortunately, Kate does not take advantage of the possibilities the discussion of the painting opens. Beryl finds the painting 'disturbing', filled with 'anxiety' and 'feeling' She tells Kate that she can 'identify with that' but ominously asks 'what does it mean?' and 'what is its meaning?' (8). Just as Kate will later humiliate Beryl, characterizing her as ridiculous, Kate shuts Beryl down now, telling her that '[p]ainting is about painting. It doesn't matter.' Beryl then retreats into memory, recalling 'blue mountains, and the sea, and sea gulls.' Beryl was ready to discuss the painting and its implications for her life. Kate clearly sees that the painting has such potential, describing the work as a collective product and insisting that it should be finished in order to help Moggie. More importantly, Kate 'performs' the production of the painting. She positions herself so that she may be seen painting and invites the other characters to '[c]ome and see' the work. However, Kate refuses to take advantage of the possibilities Beryl's observations offer and proceeds, in fact, to devalue Beryl's remarks, by telling her that any meaning contained in the painting, 'doesn't matter'. Beryl responds by discussing childhood memories that do not matter to anyone but herself. Prompted by Moggie to look at the painting Roddy, fearful, expresses hope that the painting is 'not abstract' (9) Roddy, on the surface, refers to the abstract style of a work of art. However, as his character develops throughout the play, it becomes clear that he is uncomfortable thinking abstractly about anything. Rather than engage in a discussion about meaning and the relative value of a work of art that might compel observers to think creatively and critically about their lives, Kate responds defensively. Kate tells him that 'the abstract is the easy way out of everything.' She does not challenge her brother to look beyond the obvious and into an image that might make an abstract idea or circumstance more clear. She defensively guards her aesthetic at the expense of a potentially productive conversation with her brother. He does not want to be challenged, and she does not want to challenge him. He dismisses the representation through humour, discussing only his image and calling it approvingly 'Superman. Reclining' (8). His humour reveals a sense of insecurity. He immediately focuses on the representation of himself, comically exaggerating his importance and dismissing any meaning the painting might have. However, perhaps emboldened by his comic turn, he does engage his sister in conversation, asking her about a childhood memory. Kate does not take advantage of the opening but shuts down the conversation and walks away. By closing off discussion, Kate ignores the possibilities the painting opens for meaningful exchange. She cannot open herself up to possibilities that lie beyond her aesthetic control.

Mr Kyne also has an opportunity for growth. He too can confront issues of personal development by returning to Ireland, his home, his wife, and his garden. However, at the end of the play, despite some evidence of self-awareness, he decides to stay in England.

Early in Act One, Dan establishes the association between his father's residence in England and his refusal to accept the truth. Dan tells Kate and Moggie that his father 'was working in England, and when I left the priesthood he wouldn't go home, back to Ireland anymore' (22). Dan speculates that his father is embarrassed or ashamed over the scandal – as it was in the 1960s – of a priest abandoning his vocation, but cannot be certain because his father 'wouldn't talk about it' even though Dan took the trouble to go and see him. Mr Kyne shut down a dialogue between himself and his son that would have strengthened their relationship and would have allowed the father to come to terms with his son's decision to leave the priesthood. At the end of the play, Mr Kyne seems to have grown. He tells Dan that he's 'not blaming you at all. You shouldn't have been pushed into it.' Mr Kyne adds that he and his wife, 'had a lot of high notions. We were only thinking of ourselves, and we were proud. And them things have to be paid for. Not your fault' (45). Mr Kyne confronts the issues of guilt and shame and places them on himself and his wife. His dialogue with his son suggests that Dan has no reason for shame and guilt. Essentially, he does try to relieve Dan of some of the burdens associated with his decision, but Mr Kyne's gesture still vests shame in Dan's actions; Kyne simply internalizes the guilt and blame he had visited upon his son. Kyne's gesture is well intentioned but ultimately unsatisfactory. It is likely that his reasons for confessing self-blame to Dan are akin to his reasons for not accepting a lift to the station. When Kate offers him a ride, Kyne says that he 'think[s] a bus passes soon down the road. I'd rather not be upsetting ye and slip off quiet' (44).[18] By taking Dan's shame and guilt onto himself Kyne leaves behind him a seemingly tranquil scene: he has told his son that he should not feel guilty about his choices, but, in reality, Kyne still attributes guilt to those choices, indicating that he has not really grown, that he has not confronted the truth, but rather that he has simply temporarily defused an uncomfortable moment. He leaves the house but not to return to Ireland but to a place of psychological stagnation. He too is in his way orphaned.

Dan also appears to make progress, in terms of self-analysis and growth, only to stagnate in the end. He confronts Moggie with his love for her. After listening to her tell him about her abortions and her desire to have a baby, he 'touches her – the gesture half-sexual, half blessing' and whispers her name. Act Two ends with her walking away. Rather than confront her, he 'starts to tidy up' (37).

He doesn't follow through on his gesture of love. Like his father, he wants to leave things quiet without any noticeable disturbance, and, like his father, Dan leaves the issue unresolved. Towards the end of the play, he again confronts Moggie: He tells her to come into the shed: 'Don't be afraid', he has 'thought of something else' (45), as yet unformulated. She responds nervously, telling him that she's been thinking about leaving, and this includes her husband Roddy; Dan asks her if she would give him 'a lift' (46), implying that he is interested in pursuing the conversation. But he lacks the skills. Stupidly, he tries to 'embrace Moggie, [to] pull her back into the shadows at the end of the shed', she struggles to free herself, Kate and Roddy see them, Moggie breaks free and Dan simply stands in the shed, 'face aghast' (47). Eventually, he comes out of the shed and joins the party for dinner. He never utters another word to Moggie or to Kate. He never follows through and confronts Moggie with the implications of his love for her and does not open a discussion with Kate about his feelings for her. He lives with a silent status quo that restricts growth and that will, as a consequence of repression, lead to fear and anxiety. The festering emotions will also lead to a sense that the characters do not have control over their lives. Close scrutiny reveals that Dan's gestures towards Moggie also contain elements of repression. In his effort to 'pull her back into the shadows', the play's symbolism suggests, Dan attempts to conceal (keep repressed) his feelings and relationship with Moggie. He can confess and act on his desires and love privately but cannot confront the implications of his decisions; he cannot take responsibility for his actions. Moreover, Dan persists in trying to embrace Moggie even as she is 'struggling to free herself' (46). Dan clearly does not listen to Moggie, much less enter into a relationship or dialogue with her. The inference is that he has been humanly disabled by the discipline of the priesthood and, in the presence of a woman he finds desirable, simply acts on his impulses. By not reflecting on his behaviour towards Moggie Dan reveals himself to be self-consumed and self-centred. His lack of self-analysis points towards truncated emotional development. He makes some progress, has some desire for communication, but, ultimately, he shuts himself down.

Dan's abuse also attempts to shut down Moggie and has the potential to damage her efforts at introspection and growth. Immediately preceding his 'half-sexual, half-blessing' gesture at the end of Act Two, Dan had achieved Moggie's trust. She tells him that she 'feel[s] better now', that she 'feel[s] fine now' (37). Dan had listened to her, had carefully responded to her disclosures by encouraging her to continue: Five times during her 'confession' he responded positively: 'Yes?' (36). He did not judge her. Rather, he allows Moggie to open herself up. He creates a safe and secure environment for her to talk about her troubles. Indeed, Moggie does disclose much that she has repressed, talking about her 'two abortions', about taking 'sixteen pills' (36) one night, about her relationship with Roddy, and about her new baby: she likes the idea. Her confession serves her well. It is a type of catharsis. She unburdens herself and allows herself to be vulnerable in order to talk things out. She grows, and her character is the only one who demonstrates such a level of self-awareness and understanding. Unfortunately, her sense of self confronts Dan's truncated self-awareness. He does honestly tell her about his feelings. He does make an effort to talk to her about himself and their relationship. However, by forcing himself on her, he not only demonstrates that he lacks the self-awareness to modify his behaviour in reaction to her wishes, but that also his impulse for listening and drawing Moggie out may reveal abusive tendencies.

Importantly, Dan's behaviour also corresponds with the changing views of the priesthood in Ireland that occurred in the late 1960s, anticipating the scandals what would devastate the Catholic Church in the following decades. In a scene that has now become all too familiar, Dan violates Moggie's gestures of intimacy. He used his skills as a counsellor to gain Moggie's trust. He then betrayed that trust through violation. In portraying Dan's self-indulgent violence, Murphy reveals a larger truth about the clergy in the late 1960s. In a 1971 study, Conrad Baars found that about 70% of priests were emotionally undeveloped and 25% of priests had serious psychological difficulties.[19] His study also focused on how those psychological and emotional problems manifested themselves in the form of sexual aggression and violation. Certainly, Dan's behaviour indicates at the very least an underdeveloped psychology and suggests far more serious problems. Moreover, in representing Dan as a former priest, Murphy demythologizes the role of the priest in the same way that the reforms of the Second Vatican Council 'included a demythologizing of the Church, its clergy and its rituals.' Furthermore, '[a]lthough the exalted role of clerical personages has diminished, the feeling of elitism among the clergy' remained.[20] Indeed, Dan attempts to assert his superiority over Moggie. He encourages her to make herself vulnerable to him and then attempts to confirm her vulnerability through physical intimidation. Indeed, his behaviour suggests that she may be physically appealing to him because of her vulnerability. He does continue to force himself onto her as she struggles to escape his abuse.

Moggie responds as if she had been abused. Initially, she blames herself, telling Kate that she 'slipped – I fell – I was feeling faint' (47). Though literally thrown off balance, immediately afterwards she begins to confront her fate and lashes out in rage at the 'useless forgotten shower of cock-sucking bums' and 'despicable bunch of idle twots' inhabiting this modern *Heartbreak House*. She builds on her earlier anagnorisis, moving from instinct through realization into action. She sees through the façade of the other characters, indicating that she knows they pretend to be what they are not, saying 'You don't know how to live anymore' (47). Definitively, she calls the house a 'burial ground'. In her cleansing rage, she leaves. Her self-assertion and her breaking with Roddy suggest that she has established self-awareness. Moggie alone acts morally, in a way that demonstrates volition, that reveals a level of self-understanding con-summate with genuine growth and change.[21] Even as the other characters gather for dinner, listening to the radio announcer dis-cussing the hazards of the Apollo missions, the sound of Moggie's car can be heard driving away. Kate 'remains impassive.' Dan may set the table for dinner to re-establish the old order but Moggie departs,[22] and her departure symbolically leaves the house and its inhabitants behind with their repressions and anxieties. Her de-parture also symbolizes a definitive break with the house and its inhabitants. In doing so, Moggie leaves an environment in which she was abused, which is no easy task. Her courage in leaving means that she must confront an unknown fate; the play leaves an audience on stage with Kate, Dan and the others. Moggie's future remains a mystery, in just the same way the astronauts' fate remains a mystery to those who stay behind, and those who stay behind are left with the sounds of action and self-assertion coming from the radio or from Moggie's car. For those who remain, change, self-control, and growth are matters that happen offstage.

∾   ∾

The Orphans, admittedly, did not stage well in its day. Yet it is an important text in Murphy's canon in that it addresses themes that were to find more successful dramatic settings in Murphy's other plays. Specifically, it is a moral play, in the sense that all Murphy's plays are profoundly moral: *Orphans* explores the new liberation of the 1960s, *la dolce vita* on a small scale, and with great compassion finds only lost souls incapable for the most part – Moggie being the exception – of coping either with history or with the new world, the moral space age.

Certainly, critical response to Murphy's other works touches on the same themes explored in *The Orphans*. As José Lanters observes, 'Murphy's characters are caught between two responses to the word: they are in danger of going mad unless they speak out, but they are prevented from speaking out by self-consciousness and guilt.'[23] Indeed, all the characters in *The Orphans*, with the exception of Moggie, feel both the need to speak out and the suffocating silence of guilt that prevents them from articulating their needs. *The Orphans,* however, lacks a theatrical appeal. Reading the criticism of Murphy's other works offers hints concerning why this play underperforms: Robert Welch, writing of *The Gigli Concert* notes that that play demonstrates a tendency 'to opt for a transcendence and hectic abstraction that itself is a form of toxic derangement. [...] These ambiguities, this rage, despair, and insatiable craving for something outside the daily tedium of the actual facts of bombing, cruelty, and atrocity, are gathered into the heaving and inchoate drivings of emotion in Murphy's theatre.'[24] Perhaps *The Orphans* lacks the manifest rage and insatiable craving present in Murphy's best works. Moggie ends the play with a rising crescendo of outrage that forces her to quit the stage but as she leaves she takes the emotional force of the action with her and leaves the other characters (and an audience) without an emotional resolution, resulting in a play that catalyses intellectual reflection but one that reads better as a text than it might perform as a drama.

---

[1] Robert Hogan, 'Where Have all the Shamrocks Gone,' in *Aspects of the Irish Theatre*, eds Patrick Rafroidi, Raymonde Popot, and William Parker (Paris: Éditions universitaires, 1972): 230.

[2] Christopher Griffin, 'Thomas Murphy,' in *Dictionary of Irish Literature,* ed. Robert Hogan, (Westport, CT: Greenwood Publishing, 1996): 889.

[3] Ibid.

[4] Fintan O'Toole, *Tom Murphy: Politics of Magic* (Dublin: New Island Books, 1994): 131-32.

[5] O'Toole, *The Politics of Magic*: 131.

[6] O'Toole, *The Politics of Magic*: 140.

7 Robert Hogan, *Since O'Casey and Other Essays on Irish Drama* (Gerrards Cross, Bucks.: Colin Smythe, 1983): 138.

8 Seamus Kelly, 'Record 37,000 Audience,' *The Irish Times* 9 October 1969: 10.

9 O'Toole: 134.

10 Thomas Murphy, *The Orphans* (Newark, DE: Proscenium Press, 1974): 10. Subsequent quotations from *The Orphans*, unless otherwise specified, are from this text, and page numbers supplied parenthetically will refer to this text.

11 'The Rough and Holy Theatre of Thomas Murphy,' *Irish University Review: Tom Murphy Special Issue* 12.1 (Spring 1987): 14.

12 The typescript is cut along a line that bisects the 'g'. The 'ed' is not present but suggested by the context.

13 Thomas Murphy, *The Orphans* (University of Delaware, Special Collections: Archives of the Proscenium Press, Series II, Box 5, F248): 18, my emphases.

14 Ibid.: 59.

15 Ibid.

16 O'Toole, *The Politics of Magic*: 132.

17 O'Toole: 132.

18 O'Toole: 44.

19 Conrad Baars, *How to Treat and Prevent The Crisis in the Priesthood* (Chicago: Franciscan Press, 1972): 7.

20 Thomas P. Doyle, 'Roman Catholic Clericalism, Religious Duress, and Clergy Sexual Abuse,' *Pastoral Psychology*, 51. 3 (January 2003): 189 -190.

21 Mr Kyne may also have left but his departure suggests more avoidance that awareness.

22 It is not clear whether Roddy leaves with her. He exits the house, calling after her. However, the car starts immediately and may have left him behind.

23 José Lanters, 'Playwrights of the Western World,' *A Century of Irish Drama: Widening the Stage*, ed. Stephen Watt (Bloomington: Indiana UP, 2000): 208.

24 Robert Welch, *The Abbey Theatre* (Oxford: Oxford UP, 2003): 193.

18 | 'Rituals of a Lost Faith'?: Murphy's Theatre of the Possible

Csilla Bertha

'He who wants to be a piper, must go to hell to learn how to pipe' (Hungarian folk song)

Introduction

The dynamatologist JPW King in Murphy's *The Gigli Concert* (1983), pondering on God's nature, comes to the conclusion that, instead of saying 'I am who am', God should have said: 'I am who may be [...] which means, I am the possible, or, if you prefer, I am the im-possible.'[1] The difference between the two announcements – which are actually two different possible translations of the original Hebrew text in Exodus where God speaks to Moses from the burning bush and promises him that he will bring his people out of the afflictions of Egypt – proves to be a cornerstone of understanding the nature of God in philosophy and theology and is a central issue in Murphy's drama, both in regard to its themes and also its dramaturgy.

Richard Kearney, in his book on religious hermeneutics, *The God Who May Be,* explains how the translation of the Hebrew ''ehyeh 'asher 'ehyeh' reflects different ways of understanding God. The translation into 'I am who am' provides an ontological interpretation which (from Augustine through Aquinas and the neo-Scholastics to Heidegger's 'onto-theology') images a God as a metaphysical divinity, as Being itself, eternal and unchangeable. Understanding the Exodic name as 'I am who will be', on the other hand, conditions an eschatological reading (from the Hebrew Rashi and early Christians through Martin Buber to André LaCocque and Paul Riceour) which sees the God of the burning bush as 'a saving-enabling-promising God' whose promise is granted in an 'I-Thou relationship (of God with Moses) thereby indicating *two* sides to the promise, human *as well as* divine.'[2] The promise in the divine name gives humans the option to respond, the freedom to accept or refuse the gift. Kearney's own 'onto-eschatological' reading offers a *via tertia*, moving along the lines earlier pointed out by the Christian mystic Meister Eckhart, then Nicholas of Cusa, Schelling, the late Heidegger and Ricoeur and postulates that in the 'I-am-who-may-be' annunciation

> God transfigures and exceeds being. His *esse* reveals itself, surprisingly and dramatically, as *posse*. [...] God, transfiguring himself in the guise of an angel, speaks through ... a burning bush and seems to say something like this: *I am who may be if you continue to keep my word and struggle for the coming of justice.* (37-8, emphasis in the original)

With that interpretation Kearney emphasizes not only God's possibilizing power but also human responsibility in bringing about 'the kingdom of justice and love'. (38)

In his Introduction to *The God Who May Be* Kearney recalls how in the eighties he and Tom Murphy were trying to find a term 'to convey the meaning of th[e] "logic of the dynamizing possible"' and what they hit upon was *dynamatology*. That term becomes one of the names that Kearney then offers to identify his philosophy of God which, like Murphy's, puts the words of Exodus 3:14 in the centre of speculation about the nature of the divine. And it is exactly the same name that Murphy gives to the branch of psychology JPW King pursues in *The Gigli Concert*. That name itself, as Kearney elucidates, 'derives from the Greek *dynamis*, meaning potentiality or potency, used by both Aristotle and the writers and commentators of the scriptures.' (6)

Murphy engages with making the impossible happen on the stage in his creation of dramatic reality – a co-creation with the God of possibility. As early as in *The Morning After Optimism* (1971), James envisions a beautiful, innocent, ideal girl as 'Miss Possible' who inspired his 'hidden, real, beautiful self' to manifest itself[3], but after his journey through 'mire and blood' he had to realize that this ideal remains unattainable. In many a later play a magic transformation consists in the process of a fall or descent into the depth of darkness, void, sin, desperation, followed by a possible revival. This pattern could be (and has been) identified as magic or alchemy where matter must be dissolved into its parts in order to be reshaped into precious gold, as the pagan, shamanic notion of having to go down to the darkness of the underworld, to be ripped apart in order to be reborn. It also reflects the ancient belief that the artist has to sojourn in hell before being able to create, as worded in the Hungarian folk song: 'He who wants to be a piper, must go to hell to learn how to pipe', and is consistent with the idea of St John of the Cross's 'Dark night of the soul' and, of course, with Jesus Christ's passion, death and resurrection. Such descent involves a journey full of dangers and Murphy's *oeuvre* shows just how dangerous it is because the miracle does not happen in all plays and not everybody returns redeemed or reconciled (for instance, no redemption occurs in *A Whistle in the Dark*, *Famine*, and only momentary relief is experienced in *Conversations on a Homecoming* or *The House*). That this pattern occurs in so many plays in a different manner and context, only confirms that it is a process that the playwright himself must go through each time, suffer the descent into the abyss, in order to bring up pure pearls of the imagination. Although a uniquely personal journey for each artist, it remains their common condition, as the Hungarian philosopher, Béla Hamvas, among many others, asserts: 'Great art, great philosophy, great fate is unimaginable without strong underworld relations. [...] He who did not step into the underworld at least once, [...] has nothing substantial to tell to other people because he who does not know the deepest spheres of existence, must be ignorant concerning all the dark and uncertain questions of fate.'[4]

In this essay, I will attempt to identify the kind of faith Murphy's plays foreground. I claim that, although Murphy's deviation from conventional Catholicism is clear in all his work, his dramatic world's rootedness in Christianity remains equally clear, however unorthodox and undogmatic it may be. He starts with violently rebelling against – not so much the spirit as – the institution of Christianity, scalding the church, the priests, the pharisees. In several of his plays his characters are 'painfully orphaned' in a god-forsaken world,[5] suffering from metaphysical homelessness in the Heideggerian sense. In this 'post-religious' age Murphy however, not only operates with religious imagery and vocabulary but also radiates a religious sensitivity which is clearly rooted in Catholicism but points towards a transformed understanding of Christianity closest to that formulated by some contemporary philosophers, particularly by Richard Kearney.

Revolt against the Church

The hegemony of the Catholic Church in Ireland with its privileged knowledge, providing 'a set of answers, which were the foregone conclusions of all your thoughts and all your experiences' doomed it to be so suddenly abandoned, as John Devitt asserts.[6] Devitt also singles out Murphy as being among the first playwrights creating shock-waves with his plays that gave voice to the changed feelings towards the institutional Church and to the disappearance of shared religious values in Ireland before the changes were publicly acknowledged. (106-7) With some frivolity we might conclude that in a sense Irish Catholics, seeking a more private, personal, less prescribed form of relationship with God Himself, finding the all-powerful mediation of the clergy no longer necessary, preferring to question rather than accept all the answers, themselves are becoming Protestants – or, as Roy Foster suggests, protestant 'with a lower-case p'.[7] The Protestants historically not only insisted on a personal relationship with God while protesting against the church's vindication of the right for itself to be the only means of leading people to the world of the spirit but also shared the tradition of questioning, reproaching, and arguing with God. The deep believer Endre Ady, an Hungarian Protestant poet at the beginning of the twentieth century, famously wrestled with God sometimes as a 'faithless believer', passionately rebelled against Him as 'God's mon-ster', worshipped pagan demons, accepted all the temptations of the flesh, but again and again, broken and desperate, escaped to God in his deeply-felt sinfulness and metaphysical despair. Murphy's work reflects a similar kind of constant questioning, doubting, anger, talking back – although without Ady's humility – while acknow-ledging moments of transcendental beauty when some of his characters suddenly become able to work miracles and show empathy and love transcending their limitations. The human good-ness and forgiveness that surface from some unlikely sources in his plays, radiate something of that divine grace. Or, as Richard Cave maintains: 'What is often profoundly moving in Murphy's plays is his conviction that even in a godless world humanity retains some religious instinct which compels them for good or ill to shape their own strange rituals of belief behind which one can still sense as it were a palimpsest of Western traditions of faith and practice.'[8]

The revolt of Murphy's rebels against the Church has little to do with faith itself. In simpler cases they are upset because of insti-tutional abuse, such as, for instance, the embittered Finbar in *The*

Wake (1998), '*a product of a culture*', bursts out shouting: 'Sex! Christian Brothers in the schools! [...] Faaack! Beating children, Henry, then buggering them: I was "in care", Henry, them establishments.'[9] A more extensive tirade against the 'coonics' is delivered in Francisco's famous monologue in *The Sanctuary Lamp* (1975). Or, as late as in *Too Late for Logic* (1989), when 'banks, and building societies can turn churches into – market-places'[10], Christopher still charges at the clergy with '*Egalité – liberté – fraternité*, said the bishops and princes, our royal arse ... which they replanked up on thrones.' (*Plays 5*: 3)[11] But more often the anger is caused by the failure of the church to answer people's spiritual needs. Murphy himself does not deny his enrichment due to his religious education and Catholicism. In an interview he affirms that

> The church certainly gave me and people of my generation a very positive background. [...] But [...] the church has got between man and the divine. [...] I think everybody has some form of apprehension of the spirit within himself. [...] The church has stopped what could possibly be the personal conversion to one's own spirit.[12]

The Divine and the Human

Murphy's quest appears very close to what is understood as contemporary Christianity, as 'a quest for life through which God can be found in the innermost humanity of man'[13]. Among others, Martin Buber and Emmanuel Levinas maintain the inseparability of the question of God from the sphere of the human, as Levinas asserts 'we can think of God [...] by trying to identify the particular interhuman events that open towards transcendence and reveal the traces where God has passed.'[14] Similarly Karl Barth in his *Mensch und Mitmensch* (Man and the Other Man) discusses the metaphysical dimension of interpersonal relationships. When Murphy's characters go through their long, arduous journeys towards accepting their own sinful selves and that of the others, when they achieve forgiveness and reconciliation, that experience is rendered in such a way that the interhuman is saturated with the trans-cendental and takes the characters and audiences towards a kind of faith that, 'in conjunction with hope and desire, transcends belief and unbelief.' (27) Hugh Cummins lists 'tender mercies, epiphanies of kindness and giftedness, as well as moments of obscure summons [...] human words in which something of the Word came to pass' (42), among moments when the divine and the human meet.

This movement is most clear in *The Sanctuary Lamp*. The 'half-lapsed Jew' Harry and the 'self-destructive' ex-Jesuit Francisco may defy God, commit all sorts of sacrilege, may even have murderous intentions, yet at the end they do arrive at forgiveness under the 'Presence', indicated by the sanctuary lamp, partaking in the sacraments through drinking of the altar wine and sharing bread and fish and finally, joining together in the confessional box. The mystery of the play lies in the manner Murphy uses the sacred place and objects together with scraps of the liturgical structure and language so that everything lends itself to a reading of a renouncing of Christianity but, at the same time also to that of an embracing of a faith in divinely animated interhuman relations. 'The question of mystery continues to haunt and pursue the characters' and for the audience 'there is an invitation to experience that shiver of recognition that sees the possibility that all human lives might be transformed through moments of grace, healing or forgiveness.'[15] Thus the church does not remain a venue only, despite Murphy's claiming so in an interview.[16] Nor is the denial itself total. Ironically, it is Harry who accepts the presence of Jesus indicated by the sanctuary lamp, albeit not as the Catholic doctrine of Jesus' carnal presence since he divides Jesus and his spirit.[17] Maudie's thoughts revolve around forgiveness from the beginning and the first sequence of her dreams that brought her the knowledge that her dead mother is happy and for-giveness exists, is related under the lamp – to which/whom Harry attributes this gift:

> **HARRY**. And what did your gran say?
> **MAUDIE**. She said it were forgiveness. (MAUDIE *smiles her*
> *personal triumph and* HARRY *complements.*)
> **HARRY**.(*to sanctuary lamp*) That was very successful. (*Plays 3*:
> 119)

Francisco himself, typically, fumes mostly against the clergy, 'predators that have been mass-produced out of the loneliness and isolation of people', those 'coonics' who, like 'black candles', instead of giving, 'each one drawing a little more light of the world. [...] Selling their product: Jesus. Weaving their theological cobwebs, doing their theological sums!' (*Plays 3*: 154) Harry's evocation: 'I believe ... Help' (156) sounds like an echo of Mark's famous 'I believe, help thou mine unbelief' (Mark 9:24). And Francisco's most furious reproach to God is for his assumed absence, for disappearing after creation, especially after 'they [...] turned him into a church' (128). Murphy says about *The Sanctuary Lamp* that 'it is a religious play, in the sense of personal religion, as against institutionalised religion. [...] I believe the blasphemer is perhaps closer to God than someone who is observing all the duties that the Catholic or Protestant or Christian or any form is obliged to uphold.'[18] If Murphy himself is a blasphemer, in his revolt he must stand closer to God than conventional religious people since 'God prefers honest people rather than the lackeys. [...] God admires people like Job and David – who argue with God.'[19]

Murphy's blasphemers are fully aware of their being sinful; moreover, they often boast about it, as Francisco does in *The Sanctuary Lamp*. As his plays witness, Murphy is preoccupied with sin, guilt, repentance, forgiveness and redemption. Sin, repentance and forgiveness are at the core of Christianity. Without sin there is no innocence. Without acknowledging sin there can be no salvation. In *The Morning After Optimism* James complains of the permissive society, which, when it was 'exclusive, when 'twas dangerous to be in it', was exciting, but once it became the norm, he 'uttered a prayer, Jesus, Mary and Joseph, where is the sin any more, I said! ... Irretrievably – irretrievably lost.' (*Plays 3*: 17) If God is absent, 'there's no one to bless you. And, worse, no one to curse you' (*Plays 3*: 156). If in the great existentialist freedom everything is allowed, what is the individual's responsibility? Responsibility exists only if there is choice. As the theologian Gerard Casey argues: 'God cannot make us to be free and, at the same time, consistently override the consequences of our free choices whenever they result in evil. To do so would be to refuse to take us seriously.'[20] Murphy's world did not dispense with evil. His characters endure the consequences of their sins and complain about their suffering like Job, with the difference that, as Vivian Mercier observed, Job was not a sinner.[21] But they are also seeking forgiveness which may come from the other person or rather, *through* the other person. Miracles or half-miracles happen through and within human beings – in accordance with Rudolf Bultmann's conviction that God's work goes on inside human beings.[22] Such, for example, is the lost, fallen James and Rosie's suddenly regained ability to cry after murdering the ideal couple in *The Morning After Optimism*, such is Harry's renewed strength and ability to lift the pulpit with Francisco standing in it in *The Sanctuary Lamp*. And such is the senile Mommo's recognition of her granddaughter Mary after confessing her guilt in her husband's and grandson's death at the end of *Bailegangaire* (1985). Above all, the moments of forgiveness prove to be the points where the divine shines through the humans. The human beings' willingness to forgive those who sinned against them belongs to the categories of good and evil, instead of the simple social morality of right and wrong. Murphy's dramatizing of the acts of asking for, gaining, and granting forgiveness with deliberate lack of psychological preparation, rather as unexpected and undeserved gifts, distinguishes those moments from ordinary humanism. One of the most remarkable examples of this occurs in Murphy's recently published dramatization of Liam O'Flaherty's *The Informer* (1981), which closes with the unmistakably Biblical sentence of the mother of the murdered man forgiving the informer, the murderer of her son after his confession and plea for forgiveness: 'I forgive yeh, Gypo. Yous didn't know what yiz were doin'.'[23]

'Where sin abounded, grace did much more abound' (*Romans 5.20*)

Many of Murphy's characters, as if in an inversion of God trying Job, seem to commit sin to test how far they can go and still gain redemption. In *Optimism*, James, 'while wrestling with morality, put Rosie on the game' (*Plays 3*: 17) and then becomes a murderer, indeed a fratricide. Francisco, after betraying his best friend and stealing his wife, preaches the reversal of Catholic teaching that 'all those rakish, dissolute, suicidal, fornicating goats, taken in adultery and what-have-you' will gain salvation at the Last Judgement. (*Plays 3*: 155)[24] Moreover, as if in contrast to the life-denying clergy, Francisco repeatedly, emphatically calls Jesus 'Man, total man, life-enhancing man', which, while stressing His humanity and humaneness, does not deny his divinity. 'Total man' – the totality of body, soul, and spirit, the earthly and the heavenly, Yeats's 'Unity of Being', the ideal wholeness that human beings can never reach. From the combination of this image of Jesus' completeness and Harry's individual imagination the two men invent an entirely undogmatic form of wholeness in the closing poetic image of the silhouettes, the souls of the dead joining each other 'in the silent outer wall of eternity' (158) while in the play's 'reality' they join each other to go home together. This re-found wholeness within and between the individual characters, as Shaun Richards suggests, reflects 'the triumph of *agape*, brotherly love, a concept which, while Christian in origin, is profoundly social in effect.'[25]

Through many of his characters, Murphy himself, especially in his earlier plays, roars and acts out his anger and despair about

existential loneliness, the human condition of metaphysical homelessness in general and the anomalies of Irish life in particular. The
authorities the revolts are aimed at include parent-figures, both
realistic and archetypal as the 'witch-mother' and 'dragon-father,'[26]
parental institutions such as the mother-church and father-priests
and of course social institutions. The 'noisy desperation' of the
characters' Job-like complaining[27] breaks out in actions of physical
or verbal violence germinating not so much from evil in the
characters themselves as from their deep frustration and despair.
John Joe Moran in *A Crucial Week in the Life of a Grocer's
Assistant* (1969) liberates himself from binding social conventions
but especially from his mother's dominating influence through
roaring out his, his family's, and his neighbours' shameful, hidden
secrets. James and Rosie in *Optimism* kill the ideal couple, their
own younger, innocent, 'beautiful selves' in order to be able to
accept their fallen, corrupted, real selves. Harry in *The Sanctuary
Lamp* wrestles with his own 'compulsion to kill' in revenge for being
betrayed and 'feeling of wrong-doing because I haven't gone back to
do it' (*Plays 3*: 102-3) while Francisco desecrates the church by
storming from the pulpit at the mother-church and priest-father-
figures. Vera in *The Wake*, defies the hypocritical family and its
tyranny in a series of huge, extravagant, scandalous actions that ruin
the respectability of the family before she humiliates them with her
extraordinary generosity. The acts of defiance in the mature plays
become less violent and often more sophisticated than in earlier
ones. There is no more need to kill the ideal, instead the desire
prevails to unite with it; what proved impossible in *Optimism,*
becomes fulfilled in *The Gigli Concert* if only in a momentary,
Yeatsean union, turning fantasy into creative imagination. The
'answering back [...] to everything' – as Murphy once gave as his
reason for writing plays[28] – to God, society, authorities, people, in
Bailegangaire appears in the form of laughing as part of the laughing contest, fed by the participants' own misfortunes (a possible
echo of the Beckettian 'Nothing is funnier than unhappiness'[29]).
Whether via rebellion or through complaint, violence or pursuing an
unappeasable desire, several of Murphy's protagonists reach beyond
despair, towards self-recognition, facing guilt and grief, and often
further, to repentance, asking for and sometimes gaining or granting
forgiveness. And that, in turn, might bring about little miracles,
reconciliations, and 'the possibility of communion, however alienated from majority opinion or convention.'[30]

After *The Gigli Concert* and *Bailegangaire*, with their endings on a triumphant note, in the later plays a new resignation, bleakness, and hopelessness seem to dominate. They are only partly counter-weighed by the 'tiny, almost imperceptible acts of love' in which the 'divine possible [...] comes in'.[31] Those tiny acts of love though gain their extraordinary power from the preceding descent into the darkest layers of the psyche, the deepest depths of personal hell. Vera, in *The Wake*, frees herself from family bonds that she had believed were essential to her, through revolting against the family's hypocritical morality by flaunting her being a prostitute and against their dehumanizing greed by overwhelming them with her gene-rosity as she gives over to them her inheritance, the much-coveted hotel. Literally, giving it away for a song, she forces the family members to party and sing songs, throwing bread at those who had thrown stones at her as if the prodigal daughter came home not to be celebrated but to share her riches with the rest of the family. In her noble revenge, she brings out the best in her relatives, uniting the family for a moment in sincere joy; meanwhile she reintegrates herself with her beloved grandmother, who also fell prey to the family's greed. In the course of that 'wake', Vera enables herself to face her isolation, the loss of the last bonds to family, homeland, past, and to take with her into exile only the warmth of the memory of her loving grandmother.

In its twin-play, *The House* (2000), however, Vera's counterpart the pimp Christy, another emigrant, remains doomed in his Purgatory. Where Vera gave away the house, Christy kills for it, obtains it, but loses what made it precious for him: the family that owned the house. Although Christy, like Gypo (in *The Informer*) and Francisco (in *Sanctuary Lamp*) earlier, also confesses his sin to the one he sinned against – Mrs de Burca – he asks her only not to tell on him, that is, to help save him merely from earthly, legal punishment. Her subsequent death deepens and multiplies his sin and he loses the courage needed to give relief to himself through another confession (to Marie) which might then cause more tragedy. This victory over himself, refraining from that desired but basically selfish act remains Christy's only redeeming choice in this 'morning after optimism' when, instead of killing his innocent self, he has killed his double, the prostitute Susanne, who reminded him of his lowliness.[32] In his desperate desire to complete his homecoming to childhood bliss, family and mother figure, Christy 'kills' the mother herself and thereby loses the prospect of gaining the 'ideal' – but this time earthly – woman, Marie. The real transcendental moment in this play – Christy's unexpected singing to Marie in the pub – is brutally interrupted and from then on he has to pay for his crime without the hope of forgiveness. This play, dramatizing most poignantly the desire for and failure of full homecoming (the metaphysical dimension is strengthened by the use of such vocabulary for the home place as 'glorious' and 'heaven on earth') – dooms the homecomer to gaining only the physical house he yearned for but denies him dwelling.

The 'I-am-who-am' syndrome

Sin appears not only as particular, individual evil but also as existential guilt. Murphy carries on the most extensive theological speculation, including the role and effect of original sin in *The Gigli Concert*. The burning bush revelation of Exodus 3:14 here is displaced to Eden, as an annunciation of God to Adam: that is, not to the Chosen People but to all humankind. This displacement thus merges God's self-definition with the expulsion from Paradise – as if God revealed Himself when 'taking his stroll in the Garden' and answered Adam's question of what the annunciation meant, with 'out, out!' (*Plays 3*: 211) – suggesting that that inquiry is as great a sin as the eating of the fruit of the Tree of Knowledge, learning to tell Good from Evil. What is also marked in that passage from Genesis is the first instance of humans hiding from God, hence beginning God's 'absence' which actually means humans' turning away and absenting themselves from God – another form of original sin, especially in the light of the Augustinian concept of evil being the absence of God.[33]

Among critics analyzing the passage about the 'I-am-who-am' syndrome in *The Gigli Concert*, Fintan O'Toole explores its implications to the fullest, associating with this concept of God as eternal presence what he calls the 'theatre of epiphany' which achieves its climax through the revelation of the essential nature of things as opposed to Murphy's kind of 'theatre of apocalypse' whose climax is a leap into a different reality or plane of action[34]. O'Toole argues that 'Christian thinking is profoundly anti-apocalyptic' because the act of salvation is 'located in the past [...] from which all hope and meaning continue to derive' (220), and maintains that *The Gigli Concert* goes 'against Christian thinking' (216). Joseph Swann disputes against O'Toole contending that even if *The Gigli Concert* 'may well put Christianity into a new orbit, it does nothing [...] to contradict it' and so is not 'subversive of Christianity'. The dynamism of Hebrew thought that King's re-translation of Yahweh's name into 'I am who may be' comes close, is carried further, Swann asserts, 'by the protestant rather than by the catholic tradition'.[35] Indeed, Christianity's act of salvation, although occurring in the past, offers only possibility and does not decide an individual's fate since the individual must be held responsible for embracing or rejecting it. As Bultman states, partly following Martin Luther, God's presence becomes reality only in the here and now.[36] Or, according to more radical views, the emphasis falls on future time:

> The resurrection of Jesus [...] belongs essentially to the future rather than the past. [...] It is not an achieved event but an ongoing possibility whose full realisation depends on our willingness to embody it and carry it forward in our own lives. Jesus' new body is the historical body of the community of the living and the dead, and as such it is only partly resurrected. [...] The promise is not a guarantee, nothing is pre-determined.[37]

Revelation by itself is not enough, it must be followed by conversion, a 'leap of faith' to another vision of reality, another plane of the world – just the kind of transformation that O'Toole associates with apocalyptic theatre. Rather than being a guarantee or a certainty, finding the path of redemption is often seen as an arduous task, a constant struggle, full of the danger of falling:

> Uncertainty is the very essence of Christianity. [...] The life of the soul in openness toward God, the waiting, the periods of aridity and dullness, guilt and despondency, contrition and repentance, forsakenness and hope against hope, the silent stirrings of love and grace, trembling on the verge of a certainty that if gained is loss – the very lightness of this fabric may prove too heavy a burden for men who lust for massively possessive experience.[38]

It is this creative uncertainty that lies at the heart of Murphy's plays.

As Kearney built his theory of the God of possibility in part on the annunciation in the burning bush, so Murphy's dramaturgy centres on the transforming possibility of the formula 'I am who may be'. Irish Man in *The Gigli Concert*, coming to the dynamatologist with the unquenchable desire to sing like Gigli, significantly, refuses to give his name to JPW King. (*Plays 3*: 169) He is, at this moment, both who he is and who he might be – as immediately after that, speaking about his childhood, he adopts details of Gigli's life and family as his own. Yet Irish Man remains who he is, finds a way to return to his ordinary life while it is King who at the play's end becomes who he might be by miraculously singing like Gigli. The dynamatologist succeeded in dynamizing his own potential (significantly, preceded by his newly becoming capable of loving). He achieves the Kingdom: the human participating in the creation of goodness and beauty. His famous speculation about the nature of the divine earlier in the play began with the words: 'God created the world in order to create himself. Us. We are God.' (*Plays 3*: 211) Rather than blasphemy, this passage echoes contemporary philosophical and theological concepts that regard Creation as a process and a mutual effort of God and humans, formulated by Hans Urs von Balthasar in his theory of Theo-drama as 'God does not play the world drama all on his own, he makes room for man to join in the acting.'[39] King sings, however, *like* Gigli, in Gigli's voice, not in his own – as Derek Hand reminds us – which brings 'fact and illusion powerfully together' and involves the audience in 'producing magic' through the willing act of imagination and thereby 'transcendence occurs [...] not only for JPW, but for us the audience.'[40]

O'Toole persuasively parallels *The Gigli Concert* to *Faust*, pointing out the many correspondences between characters, relationships, situations. Yet Murphy both establishes and simultaneously complicates such correspondences. Irish Man may bring temptation to JPW King as Mephistopheles does to Faust, yet there remains an important difference in that Irish Man, full of dark thoughts and feelings, is himself rather another version of the fallen, suffering, frustrated Murphy characters, painfully aware of his own sinfulness, full of aspiration for higher beauty. Just as he and King often reverse roles, so the Mephistopheles–Faustus roles also often become exchanged, as, for example, when King says to Irish Man: 'You may never come back to the poxy, boring anchor of this everyday world you have sold your soul for.' (*Plays 3*: 203) A counterpoint and double of King, and an inspiration stirring him to life indeed, but not quite a Jungian Shadow figure; rather than the Lord of Darkness attempting to destroy the world of God's creation, he is but another aspect of humanity fallen prey to temptation out in the great world of material corruption.

Patrick Mason, the director of *The Gigli Concert* in the 1983 Abbey premiere, discussing whether the end of the play brings salvation or only a humanistic resolution, asserts that 'there is great belief, I mean depths of belief' in the play, and emphasizes that the bells that begin to strike at the end echo the Easter bells marking Faust's salvation.[41]

Exile and Homecoming

If Murphy's plays testify to the metaphysical homelessness where 'to be in exile is our permanent condition on earth,'[42] they also dramatize the possibility of finding a dwelling in the truth. James and Rosie, Harry and Francisco, Vera, Christy – emigrants, exiles, sinners all – when reclaiming their home, lose it; King and Christopher – dried out, burnt out or (as the latter) perhaps-even-dead protagonists – have abandoned their homes. The only home is often found in the other person(s). Even in *Bailegangaire,* although exceptionally uniting the physical, emotional and metaphysical aspects of home, the crucial moment of reaching it involves grand-daughter's and (grand)mother's warm reconciliation and re-embracing love, in *Too Late for Logic* 'a kind of resurrection of the father'[43] occurs, in *Alice Trilogy* love for others, including the husband, is re-born. The protest against the church has turned into ironic dismissal while resignation at the indifference of the universe towards human suffering indicates Murphy's further distancing of himself from institutional forms of faith, from conventional Christianity. After her son died in an accident, Alice muses: 'God is the name given to the unknown. The unknown is possibly – and probably – nothing. [...] There is no explanation for what cannot be explained, no comfort for what cannot be comforted.' [44] In *Alice Trilogy* tragedy is no longer treated as something related to sin but – as Alice speculates – 'things occur, not because a divine power wills them ... but simply because that is the way things occur, they just happen. [...] for no particular reason, for no purpose.' (358) After 'the worst has happened' to her and, as a consequence, she lost all capacity for feeling and communicating, she is jolted out of her stupor by being called to sympathize with another grieving human being. This moment, transforming her back into someone capable of sympathy and empathy, exactly by its under-psychologized appearance, becomes the sign of its mysteriousness, of its bordering on the miraculous.

Instead of the earlier anger in Murphy's plays, singing and crying increasingly provide the terrain for homecoming. Since the immense role of music and singing in Murphy's whole *oeuvre* has been amply explored, here only a few examples will suffice to illustrate its expressiveness of homecoming to the self or to the other. Apart from its most elaborate dramatization in *The Gigli Concert*, in many other plays singing (both on records and by characters onstage) offers redeeming moments and articulates emotions that are impossible to verbalize. In *Conversations on a Homecoming* the abandoned, neglected, desperate Peggy's unexpected singing of a religious song miraculously beautifies her figure. Similarly, in *The House* Christy transforms for a moment when gently singing of his love to Maire in the pub, and in *The Wake* the warring family members forced to sing by Vera's command gradually begin to enjoy their togetherness and warm up towards each other, regaining some of the human feelings that they had all but lost in their pursuit of money. The priest's partaking in the wake through singing and playing music, being the best singer and also a piano-player, signifies not only his inadequacy as a spiritual leader but, simultaneously, also his ministering rituals of a half-lost, half-transformed faith, sharing some sort of spirituality which then results in moving the alienated people out of their fossilized hostilities. In *Too Late for Logic* in addition to the songs from Gluck's *Orpheus and Eurydice* and Dvorak's *Russalka* highlighting the play's theme, Jack composing his songs leads to his becoming 'the re-born Orpheus, with a banjo or guitar instead of a lyre, singing his own psychedelic lyrics'[45] in the closing scene of father-son reconciliation at the borderline of death and life where 'the nightmare ends, the magic begins'.[46]

Singing, as shouting or acting violently in some earlier plays, enables characters to cry. Crying may be a sign of grief, pain and mourning, of repentance or despair over one's own evil, but as often also of relief at the breakdown of the walls of silence dividing people from each other, hence another location where 'the traces where God has passed' can be detected. Crying may come as a gift when some blockage to one's own emotions is broken as happens to James and Rosie at *Optimism*'s end, to Vera in the closing moments of *The Wake*, to the Irish Man sobbing in King's office in *The Gigli Concert*, likewise to Christopher sobbing after his visit to the school bully whom he wants to shoot in *Too Late for Logic*. Most beautifully, in the resolution of *Bailegangaire*, prayer and crying merge in Mommo's: 'To thee do we cry. Yes? Poor banished children of Eve', once she accepts life as '[m]ourning and weeping in this valley of tears' and then Mary finally breaks down in 'tears of gratitude', accompanied by Mommo's famous words: 'And sure a tear isn't such a bad thing, Mary.[47] *Alice Trilogy*, similarly closes with the heroine's weeping, who through sharing another person's tragedy finds the way back to her own ability to feel. The third part of *Alice Trilogy* is set in a no-man's land, at an airport, a particularly non-homely place, which still features a homecoming of sorts – not only the sorrowful homecoming of the son in the coffin but – a homecoming to love, sympathy, empathy, stepping over one's limitations.

Murphy's discourse leaves his plays open to readings of his human miracles as manifestations of the divine presence within the human, especially in the interpersonal relationships. Instead of 'rituals of a lost faith' *à la* Yeats[48], then, Murphy's plays feature rituals of a transformed faith that guide the characters and audiences towards the God of the possible whose divine plan may become fulfilled if humans learn to behave as humans and participate in creating goodness. 'One of the many ways in which the infinite comes to be experienced and imagined by our finite minds is as possibility – the ability to be. Even, and especially, when such possibility seems impossible to us.'[49]

[1] Tom Murphy, *The Gigli Concert* in *Plays: Three* (London: Methuen, 1994): subsequent quotations are from this edition, to which page numbers will refer.

[2] Richard Kearney, The *God Who May Be: A Hermeneutics of Religion* (Bloomington IN: Indiana UP, 2001): 28, emphasis in the original. Subsequent references are cited in the text.

[3] Tom Murphy, *The Morning After Optimism*, in *Plays 3*: 12.

[4] Béla Hamvas, *Szellem és egzisztencia* [Spirit and Existence] (Pécs: Baranya Megyei Könyvtár, 1987): 17, my translation.

[5] Christopher Murray, 'Introduction: The Rough and Holy Theatre of Thomas Murphy', *Irish University Review* 17.1 (1987): 14.

[6] John Devitt in conversation with Nicholas Grene and Chris Morash, *Shifting Scenes* (Dublin: Carysfort Press, 2008): 106.

[7] Quoted in Christopher Murray, 'The Representation of Suicide in Modern Irish Drama 1960-2007', *A New Ireland in Brazil*, eds Laura P.Z. and Beatriz Kopschitz X. Bastos (Sao Paolo: Humanitas, 2008): 179.

[8] Richard Cave, 'Tom Murphy: Acts of Faith in a Godless World', *British and Irish Drama Since 1960,* ed. James Acheson (London: Macmillan, 1993): 89.

[9] Tom Murphy, *The Wake*, in *Plays: 5* (London: Methuen, 2006): 85, 140. Subsequent references are cited in the text.

[10] Tom Murphy, *Too Late for Logic* in *Plays: 5*: 19. Subsequent references are cited in the text.

[11] Fintan O'Toole comments that this conjures up for an Irish audience 'the re-establishment of Catholic orthodoxy' in the 1980s. *The*

Politics of Magic, revised edition (Dublin: New Island; London: Nick Hern, 1994) : 259.

[12] Tom Murphy in interview with John Waters, *In Dublin* (May 1986): 27.

[13] Catherine Maignant, 'The New Prophets: Voices from the Margins', *Contemporary Catholicism in Ireland*, eds. John Littleton and Eamon Maher (Blackrock: Columba, 2008): 104.

[14] Quoted in Hugh Cummins, 'Beyond Belief and Unbelief', *Credo: Faith and Philosophy in Contemporary Ireland*, ed. Stephen J. Costello (Dublin: Liffey, 2003): 40.

[15] Anne F. O'Reilly, *Sacred Play* (Dublin: Carysfort Press, 2004): 119-20.

[16] Tom Murphy, In interview with Mária Kurdi, *Irish Studies Review* 12.2 (2004): 237.

[17] Tom Murphy, *The Sanctuary Lamp* , in *Plays 3*: 113. Subsequent references are cited in the text.

[18] In interview with John Waters, *In Dublin*: 27.

[19] Richard Kearney, 'Philosophising the Gift', an interview with Mark Manolopoulos, in *Credo*, ed. Stephen J. Costello: 104.

[20] Gerard Casey, 'Faith in Search of Understanding', in *Credo*, ed. Costello: 9.

[21] Vivian Mercier, 'Noisy Desperation: Murphy and the Book of Job', *Irish University Review* 17.1 (1987): 20.

[22] Rudolf Bultman, *Jézus Krisztus és a mitológia*, transl. of *Jesus Christus und die Mythologie* by Zelma Takácsné Kovácsházi (Budapest: Teológiai Irodalmi Egyesület, 1996): 68, my translation from the Hungarian.

[23] A similar sentence is said in the original, too, but Murphy makes it more emphatic by making it the closing sentence of the play and with the stage image: '*She is kneeling beside him, cradling his head upon her lap.*' Tom Murphy, *The Informer* (Dublin: Carysfort Press, 2008): 81.

[24] Interestingly, a similar reversal of judgment occurs in the vision of a character of the Protestant Stewart Parker's *Pentecost* (1987).

[25] Shaun Richards, 'Response', *Talking about Tom Murphy*, ed. Nicholas Grene (Dublin: Carysfort Press, 2002): 65.

[26] See Fintan O'Toole, *The Politics of Magic*: 77, and Alexandra Poulain, 'Fable and Vision: *The Morning after Optimism* and *The Sanctuary Lamp*', in *Talking about Tom Murphy*, ed. Grene: 45.

[27] Vivian Mercier, 'Noisy Desperation': 18-19.

[28] Ivor W. Browne, 'Thomas Murphy: The Madness of Genius', *Irish University Review* 17.1 (1987): 129.

[29] Samuel Beckett, *Endgame* (New York: Grove, 1958): 18.

30 Christopher Murray, 'Introduction: The Rough and Holy' : 17.

31 Richard Kearney, 'Philosophising the Gift', in *Credo*, ed. Costello: 102.

32 See more detailed analysis in Csilla Bertha, 'Poetically Dwelling: The Mythic and the Historical in Tom Murphy's *The House*', *Hungarian Journal of English and American Studies* 8.1 (2002).

33 'And they heard the voice of the Lord God walking in the garden in the cool of the day; and Adam and his wife hid themselves from the presence of the Lord God amongst the trees of the garden' (Genesis 3: 8).

34 Fintan O'Toole, *The Politics of Magic*: 221.

35 Joseph Swann, 'Language and Act: Thomas Murphy's Non-Interpretive Drama', *Perspectives of Irish Drama and Theatre*, eds Jacqueline Genet and Richard Allen Cave (Gerards Cross: Colin Smythe, 1991): 151.

36 Rudolf Bultmann: 78.

37 Hugh Cummins, 'Beyond Belief and Unbelief': 46.

38 Eric Voegelin, quoted in Cummins, *Credo*: 43-44.

39 Hans Urs von Balthasar, quoted in Eric Voegelin, *The Drama of Doctrine* (Louisville, Kentucky: Westminster John Knox, 2004): 49.

40 Derek Hand, '*The Gigli Concert*: The Necessity of the Imagination', in *The Irish Reader: Essays for John Devitt*, eds Michael Hinds, Peter Denman and Margaret Kelleher (Dublin: Otior/Mater Dei, 2007): 36.

41 Patrick Mason, 'Directing *The Gigli Concert*', interview with Christopher Murray, *Irish University Review* 17.1 (1987): 105-6.

42 Leszek Kolakowski, quoted in Cummins, 'Beyond Belief and Unbelief', *Credo*: 27.

43 O'Toole, *The Politics of Magic*: 252.

44 Tom Murphy, *Alice Trilogy*, in *Plays: 5*: 357. Subsequent references are cited in the text.

45 O'Toole, *The Politics of* Magic: 264.

46 Tom Murphy, *Too Late for Logic* (London; Methuen, 1990): 51. In the revised edition (*Plays 5*: 71) this line in Jack's song is altered, omitting 'the magic begins'.

47 Tom Murphy, *Bailegangaire, Plays: Two* (London: Methuen, 1993): 169.

48 'I always feel my work is not drama but the ritual of a lost faith.' *W.B. Yeats and T. Sturge Moore: Their Correspondence 1901-1937*, ed. Ursula Bridge (London: Routledge and Kegan Paul, 1953): 156.

49 Richard Kearney, 'Re-Imagining God', in *Credo*, ed. Costello : 73.

Tom Murphy: A Bibliography

(in order of date of first production on stage, indicated in brackets, followed by date of first publication)

A Whistle in the Dark (1961), published New York: Samuel French, 1970; Dublin: Gallery Press, 1984.

The Orphans (1968), published Newark, DE: Proscenium Press, 1974.

Famine (1968), published Dublin; Gallery Press, 1977.

A Crucial Week in the Life of a Grocer's Assistant (1969), published Dublin: Gallery Press, 1978

(Originally titled *The Fooleen*, published Dixon, CA: Proscenium Press, 1968).

The Morning after Optimism (1971), published Cork: Mercier Press, 1973.

'The White House' (1972), unpublished. Later rewritten as *Conversations on a Homecoming* below.

On the Outside (in collaboration with Noel O'Donoghue), RTE radio 1962, staged 1974, published 1976 with preface by Tom Murphy, together with:

On the Inside (1974), Dublin: Gallery Press, 1976, London: Methuen, 1989 in *A Whistle in the Dark and Other Plays*.

(*On the Inside* premiered in a double bill with *On the Outside* at the Peacock, 1974.)

The Vicar of Wakefield (1974), adapted from the novel by Oliver Goldsmith, and unpublished. (This adaptation was later re-titled *She Stoops to Folly* in revival, published London: Methuen, 1996; revised for *Plays 6*, Methuen, 2010).

The Sanctuary Lamp (1975), published Dublin: Poolbeg Press, 1976, revised edition Dublin: Gallery Press, 1984.

'The J. Arthur Maginnis Story' (1976), unpublished.

'Epitaph under Ether' (1979), adapted from J.M. Synge, unpublished.

The Blue Macushla (1980), published London: Methuen, 1992, in *Plays: One*.

The Informer (1981), adapted from the novel by Liam O'Flaherty, revised text published Dublin: Carysfort Press, 2008.

She Stoops to Conquer (1982), transferred to an Irish setting from Goldsmith's 1773 play and unpublished in Murphy's version.

The Gigli Concert (1983), published Dublin, Gallery Press, 1984.

Conversations on a Homecoming (1985), published Dublin:
   Gallery Press, 1986.
Bailegangaire (1985), published Dublin: Gallery Press, 1986.
A Thief of a Christmas (1985), published London: Methuen,
   1993, in *Plays: Two.*
Too Late for Logic (1989), published London: Methuen, 1990,
   revised edition 2006, in *Plays: 5.*
The Patriot Game (1991), published London: Methuen, 1992, in
   Plays: One.
The Seduction of Morality (a novel), published London: Little,
   Brown, 1994.
The Wake (1998), published London: Methuen, 1998.
The House (2000), published with introduction by Fintan
   O'Toole, London: Methuen, 2000.
The Drunkard (2003), adapted from the 1844 melodrama by
   W.H. Smith and A Gentleman and published Dublin:
   Carysfort Press, 2004.
The Cherry Orchard (2004), adapted from Anton Chekhov and
   published London: Methuen, 2004.
Alice Trilogy (2005), published London: Methuen, 2005.
The Last Days of a Reluctant Tyrant (2009), 'inspired by' the
   novel *The Golovlyov Family* (1876) by Mikhail Saltykov-
   Shchedrin and published London: Methuen, 2009.

Television plays

The Fly Sham (BBC, 1962).
Veronica (BBC, 1962).
Snakes and Reptiles (BBC, 1965).
A Crucial Week in the Life of a Grocer's Assistant (BBC, 1966).
Young Man in Trouble (Thames, 1969).
Famine, three-part series (RTÉ, 1973).
The White House (RTÉ, 1977).
Brigit (RTÉ, 1988).

Other

'Introduction', *Plays: One* (London: Methuen, 1992): ix-xxi.
'The Creative Process', in Jacqueline Genet and Wynne
   Hellegouarc'h (eds), *Irish Writers and Their Creative Process*
   (Gerrards Cross: Colin Smythe, 1996): 78-86.

A Selected Bibliography of Criticism

Arrowsmith, Aidan, '"To Fly By Those Nets": Violence and Identity in Tom Murphy's *A Whistle in the Dark*', *Irish University Review* 34.2 (2004): 315-31.

Bertha, Csilla, 'Poetically Dwelling: The Mythic and the Historical in Tom Murphy's *The House*', *Hungarian Journal of English and American Studies* 8.1 (2002): 213-26.

Billington, Michael, interview, in Nicholas Grene (ed.), *Talking about Tom Murphy* (Dublin: Carysfort Press, 2002): 91-112.

Browne, Ivor W., 'Thomas Murphy: The Madness of Genius', *Irish University Review* 17.1 (1987): 129-36.

Cave, Richard Allen, 'Tom Murphy: Acts of Faith in a Godless World', in James Acheson (ed.), *British and Irish Drama since 1960* (Basingstoke: Macmillan, 1993): 88-102.

Etherton, Michael, *Contemporary Irish Dramatists* (Basingstoke: Macmillan, 1989): 107-46.

Fitzgibbon, T. Gerald, 'Thomas Murphy's Dramatic Vocabulary', *Irish University Review* 17.1 (1987): 41-50.

Fogarty, Anne, 'Tom Murphy in Conversation', in Lilian Chambers et al (eds.), *Theatre Talk: Voices of Irish Theatre Practitioners* (Dublin: Carysfort Press, 2001): 355-64.

Gleitman, Claire, 'Clever Blokes and Thick Lads: The Collapsing Tribe in Tom Murphy's *A Whistle in the Dark*', *Modern Drama* 42 (Fall 1999): 315-25.

Grene, Nicholas, *The Politics of Irish Drama: Plays in Context from Boucicault to Friel* (Cambridge: Cambridge UP, 1999): 219-41.

---, 'Talking it through: *The Gigli Concert* and *Bailegangaire*', in Grene (ed.), *Talking about Murphy* (Dublin: Carysfort Press, 2002): 67-81

---, 'Tom Murphy and the Children of Loss', in Shaun Richards (ed.). *The Cambridge Companion to Twentieth-Century Irish Drama* (Cambridge: Cambridge UP, 2004): 204-17.

---, 'Tom Murphy: Famine and Dearth', in George Cusack and Sarah Goss (eds.), *Hungry Words: Images of Famine in the Irish Canon* (Dublin: Irish Academic Press, 2006): 245-62.

---, 'Introduction', *Plays: 5* (London: Methuen, 2006): ix-xiii

Griffin, Christopher, '"The Audacity of Despair": *The Morning after Optimism*', *Irish University Review* 17.1 (1987): 62-70.

Hand, Derek, '*The Gigli Concert*: The Necessity of the Imagination', in Michael Hinds, Peter Denman and Margaret Kelleher (eds.), *The Irish Reader: Essays for John Devitt* (Dublin: Otior Press / Mater Dei Institute, 2007): 31-37.

Harrington, John P. (ed.), *Irish Theater in America: Essays on Irish Theatrical Diaspora* (Syracuse: Syracuse UP, 2009).

Henderson, Lynda, 'Men, Women and the Life of the Spirit in Tom Murphy's Plays', in Jacqueline Genet and Wynne Hellegouarc'h (eds.), *Irish Writers and Their Creative Process* (Gerrards Cross: Colin Smythe, 1996): 87-99.

Hickey, Des, and Gus Smith (eds.), interview, *A Paler Shade of Green* (London: Leslie Frewin, 1972): 225-27.

Hunt, Hugh, *The Abbey: Ireland's National Theatre 1904-1979* (Dublin: Gill and Macmillan, 1979).

Jordan, Eamonn, *Dissident Dramaturgies: Contemporary Irish Theatre* (Dublin and Portland, OR: Irish Academic Press, 2009).

Kearney, Richard, 'Tom Murphy's Long Day's Journey into Night', *Studies* LXXII (winter 1983): 327-35 , reprinted in Kearney, *Transitions: Narratives in Modern Irish Culture* (Manchester: Manchester UP, 1988): 161-71.

Kelly, Anne F., 'Bodies and Spirits in Tom Murphy's Theatre', in Eamonn Jordan (ed.), *Theatre Stuff: Critical Essays on Contemporary Irish Theatre* (Dublin: Carysfort Press, 2000): 159-71.

Kiberd, Declan, 'Theatre as Opera: *The Gigli Concert*', in Eamonn Jordan (ed.), *Theatre Stuff: Critical Essays on Contemporary Irish Theatre* (Dublin: Carysfort Press, 2000): 145-58.

Kuch, Peter, '*The Gigli Concert* in Brisbane and Sydney', in Laura P. Z. Izarra and Beatriz Kopschitz X. Bastos (eds.), *A New Ireland in Brazil: Festschrift in Honour of Munira Hamud Mutran* (São Paulo: Humanitas, 2008): 163-76.

Kurdi, Mária, 'An Interview with Tom Murphy', *Irish Studies Review* XII:2 (2004): 233-240.

Lanters, José, 'Schopenhauer with Hindsight: Tom Murphy's *Too Late for Logic*', *Hungarian Journal in English and American Studies* 2.2 (1996): 87-95.

---, 'Thomas Murphy', in Bernice Schrank and William W. Demastes (eds.), *Irish Playwrights, 1880-1995: A Research and Production Sourcebook* (Westport, CT: Greenwood Press, 1997): 231-42.

---, 'Playwrights of the Western World: Synge, Murphy, McDonagh', in Stephen Watt et al (eds.), *A Century of Irish Drama: Widening the Stage* (Bloomington: Indiana UP, 2000): 204-22.

Lonergan, Patrick, *Theatre and Globalization: Irish Drama in the Celtic Tiger Era* (Basingstoke: Palgrave Macmillan, 2009).

McDonald, Marianne, interview in *Ancient Sun, Modern Light: Greek Drama on the Modern Stage* (New York: Columbia UP, 1992): 199-200.

Mason, Patrick, 'Directing *The Gigli Concert*: An Interview', *Irish University Review* 17.1 (1987): 100-13.

Maxwell, D.E.S., *A Critical History of Modern Irish Drama 1891-1980* (Cambridge: Cambridge UP, 1984): 162-68.

---, 'New Lamps for Old: The Theatre of Tom Murphy', *Theatre Research International*, 15.1 (1990): 57-66.

---, 'Introduction: Contemporary Drama 1953-1986', *Field Day Anthology of Irish Writing*, vol. 3, ed. Seamus Deane et al. (Derry: Field Day Publications, 1991): 1137-43.

Mercier, Vivian, 'Noisy Desperation: Murphy and the Book of Job', *Irish University Review* 17.1 (1987): 18-23.

Mikami, Hiroko, '"The Saga Will Go On": Story as History in *Bailegangaire*', in Hiroko Mikami, Minako Okamuro and Naoko Yagi (eds.), *Ireland on Stage: Beckett and After* (Dublin: Carysfort Press, 2007): 135-51.

Morash, Christopher, 'Sinking Down into the Dark: The Famine on Stage,' *Bullán* 3.1 (1997): 75-86.

---, 'Murphy, History and Society', in Nicholas Grene (ed.), *Talking about Murphy* (Dublin: Carysfort Press, 2002): 17-30.

Murray, Christopher, 'The Rough and Holy Theatre of Thomas Murphy', Introduction *Tom Murphy Special Issue, Irish University Review* 17.1 (1987): 9-17, reprinted in Eberhard Bort (ed.), *'Standing in their shifts itself': Irish Drama from Farquhar to Friel* (Bremen: European Society for Irish Studies, 1993): 211-19.

---, *Twentieth-Century Irish Drama: Mirror Up to Nation* (Manchester: Manchester UP, 1997).

Neil, Ruth, 'Thomas Murphy and Federico Garcia Lorca', in Joseph McMinn (ed.), *The Internationalism of Irish Literature and Drama* (Gerrards Cross: Colin Smythe, 1992): 94-106.

Ní Anluain, Clíodhna (ed.), *Reading the Future: Irish Writers in Conversation with Mike Murphy* (Dublin: Lilliput Press, 2000): 173-86.

O'Dwyer, Riana, 'Play-Acting and Myth-Making: The Western Plays of Thomas Murphy', *Irish University Review*, 17.1 (1987): 31-40.

O'Leary, Joseph S., 'Looping the Loop with Tom Murphy: Anticlericalism as Double Bind', *Studies* LXXXI (spring 1992): 41-48.

O'Toole, Fintan, 'Homo Absconditus: The Apocalyptic Imagination in *The Gigli Concert*,' *Irish University Review*, 17.1 (1987): 90-99.

---, Tom Murphy: *The Politics of Magic* [1987] updated and expanded edition (Dublin:New Island; London: Nick Hern, 1994).

---, 'The Tom Murphy Papers in Trinity College Dublin', in Nicholas Grene (ed.), *Talking about Murphy* (Dublin; Carysfort Press, 2002): 9-16.

---, Introductions to *Plays: Two* (London: Methuen, 1993), *Plays : Three* (London: Methuen, 1994), and *Plays: 4* (London: Methuen, 1997).

Pilkington, Lionel, '"The Superior Game": Colonialism and the Stereotype in Tom Murphy's *A Whistle in the Dark*', in C.C. Barfoot and Rias van den Doel (eds.), *Ritual Remembering: History, Myth and Politics in Anglo-Irish Drama* (Amsterdam: Rodopi, 1995): 165-79.

Poulain, Alexandra, '"A Voice and Little Else": Talking, Writing and Singing in *The Gigli Concert*', in Patrick Lonergan and Riana O'Dwyer (eds.), *Echoes Down the Corridor* (Dublin: Carysfort Press, 2007): 107-16.

---, *Homo Famelicus: Le Théâtre de Tom Murphy* (Caen: Université de Caen Basse-Normandie, 2008).

Richards, Shaun, '"There's No Such Thing as the West Anymore": Tom Murphy and the Lost Ideal of the Land of the Free', *Études Irlandaises* XV.2 (December 1990): 83-94.

---, 'Response', in Nicholas Grene (ed.), *Talking about Murphy* (Dublin: Carysfort Press, 2002): 57-65.

Roche, Anthony, '*Bailegangaire*: Storytelling into Drama', *Irish University Review* 17.1 (1987): 114-28.

---, *Contemporary Irish Drama*: Second Edition (Basingstoke: Palgrave Macmillan, 2009): 84-129.

Roche, Billy, 'Tom Murphy and the Continuous Past', *Princeton Library Chronicle* LXVIII (2006-7): 620-31.

Ryschka, Birgit, *Constructing and Deconstructing National Identity: Dramatic Discourse in Tom Murphy's* The Patriot Game *and Felix Mitterer's* In der Löwengrube (Frankfurt: Lang, 2008).

Stembridge, Gerard, 'Murphy's Language of Theatrical Empathy', *Irish University Review* 17.1 (1987): 51-61.

Swann, Joseph, 'Language and Act: Thomas Murphy's Non-Interpretive Drama', in Jacqueline Genet and Richard Allen Cave (eds.), *Perspectives of Irish Drama and Theatre* (Gerrards Cross: Colin Smythe, 1991): 145-54.

Tóibín, Colm, 'Thomas Murphy's Volcanic Ireland', *Irish University Review* 17.1. (1987): 24-30.

Waters, John, 'The Frontiersman' [interview with Tom Murphy], *In Dublin* 15 May 1986: 28-29.

Welch, Robert, *The Abbey Theatre 1899-1999: Form and Pressure* (Oxford: Oxford UP, 1999).

White, Harry, '*The Sanctuary Lamp*: An Assessment', *Irish University Review* 17.1 (1987): 71-81.

Contributors

Aidan Arrowsmith is a Senior Lecturer in English at Manchester Metropolitan University. He has published on various aspects of Irish diaspora culture, including prose, drama, photography, painting and football. His *Fantasy Ireland: Irish Diaspora Culture* is published by Liverpool UP (2010). He is currently researching 'Ireland's Drama in Britain's Cities'.

Ben Barnes curated a major retrospective of the work of Tom Murphy at the Abbey Theatre in 2001, for which he directed *The Gigli Concert*. He also directed the American premiere of Murphy's version of *The Cherry Orchard* (2009). His *Plays and Controversies: Abbey Theatre Diaries 2000-2005* (Carysfort Press, 2008) covers the years of his artistic directorship of the Abbey.

Csilla Bertha teaches Irish and English Literature at Debrecen University, Hungary. Her publications on Irish drama include, apart from numerous essays on modern Irish dramatists, *Yeats the Playwright* (in Hungarian), volumes co-authored or co-edited with Donald E. Morse: *Worlds Visible and Invisible; A Small Nation's Contribution to the World; More Real than Reality;* and, with also Mária Kurdi, *Brian Friel's Dramatic Artistry* (Carysfort Press, 2006). Selected and edited *Homeland in the Heights*, an anthology of Hungarian poetry in English, and with Morse co-translated and co-edited *Silenced Voices*, a volume of Transylvanian-Hungarian plays (Carysfort Press, 2008).

Patrick Burke lectured in English, Drama and Theatre for 36 years at St Patrick's College, Dublin City University, where from 1997 to 2007 he was first director of the MA in Theatre Studies. His research interests include Friel (the subject of his PhD), Murphy, Synge and T.C. Murray, on all of whom he has published widely. He is a frequent speaker at international conferences. He is also an experienced actor and director with the Dublin Shakespeare Society, and includes *Conversations on a Homecoming* and *Bailegangaire* among his best productions.

Zsuzsa Csikai is an assistant lecturer in the Department of English Literatures and Cultures, University of Pécs, Hungary, and has recently completed her PhD on Irish translations and adaptations of Chekhov's plays. Her academic interests include Irish drama, Irish culture and translation studies.

Nicholas Grene is Professor of English Literature at Trinity College Dublin. He has written widely on drama and on Irish litera-ture: his books include *The Politics of Irish Drama* (Cambridge University Press, 1999), *Shakespeare's Serial History Plays* (Cambridge University Press, 2002) and *Yeats's Poetic Codes* (Oxford University Press, 2008). He edited *Talking About Tom Murphy* (Carysfort Press, 2002) and has since co-edited three other books published by Carysfort.

Peter James Harris is lecturer in English at São Paulo University (UNESP), San José do Rio Preto, Brazil. He is the author of *Sean O'Casey's Letters and Autobiographies: Reflections of a Radical Ambivalence* (Trier: WVT, 2004). He has also published articles on twentieth-century Irish playwrights and on Roger Casement's 1910 Amazon expedition. He is currently researching Irish dramatists on the London stage since 1922.

José Lanters is professor of English at the University of Wisconsin-Milwaukee, where she also co-directs the Center for Celtic Studies. She serves on the editorial boards of the electronic interdisciplinary journal *e-Keltoi*, and the University of Wisconsin Press. Her numerous publications in the field of Irish literature and culture include *Unauthorized Versions: Irish Menippean Satire, 1919-1952* (Catholic University of America Press, 2000) and *The 'Tinkers' in Irish Literature: Unsettled Subjects and the Construction of Difference* (Irish Academic Press, 2008). She is the vice chair for North America of the International Association for the Study of Irish Literatures (IASIL), and past president of the American Conference for Irish Studies (2007-09).

Helen Heusner Lojek retired in June from Boise State University (Idaho), where she was Associate Dean of the College of Arts and Sciences and Professor of English. Among her publications on Irish drama is *Contexts for Frank McGuinness's Drama* (Catholic University of America Press, 2004). She is working on a book about the use of space in contemporary Irish drama.

Bernard McKenna is an assistant professor at the University of Delaware. His work has appeared in *Eire-Ireland*, *The New Hibernia Review* and *Etudes Irlandaises*. He has also published *Rupture, Representation, and the Refashioning of Identity in Drama from the North of Ireland, 1969-1994* (Greenwood/Praeger, 2003).

Hiroko Mikami is Professor of Irish Studies in the School of International Liberal Studies, Waseda University, Tokyo. She is the author of *Frank McGuinness and His Theatre of Paradox* (Colin Smythe, 2002) and co-editor/author of *Ireland on Stage: Beckett and After* (Carysfort, 2007). She has translated many contemporary Irish plays into Japanese, including Murphy's *Bailegangaire* and *A Thief of a Christmas*.

Paul Murphy is Lecturer in Drama Studies at Queen's University Belfast, and President of the Irish Society for Theatre Research. His book *Hegemony and Fantasy in Irish Drama, 1899-1949* was published by Palgrave Macmillan in 2008

Christopher Murray is Emeritus Professor of Drama and Theatre History in the School of English, Drama and Film, University College Dublin. A former editor of *Irish University Review* and chair of the International Association for the Study of Irish Literatures (IASIL), he is author of *Twentieth-Century Irish Drama: Mirror Up to Nation* (1997) and *Sean O'Casey, Writer at Work: A Biography* (2004) He has edited *Brian Friel: Essays, Diaries, Interviews 1964-1999* (1999) and *Beckett at 100: The Centenary Essays* (2006). His *Selected Plays of George Shiels* was published by Colin Smythe in 2008. During 2008-9 he was adjunct lecturer in drama at the School of English, Trinity College Dublin.

Riana M. O'Dwyer is Senior Lecturer in English at the National University of Ireland, Galway. She has served as Chair of the International Association for the Study of Irish Literatures (IASIL) from 2003 to 2009. She has lectured and published on Joyce, modern Irish drama, Irish studies, and Irish women novelists of the nineteenth century. Articles on Lady Blessington and on Emily Lawless have been published recently (2008). She has also co-edited a number of volumes, including a section in the *Field Day Anthology of Irish Writing* Vol. 5 (2002) and *Echoes Down the Corridor: Irish Theatre – Past, Present* *and Future* (Carysfort Press, 2007) in the series IASIL Studies in Irish Writing.

Alexandra Poulain is Professor of Irish Studies at the University of Charles-de-Gaulle, Lille 3. Recent publications include *Homo Famelicus: le théâtre de Tom Murphy, Hunger on the Stage* (co-edited with Elisabeth Angel-Perez), and (co-edited with Martine Pelletier) a special issue of *Etudes Irlandaises* under the title *French and Irish Theatres: Interactions and Influences*, papers given at the ITD conference in Lille in 2008. In addition, she has written many articles on Irish theatre and has translated several Irish plays into French.

Shaun Richards is Professor of Irish Studies at Staffordshire University. He is the co-author (with David Cairns) of *Writing Ireland: Colonialism, Nationalism* (1988) and editor of *The Cambridge Companion to Twentieth-Century Irish Drama* (2004). His primary research is on Irish drama, particularly its cultural politics, and he has published extensively on the subject in major journals and edited collections.

Harry White is Professor of Music at University College Dublin and a Fellow of the Royal Irish Academy of Music. He was inaugural President of the Society for Musicology in Ireland 2003-2006 and is general editor (with Barra Boydell) of the forthcoming *Encylopaedia of Music in Ireland*. His publications include *The Keeper's Recital* (1998), *The Progress of Music in Ireland* (2005), and *Music and the Irish Literary Imagination* (2008). He was elected to the Royal Irish Academy in 2006 for his services to musicology.

Index

Carysfort Press was formed in the summer of 1998. It receives annual funding from the Arts Council.

The directors believe that drama is playing an ever-increasing role in today's society and that enjoyment of the theatre, both professional and amateur, currently plays a central part in Irish culture.

The Press aims to produce high quality publications which, though written and/or edited by academics, will be made accessible to a general readership. The organisation would also like to provide a forum for critical thinking in the Arts in Ireland, again keeping the needs and interests of the general public in view.

The company publishes contemporary Irish writing for and about the theatre.

Editorial and publishing inquiries to:
Carysfort Press Ltd.,
58 Woodfield,
Scholarstown Road,
Rathfarnham,
Dublin 16,
Republic of Ireland.

T (353 1) 493 7383
F (353 1) 406 9815
E: info@carysfortpress.com
www.carysfortpress.com

HOW TO ORDER

TRADE ORDERS DIRECTLY TO:
CMD/BookSource
55A Spruce Avenue,
Stillorgan Industrial Park
Blackrock,
Co. Dublin

T: (353 1) 294 2560
F: (353 1) 294 2564
E: cmd@columba.ie

INDIVIDUAL ORDERS DIRECTLY TO:
eprint Ltd.
35 Coolmine Industrial Estate,
Blanchardstown, Dublin 15.
T: (353 1) 827 8860
F: (353 1) 827 8804 Order online @
E: books@eprint.ie
www.eprint.ie

FOR SALES IN NORTH AMERICA AND CANADA:
Dufour Editions Inc.,
124 Byers Road,
PO Box 7,
Chester Springs,
PA 19425,
USA

T: 1-610-458-5005
F: 1-610-458-7103

Performing Violence in Contemporary Ireland

Lisa Fitzpatrick

This interdisciplinary collection of fifteen new essays by scholars of theatre, Irish studies, music, design and politics explores aspects of the performance of violence in contemporary Ireland. With chapters on the work of playwrights Martin McDonagh, Martin Lynch, Conor McPherson and Gary Mitchell, on Republican commemorations and the 90th anniversary ceremonies for the Battle of the Somme and the Easter Rising, this book aims to contribute to the ongoing international debate on the performance of violence in contemporary societies.

ISBN 978-1-904505-44-0 (2009)   €20

Ireland's Economic Crisis - Time to Act. Essays from over 40 leading Irish thinkers at the MacGill Summer School 2009

Eds. Joe Mulholland and Finbarr Bradley

Ireland's economic crisis requires a radical transformation in policymaking. In this volume, political, industrial, academic, trade union and business leaders and commentators tell the story of the Irish economy and its rise and fall. Contributions at Glenties range from policy, vision and context to practical suggestions on how the country can emerge from its crisis.

ISBN 978-1-904505-43-3 (2009)   €20

Deviant Acts: Essays on Queer Performance

Ed. David Cregan

This book contains an exciting collection of essays focusing on a variety of alternative performances happening in contemporary Ireland. While it highlights the particular representations of gay and lesbian identity it also brings to light how diversity has always been a part of Irish culture and is, in fact, shaping what it means to be Irish today.

ISBN 978-1-904505-42-6 (2009)   €20

Seán Keating in Context: Responses to Culture and Politics in Post-Civil War Ireland

Compiled, edited and introduced by Éimear O'Connor

Irish artist Seán Keating has been judged by his critics as the personification of old-fashioned traditionalist values. This book presents a different view. The story reveals Keating's early determination to attain government support for the visual arts. It also illustrates his socialist leanings, his disappointment with capitalism, and his attitude to cultural snobbery, to art critics, and to the Academy. Given the national and global circumstances nowadays, Keating's critical and wry observations are prophetic – and highly amusing.

ISBN 978-1-904505-41-9   €25

Dialogue of the Ancients of Ireland: A new translation of Acallam na Senorach

Translated with introduction and notes by Maurice Harmon

One of Ireland's greatest collections of stories and poems, The Dialogue of the Ancients of Ireland is a new translation by Maurice Harmon of the 12th century *Acallam na Senorach*. Retold in a refreshing modern idiom, the *Dialogue* is an extraordinary account of journeys to the four provinces by St. Patrick and the pagan Cailte, one of the surviving Fian. Within the frame story are over 200 other stories reflecting many genres – wonder tales, sea journeys, romances, stories of revenge, tales of monsters and magic. The poems are equally varied – lyrics, nature poems, eulogies, prophecies, laments, genealogical poems. After the *Tain Bo Cuailnge*, the *Acallam* is the largest surviving prose work in Old and Middle Irish.

ISBN: 978-1-904505-39-6 (2009)   €20

Literary and Cultural Relations between Ireland and Hungary and Central and Eastern Europe

Ed. Maria Kurdi

This lively, informative and incisive collection of essays sheds fascinating new light on the literary interrelations between Ireland, Hungary, Poland, Romania and the Czech Republic. It charts a hitherto under-explored history of the reception of modern Irish culture in Central and Eastern Europe and also investigates how key authors have been translated, performed and adapted. The revealing explorations undertaken in this volume of a wide array of Irish dramatic and literary texts, ranging from *Gulliver's Travels* to *Translations* and *The Pillowman*, tease out the subtly altered nuances that they acquire in a Central European context.

ISBN: 978-1-904505-40-2 (2009)   €20

Plays and Controversies: Abbey Theatre Diaries 2000-2005

By Ben Barnes

In diaries covering the period of his artistic directorship of the Abbey, Ben Barnes offers a frank, honest, and probing account of a much commented upon and controversial period in the history of the national theatre. These diaries also provide fascinating personal insights into the day-to- day pressures, joys, and frustrations of running one of Ireland's most iconic institutions.

ISBN: 978-1-904505-38-9 (2008)   €35

Interactions: Dublin Theatre Festival 1957-2007. Irish Theatrical Diaspora Series: 3

Eds. Nicholas Grene and Patrick Lonergan with Lilian Chambers

For over 50 years the Dublin Theatre Festival has been one of Ireland's most important cultural events, bringing countless new Irish plays to the world stage, while introducing Irish audiences to the most important international theatre companies and artists. Interactions explores and celebrates the achievements of the renowned Festival since 1957 and includes specially commissioned memoirs from past organizers, offering a unique perspective on the controversies and successes that have marked the event's history. An especially valuable feature of the volume, also, is a complete listing of the shows that have appeared at the Festival from 1957 to 2008.

ISBN: 978-1-904505-36-5   €25

The Informer: A play by Tom Murphy based on the novel by Liam O'Flaherty

The Informer, Tom Murphy's stage adaptation of Liam O'Flaherty's novel, was produced in the 1981 Dublin Theatre Festival, directed by the playwright himself, with Liam Neeson in the leading role. The central subject of the play is the quest of a character at the point of emotional and moral breakdown for some source of meaning or identity. In the case of Gypo Nolan, the informer of the title, this involves a nightmarish progress through a Dublin underworld in which he changes from a Judas figure to a scapegoat surrogate for Jesus, taking upon himself the sins of the world. A cinematic style, with flash-back and intercut scenes, is used rather than a conventional theatrical structure to catch the fevered and phantasmagoric progression of Gypo's mind. The language, characteristically for Murphy, mixes graphically colloquial Dublin slang with the haunted intricacies of the central character groping for the meaning of his own actions. The dynamic rhythm of the action builds towards an inevitable but theatrically satisfying tragic catastrophe. ' [The Informer] is, in many ways closer to being an original Murphy play than it is to O'Flaherty...' Fintan O'Toole.

ISBN: 978-1-904505-37-2 (2008)   €10

Shifting Scenes: Irish theatre-going 1955-1985

Eds. Nicholas Grene and Chris Morash

Transcript of conversations with John Devitt, academic and reviewer, about his lifelong passion for the theatre. A fascinating and entertaining insight into Dublin theatre over the course of thirty years provided by Devitt's vivid reminiscences and astute observations.

ISBN: 978-1-904505-33-4 (2008)   €10

Irish Literature: Feminist Perspectives

Eds. Patricia Coughlan and Tina O'Toole

The collection discusses texts from the early 18th century to the present. A central theme of the book is the need to renegotiate the relations of feminism with nationalism and to transact the potential contest of these two important narratives, each possessing powerful emancipatory force. Irish Literature: Feminist Perspectives contributes incisively to contemporary debates about Irish culture, gender and ideology.

ISBN: 978-1-904505-35-8 (2008) €25

Silenced Voices: Hungarian Plays from Transylvania

Selected and translated by Csilla Bertha and Donald E. Morse

The five plays are wonderfully theatrical, moving fluidly from absurdism to tragedy, and from satire to the darkly comic. Donald Morse and Csilla Bertha's translations capture these qualities perfectly, giving voice to the 'forgotten playwrights of Central Europe'. They also deeply enrich our understanding of the relationship between art, ethics, and politics in Europe.

ISBN: 978-1-904505-34-1 (2008) €25

A Hazardous Melody of Being:
Seóirse Bodley's Song Cycles on the poems of Micheal O'Siadhail

Ed. Lorraine Byrne Bodley

This apograph is the first publication of Bodley's O'Siadhail song cycles and is the first book to explore the composer's lyrical modernity from a number of perspectives. Lorraine Byrne Bodley's insightful introduction describes in detail the development and essence of Bodley's musical thinking, the European influences he absorbed which linger in these cycles, and the importance of his work as a composer of the Irish art song.

ISBN: 978-1-904505-31-0 (2008) €25

Irish Theatre in England: Irish Theatrical Diaspora Series: 2

Eds. Richard Cave and Ben Levitas

Irish theatre in England has frequently illustrated the complex relations between two distinct cultures. How English reviewers and audiences interpret Irish plays is often decidedly different from how the plays were read in performance in Ireland. How certain Irish performers have chosen to be understood in Dublin is not necessarily how audiences in London have perceived their constructed stage personae. Though a collection by diverse authors, the twelve essays in this volume investigate these issues from a variety of perspectives that together chart the trajectory of Irish performance in England from the mid-nineteenth century till today.

ISBN: 978-1-904505-26-6 (2007) €20

Goethe and Anna Amalia: A Forbidden Love?

By Ettore Ghibellino, Trans. Dan Farrelly

In this study Ghibellino sets out to show that the platonic relationship between Goethe and Charlotte von Stein – lady-in-waiting to Anna Amalia, the Dowager Duchess of Weimar – was used as part of a cover-up for Goethe's intense and prolonged love relationship with the Duchess Anna Amalia herself. The book attempts to uncover a hitherto closely-kept state secret. Readers convinced by the evidence supporting Ghibellino's hypothesis will see in it one of the very great love stories in European history – to rank with that of Dante and Beatrice, and Petrarch and Laura.

ISBN: 978-1-904505-24-2 €20

Ireland on Stage: Beckett and After

Eds. Hiroko Mikami, Minako Okamuro, Naoko Yagi

The collection focuses primarily on Irish playwrights and their work, both in text and on the stage during the latter half of the twentieth century. The central figure is Samuel Beckett, but the contributors freely draw on Beckett and his work provides a springboard to discuss contemporary playwrights such as Brian Friel, Frank McGuinness, Marina Carr and Conor McPherson amongst others. Contributors include: Anthony Roche, Hiroko Mikami, Naoko Yagi, Cathy Leeney, Joseph Long, Noreem Doody, Minako Okamuro, Christopher Murray, Futoshi Sakauchi and Declan Kiberd

ISBN: 978-1-904505-23-5 (2007) €20

'Echoes Down the Corridor': Irish Theatre - Past, Present and Future

Eds. Patrick Lonergan and Riana O'Dwyer

This collection of fourteen new essays explores Irish theatre from exciting new perspectives. How has Irish theatre been received internationally - and, as the country becomes more multicultural, how will international theatre influence the development of drama in Ireland? These and many other important questions.

ISBN: 978-1-904505-25-9 (2007) €20

Musics of Belonging: The Poetry of Micheal O'Siadhail

Eds. Marc Caball & David F. Ford

An overall account is given of O'Siadhail's life, his work and the reception of his poetry so far. There are close readings of some poems, analyses of his artistry in matching diverse content with both classical and innovative forms, and studies of recurrent themes such as love, death, language, music, and the shifts of modern life.

ISBN: 978-1-904505-22-8 (2007) €25 (Paperback)
ISBN: 978-1-904505-21-1 (2007) €50 (Casebound)

Brian Friel's Dramatic Artistry: 'The Work has Value'

Eds. Donald E. Morse, Csilla Bertha and Maria Kurdi

Brian Friel's Dramatic Artistry presents a refreshingly broad range of voices: new work from some of the leading English-speaking authorities on Friel, and fascinating essays from scholars in Germany, Italy, Portugal, and Hungary. This book will deepen our knowledge and enjoyment of Friel's work.

ISBN: 978-1-904505-17-4 (2006) €30

The Theatre of Martin McDonagh: 'A World of Savage Stories'

Eds. Lilian Chambers and Eamonn Jordan

The book is a vital response to the many challenges set by McDonagh for those involved in the production and reception of his work. Critics and commentators from around the world offer a diverse range of often provocative approaches. What is not surprising is the focus and commitment of the engagement, given the controversial and stimulating nature of the work.

ISBN: 978-1-904505-19-8 (2006) €35

Edna O'Brien: New Critical Perspectives

Eds. Kathryn Laing, Sinead Mooney and Maureen O'Connor

The essays collected here illustrate some of the range, complexity, and interest of Edna O'Brien as a fiction writer and dramatist. They will contribute to a broader appreciation of her work and to an evolution of new critical approaches, as well as igniting more interest in the many unexplored areas of her considerable oeuvre.

ISBN: 978-1-904505-20-4 (2006) €20

Irish Theatre on Tour

Eds. Nicholas Grene and Chris Morash

'Touring has been at the strategic heart of Druid's artistic policy since the early eighties. Everyone has the right to see professional theatre in their own communities. Irish theatre on tour is a crucial part of Irish theatre as a whole'. Garry Hynes

ISBN 978-1-904505-13-6 (2005) €20

Poems 2000-2005 by Hugh Maxton

Poems 2000-2005 is a transitional collection written while the author – also known to be W.J. Mc Cormack, literary historian – was in the process of moving back from London to settle in rural Ireland.

ISBN 978-1-904505-12-9 (2005) €10

Synge: A Celebration

Ed. Colm Tóibín

A collection of essays by some of Ireland's most creative writers on the work of John Millington Synge, featuring Sebastian Barry, Marina Carr, Anthony Cronin, Roddy Doyle, Anne Enright, Hugo Hamilton, Joseph O'Connor, Mary O'Malley, Fintan O'Toole, Colm Toibin, Vincent Woods.

ISBN 978-1-904505-14-3 (2005) €15

East of Eden: New Romanian Plays

Ed. Andrei Marinescu

Four of the most promising Romanian playwrights, young and very young, are in this collection, each one with a specific way of seeing the Romanian reality, each one with a style of communicating an articulated artistic vision of the society we are living in. Ion Caramitru, General Director Romanian National Theatre Bucharest.

ISBN 978-1-904505-15-0 (2005) €10

George Fitzmaurice: 'Wild in His Own Way', Biography of an Irish Playwright

By Fiona Brennan

'Fiona Brennan's introduction to his considerable output allows us a much greater appreciation and understanding of Fitzmaurice, the one remaining under-celebrated genius of twentieth-century Irish drama'. Conall Morrison

ISBN 978-1-904505-16-7 (2005) €20

Out of History: Essays on the Writings of Sebastian Barry

Ed. Christina Hunt Mahony

The essays address Barry's engagement with the contemporary cultural debate in Ireland and also with issues that inform postcolonial critical theory. The range and selection of contributors has ensured a high level of critical expression and an insightful assessment of Barry and his works.

ISBN: 978-1-904505-18-1 (2005) €20

Three Congregational Masses

By Seoirse Bodley

'From the simpler congregational settings in the Mass of Peace and the Mass of Joy to the richer textures of the Mass of Glory, they are immediately attractive and accessible, and with a distinctively Irish melodic quality.' Barra Boydell

ISBN: 978-1-904505-11-2 (2005)   €15

Georg Büchner's Woyzeck,

A new translation by Dan Farrelly

The most up-to-date German scholarship of Thomas Michael Mayer and Burghard Dedner has finally made it possible to establish an authentic sequence of scenes. The wide-spread view that this play is a prime example of loose, open theatre is no longer sustainable. Directors and teachers are challenged to "read it again".

ISBN: 978-1-904505-02-0 (2004)   €10

Playboys of the Western World: Production Histories

Ed. Adrian Frazier

'The book is remarkably well-focused: half is a series of production histories of Playboy performances through the twentieth century in the UK, Northern Ireland, the USA, and Ireland. The remainder focuses on one contemporary performance, that of Druid Theatre, as directed by Garry Hynes. The various contemporary social issues that are addressed in relation to Synge's play and this performance of it give the volume an additional interest: it shows how the arts matter.' Kevin Barry

ISBN: 978-1-904505-06-8 (2004)   €20

The Power of Laughter: Comedy and Contemporary Irish Theatre

Ed. Eric Weitz

The collection draws on a wide range of perspectives and voices including critics, playwrights, directors and performers. The result is a series of fascinating and provocative debates about the myriad functions of comedy in contemporary Irish theatre. Anna McMullan

As Stan Laurel said, 'it takes only an onion to cry. Peel it and weep. Comedy is harder'. 'These essays listen to the power of laughter. They hear the tough heart of Irish theatre – hard and wicked and funny'. Frank McGuinness

ISBN: 978-1-904505-05-1 (2004)   €20

Sacred Play: Soul-Journeys in contemporary Irish Theatre

by Anne F. O'Reilly

'Theatre as a space or container for sacred play allows audiences to glimpse mystery and to experience transformation. This book charts how Irish playwrights negotiate the labyrinth of the Irish soul and shows how their plays contribute to a poetics of Irish culture that enables a new imagining. Playwrights discussed are: McGuinness, Murphy, Friel, Le Marquand Hartigan, Burke Brogan, Harding, Meehan, Carr, Parker, Devlin, and Barry.'

ISBN: 978-1-904505-07-5 (2004) €25

The Irish Harp Book

by Sheila Larchet Cuthbert

This is a facsimile of the edition originally published by Mercier Press in 1993. There is a new preface by Sheila Larchet Cuthbert, and the biographical material has been updated. It is a collection of studies and exercises for the use of teachers and pupils of the Irish harp.

ISBN: 978-1-904505-08-2 (2004) €35

The Drunkard

By Tom Murphy

'The Drunkard is a wonderfully eloquent play. Murphy's ear is finely attuned to the glories and absurdities of melodramatic exclamation, and even while he is wringing out its ludicrous overstatement, he is also making it sing.' The Irish Times

ISBN: 978-1-90 05-09-9 (2004) €10

Goethe: Musical Poet, Musical Catalyst

Ed. Lorraine Byrne

'Goethe was interested in, and acutely aware of, the place of music in human experience generally - and of its particular role in modern culture. Moreover, his own literary work - especially the poetry and Faust - inspired some of the major composers of the European tradition to produce some of their finest works.' Martin Swales

ISBN: 978-1-9045-10-5 (2004) €40